Essays in Swedish History

Essays in
Swedish History

MICHAEL ROBERTS

Professor of Modern History,
The Queen's University, Belfast

UNIVERSITY OF MINNESOTA PRESS
Minneapolis

Printed in Great Britain

To
A. and J.

Contents

Preface

With two exceptions (nos. 1 and 9) all the papers in this volume began life as lectures and were subsequently expanded into articles. All have been published before, and I am indebted to The Athlone Press, Messrs A. & C. Black, the Irish Committee of Historical Sciences, Messrs Routledge and Kegan Paul, the Royal Historical Society, and the editors of *The English Historical Review*, *History*, *The Historical Journal*, and *Past and Present*, for permission to reprint them. They reappear, for the most part, in the form in which they were originally printed. Here and there a little new matter has been added, but most of the alterations have been by way of excision – partly because some things now seemed superfluous, but also in order to avoid repetition from one paper to another.

JUNE 1966   M.R.

On Swedish History in General

Few fields of historical research have been more neglected by English scholars than the history of Scandinavia. While our historians have in recent years made notable contributions to the history of most of the smaller countries of Europe, from Holland to Rumania, from Portugal to Poland, the Scandinavian countries have attracted the merest handful of enquirers. The majority of English historians derive their ideas of Swedish history either from the austere pages of large-scale co-operative enterprises, or from such introductions to the subject – admirable in themselves, but all too short – as Svanström and Palmstierna's *History of Sweden*. Whence they draw their information upon the history of Denmark it would be difficult to conjecture, and probably profitless to enquire. At all events, a history of Sweden in English, covering the ground in one volume on a generous scale, and representative of informed contemporary Swedish opinion, has long been an urgent need. And it has been obvious for more than a decade that what we really wanted was a good translation of Ingvar Andersson's *Sveriges historia*. Now at last we have it.[1]

The late Professor Eli Heckscher once remarked that a small country has no right to demand that its history be studied, merely because it has happened.[2] And it may be that some historians would willingly borrow his dictum to excuse the a neglect of Scandinavian history in this country. Yet even cursory reading of Dr Andersson's book must suggest that there is much in the history of Sweden which is of interest to a non-Swedish public. For Sweden's history is indeed a history unusual and in some ways unique; and though in a number of important respects it may be held to show similarities with the history of England, it differs markedly from that of the general run of continental countries. We are immediately struck, for instance, by the circumstance that in Sweden so many developments appear to come so late: by western standards the whole history of Sweden seems to be retarded. Man came late to Sweden; the Romans never came at all; Christianity did not finally triumph till half a millennium after St Augustine came to Britain. The founding of the University of Uppsala comes more than two centuries after the time when Oxford had emerged as one of the great centres of European scholarship. Lying on the periphery of the world of the western Church, rescued from heathendom only when the renaissance of the twelfth century was in full flower, Sweden escaped those great clashes between *regnum* and *sacerdotium* which provide much of the dynamic of the mediaeval history of the West. No investiture contest, no statutes of Provisors or Praemunire, mark the history of Church-state relations; and the relatively brief supremacy of Rome is untroubled by a single important heretic. And just as Sweden was late in being incorporated into the unity of western Christendom, so she was late in achieving her own unity – late, at least, by English standards. For a true capital she had to wait till the mid-thirteenth century; for a common law till the middle of the fourteenth. Provincial feeling remained strong for centuries thereafter; and was a political force to be reckoned with perhaps as late as 1743. Indeed, the successive ascendancies of this province or that – now Uppland, now Västergötland, now Dalarna – may almost be said to resemble the rise and decline of Kent and Northumbria, Mercia and Wessex, four or five centuries earlier.

Even more remarkable, to an English observer, is the slowness with which the country emerged from a relatively primitive economic condition. Whatever may have been the case during the Viking period, when that period was over Sweden found herself in a blind-alley, at the end of the trade routes rather than at their centre. Her commerce came to be conducted, her larger towns to be peopled, mainly by Hanseatic merchants; and the economic life of the rest of the country became less subject to international influences than that of any western state. Even in the sixteenth century, and under a monarch with so sharp an eye to his own advantage as Gustav Vasa, Sweden was content with a 'passive' trade; content that foreign merchants should resort to her, rather than that her own should venture out to engage in commercial enterprises. In a striking comparison, Eli Heckscher once estimated the level of economic development of sixteenth-century Sweden as about equivalent to that of Carolingian France in the year 1000. A barter economy was still dominant. Taxes were collected, salaries assigned, interest upon loans was paid, in commodities (and perishable commodities at that). The fiscal reforms of Gustav Adolf and Axel Oxenstierna temporarily substituted cash for commodities as the main constituent of the revenues of the crown; but fifty years later Charles xi's *indelningsverk* marked a partial reversion to the old system. Throughout the eighteenth century a good deal of this natural economy survived; so that even at the end of it a professor at Uppsala might have his emoluments calculated and paid in grain. It was not until the abolition of *grundskatterna* in 1892 and of the *indelningsverk* in 1901 that Sweden saw the disappearance of the last traces of a fiscal system which had probably vanished in England at least six hundred years earlier. So too with the gilds; which in Sweden became general only at the end of the sixteenth century, and flourished mainly in the seventeenth and eighteenth, when their day in England was already over.

The slowness of this progress towards a modern type of economy is in part to be explained by the social structure of the country. Sweden has throughout her history been a rural country; and she remains a rural country today, despite her industries. In 1885 there were only some 100,000 industrial workers; and even in 1940 only about forty-four per cent. of the population could be reckoned as urban. And that forty-four per cent. was (as to a great part of it, at least) urban only in a very limited sense. Sweden has still only two or three really large centres of population; and a great part of Swedish industry is located in quite small towns. In Västerås, in Huskvarna, in Borås, in Sundsvall, you feel the country all around you – the skerries and the forest, the curve of the river, the broad expanse of the lake, are at your door, or at least just

3

round the corner. Gällivare and Gusum are not much more than overgrown villages; Lessebo not even that. The fathers or grandfathers of a majority of urban dwellers may probably have worked on the land. This rural strain colours all Swedish history: Gustav Vasa's letters put one in mind of Sir Robert Walpole and his bailiff; a century later, Johan Ekeblad, in waiting at the court of Christina, is greedy for news from his father of horses and dogs and country matters; even the elegant Tessin sighs to quit Stockholm for the rustic pleasures of Åkerö. Urban society is predominantly the society of the small country town; and the small-town atmosphere is no less characteristic than the rural, whether we seek it in the materials of history – Tersmeden arranging picnics in his leisure-hours at Karlskrona, Malla Silfverstolpe presiding over her miniature *salon* in Uppsala – or in the half-real world of Gustaf Hellström's Kristianstad, or Hjalmar Bergman's Örebro, or Birger Sjöberg's Vänersborg: it is, indeed, one of the fundamental constituents of Swedish humour.

Swedish history is, in one aspect, the history of the conflicting influences of forest and water. The forests divided and isolated: they ruralized industry, impeded traffic, hindered invasion, preserved provincialism. The waters united: the immense indented coastline offered a highway by sea; the frozen lakes a winter-way through the land; and both, it has been suggested, saved Sweden – as the sea saved England – from those internal barriers of tolls and Customs which were the curse of continental countries. Or to look at it from a slightly different angle: the history of Sweden, until quite recent times, has been a history of internal colonization, of man's gradual subjugation and exploitation of his environment. For the last three centuries Swedish rulers have been forced to hold a nice balance between the enterprise of the colonist, increasing the arable by clearing the woods, and the needs of the settled communities, who looked to the woods for grazing, pannage, timber, and fuel for domestic or industrial purposes. But whichever way you look at it, the central figure in the picture, the man upon whose relationship with his environment the nation's welfare depended, has always been the Swedish peasant.

It may well be that the idealization of the yeoman peasant by such writers as E. G. Geijer has been proved to have but a

4

shaky historical basis; it is certainly true that the earliest Swedish society of which we have a clear picture was not that egalitarian society of peasant proprietors which earlier historians believed in; but it is still safe to say that the peasant in mediaeval Sweden retained his social and political freedom to a greater degree, played a greater part in the politics of the country, and was altogether a more considerable person, than in any other western European country. At the close of the Middle Ages the class of free peasant proprietors was still the largest class in the community; it owned more land than any other; it was strong enough to tip the balance in the swaying constitutional struggle between monarchy and nobility. And this, it seems, because Sweden had never been in any true sense a feudal country. Between a nobility which had already by the close of the Middle Ages become hereditary and the free taxpaying and landowning peasantry were no intermediate gradations of any consequence. No tenurial pyramid existed: the distinction was only between those who paid taxes (the free peasantry) and those who did not (the nobles, their tenants, and the crown's tenants). There could be no question of a gentry class such as existed in England, no instinctive alliance between squire and parson. After the Reformation the clergy either drew their recruits from the peasantry, or were self-recruiting within their own order. The towns, always the weakest of the four Estates, never played a part in Swedish history comparable with that played by the towns of England, France, and Germany – to say nothing of Italy and the Netherlands. It was not to them that the monarchy looked for a counterpoise to aristocratic faction: even Stockholm was perhaps of less importance to its possessor than was the capital of any western monarchy. In Sweden the crown's ally, or its tool, came more and more to be the peasantry; and from Karl Knutsson to Gustav III successive rulers turned to it for support when they ran up against a major difficulty. Hence the demagogic tradition of Swedish kingship, which crops up again and again: Sten Sture the younger, Gustav Vasa, Erik xiv, Charles ix, Gustav Adolf – they all had it, in greater or less degree; all developed a style of oratory which, whatever may have been its literary merits (and on occasion they were considerable), was essentially popular. Even over-civilized and over-intellectualized monarchs such as Christina and Gustav III could strike this note surely and without effort when they chose. When Gustav III spoke to the soldiers in the guard-room on the morning of 19 August 1772, or stood on the churchyard walls of Dalarna to rally the people, seventeen years later, he was only the last (and not the least eloquent) representative of a tradition which had become part of the stock-in-trade of Swedish kingship.

But even in the nineteenth century, when the tides of politics were setting strongly in favour of the emergent middle class, it was the country, rather than the town, that provided the great issues. The social crisis of nineteenth-century Sweden was mainly a rural crisis; the consolidation of strips in the common field was as great a revolution in rural Sweden as in rural England (though Sweden managed it much more intelligently); and the great emigration of the second half of the century – as in Ireland or Scotland – was the reaction to a rural rather than an urban problem. And though the constitutional reform of 1865 may have resulted from the pressure of those middle classes who had found no representation within the framework of the old system of Estates, it was the peasantry, now organized as a political party, that reaped the main political advantage of the change.

All this is in strong contrast to the course of English history. Yet in some respects the history of Sweden has much in common with our own. And perhaps the most important of these common factors is the long tradition, shared by both countries, of personal and political freedom, and a profound respect for the rule of law. The feeling for law and liberty, the consciousness of having managed to preserve them when most other countries failed to do so, the pride in their unbroken transmission, more or less intact, from a remote past – this is something which, even if at times it verges on mythology rather than history, is nevertheless part of the national ethos of each country. Magnus Eriksson's *landslag* of the mid-fourteenth century was not merely a codification, valid for the whole realm, of criminal and civil law: it was, even more importantly, a statement of the law of the constitution; and it meant much the same to constitutional antiquarians such as Hogenskild Bielke as Magna Carta meant to the contemporaries of Sir Edward Coke. 'The land shall be built upon law' was thus a political tradition handed down from the Middle Ages, firmly grasped, and never abandoned. Sweden was indeed to experience more than one attempt at absolutism; but such attempts were successful only if they kept within the letter of the law; and the rights of the subject were respected even under such kings as Charles XI and Charles XII. Because it was not until the seventeenth century that Sweden developed a professional class of advocates, the administration of the law, and the custody of the tradition of observance of the law, fell to a great extent upon the nobility; and the mind of the Swedish aristocracy was from an early period soaked in Swedish law. And this in turn strengthened the rule of law, by enlisting among the champions of legality a class which in other countries was sometimes disposed to override it.

Equally ancient is the tradition of self-government. Local self-government, indeed, has roots stretching down to the earliest days of state and Church. The democracy of the *ting*, the co-operation of all classes in the parochial council, are among the fundamental facts of Swedish history; and they proved strong enough in the seventeenth century to resist successfully the contradictory threats of the efficient centralizing officials of the monarchy, on the one hand, and those aristocratic tendencies towards social oppression of the type prevalent in Germany, on the other. Parliamentary self-government is much younger; but it is still of respectable antiquity. Before the end of the fourteenth century the *riksdag* had begun to take shape; before the end of the fifteenth it had become an important element in the political life of the nation. It was of high significance that the Diet should have included, from an early date, a separate Estate of Peasants. As with the English parliament, it was only gradually that the *riksdag* took over the task of safeguarding the liberties of the nation, and no notion of that sort lay behind its early summonses. The constitutional opposition, the guardian of the law, the check upon royal aggression, was at first the nobility, in Sweden as in England. They strove to keep the monarchy elective; they made the *råd* the watch-dog of the constitution.

The political accidents which led to the breach of the union with Denmark at the opening of the sixteenth century were utilized by the new monarchy to destroy this constitutional resistance: Gustav Vasa and Erik XIV, reaping where the Stures had sown (much as the early Tudors built on Yorkist foundations), made the monarchy hereditary, stopped the mouth of the nobility with the plunder of the Church, and began the erection of a parliamentary despotism of the Tudor type. Their work was, however, but a half-success. The *riksdag* in the end did not become the obedient instrument of the monarchy, as the Cortes did in Castile; the crises at the end of the sixteenth century proved that aristocratic constitutionalism was still very much alive; and throughout the whole of the seventeenth century, Sweden was engaged in a protracted constitutional struggle between monarchy and aristocracy. In the course of that struggle the *riksdag* emerged as a truly national representative organ; it crystallized into four Estates; it developed parliamentary procedure. There were times – in 1650, in 1680 – when for reasons social or economic a majority of the Estates was willing to back the monarchy against the aristocracy. But what was important was that the *riksdag*'s monopoly of legal legislation was established; its control of the executive began to be asserted; its regular meeting was secured; and above all its exclusive right to grant new taxes was successfully maintained. When the death of Charles XII in the trenches of Fredrikshald brought the so-called absolutism to a close, the Estates were ready, with a constitutional tradition, a theory of government, and a long experience, to shoulder the burden of parliamentary rule. This triumphant maintenance of parliamentary constitutionalism, throughout a century which saw the general prevalence of absolutism on the Continent and in Denmark, was a great achievement. It may, perhaps, be related to another peculiarity of Swedish history: the establishment, in 1544, of a truly national army – the first national army of modern times.

On the whole, the constitutional development of every country seems to be related – sometimes closely related – to its military system; and the fact that a great part of the Swedish population took an active part in the armed forces of the country certainly interposed a real obstacle in the way of the establishment of any absolute form of government. Constitutional conflicts in the seventeenth century tended to centre upon the right to control the resources which were required to maintain a standing army, and on the whole the struggle went in favour of absolutism, security and efficiency, and against constitutionalism, which now appeared risky and outmoded. But the nature of the Swedish army, and (not least) the way it was paid, protected Sweden from the perilous choice between military efficiency and civil liberty; and the country's backward economy, based as it still was upon goods rather than cash, preserved it from the controversy about army finance – a controversy which (if it had arisen) might well have ended no better for the *riksdag* than for the Estates in Brandenburg. Hence it happened that the warlike enthusiasms of the Age of Greatness left no constitutional neuroses or complexes behind them; and the Age of Liberty remained serenely untroubled by the Whigs' nightmare fears of a standing army. Englishmen remembered Strafford, and Cromwell's Major-Generals, and James II's Irish army; but Swedes continued to be almost oblivious of the possibility of a cleavage between the civil and military authorities within the state. After a century and a half of terrible wars Sweden emerged into the tranquil airs of the eighteenth century as a surprisingly unmilitary society.

The Age of Liberty saw an extraordinary efflorescence of parliamentary life and habits. Its statesmen combined a common sense and flexibility in practice which recalls the evolutionary and pragmatic methods of English constitutional advance, with a rigour and logic in political theory reminiscent of revolutionary France. Before that age ended, they had established techniques of parliamentary control more varied and effective than any that existed in eighteenth-century England; they had grasped the notion of unwritten conventions of the constitution; they had developed true political parties, genuinely divided upon issues of national policy; they had enforced the doctrine of ministerial responsibility to parliament; and they had enunciated the theory of cabinet solidarity. The cumbrous machinery of four Estates had been made to work, if not wholly without friction, still at least with tolerable success. Sweden was the only country in Europe (with the possible exception of Württemberg) in which the old mediaeval Estates were able to transform themselves into something like a modern parliament. The Age of Liberty brought about its own destruction by its vices and its follies, and no retrospective enthusiasm for its constitutional achievements (or, even more, for its constitutional possibilities) can alter the plain fact that the revolution of 1772 was necessary for the health and safety of Sweden; but with all its odiousness the *régime* of the Hats and Caps had reached a stage of constitutional advance which was unequalled in pre-revolutionary Europe, and which was not attained again in Sweden for many decades after 1772.

The fratricidal strife of Hats and Caps – the political excesses of the one after 1756, and of the other in 1771–2 – suggest a further reflection: that excesses of this kind have been extraordinarily rare in Sweden. The history of modern Sweden shares with the history of modern Britain a quite unusual quality of moderation. There are no great upheavals, no crises which seem to throw the very bases of the state into confusion, no violent outbreaks of lawlessness on a large scale. Unlike most European countries, Sweden has never experienced a *jacquerie*; but neither has she been shaken by great subversive movements of the proletariat. The vision or opportunism of Gustav III enabled her to escape the repercussions of the French Revolution; and in the epidemic of 1848 she came off with the mildest of attacks. Since the battle of Stångebro in 1598 there has been no civil war in Sweden; nor has there been any really dangerous rebellion. Gustav III provided the only victim of political assassination; and the rabbling of the younger Fersen in 1810 the only serious example of mob-murder. The twin spirits of compromise and conservatism, it would seem, have now presided over Sweden's history for something like three centuries; and they have given it a continuity which has survived many abrupt changes of course. Swedish lawyers have been as reluctant as English to interfere unnecessarily with what has grown venerable by age: it took a century and a quarter of intermittent effort to produce the great recodification of the law which finally appeared in 1734. The revolution of 1809 was as peaceful as the Glorious Revolution in England: James II's nose is said to have bled, Gustav IV certainly vomited; but neither of them otherwise suffered physical discomfort. And the constitution of 1809 had its roots as firmly set in the old order as had the Bill of Rights. No single sharp enactment destroyed the privileges of the Swedish nobility: the process of social levelling went on gradually, with notable accelerations here and there (as for instance in 1789) from 1723 until the Estates themselves came to an end in 1865. The expansion of the electorate after that year proceeded at a pace which would not have appeared unduly hectic to Sir Robert Peel, and might even have seemed sluggish to Disraeli. On all sides there has been a reluctance to draw the uttermost logical consequences from a principle. The absolutism of Charles xi was always bounded by the law; the rule of the Estates after 1718 was carefully declared to be something short of sovereignty. It is noteworthy that the Social Democrats soon abandoned the pure dogma of Marxism, as too rigid for Swedish political conditions; while Swedish conservatives have shown a Wellingtonian readiness to swallow reforms which have become inevitable, and even to assist in putting them through.

If we turn now from internal affairs to the part played by Sweden in the general history of Europe, her peculiar contribution is not difficult to isolate. It does not consist in her brief but glorious career as a great power; it does not consist even in Gustav Adolf's deliverance of German Protestantism from the threat of the Counter-Reformation: by 1660 Sweden was already struggling to maintain the position which Gustav Adolf and Charles x had won, and all that followed was a long-drawn epilogue; while as to Germany, it may be plausibly argued that sooner rather than later much the same result might have been expected by other means. The true international importance of Sweden's part in history is rather that she has always stood, as she still stands, in the gate between East and West. Swedish statesmen have always aimed at keeping open their window to the west, while at the same time establishing some system of security to the east. They have tried on occasion to make Sweden the economic, as well as the political, entrepôt between the two. They have sought – as the elder Sture sought, and Gustav Adolf, and Charles xii, and Gustav iii – to find securityagainst Russia by a system of outposts in the eastern Baltic, and by driving back the Muscovite from the sea: it is possible to explain the whole history of Sweden's Baltic empire on the theory that it was essentially a defensive policy from first to last. At times they have tried the other tack – Erik xiv tried it, and so did the Caps, and Gustav iii at the close of his reign, and the men of 1812 – and made a bid for security by courting Russian friendship. They have even fought to neutralize Russia by putting a Swedish prince on the throne of the Tsars. But whatever the method employed, they have always been conscious of the ultimate importance of the geopolitical problem which they cannot escape.

These, then, are some of the reflections provoked by a reading of Dr Andersson's account of his country's history. The military historian might well have dwelt on aspects no less interesting and important: on Erik xiv's brilliant anticipation of the military reforms of Maurice of Orange; on Gustav Adolf's amendment of what was lacking in those reforms, so that he was able, as Maurice was not, to transform the whole art of war for more than a century; on Charles xii's use of attack in column, transmitted as a direct legacy to the armies of revolutionary France. The naval historian would have noted the remarkable fact that in the sixteenth century Sweden acquired a formidable fleet at a time when she had scarcely the beginnings of a mercantile marine – a feat to which perhaps only Peter the Great can show a parallel; he could hardly have failed to advert to Erik xiv's experiments in shipbuilding; and he would probably have added a timely warning (by no means superfluous for an English reader) against over-hasty generalization about the ineffectiveness of galleys, in the light of Baltic experience. The economic historian would have called attention to the close correlation between Sweden's monopoly of the European copper-market and her political ascendancy; to the remarkable experiments in state control by Görtz; to the successful efforts throughout the eighteenth century to ensure a stable price for iron; and to the economic writings of Chydenius. And the ecclesiastical historian might have drawn fruitful comparisons between the English Reformation and the Swedish, between Cranmer and Laurentius Petri, between Pyhy and Thomas Cromwell. But apart from all such individual facets, which will gleam with varying brightness according to the angle from which we approach them, there remains the general impression produced by the whole story; a story so various, so rich in great moments, so violent in its contrasts. Is it possible to read without excitement the extraordinary epic of Sweden's rise to greatness, or to follow without emotion the story of her last desperate struggles under Charles XII? Extraordinary the transformation of the Sweden of Axel Oxenstierna to the Sweden of Per Albin Hansson! Swedish history has this challenging quality: that it is almost impossible to approach it without taking sides. Gustav Adolf or Charles XI? For Charles XII, or against? Royalist or aristocrat-constitutionalist? Hat or Cap? And the record is strewn with great actions and peopled with great men. It is not necessary to be a Swede to glory in Breitenfeld, to admire Fraustadt (the perfect victory), to applaud Svensksund. The sixteenth century produced few greater rulers than Gustav Vasa, and none more remarkable than Erik XIV; Gustav Adolf has a good claim to be regarded as among the greatest kings of any age, and Oxenstierna as the greatest of his contemporaries; Gustav III is the most baffling, the most fascinating, and perhaps in the long run not the least successful, of the benevolent despots.

But there is no need to prolong the catalogue. There have been moments – not more than two or three, perhaps – when the history of Sweden was also the history of Europe; and at such moments a knowledge of the history of Sweden has always been obligatory upon historians. But between these peaks lie long valleys, secluded from the eye of foreign observation, neglected hitherto by the historical explorer, but crowded with their own peculiar and fascinating forms of life. The man who finds Swedish history dull had better not read history at all.

NOTES

[1] Ingvar Andersson, *A History of Sweden* (trans. Carolyn Hannay), London, 1956, to which this essay was originally written as an Introduction.

[2] E. F. Heckscher, 'Un grand chapitre de l'histoire du fer: le monopole suèdois', *Annales d'histoire économique et sociale*, Paris, 1932, p. 128: as he observed, 'ne compliquons pas sans nécessité la tâche de la science'.

2

On Aristocratic Constitutionalism in Swedish History, 1520–1720[1]

I

It is just a hundred and twenty years since Anders Fryxell, goaded beyond endurance by the historiography of his day, was provoked into publishing the first of a series of pamphlets entitled *On Anti-Aristocratic Prejudice in Swedish History*.[1a] Fryxell's object was to enter a protest against the school of thought which subscribed to Geijer's dictum that the history of Sweden is the history of her kings, and which saw the nobility as the villain of the piece. And it must be conceded, even by those who do not think well of Fryxell, that his protest was essentially dignified and temperate. The ensuing academic *fracas*, alas, was neither the one nor the other, at least on Geijer's side. But it did give rise to two vigorous and long-lived schools of historians, both of them happily still with us; and in the first decade of the present century their learned wrangles became for a time part of the stuff of contemporary politics, in a manner familiar from the historiography of the French Revolution.[2] The controversy, among its other effects, helped to confirm Swedish historians in a habit which was already well established: the habit of viewing the constitutional history of their country, from the fourteenth century to the eighteenth, as essentially a struggle between monarchy and aristocracy. And until quite recently this view of the matter has passed almost without question. In the last few years, however, there has been a tendency to see the problem

14

in less clear-cut terms: monarchy and aristocracy, it is argued, had more in common, were less absolutely opposed (even in the domain of political theory) than was allowed for in the older stereotypes.[3] This is undoubtedly a salutary and overdue exercise in historical revision; but those who practise it can scarcely contend that they are doing more than putting *nuances* and perspective into an historical picture which had hitherto been a trifle flat: the main outlines have not really been disturbed. There is no denying that for some four hundred years much of the inner tension of Swedish history is provided by the clash of crown and nobility; that the nobility did aspire to set bounds to the power of the monarchy, by devices which make it plausible to think of them as the proponents of something which may be very loosely termed a constitutional programme; and that the only alternative to that programme for long seemed to be a form of government which without any pejorative intention can be called absolutism. There was, certainly, an aristocratic constitutional tradition. It will be the object of this lecture to try to gauge the importance of that tradition within a limited period of Swedish history, and to view it, not from the point of view of the historian of political thought – on which quite enough has been written already[4] – but with the more pedestrian and pragmatic purpose of attempting to determine its practical effectiveness. The question I ask myself, then, is this: what share has the aristocratic tradition in the establishment of a constitutional *régime* in Sweden, and what did it do during these two centuries to secure those basic liberties of the subject which a constitutional *régime* is designed to provide?

The fundamental document in Swedish constitutional history is Magnus Eriksson's Land Law, drawn up about the year 1350.[5] It was the first general code of law for all the Swedish provinces; but for our present purpose its importance lies rather in the fact that it also defined for the first time the law of the constitution. In this respect it had an influence upon Swedish history similar in kind to that exerted by Magna Carta upon the history of England. The Land Law laid it down that the monarchy was to be elective, and that the king's accession was to be conditional upon his acceptance of a coronation oath. By that oath he undertook that no subject should suffer loss of life, liberty or property save by due process of law; that no new law should be made save with the consent of the commonalty; and that the country should be defended out of the ordinary revenues of the crown: except in four specially enumerated cases the king was to impose no new taxes, but was to live of his own. He was to be advised by a council (*råd*) comprising the archbishop and bishops, together with twelve lay magnates. But this body was not the *king*'s council: it was, and was already called, the council of the realm (*riksråd*). Though the king selected its lay members, they were in no sense his ministers; they held office, in all ordinary circumstances, for life; their responsibility was not to him but to the community of the realm. And their most important function was to see to it that the king and his subjects observed the pledges which each had given to the other at the coronation; to act as mediators between monarch and people; to maintain the balance of the constitution. Upon the demise of the crown the royal authority reverted to them: in an electoral monarchy they occupied the position of a permanent residuary sovereign power.

It is here, then, in the council as the Land Law defined it, that the tradition of aristocratic constitutionalism takes its rise; and until late in the seventeenth century the heart of that tradition was what Swedish historians call 'council-constitutionalism' (*rådskonstitutionalism*).[6] In the century and a half which intervened between the Land Law and the accession of Gustav Vasa it acquired increasing strength and consistency. In 1371 the council extorted from an alien king (Albert of Mecklenburg) the first of those Accession Charters (*konungaförsäkran*) which were designed to provide guarantees for the redress of grievances, or explanatory glosses upon the general formularies of the coronation oath. It deposed Erik of Pomerania in 1439 because he showed signs of trying to make himself an absolute ruler. It forced Christopher of Bavaria, in the 1440s, to admit its right to veto appointments and grants of fiefs; and the revised version of the Land Law which was issued in this reign[7] contained for the first time a royal promise to rule 'with the council's counsel' (*med råds råde*) – a formula destined to echo through the constitutional debate for centuries to come. In the 1430s the council secured the custody and control of the great seal of the realm; and, at a time when the administrative machinery of the monarchy was still primitive, established its own chancery, with the bishop of Strängnäs as permanent *ex officio* chancellor. It was already customary for the king to obtain the council's assent to taxation, as a necessary preliminary to approaching the provincial assemblies. The circumstances of the Scandinavian Union, especially after 1440 – with an absentee king in Copenhagen, and a regent in Stockholm precariously maintaining a semi-independence – afforded political opportunities of which the council took full advantage; and in the 1470s and 1480s the pretensions of the magnates reached a climax. In 1476 they tried to force Christian 1 to concede the right to legal rebellion;[8] in 1483 they drew up, in the Recess of Kalmar, the most extreme statement of council-constitutionalism ever to be formulated.[9] It included the demand that the council should have the right to judge between the king and his subjects; that councillors should be free to afford refuge on their manors (which they were to be allowed to fortify) to persons arraigned by the king; that they should have control over their own membership, be recognized as sovereign authority in the king's absence, and be 'kings over their own peasants' – by which was meant that any fines imposed on such persons should go, not into the king's pocket, but into the lord's. It is no wonder that Anders Schönberg, contemplating this document in the euphoric atmosphere of the autumn of 1772, should have exclaimed in horror that 'if Anarchy could be established by Law, this should surely be called an anarchical constitution'.[10] No king ever accepted the terms of the Recess of Kalmar *in toto*; but its historical significance was very great. For two centuries it was a constitutional ideal to which the high nobility intermittently recurred, sometimes in curiously inappropriate circumstances.

Such was the basis of the aristocratic-constitutional tradition, as it came down to the Sweden of Gustav Vasa. It was in one important aspect an inter-Scandinavian tradition, common to the councils of all three realms; but it had also evident affinities to those ideas of a *regimen politicum* which were generally current in the fifteenth century. It commanded the support of an episcopate fearful of royal interference in the processes of canonical election; and it was, quite obviously, a useful stalking-horse for the economic interests and political ambitions of the closely-interrelated clique of great landowners from whom the council was recruited. But by 1520 there was set over against it another political trend, more modern, more broadly based, and as the event proved more powerful: the trend to a hereditary monarchy, emancipated from the restraints of election-pledges, centralizing rather than provincial in emphasis, domain-acquiring rather than fief-granting, *étatiste* in its attitude to the church, prepared to harness an instinctive xenophobia and stand forth as leader of a 'national' cause. And, not least, prepared to look for political support outside the circle of the high aristocracy and the upper *échelons* of the church – to the miners of Dalarna, the burghers of Stockholm, the lesser nobility and the ecclesiastical careerists – and to seek legal sanction for its actions not so much in the approval of the council as in the backing of a relatively new body, the *riksdag*. In the last half-century of the Scandinavian Union the regents (*riksföreståndare*) of the Sture family all at one time or another cultivated these allies. Sten Sture the younger, especially, sought their support in the pursuit of his dynastic ambitions. His method was to unite the Estates in a formal act of conjuration, in which he and they swore to stand together, 'one for all, and all for one', and so to leave his aristocratic rivals in the position of being dissidents from something that could be represented to be a national front.[11] The constitutional issue thus became entangled in the controversy over the continuance or rupture of the Union. But this aspect of the question was not essential to it. What was essential, was the confrontation of antagonistic political ideals: on the one hand limited monarchy under oligarchical control, on the other popular absolutism. The Stures had in fact posed the great question which was to dominate Sweden's domestic history for the next two centuries. They had established that tradition of demagogic kingship which was to endure until 1789;[12] they had forged the long-lasting alliance between king and Estates. As long as that alliance subsisted, no victory for constitutional principles could be otherwise than precarious and fragile. The way forward to a modern constitutional *régime* could henceforth lie only along one of two roads: either the council and the aristocracy must be able to enlist the *riksdag* in support of their programme; or the *riksdag* itself must mature sufficiently to fight the battle of liberty on its own account, without regard to the magnates' leadership. The constitutional history of the Vasa period is the record of Sweden's failure to advance in either direction.

2

Gustav Vasa was the political heir of Sten Sture, inheriting his ambitions, employing his tactics, succeeding where he had failed. His reign seemed to mark the final defeat of aristocratic constitutionalism; which did, in fact, go underground for more than forty years. The great council families had been hard hit by Christian II's 'Blood-bath of Stockholm'; the council itself was weakened by the exclusion of the episcopate after 1527; while the king, immensely strengthened by the plunder of the church, was able to resume the great fiefs, amass a vast accumulation of manors in his own hands, and rule the country through his bailiffs. The royal pledges imposed by the Land Law were robustly brushed aside whenever the king found it inconvenient to adhere to them; the council ceased altogether to act as regulator of the constitutional machine; the king followed its advice, or ignored it, as he thought proper.[13] Even the *ultima ratio* of rebellion availed nothing against a monarch with money to buy guns and mercenaries. When Gustav Vasa felt the need to provide his actions with an emphatic stamp of legality – as in 1527, or 1544, or 1560 – it was to the *riksdag* rather than to the council that he turned to obtain it; and the Estates on their side made no difficulty about throwing an occasional and transparent veil over what had in fact become a paternal absolutism. A decisive moment came in 1544, when the king, fresh from his triumph over the most serious rebellion of the reign, secured their acceptance of the Succession Pact (*arvförening*).[14] This was, indeed, one of the great turning-points of Swedish history. By transforming Sweden into a hereditary monarchy (as the Stures and the Oldenburgs had both failed to do) Gustav Vasa destroyed the very basis upon which aristocratic constitutionalism rested; for in fifteenth-century Sweden hereditary monarchy had generally been taken to imply unlimited monarchy.[15] Henceforward, it seemed, there could be no pledges exacted as a condition of accession, no Charter extorted to reinforce those pledges. The battle which the council had fought all through the fifteenth century seemed lost. And if the Succession Pact was thus the sign of the crown's victory, the solidity of the success was guaranteed by the character and policy of the victor – by Gustav Vasa's intense personal application to the business of government, and by his long-headed caution in avoiding foreign adventures. The first enabled him to run the country with the assurance and authority of an improving landlord; the second, by making it possible for him to retain in his hand the gains of the Reformation, left him at the end of his reign richer than any Swedish king before or since. He may at times have behaved like a greedy and ruthless tyrant; but at least he conformed to the Land Law's requirement that the king should live of his own.

By 1560, then, the tradition of council-constitutionalism seemed as good as dead. Gustav Vasa's Testament did indeed provide for checks upon the king's freedom of action;[16] but they were checks to be applied within the dynasty, by the royal dukes. And even these were swept away by Erik xiv.[17] Erik's absolutism was more obvious, more explicit and more capricious than his father's: his coronation-oath was so brief and so vague as to be almost perfunctory.[18] He imported into Swedish kingship the practices of Machiavelli[19] and the high prerogative claims of the Roman Law. His rule bore with especial severity upon the high nobility; for his pathological suspiciousness led him to see, in the surviving members of the Sture family, rivals who were plotting to deprive him of his throne. These morbid fears, and his exalted notions of his royal rights, combined to produce the catastrophe of 1567; when Erik, doubling the parts of judge and executioner, murdered Nils Sture with his own hand, and forthwith lapsed into insanity.[20]

It is probably as a direct outcome of these tragic events that we must see the vigorous and unexpected revival of aristocratic constitutionalism in the last three decades of the century. The rising which led to Erik's deposition in 1568 may very well have been no more than the defensive reaction of an aristocracy which felt its neck endangered by Erik's incalculable proceedings. But it was the beginning of a renewal of conscious political activity by the high nobility as a class. They were deeply wounded and disturbed by the advance to power of a new class of royal secretaries, often of mean extraction and few scruples. In the two decades after 1570 they grew progressively more exasperated by the muddle and inefficiency which marked the rule of John III.[21] They hankered for the good old days of liberal aristocratic privilege;[22] and they were conscious of a reviving ambition to recover the dominant position in the state which they had lost since 1529. These sentiments were given a solid intellectual basis by the antiquarian researches and widened reading of a new generation of nobles, who combined a passion for mediaeval precedents with a leaning to monarchomachist political theory. In the light of Duplessis-Mornay, the Recess of Kalmar acquired a fresh and topical relevance.

The leaders of this new generation were Erik Sparre and Hogenskild Bielke.[23] Their programme had two aspects. On the one hand it was a protest against lack of governance, a demand for order and efficiency, a plea for modern administrative techniques. Sparre wanted an administration which should be properly articulated, specialized, regularly paid, and above all national, as opposed to the domestic, cameral, *ad hoc* methods which had been good enough for the first Vasas: his proposal to link the central administration to the five great offices of state looks forward to the collegial structure of 1634.[24] On the other hand it was an attempt to repair the damage to the constitutional cause which had been the consequence of the Succession Pact of 1544. And this could be done only by establishing the doctrine that the change from electoral to hereditary monarchy had not absolved the king from his obligation to rule within the limits of the law.[25] The deposition of Erik XIV had given a severe jolt to the hereditary principle, and John III, in a natural effort to redress the balance, had advanced provocative claims to be an absolute monarch.[26] Sparre fought those claims, in theory and in practice. In practice, like so many reformers, he was at heart a conservative, wishing to restore rather than to innovate: his ideal was a return to monarchy under the Land Law as the fifteenth century had conceived it.[27] In theory he was attracted by the fashionable notion of a 'mixed monarchy'; and he seems to have believed that the royal authority was derived from the people, not by a *translatio*, but by a *concessio*.[28] The king, therefore, must rule with the consent of his subjects. But the difficulty was to define the body through whom that consent should be conveyed. At first Sparre had no doubt that it should be the *riksdag*: in his pamphlet *Pro Lege Rege et Grege* (1587) he clearly recognized this.[29] But the Stures and Gustav Vasa had shown how easily the Estates could be captured and used by a skilful and unscrupulous ruler; and Erik XIV, very recently, had employed them as a weapon against his aristocratic enemies. The experience of the 1590s was to provide ample confirmation of these disquieting examples; and already by 1594 Sparre seems to have been doubtful whether the *riksdag* could be trusted to uphold the rule of law against the crown.[30] Duke Charles of Södermanland was reviving, with terrifying and sinister virtuosity, the tumultuary parliamentarism of Sten Sture; and his crude, emotive eloquence could sway the Estates as might best suit with his obscure ambitions. Since this was so, Sparre had no option but to fall back on the safeguard provided by 'the leading personages of the realm' (*de förnämsta*)[31] – to stand fast, that is, upon the Land Law's remedy: the council, rather than the *riksdag*, must be the watchdog of the constitution. Thus, once again, political necessity forced the council party into a position in which the popular representative element in the constitution was divorced from its obvious leaders. It was a misfortune which henceforward was to weaken the cause for which Sparre stood.

The political confusion of the 1590s brought to the front another difficulty closely related to that of defining consent. This was the problem of the proper body to apply sanctions, if sanctions should be needed. With whom, in the last resort, lay the right of rebellion? In the terminology which Althusius was shortly to popularize, who were the ephors? Sparre seems to have equated the ephorate with the council. But there were other candidates for inclusion: the episcopate, for instance, and above all the royal dukes. The question became of importance after 1595, when Duke Charles, backed by the church and the 'grey multitude', began a course of opposition to King Sigismund which eventually led to that monarch's deposition. It is easy to see that Charles was exploiting Protestant panic and class animosities for his own purposes: the religious crisis, at least, was largely factitious.[32] What was at stake was, in the first place, constitutional propriety, and in the second, the rule of law itself. And on this the council rightly refused to compromise. They declined to violate their oath of loyalty to their sovereign by following the duke into rebellion: the ephorate, in fact, refused to revolt. But by taking this line they offered their adversary a chance to un-Whig them, and Charles was not the man to miss it. It was easy to represent Sparre and his friends as the supporters of popish despotism; it was scarcely less easy to enlist the *riksdag* to override the reluctant ephors. The real constitutionalism of the council was over-trumped by the sham constitutionalism of the duke. He was able to contend that the *riksdag* had inherited the functions of those electoral assemblies which in the Middle Ages had been charged with the task of 'taking and breaking' kings; that in them inhered the right to doom Sigismund from his kingdom, if they thought proper.[33] At Linköping, in 1600, this theoretical dispute was settled in a severely practical manner: the heads of Erik Sparre and three of his colleagues fell to the axe of the executioner, and the shouts of *Herr Omnes* summoned Charles to a throne which was declared vacant. It was a political murder worthy of Henry VIII.

The blood shed at Linköping, like Erik's killing of the Stures, poisoned the monarchy's relations with the high aristocracy; and Charles's propaganda found it expedient to take the line that the council had sought to compass the extinction of the Vasa dynasty in order to revive elective monarchy, or even to set up an aristocratic republic. The young Gustav Adolf was brought up to believe that Sparre and his friends had aimed at a constitution which would have given them a status equivalent to that of the Electors in the Empire.[34] There was just enough of truth in this to make it credible; and henceforth such accusations would be among the standard weapons in the royalist armoury. Erik XIV in his day had found the explanation for his repeated matrimonial failures in the sinister intrigues of the aristocracy;[35] John and Charles had blamed their fraternal quarrels upon the deliberate fomentation of the council.[36] In Christina's time Axel Oxenstierna would be suspected of aiming at a Polish republic,[37] and Magnus de la Gardie accused of trying to prevent the queen's marriage.[38] Thirty years after that Johan Gyllenstierna's enemies asserted that it was his object to ensure the extinction of the dynasty by involving Charles XI in war, debauchery and political follies;[39] and when Charles XII fell in the trenches before Fredrikshald the suspicion of a murder instigated by factious interests long persisted.[40] Tales such as these did not lack believers; and this is perhaps one reason why council-constitutionalism was never a really popular cause.

Meanwhile, it might seem that Erik Sparre had lived and died in vain. For a decade after 1600 Charles ruled Sweden much as Gustav Vasa had ruled it, through secretaries and bailiffs; extorting, by periodic threats of abdication, parliamentary support for unpopular policies and parliamentary condonation of actions more high-handed than any that had ever been laid to Sigismund's charge. The council was drastically remodelled; and a *riksdag* resolution of 1602 laid it down that 'henceforth the council shall give counsel, and shall *not* govern'.[41] But in fact Sparre had gained one victory of the utmost significance. By forcing Sigismund in 1594 to grant an Accession Charter[42] as a condition of his recognition as king, and as a preliminary to his coronation, he had in fact established the principle that hereditary monarchy did not mean absolute monarchy: the king was still to be bound by the fundamental law of the constitution. It is true that he had been able to gain his point only because Charles for his own purposes concurred in pressing it, and because the constitutional question was mixed up with a religious issue. It is true too that Charles himself gave *his* Charter only *after* his coronation, and that the only important guarantees in it concerned religion. Nevertheless, some of the ideas of the 'nineties did survive the destruction of the men who had propounded them. The so-called 'Rosengren Draft' of a revision of the Land Law (1605) would have given the council the right to try causes in which a subject complained that the crown had illegally deprived him of his property; and would even have made the king's power of granting patents of nobility subject to the nobility's consent. Erik Sparre's theories crop up surprisingly in the writings of men in close touch with Charles IX; and though this had little effect on Charles's actions, it can at least be said that Sparre's principles had to some extent become the common cant of his enemies.[43] And it was a matter of real importance that from 1611 to 1697 every Swedish sovereign should have accepted the obligation to subscribe to a Charter as a condition of accession. Nothing more plainly reveals the despotic nature of Charles XII's government than his refusal to conform to this precedent.[44]

The circumstances of the accession of Gustav Adolf did

indeed appear to provide Sparre with a posthumous triumph. The council and the Estates, as in 1594, dictated terms to the monarchy. The Charter of 1611,[45] with its detailed exposition of the abuses and illegalities of Charles IX's reign, was an almost explicit vote of censure. Gustav Adolf was made to promise to abstain from such practices in future; the council was given a guarantee that its members should be free to discharge their constitutional functions without hazard;[46] the great officers of state were promised security of tenure during good behaviour; the principles of the Land Law were reaffirmed. Axel Oxenstierna seemed to be emerging as Erik Sparre's political heir. In the sequel, it did not turn out quite like that. The crisis of 1611 was followed by twenty years of constitutional harmony. The monarchy appeared to have learned its lesson. Gustav Adolf on the whole took care to stick to the spirit of the Charter, and Oxenstierna was wise enough to avoid any pedantic attempts to tie him to the letter of it. No doubt Gustav Adolf was less complaisant to the men of 1611 than has sometimes been imagined;[47] and Oxenstierna, as was to appear after 1632, had not forgotten the experiences of Charles IX's time. But still, for a whole generation the intimate collaboration of king and chancellor came near to masking the underlying constitutional conflict. It was only when the great king was dead that the tradition of council-constitutionalism revived; to produce, in the Form of Government (*regeringsform*) of 1634, its most elaborate achievement – and, as it proved, its last.

The Form of Government[48] implemented simultaneously both wings of Erik Sparre's programme. On the one hand it provided Sweden with an orderly, logical and modern machinery of government,[49] and thus brought to a culmination the great administrative reforms which Oxenstierna had inaugurated in the preceding reign: in its concern for efficiency, in its belief in centralization as a means to efficiency, it was a typical example of the 'progressive' thought of the age. On the other hand it put the control of the country into the hands of the regents and the council, with more than a suggestion that it might remain there after the minority was over: it was, after all, declared to be an 'eternal' law; and one contemporary legal expert compared it to the Golden Bull.[50] Its preamble stated, in words which were to acquire classic authority, the

25

ideal of mixed monarchy.[51] But in every mixed monarchy, as the political theorists were wont to point out, one element tended to predominate; and friends of the Vasa dynasty had an uneasy feeling that that element would prove to be the council and the high aristocracy. The automatically-functioning machinery of council and colleges seemed indeed to make a king superfluous, a mere Venetian Doge: the contrast between a mortal *rex* and an immortal *regnum* was pointed too plainly to be mistaken.[52] Royalists such as Karl Karlsson Gyllenhielm saw the imminent threat of an aristocratic republic, to be run by Oxenstierna and his relatives in their own interest.[53] At no time during the regency were there less than three members of the Oxenstierna family in the council; towards the end of it there were four; and in the face of this situation it was no great comfort to be assured: '*statum manere monarchicum, sed aristocratice administrari*'.[54]

In reality, far from announcing the triumph of council-constitutionalism, the Form of Government was the herald of its decline. In the course of Gustav Adolf's reign the council had gradually but decisively changed its character. Under the early Vasas it had been a loosely constituted group of great magnates, meeting irregularly at the king's summons, normally resident on their estates in the country, entrusted with no regular or defined functions. By 1634 it had become a standing executive comparable with the Tudor council, sitting in almost continuous session in Stockholm, developing its own specialisms, 'slaving away' (to use Skytte's expression)[55] at routine business, the supreme policy-making body.[56] The change was due, of course, mainly to Gustav Adolf's prolonged absences abroad, and later to Christina's long minority. The unforeseen effect was to compromise the council's traditional position as regulator of the constitutional machine. It had become a part of the government, if not the government itself; and its members developed very clear insights into the value of prerogative action. As always, a major concern of the council-constitutionalists was good government: when the conduct of the state passed into their hands, they were not slow to find that good government might imply strong government. And if this was true of the council-members in general, it was still truer of those of them who were also regents. Not the least remarkable feature of the regency for Christina is the conscientious care of the regents to safeguard the prerogatives and interests of the crown: it was no part of the duty of an ephorate, they considered, to allow the monarchy to be robbed of its just rights, or permit the balance of the state to be tilted towards a democracy.[57] As *de facto* head of the government Oxenstierna adopted some of the techniques and mental attitudes of his royal predecessors – even to silencing opposition by a threat of abdication.[58] It was significant that on one crucial issue – the question whether the council's approval was necessary for appointments to senior posts – he now took the side of the monarchy.[59] He may for a time have had some notion of making his son Prince Consort: what he quite obviously was not contemplating was a republic.

In another way, too, the constitutional situation had undergone alteration in the years since 1600: I mean, in the steady growth of the powers and pretensions of the *riksdag*. Where the Land Law had spoken of the need for the assent of the commonalty, the tendency now was to equate this vague term with the Estates. The attitude of the council to this development had varied with political circumstances; but there had been signs in 1611 that they would have been glad to reduce the frequency of meetings of the *riksdag*,[60] and the Form of Government of 1634 obviously contemplated fewer and more formal sessions, with the diversion of much business to smaller 'committee-meetings'[61] – a development which might well have been as fatal to the cause of parliamentarism in Sweden as it was to prove in Germany. But when Oxenstierna at last came home for good in 1636 he was not long in realizing that the time for any such idea had gone by.[62] The *riksdag* in the 1630s and 1640s was vigorous, alert, jealous of its supposed rights, on the aggressive to extend them. Great bishops such as Rudbeckius and Lenaeus appeared as spokesmen for what at times resembled a constitutional opposition to government measures. It could no longer be assumed, moreover, that the interests and attitudes of the Estate of Nobility coincided broadly with those of the council. It had been true when Erik Sparre produced the *Postulata Nobilium* in 1594; it had been true when Oxenstierna drew up the Nobility's demand for privileges in 1611; but it was now true only with qualifications. Since the acceptance of the *Riddarhusordning* of 1626 the members of the council no longer sat in the first Estate, and the distinctions of rank within that Estate had been emphasized by its division into three classes, voting separately. In theory, the council was still an essential constituent part of any *riksdag*; in fact, a cleavage was opening between them.[63] After 1634, indeed, the council is almost as likely to be the target of constitutionalist opposition as to be its spearhead. The political theorists of the day expressed the situation when they urged – as Archbishop Paulinus urged – that the ephorate must be understood to include all the Estates; and the claim was even put forward that during a minority the *summa majestas* inhered not in the council but in the *riksdag*.[64] In the middle decades of the century, indeed, it was the *riksdag* rather than the council that tended to set the pace of constitutional advance. In the 1640s they began to put forward a claim to a share in the appointment of ministers – a claim which won limited acceptance when the *jus improbandi et approbandi* was conceded to them for the period of Charles XI's minority.[65] In 1650 the three lower Estates, with the connivance and encouragement of the queen, successfully asserted the right to the initiative.[66] On the death of Charles X the *riksdag* implicitly rejected the council's right to be the custodian of the immortal *regnum* and the ultimate depositary of sovereign power. It refused to be bound by the provisions of Charles X's will, and thus pronounced against the implied theory that the realm was a kind of royal property which could be made the subject of private testamentary dispositions. It resolved that the regents should be responsible to 'God, H.M., and *all the Estates of the Realm*';[67] and that the Form of Government, with the *Additamentum* which modified it, should have force only during the minority: it thus ruled out the possibility of any permanent oligarchical *régime*.[68] At the same time the *Additamentum* secured (at least on paper) the principle of triennial diets.[69] Fifteen years later, in 1675, the principle of redress before supply was effectively asserted for the first time; a demand for appropriation of supply was conceded; and the crown accepted the concept of ministerial responsibility, to be brought home by parliamentary scrutiny of the minutes of council and government offices.[70] There was even some talk, in 1678, of refusing to dissolve until grievances had been redressed.[71]

In most of these questions the leading part had been taken by the first Estate,[72] and it might well have seemed that as the old type of council-constitutionalism declined, a new type of aristocratic constitutionalism was growing up in its place. But any chance there might have been of the Nobility's emerging as a body of Whiggish parliamentarians was scotched by social tensions and economic struggles, both within the Estate of Nobles, and between the Nobles and the lower Estates. By the second quarter of the seventeenth century there had emerged within the nobility an imprecise but real line of division between the haves and the have-nots: on the one hand the great council families, now taking their ease in the best jobs (and often pluralists and sinecurists into the bargain), together with their allies and connections among the new men who had recently risen to the top, and won a title and a fortune out of the wars of Germany; on the other hand the mass of middling and lesser nobles, often of good old family, who were edged out in the scuffle for offices, and who bitterly resented the magnates' virtual monopoly of all the most eligible employments – the more so, since to them the wages of office were often a necessity rather than a bonus.[73] It was a typical court-country situation; but it differed from some of its analogues in that the court party was not led by the king, and that the country party was prepared to fling itself into the king's arms in order to gain its objectives. And it was against the council, especially, that the resentment of the hungry place-hunters was directed; for it was the council that openly maintained a policy of job-reservation for its members and their offspring.[74] Thus, apart from purely political developments, economic and social maladjustments made nonsense of any hopes that the council might retain its position as leader of the anti-absolutist cause. The mass of the aristocracy was not prepared to curb the prerogative of a monarchy which offered the best chance of righting its social grievances. When set against the prospect of a secure if modest income in the civil service or the army, the declamation of constitutional theorists such as Clas Rålamb made little appeal; *aurea libertas* had few attractions for those to whom it might mean liberty to live in penury.

If the lesser nobility were thus driven to connive at absolutism, the same was still more true for the three lower Estates.

They too aspired to office, and resented the predominant share of it that went to the nobility. The Recess of Kalmar had long ago insisted that no 'base-born' (*vanbördig*) person be placed over the head of a nobleman; the *Postulata Nobilium* of 1594 had reiterated the demand; as recently as 1612 Gustav Adolf's Privileges had contained a clause of similar tenor;[75] but in 1650 the non-noble Estates forced the Nobility to take refuge in shuffling equivocations and semantic gymnastics in an attempt to explain that the phrase had no derogatory implications.[76] For Erik Sparre, *vanbördig* meant Johan Henriksson; in the Privileges of 1612 it meant Nils Chesnecopherus or Erik Göransson Tegel; in 1650 it meant a whole new middle class, angrily knocking at the gates of power. The wars did indeed bring promotion, in the field and at home, to many men of non-noble origin. A few of them – Johan Skytte and Johan Adler Salvius, for instance – even fought their way up, with royal patronage, to membership of the council itself. But the prospect of office was clouded, first by the attempts of the high nobility to pre-empt the best places, and secondly by the progressive impoverishment of the crown, which was the consequence of its alienation of lands and revenues into noble hands. This meant, only too often, that the king could not pay his servants' wages.[77] The Peasantry, for their part, complained that alienations and donations were depressing them into servitude; the Clergy and Burghers feared that the social and economic preponderance of the Nobility might lead to a constitutional revolution in which crown and commons would alike be reduced to political insignificance.[78] In the light of these discontents and apprehensions it is not difficult to understand why, in 1680, the lower Estates and the serving nobility should have united to support Charles xi in carrying through a *reduktion*, nor why the *riksdag* in the years that followed should have allowed itself to sink into complaisant inertia, preferring the order and security of absolutism to the distracted finances and social discrimination of liberty.

It was only slowly that the council came to realize the implications of these changes. It still felt itself to be the bearer of a great historic mission: indeed, in the 1660s and 1670s it pushed its constitutional pretensions with unwonted vigour. In Clas Rålamb it found a leader who personified the old tradition more forcefully and more eloquently than any man since the death of Erik Sparre: for him, at least, the Recess of Kalmar still had more than an antiquarian interest.[79] There had been a persistent undercurrent of antagonism between council and regents even in Oxenstierna's time, though the great chancellor had usually been able to impose his authority to prevent its emergence into the open. After 1660 Magnus de la Gardie, less able and less sure of himself, was hard put to it to preserve even a semblance of harmony. In this situation the council remembered again its duty to be jealous of the prerogative, now for the time being in the regents' care: it remembered too its claim to a voice in the disposal of offices.[80] When the time came for Charles xi to give his Accession Charter, it made a last effort to impose limitations on the monarchy in the spirit of 1611. The attempt failed. For the Estates had taken the part of the regents against the council in the 'sixties, precisely *because* the regents represented the prerogative; and they insisted on an innocuous Charter in 1672 precisely because they feared a persistence of council influence – and especially of influence on appointments – after the minority was over. The council, in fact, was now fighting on two fronts; the one facing the crown, the other facing the Estates. Its fate was to be distrusted by both sides. The monarchists waited their opportunity to throw off the council's constitutional tutelage. The Estates disliked it as the citadel of the high aristocracy; blamed it for the fiasco in foreign policy, the ruinous finances, and the disasters of the war against Brandenburg; and sharpened their knives against the day of reckoning. That day came in 1680. But to the very last the council preserved its historic constitutional position; to the very last it fought a tenacious rearguard action against advancing absolutism; and from the last ditch of conciliar resistance the trumpets of 1483 still sounded flatly upon the echo-less air.[81]

The years after 1680 seemed to close a long historical perspective. The council was stripped of its political authority, and became, for the first time in its history, the king's council; its claim to be a mediator between king and people, its more recent pretension to be an Estate in itself,[82] were both explicitly rejected; the great offices of state were left unfilled; the high aristocracy was ruined by political prosecutions and the operation of the *reduktion*; a new 'rule of secretaries' seemed to revive all those aspects of monarchical government which Erik Sparre and Hogenskild Bielke had found most odious in the reigns of Gustav Vasa's sons. The Land Law, indeed, still stood, as the moveless foundation of the state; but the king's legists now interpreted it in a way which allowed him greater liberty of action than its framers had ever dreamed of. Under Charles XII that liberty extended so far, that the reign seemed the realization of all the most sinister implications which council-constitutionalism had perceived in hereditary monarchy. But the political catastrophe and the economic sufferings which it entailed in the end nerved the nation to sweep absolutism away. The idea of electoral monarchy had never wholly died, even in the mid-seventeenth century;[83] and the death of Charles XII without heirs qualified to succeed him provided an opportunity for a new election and a fresh start. And with the return of electoral monarchy, constitutionalism too returned. The service-nobility deserted the crown; a constitution was adopted which established the virtual sovereignty of the *riksdag* for more than half a century. But the attempt of the high aristocracy to use the opportunity to reassert the council's claim to speak for the nation failed ignominiously. The day when they could stand forth as the champions of constitutionalism had gone for ever; and the sign of its passing was provided by the nickname given to their supporters in 1719: their opponents called them – 'Tories'.[84]

3

We are now, perhaps, in a position to approach an answer to the question which I posed at the beginning of this lecture, and to attempt some estimate of the contribution of aristocratic constitutionalism to the development of Swedish liberty. Seen thus in perspective, it appears much less impressive than the reader of Lagerroth or Erland Hjärne might suppose. Between 1560 and 1718, the limitations which the high aristocracy imposed upon the monarchy, the bulwarks they built up against royal absolutism, proved fragile indeed. Their efforts were fairly effective against sovereigns who were minors, as in 1611, 1634, 1660; but when a ruler reached his majority the ground which had been gained during his nonage was lost quickly, and with scarcely a struggle. With the solitary exception of the Charter extorted from Sigismund in 1594, no constitutional victory was ever won over a king of full age. In 1590 John III purged his council, and exacted from its members a declaration of abject servility;[85] Charles IX and his secretaries maintained the royal authority in the face of widespread discontent even after Charles had been disabled by a paralytic stroke; Christina shrugged off the Form of Government when she came of age without the smallest hint of resistance from the men who had made it, and followed this up by imposing, by sheer will-power, a dynastic settlement almost unanimously opposed by her council. Charles X gave short shrift to mediators;[86] Charles XI dealt the council a blow from which it never recovered. It needed Charles XII's death to break the spell of obedience which his absolutism had cast upon the country in his lifetime. No reigning monarch ever subscribed to the Form of Government of 1634. Until 1719 no Charter on the lines of that of 1611 was ever extracted from Gustav Adolf's successors.

But if the power of the monarchy thus remained remarkably constant, it would be rash to assume that the liberties of the subject were retarded by this state of affairs. Some liberties were fairly secure in any event; others, though in jeopardy, would have been none the safer if the council had been able to make good all its claims. Take, for instance, that clause in the Land Law which bound the king to impose no new law upon the people without their consent. It was not a clause which came into play very often, for 'new law' meant in fact only major pieces of legislation which affected the Land Law itself in important respects: as, for example, the Succession Agreements of 1544 or 1604, or the Judicature Ordinance of 1614, or the Form of Government of 1634. Now in fact all these were submitted to, and accepted by, the *riksdag*; and it is not easy to think of legislation of this sort (apart, perhaps, from some ecclesiastical legislation in Gustav Vasa's time) which did not comply more or less with the Land Law's provisions. Side by side with statutes of this kind, however, was a large body of what may be called proclamations, ordinances or regulations, which the king could promulgate without the consent of anybody at all – though to be sure the Land Law obliged him to take his council's counsel upon them. Practically all legislation of an economic or administrative nature fell into this category, and so too did legislation affecting one Estate only, for which it was sufficient that the king should consult the Estate concerned. The kings used this power of ordinance-making freely, as their duty was, and the council accepted the practice without question. Many of the great reforms of Gustav Adolf's reign were put out in this way. Axel Oxenstierna, who drafted most of them, was certainly not the man to object to it.[87]

What then was the position in regard to illegal taxation? To this the answer must be that illegal taxation really was surprisingly rare. The king might bargain for an aid with individual provincial assemblies, he might ask the assembled *riksdag* for a tax, he might even harangue the crowd at the great markets with a view to trying the effect of royal oratory upon the commonalty;[88] but almost always he sought and obtained consent of some sort.[89] Illegal taxation is simply not a major issue in Swedish constitutional history, and the roll of national heroes is surprisingly poor in village Hampdens. There were tumults and demonstrations against *heavy* taxes, certainly; and it was always fairly probable that some of the king's bailiffs would abuse their position to fleece the taxpayer in order to line their own pockets. But the victims of this situation did not make a constitutional issue of it: they applied the standard remedy, and massacred the bailiff; and most kings were not insensitive to a hint so vicariously administered. After Gustav Vasa no king lived of his own, as the Land Law directed that he should; and when in the seventeenth century the question of a *reduktion* came to be a burning issue its advocates were able to make the point (and it was not altogether a mere debating point) that members of the high aristocracy, by defending alienations of lands and revenues, were making it impossible for the king to live without extraordinary taxation, and so were tempting him to violate his coronation oath.[90]

Illegal taxation might be rare; arbitrary imprisonment – that is, imprisonment otherwise than after formal trial and sentence – was more common, especially for crimes of a political nature. But this was not a matter about which the council was disposed to make any fuss. Nothing like a writ of *habeas corpus* existed;[91] and if it had, a return to the effect that imprisonment was *per speciale mandatum domini regis* would have seemed perfectly in order to almost everybody. The king, after all, was the highest officer of justice in his kingdom, entitled to doom his own dooms personally[92] – as Monaldesco found to his cost; and even Erik Sparre conceded that the King had the right to be judge in his own cause, if it were a question *de regalibus*.[93] The council, for its part, had no sympathy with persons who 'employed an unprofitable mouth' in lewd and naughty words. Censorship was vigorous and vigilant, and remained so until 1766.[94] The idea of freedom of speech in parliament was indeed growing, but only rather slowly;[95] and in this matter the council was as ready as the monarch to take a strong line with pert and froward members.[96]

Liberties of the subject of this kind were not really at the centre of constitutional controversy in the sixteenth and seventeenth centuries. They never became popular grievances, and they make no figure in the lists of 'burdens' (*besvär*) which the lower Estates presented to each *riksdag*; in part because abuses of this sort were not vital issues in Sweden, in part because Sweden lacked an economically strong, politically mature and habitually litigious middle class, able and willing to resent them. There are no analogues in Sweden to Bate and Cony; a Prynne or a Lilburne is scarcely conceivable; the crucial constitutional issues never seem to hang upon decisions in the courts; and if any historian were to attempt to compile a volume of *Cases in the Constitutional Law*, of the type familiar to English undergraduates, the crop he would glean from the sixteenth and seventeenth centuries would be meagre indeed.

Turning to another field, we can see that the attempt to impose some control upon the king's conduct of foreign policy had certainly a limited measure of success: Gustav Adolf took *riksdag* and council fully into his confidence before embarking upon the German expedition (and indeed seemed glad enough to spread the burden of responsibility);[97] Oxenstierna followed the same line in 1644. But neither of them paid any heed to the complementary obligation to seek approval for a truce or a peace;[98] and just how little king or council could feel bound in the matter of declaring war can be seen from Charles x's attack on Denmark in 1658, and de la Gardie's attack on Brandenburg in 1674 – in the one case without consulting the Estates, in the other in express defiance of their wishes.

35

It might appear, then, that the tangible achievements of aristocratic constitutionalism were scarcely proportionate to the pother that has been made about it. At best the king was kept firmly pegged to the letter of the Land Law. But it was one of the difficulties of those who sought to set bounds to the king's power that the Land Law, unshakably embedded as it was in the fabric of the constitution, was drawn in antique terms which no longer had relevance to existing conditions, or were at best vague. In regard to extraordinary taxation, for instance, it stipulated for the consent of each province, given through a body consisting of the bishop, the *lagman*, and a jury of six nobles and six peasants. By the second half of the sixteenth century such bodies had long since ceased to meet. One of the purposes of Charles ix's proposed revision of the Land Law was to remove this antique anomaly and bring the law into conformity with existing constitutional practice.[99] It was still common ground that taxation and legislation required popular consent of some sort; but nobody now was certain of precisely what sort. Until the *riksdag* established an undisputed claim to be the only organ through which that consent was to be given – and it can hardly be said to have done this much before 1660 – the constitutional situation was in this respect remarkably fluid: hence the use, in the Charter of 1611 and the Form of Government of 1634, of such imprecise formularies as 'the consent of those whom it concerns'.[100] The king was left with a wide area for manoeuvre: as late as Charles x's time he negotiated with provincial gatherings, as well as with the *riksdag*.[101] The prerogative was admitted to be elastic; and perhaps one reason for the long continuance of this situation was that it was never outrageously abused. Few kings in this period were sufficiently arbitrary or tyrannical to provoke much popular support for a constitutional movement. Apart from Erik xiv, who was mentally ill, none was a really intolerable ruler. When John iii boasted that he intended to rule absolutely 'hereafter as heretofore',[102] it was not a threat to make anyone's blood run hot or cold. Sigismund's 'tyranny' was a political myth propagated by his enemies; Charles ix's – like Gustav Vasa's – was a shrewd trading upon his political indispensability. The absolutism of Charles xi after 1680 was always kept carefully within the letter of the law, and in any case had the nation behind it. And even

Charles XII – the most despotic of them all – provoked no serious discontent until his desperate final years. The monarchy did indeed lay very heavy burdens on the Swedish people. But it is impossible to be blind to the fact that, on the whole, it was popular. And it was popular because it was personal and paternal – the very qualities which were threatened by Erik Sparre's plans for a civil service which should be national, rather than a haphazard collection of royal servants. The crown was the common man's refuge, his ally, his safeguard against injustice and oppression; and this concept of monarchy persisted until far into the eighteenth century, as the popularity of Adolf Frederick and the support for Gustav III make clear. As supreme dispenser of justice, the king must be accessible to those of his subjects who might need his aid. All good kings were so: it is ironical to find the *council* remonstrating with John III because of his slackness in this regard.[103] The burden which this accessibility imposed was one main reason for the creation of the supreme court in 1614.[104] To 'go to the king' (*att gå till kungs*) was a precious last resort for those who were exposed to the violence of the strong, or who found their simplicity ensnared in the meshes of the law. And what drove them to the king, often enough, was the greed or oppression of the nobility – and not least of that high nobility which provided council-constitutionalism with its leaders. The nobleman had his private manorial code (*gårdsrätt*), and his manorial prison too; alleging that the long intervals between sessions of the ordinary courts made these adjuncts to agriculture a necessity.[105] When sessions-time at last came round, the peasant might well feel that his chances were not much improved, for the nobleman would probably preside, in person or by deputy, in the county court (*häradsting*). The lord's power of designating his peasants for the militia enabled him to discipline his tenants; his acquisition, by alienation from the crown, of the right to the fiscal contributions of tax-peasants, threatened them (if they were tardy in payment) with the loss of their rights of ownership. The townsman resented noble encroachments upon municipal privileges; the clergy, drawn largely from the peasantry, sympathized with the peasant's plight. To all the lower Estates the main danger to liberty, by the middle of the seventeenth century, came not from the unconstitutional actions of the king,

37

but from the threat – real or prospective – of subjection to an overwhelmingly powerful aristocracy. What was the Recess of Kalmar to them? To which of them, save to a few bishops, was it of any concern who was included in the ephorate, and who not? It was not until the Age of Liberty that the ordinary member of the *riksdag* came to feel vividly the relevance of political theory to political life, and was ready to translate the speculations of the study into the parrot-cries of the clubs; for only then did 'constitutionalism' chime in with the real needs and aspirations of the *pays légal*. The crown, on the other hand, seemed to have its feet much more firmly planted in the common earth. It offered not only protection, but the hope of better days: the abhorred 'rule of secretaries', from Jöran Persson to Johan Hoghusen, opened a career to ambition and ability; the king, far more than the nobility (though they had their clients too) was favourable to social mobility. How sharp the contrast between the new men around Charles XI, and the narrow, socially exclusive circle of great council-families which he overthrew! That circle had indeed been widening a little, especially after 1660; but the same small handful of names recurs, decade after decade, century after century: Brahe, Bonde, Bielke, Banér, de la Gardie, Fleming, Oxenstierna, Sparre, Posse, Tott; ringing the changes on office in endless variety, yet always essentially the same, like some genealogical treble-bob-major. When Gustav Bonde was called to the council in 1727, he was the twentieth member of his family, in unbroken succession, to sit in that body.[106]

A sceptic might at this point feel justified in doubting whether the aristocracy had any truly *constitutional* programme at all, in the sense of a commitment to the defence or expansion of fundamental liberties. They had indeed programmes of administrative reform; they reacted appropriately to lack of government. But mainly (it might be urged) they saw things through the medium of the interests of their class. The men who opposed John III and Charles IX in the name of the ideal polity of the fifteenth century may have been deluding themselves; but that is no reason why they should be permitted to delude posterity. The political arrangements of the age of Christian I, which they represented as being based on a respect for law, were arrangements devised to secure the almost total immunity of the

Nobility from the burdens of society. From the beginning it had been a main weakness of council-constitutionalism that its programme was so obviously explicable as a scheme to advance the interests of a narrow clique of great magnates. It was an explanation which did them less than justice; but there was a core of truth in it. The constitutional struggles of the fifteenth century were but one facet of a fierce competition for fiefs, for the right to dispose of fiefs, and for the solid economic advantages which could be a consequence of fief-holding. A century later, when fiefs in the old style were no more than a poignant memory lingering in the minds of an aristocracy which felt obscurely that it had been denied its reward for existing, Erik Sparre and his associates hoped to find, in the revenue-assignments and wages (*förläningar* and *beställningar*) which were now the return for government service, some compensation for the fiefs which were no longer given to them; and hence they demanded a monopoly of high office. It was a nostalgia for the withered blooms of privilege, rather than a passion for constitutional rights, that inspired Hogenskild Bielke to rummage in the archives and the muniment-rooms; and even Erik Sparre's more sophisticated political theory was in part a cloak for class-advantage.[107] They importuned the monarchy for more generous privileges on two main grounds. The first ground was that they sought no more than the recovery of their prescriptive rights, as those rights had existed in the fifteenth century; and to this argument Erik Sparre himself provided a succinct reply, when he said, in rebuttal of royal pretensions, 'We should look not so much to what was done here aforetime, but rather to what ought to be done.'[108] The second ground was that their acceptance of the Succession Pact of 1544 gave them a claim upon the crown's gratitude.[109] It was a claim which had no chance of being admitted, since the Vasas on their side always argued that the Succession Pact really was to be looked upon as a kind of testimonial from a grateful people.[110] To Erik Sparre, however, the Pact was an implied contract; and in terms of that contract the crown was bound to give the Nobility better privileges, wider immunities, and a monopoly of office. But this was an argument which knocked the bottom out of their claim to be a constitutional opposition; for it implicitly admitted that in 1544 they had sold their constitutional birthright for a mess of pottage. If they did so, it was by no means the only example of such a bargain. The success of Charles ix, for instance, was based upon his ability to bribe the aristocracy to forgo constitutional principles in return for donations, enfeoffments and wages.[111] On the accession of Charles x in 1654 Oxenstierna was quite prepared to strike a bargain with him on terms which would have sacrificed constitutional principle for class interest and private ambition: the king was to be let off with a vague and innocuous Accession Charter, and in return was to give a guarantee against a *reduktion*, and sanction administrative arrangements which would have given to the chancery – Oxenstierna's own department – a primacy over its rivals.[112] In 1686, when Charles xi's *indelningsverk* seemed likely to diminish the aristocracy's tied labour force, they tried to wreck the scheme by offering to throw overboard all the constitutional checks upon troop-raising which had been slowly built up in the preceding half-century.[113] The revival of aristocratic constitutionalism in the closing decades of the sixteenth century may seem to the historians of political thought to be important for the theories, domestic or imported, which lay behind it; but what gave it its cutting edge was indignation at the crown's calculated neglect to provide the high aristocracy with suitably juicy substitutes for the fiefs which they had lost.[114] If it came to a pull between private interest and public principle, in fact, the Swedish aristocracy was by no means always to be relied on to choose the latter. Charles ix may have been hitting below the belt when he played on class hatreds to defeat Erik Sparre; but he would scarcely have succeeded unless the aristocracy's conduct had made his accusations plausible. The *Postulata Nobilium*, after all, was not only a constitutional programme: it included a demand that the peasants of the nobility should be withdrawn from the jurisdiction of the ordinary courts, and abandoned to the justice of their lords.[115] For an old-fashioned patriarchal magnate such as Per Brahe the elder, this no doubt implied no more than a recognition of the good old Nordic custom of paternal correction (*husaga*); but two generations later it might mean riding the wooden horse, or other imported refinements of Teutonic culture;[116] and in the 1640s a younger Per Brahe would protest that it was insulting to refer to the nobility as 'subjects'.[117] The crisis at the time of Gustav Adolf's accession was not only, or even mainly, a constitutional crisis: it was a crisis which turned on the demands, the sufferings and the wrongs of a dominant and resentful class; and the privileges which Gustav Adolf was forced to concede to them in 1612 proved a good deal more durable than the Charter which he granted in 1611. How should such a class feel strongly about illegal taxation, when they were to so great an extent exempt from paying it? Why should they seek to restrain an aggressive foreign policy? They were likely to be its main beneficiaries![118] As to free speech, they were against it, at least in their social inferiors; as to illegal punishments, they were themselves among the chief offenders. The Land Law's ban upon the employment of foreigners was no more than the principle of the closed shop, common to half the aristocracies of continental Europe. And the first Estate's claim to a *votum decisivum* – later to be justified on the ground that they alone were their own constituents – was a standing threat to the development of a healthy parliamentary system.[119]

But this is too simple and superficial a judgment. One of the salient characteristics of Swedish history, and one which links it most closely to our own, is the pertinacity and success with which the Swedish people have maintained the concept of the rule of law. And of that concept the Swedish aristocracy, from the fourteenth century to the eighteenth, were the most effective custodians. Sweden had no long legal tradition stretching far back into the Middle Ages; no Year Books, no Inns of Court; until the middle of the seventeenth century there was no class of professional lawyers and advocates at all; until the setting up of *Svea Hovrätt* in 1614 no judge-made law, no regular record of decided cases, no treasury of legal precedents.[120] The law-bearing class was the nobility, who served the community as a matter of course in the capacity of provincial or county-court judges (*lagmän* or *häradshövdingar*). The legal antiquarianism of Coke or Spelman is represented in Sweden by the researches and collections of Erik Sparre and Hogenskild Bielke. It was no accident that in the greatest and most protracted civil suit of the sixteenth century – the case of the Gyllenstierna estate – it was just these two who appeared as pleaders for the main parties to the cause.[121] It was no accident, either, that when *Svea Hovrätt* was instituted, all the judges, and half the assessors, were members of the nobility:[122] the arrangement was natural, sensible and traditional. For the nobility were, and had always been, the natural buttresses of the rule of law. It was a matter of history that when Erik xiv's High Court lost its aristocratic character after 1562 the only real barrier to royal bending of justice was removed. After that experience it was no wonder if the nobility felt that they must not only be tried by their peers, but also dominate the supreme judiciary.[123] As time went by, it is true, the office of county-court judge (*häradshövding*) came to be regarded more as a lucrative sinecure than as a real responsibility;[124] and until Charles xi enforced residence its holders were often absentees who discharged their functions by deputy. But such things by no means diminished the aristocracy's respect for, and knowledge of, the law. Moreover, as long as the nobility continued to exercise important judicial functions – in the council (as supreme appellate court), in the *hovrätter*, and in the local courts – the security of tenure of the judiciary was pretty safe from attack by the crown.[125] And the best opinion nowadays is that even in the dark days of the mid-seventeenth century the peasant could as a rule be sure that the courts and the council would give him justice against his lord.[126]

It would be a mistake, moreover, to assume that the aristocracy's pursuit of its own advantage was incompatible with the advancement of the constitutional cause. On the contrary, the two often enough went hand in hand. The Recess of Kalmar itself embodied an important guarantee of the liberty of the subject, when it demanded security against arbitrary imprisonment, and a promise that the king would take no punitive action upon the strength of unsubstantiated delations.[127] These demands were repeated almost *verbatim* in the *Postulata*,[128] and finally acquired legal sanction in the Charter of 1611.[129] The draft privileges of 1567, King John's privileges of 1569, the council's draft of 1594, all included clauses designed to safeguard the rule of law;[130] and in 1594 the nobility expressly stipulated that there should be no legislation without the consent of the Estates.[131] A claim which may at first sight appear to be wholly dictated by sectional interests may well turn out on closer examination to be the assertion of a genuine constitutional principle. For instance, there was a reiterated demand (not finally conceded until 1612) that the king be debarred from negotiating directly with the peasantry of the nobility when he wished to obtain a grant of men, money or labour services from them: the request, it was contended, must be made not to the peasants but to their lords. This looks like an attempt to preserve the fiscal immunity of the nobility, and to degrade their peasants to mediate status. But in fact it is a statement of the general principle of no taxation without consent. For even though the peasants might make the grant, the burden would in reality fall upon their landlords; since the more the crown took the less the lord would get.[132]

It was certainly unfortunate that successive regents and kings should have been able to drive a wedge between the council-constitutionalists and the Estates. But in the existing circumstances it is difficult to deny that constitutional principles, at least until the seventeenth century, were safer in aristocratic hands. Erik Sparre and his friends could have contended, with much justice, that by opposing Charles IX's tactics of treating all dissentients as 'unruly and lopped-off members'[133] of the body politic – by upholding the right of a minority to differ, as against Charles's totalitarian notion of obligatory unanimity – they were championing a more truly democratic system of government than their adversary. No doubt the aristocracy, like the *riksdag*, could on occasion be bribed. But it is still true, that while the Strife of Estates (*ståndstriden*) continued the council was the only element in the state which could normally be relied upon to provide a constitutional opposition: the events of the 1680s made that quite plain. It was precisely because Charles XI's *reduktion* brought the Strife of Estates more or less to a close that a *nationally*-based constitutionalism became possible for the first time, in the years after 1718.

And this must be added, in conclusion: the Swedish aristocracy, for all its heavy faults, had the high virtue of a genuine patriotism which in the last resort was prepared to put country before class.[134] In this it contrasts strikingly with the aristocracies of Poland, Denmark, and perhaps Holland too, to name no more. It could always be relied upon to waive its privileges and its fiscal immunities if the national interest seemed to demand it: indeed, its readiness to do so sometimes provided monarchs with a useful argument for screwing a grant out of the ordinary taxpayer. It was not infected with the *servicio-merced* mentality which enervated the aristocracies of the Spanish kingdoms. Despite all the conquests of the seventeenth century, it never really became militarized. It was accustomed to pursue its political objects within the limits of the law: between 1529 and 1718 there is but one instance of its resorting to violence to gain its ends or defend its interests, and that was the wholly exceptional case of the rising against Erik xiv in 1568. It produced no Bouillon, no Montmorency, no Condé. An Oxenstierna or a de la Gardie would as soon have turned Leveller as *frondeur*.[135]

In the year 1439 Bishop Thomas of Strängnäs, in the course of a political poem devoted to the support of Karl Knutsson, wrote some stanzas which are among the best-known passages of early Swedish literature. Their theme is the praise of liberty; and though historians still dispute among themselves as to the nature of the liberty intended, the dust of that controversy cannot altogether obscure the passion that lies behind them.[136]

> Frihet är den bästa ting
> Der sökas kan all världen kring,
> Den frihet kan väl bära.
> Vill du vara dig själva huld,
> Du älskar frihet mer än guld,
> Ty frihet följer ära.

Those lines were written when the tide of aristocratic constitutionalism was flowing strongly towards its flood. They were written by a man who was himself a member of the council of the realm. And perhaps it is not wholly inappropriate that the first literary expression of an ideal which has so strong a hold upon the Swedish people should have come from a representative of the class which did so much to lay the foundations upon which the fabric of Swedish law is built. In the long run – at least for the period I have been considering – it is Fryxell, rather that Geijer, who has had the better of the argument.

NOTES

[1] This paper is an expanded version of the Creighton Lecture for 1965, delivered in the University of London, 15 November 1965, and published by the Athlone Press, 1966.

[1a] Anders Fryxell, *Om aristokrat-fördömandet i svensk historia*, i–iv, Uppsala, 1845–50.

[2] Ulf Sjödell, 'Kungamakt och aristokrati i svensk 1900-tals debatt', *Historisk Tidskrift*, 1965, p. 5: the article offers a full discussion of the whole Geijer-Fryxell controversy and its historiographical consequences. See also Carl-Arvid Hessler, ' "Aristokratfördömandet". En riktning i svensk historieskrivning', *Scandia*, xv (1943), 209–97.

[3] See, especially, Åke Hermansson, *Karl IX och ständerna. Tronfrågan och författningsutvecklingen i Sverige 1598–1611*, Uppsala, 1962, and Nils Runeby, *Monarchia mixta. Maktfördelningsdebatt i Sverige under den tidigare stormaktstiden*, Uppsala, 1962.

[4] See, e.g., Karl Nordlund, *Den svenska reformationstidens allmänna statsrättsliga ideer*, Stockholm, 1900; Fredrik Lagerroth, *Frihetstidens författning. En studie i den svenska konstitutionalismens historia*, Stockholm, 1915; Erland Hjärne, *Från Vasatiden till Frihetstiden. Några drag ur den svenska konstitutionalismens historia*, Uppsala, 1929; Kerstin Strömberg-Back, *Lagen, rätten, läran. Politisk och kyrklig debatt i Sverige under Johan III:s tid*, Lund, 1963; Runeby, *op. cit.*

[5] A conveniently accessible edition is *Utdrag ur Magnus Erikssons Landslag*, ed. Emil Olsson, Lund, 1927.

[6] Dr Strömberg-Back (*op. cit.*, p. 33) deprecates the use of terms such as 'constitutionalism', or 'council-constitutionalism', on the ground that they are too suggestive of nineteenth-century Liberalism; but an English reader brought up on Stubbs can perhaps be relied upon to make the necessary mental adjustment.

[7] The relevant portions of Christopher's Land Law are printed in *Sveriges regeringsformer 1634–1809 samt konungaförsäkringar 1611–1800*, ed. Emil Hildebrand, Stockholm, 1891: this is clause 4, p. 279.

[8] Gottfrid Carlsson, *Kalmar Recess 1483*, Stockholm, 1955, p. 5. For the growth of the council's power in the fifteenth century, see in general Emil Hildebrand, *Svenska statsförfattningens historiska utveckling*, Stockholm, 1896, pp. 84–141.

[9] Gottfrid Carlsson, *op. cit., passim.*; Sven Ulric Palme, *Sten Sture den äldre*, Stockholm, 1950, pp. 98–111.

[10] Anders Schönberg, *Historiska bref om det svenska regeringssättet, i äldre och nyare tider* (new edn), Stockholm, 1849, i. 196.

[11] For recent assessments of the younger Sten's character and policies, see Gottfrid Carlsson, 'Sten Sture den yngre', *Scandia*, ii (1929); Greta Wieselgren, *Sten Sture d.y. och Gustav Trolle*, Lund, 1949; Gunnar T. Westin, *Riksföreståndaren och makten. Politiska utvecklingslinjer i Sverige 1517–1521*, Lund, 1957.

[12] Its real initiator, however, was Karl Knutsson.

[13] As, for example, in regard to the question of billeting of troops (*borgläger*) in 1524; or in regard to policy towards Lübeck in 1533–4; or in regard to the Russian war of 1554. It was significant that the oath sworn by members of the council at Gustav Vasa's coronation omitted any mention of their duty to ensure the observance by king and people of the pledges each had given to the other: *Svenska riksdagsakter*, I Series, Stockholm, 1888, i, 111.

[14] Printed in *Svenska riksdagsakter*, I Series, i, 378–89.

[15] As Professor Lönnroth has remarked, 'The difference between hereditary

and elective monarchy was quite simply the difference between uncon-
ditional or conditional handing over of castles – that is, of the country's
military and financial resources – to the new king': Erik Lönnroth, 'Är
Sveriges historia oföränderlig?', *Historisk Tidskrift*, 1950, p. 386. When the
riksdag in 1693 declared Charles XI to be absolute, they explicitly based
absolutism upon the hereditary character of the monarchy: Lennart Thanner, 'Suveränitetsförklaring år 1693', *Karolinska förbundets årsbok*, 1954.

[16] Printed in *Svenska riksdagsakter*, I Series, i, 675–700: the check referred
to is on p. 687. And see Birgitta Odén, 'Gustav Vasa och testamentets
tillkomst', *Scandia*, xxix (1963), pp. 114, 136.

[17] By the Articles of Arboga, 1561: they are printed in *Svenska riksdagsakter*,
I Series, ii, 9–19.

[18] *Ibid.*, p. 33.

[19] See Ingvar Andersson, 'Erik XIV och Machiavelli', *Scandia*, iv (1931),
pp. 1 ff., but also the criticism of this point of view in Gunnar Annell,
Erik XIV:s etiska föreställningar och deras inflytande på hans politik, Uppsala,
1945, pp. 59–64.

[20] Erik's motives, and his state of mind at the time of the killing, are
matters of controversy: see Ingvar Andersson, *Erik XIV* (2nd edn, Stockholm, 1948), pp. 191–248 (a classic biography); Viktor Wigert, *Erik XIV:
historisk-psykiatrisk studie*, Stockholm, 1920; Rudolf Elander, *Sturemordens
gåta*, Stockholm, 1928; Jerker Rosén, *Studier kring Erik XIV:s höga nämnd*,
Lund, 1955, pp. 65–84; Gunnar Annell, *op. cit.*; and the collection of documents in *Handlingar rörande Skandinaviens historia*, v, Stockholm, 1817.

[21] For example of the council's protests and remonstrances on this
account, see *Svenska riksdagsakter*, I Series, ii, 510–14, 571, 668, 670–7, 811–
16, 827.

[22] In 1593 the nobility asked the council ('since there are very few of us
who have any knowledge of our ancient liberties'), to give them information
about them, 'for we gather that our forefathers were a very free people,
beyond all others, which now (God amend it) is much altered': *ibid.*,
iii, 177–8; and see the revealing letter from Hogenskild Bielke to his brother
Ture, 11 June, 1593, where he writes: 'King Gustav degraded the Estate of
Nobility, which was the foremost in the realm . . . After that there were not
many left who dared to say a word against it [*sc.* the Vasa *régime*] and so
liberty declined the one year after the other, so that it came to be clean
forgot what the old freedom had been, and no one cared to look into it and
consult old documents, and such as were found in cathedrals and monas-
teries were all confiscated and kept hidden from others, so that they might
not come to the eyes of those whom they most concerned': *Handlingar
rörande Skandinaviens historia*, viii, 56.

[23] On Sparre's political theories, K. Strömberg-Back, *Lagen, rätten, läran*,
now supersedes all others; but see also Lagerroth, *Frihetstidens författning*,
pp. 80–105.

[24] *Svenska riksdagsakter*, I Series, iii, 394.

[25] *Ibid.*, iii, 385–6.

[26] *Ibid.*, ii, 845.

[27] This, it seems to me, weakens the force of the distinction which Dr

ON ARISTOCRATIC CONSTITUTIONALISM

Strömberg-Back (*op. cit.*, p. 19) draws between Sparre's views and those of his fifteenth-century predecessors. The attempt to present alteration as restoration is a feature common to Swedish and English constitutional history: the revolutions of 1680, 1719, and 1772 all represented themselves to be returns to a previously-existing constitutional norm.

[28] Strömberg-Back, pp. 64–6.

[29] Erik Sparre, *Pro Lege Rege et Grege*, ed. J. E. Almquist: Historiska Handlingar, 26: 1 Stockholm, 1924, pp. 30–3, 54; Strömberg-Back, pp. 121, 147–9.

[30] In the *Postulata Nobilium: Svenska riksdagsakter*, I Series, iii, 393–405; and *cf. ibid.*, pp. 377–91. Sparre was not alone in fearing royal influence on the *riksdag*. In a remarkable constitutional project, drawn up (probably early in 1593) by Axel Leijonhufvud – which among other things asserted the right of rebellion – it was suggested that this danger could be averted by restricting the numbers summoned to a *riksdag*, presumably at the expense of the two lower Estates. Such a *riksdag*, thus rendered immune to royal influence, was by Leijonhufvud given control over taxation and foreign policy: he would also have made it the supreme court of appeal. It would have been summoned automatically once every three years. But the real power would have lain with the seven great officers of state, who were to be drawn from the highest nobility, and were to be irremovable. The project remained without influence, perhaps because Leijonhufvud's political record was not such as to inspire much confidence in his judgment. For an account of it, see Birger Lövgren, 'Ett författningsprojekt från 1590-talet', *Historisk Tidskrift*, 1913, pp. 104–16.

[31] A term which seems to have come into current use in politics with Gustav Vasa's Testament.

[32] As Sigismund always contended: see, e.g., *Svenska riksdagsakter*, I Series, iii, 265, where he writes, 'under the cloak of religion much was demanded of us which touched our royal majesty too nearly'; and *cf. ibid.*, iii, 887, 981. A curious confirmation of this view came half a century later in a council-debate of 21 Feb. 1649, when, in a discussion of the troubles in England, the following dialogue took place:
Christina: Religio is a *praetextus* . . . a sort of raincoat.
De la Gardie: Not to be put on save in case of necessity – as the late King Charles did against Sigismund.
Christina: Hoc non propter amorem religionis, sed propter statum.
S[venska] R[iks-] R[ådets] P[rotokoll], Stockholm, 1878–, xiii, 17.

[33] Petrus Petrejus took this line in 1609: Åke Hermansson, *Karl IX och ständerna*, p. 254. The *riksdag*, after all, had deposed Erik xiv in 1568. Or, alternatively, Charles could contend that he was himself the chief ephor, and so entitled to call the tune: Nils Runeby, *Monarchia Mixta*, p. 98.

[34] C. G. Styffe, *Konung Gustaf II Adolfs skrifter*, Stockholm, 1861, pp. 78, 88. The idea had a basis in reality. The statute of Kalmar (1587), which embodied a plan for the government of Sweden when Sigismund (already King of Poland) should succeed his father on the Swedish throne, had provided for a regency '*ab aliquot personis primatibus, consiliariis et extra consiliariis, videlicet septem numero*' (the 'leading personages' once again).

47

Charles, whose share in this arrangement would have been limited to the nomination of one of the seven, chose to see it as evidence of the sinister purposes of Sparre and his circle, and transmitted the idea to Gustav Adolf: see *Svenska riksdagsakter*, I Series, ii, 792 (for the relevant clause of the statute), and *ibid.*, ii, 867; iii, 775, 934; iv, 122, 165, for characteristic comments by Charles. John himself, though he had agreed to the statute, later associated himself with Charles's accusations: *ibid.*, ii, 896.

[35] See the letter which Svante Sture wrote at Erik's dictation: printed in *Handlingar rörande Skandinaviens historia*, iv, 119–23.

[36] *Svenska riksdagsakter*, I Series, ii, 967–8, 894–5, 909; iv, 75.

[37] See the tense debates in the council on 26 and 27 Feb. 1649, and 24 Sep. 1650; *RRP*, xiii, 343–6; xiv, 309. 'Poland' was an emotive word, used by both sides: e.g. Jakob de la Gardie's condemnation of the privileges of the Polish nobility (*ibid.*, xiii, 259); or Oxenstierna, urging better observance of the rules of order in the *Riddarhus* (29 Jan. 1642): '. . . and not do as is done in Poland . . . where when they hold a diet, one says "write this", and another gets up and says "write that", and so one after the other until at last somebody says "tear the whole thing up", and they depart no better than they came': *S[venska] R[idderskaps och] A[dels] R[iksdags] P[rotokoll]*, I Series, Stockholm, 1855–, iii, 211.

[38] R. Holm, *Johannes Elai Terserus*, Lund, 1906, p. 304.

[39] *Les Anecdotes de Suède*, The Hague, 1716, pp. 105–6; Sven Grauers, 'Kring förspelet till 1680 års riksdag': *Historiska studier tillägnade Nils Ahnlund*, Stockholm, 1949, p. 145.

[40] One of the things that annoyed Fryxell was Geijer's remark that it was not the *people* that had been untrue to Charles XII: Fryxell, *Om aristokratfördömandet*, i, 23.

[41] A. A. von Stiernman, *Alla Riksdagars och Mötes Besluth*, Stockholm, 1728, i, 536.

[42] Printed in *Svenska riksdagsakter*, iii, 328. Lagerroth, logically but surprisingly, considered that the demanding of a Charter as a precondition for the accession of a hereditary king was unconstitutional: F. Lagerroth, 'Revolution eller rättskontinuitet?' *Scandia*, ix (1936), p. 7.

[43] Hermansson, pp. 183–4; Runeby, pp. 45–78. An indication of Charles's personal taste in political theory is perhaps afforded by the fact that the first book to be published as a result of his commission to Erik Schroderus to translate notable foreign works into Swedish was James I's *Regium donum*: Lars Gustafsson, *Virtus politica. Politisk etik och nationellt svärmeri i den tidigare stormaktstidens litteratur*, Uppsala, 1956, p. 48.

[44] Lagerroth wrote: 'Our history can show no more provocative a crime against the principle of legal continuity': *op. cit.*, p. 9.

[45] Printed in *Svenska riksdagsakter*, II Series, Stockholm, 1932–, i, 69–76.

[46] In particular, that their advice should not be judged *ex eventu*, and themselves be liable to disfavour if it turned out ill. This is not explicitly stated in the Charter, but it formed a prominent item in the council's schedule of grievances, and was no doubt covered by the promise not to degrade or deprive of office without lawful judgment: for the council's grievances, see *Svenska riksdagsakter*, II Series, i, 69.

[47] As Johan de la Gardie observed in 1636: 'It was in general H.M. nature, that he was very ready to augment his *regalia* and royal prerogative, and to diminish and cut down the privileges of others': *RRP*, vi, 361. And *cf.* Sven A. Nilsson, 'Reaktionen mot systemskiftet 1611. En linje i Gustav II Adolfs politik', *Scandia*, xx (1950), *passim*.

[48] Text in E. Hildebrand, *Sveriges regeringsformer*, pp. 1–41.

[49] As Oxenstierna himself rightly claimed in 1644: *RRP*, x, 680.

[50] Runeby, p. 239.

[51] Gustav Adolf's intention (ran the preamble) had always been 'an ordered constitution, wherein the king's majesty, the council's authority, and the reasonable rights and liberties of the Estates were properly preserved and defined': Hildebrand, *Sveriges regeringsformer*, p. 2.

[52] Erik Sparre had drawn the distinction too: Strömberg-Back, p. 188.

[53] B. Lövgren, *Ståndstridens utdaning*, Uppsala, 1915, pp. 18–26; N. Ahnlund, *Ståndsriksdagens utveckling*, Stockholm, 1933, pp. 229–30. Gyllenhielm, who was Charles IX's illegitimate son, was a leading champion of the dynasty's interests during Christina's minority, and a prickly defender of his father's reputation: see the sharp clash about this in *RRP*, viii, 592 (5 May 1642).

[54] Salvius to Oxenstierna, 18 August 1634, quoted in C. T. Odhner, *Sveriges inre historia under Drottning Christinas förmyndare*, Stockholm, 1865, p. 31, n. 1. Compare the following exchanges in the council, 21 June 1636:

> *Episcopus Arosiensis: Officiorum constitutio* nowadays, since *regnum* has become *successivum, pertinet ad Regem*. When it was *electivum*, it inclined more to *democraticum statum*. But now it inclines more to *monarchicum statum, sive status* inclines more to *formam monarchicam*.
>
> *Herr Johan Skytte: Aliud est status, aliud administratio status; status* has not been changed, but *administratio status*.
>
> *Episcopus Arosiensis: Dantur gradus in monarchico statu ... Alius status monarchicus* is *in Polonia, alius in Gallia: RRP*, vi, 309.

Karl IX's draft of a revised version of the Land Law had taken care to debar father and son, or two brothers, from sitting in the Council at the same time: Severin Bergh, *Karl IX och den svenska adeln, 1607–9*, Uppsala, 1882, p. 107. The *Additament* of 1660 enacted that not more than one of each family should be a member of the regency, nor more than three be members of the *råd* (clause 3): E. Hildebrand, *Sveriges regeringsformer*, p. 46: when the provision was violated there were strong protests: see Stiernman, *Alla Riksdagars och Mötes Besluth*, Bihang, p. 421.

[55] *RRP*, v, 330. Strong pressure was brought to bear on members who were slack in attendance: *ibid.*, v, 156, 167, 172; vi, 2, 39.

[56] For the development of the council after 1611, see *RRP*, i, 9–10; J. E. Nordwall, *Om svenska riksrådets utveckling mot centralisation under Gustaf II Adolf*, Uppsala, 1891, *passim*; Nils Edén, *Den svenska centralregeringens utveckling till kollegial organisation i början af sjuttonde århundradet*, Uppsala 1902, pp. 117–44.

[57] Salvius reported Oxenstierna as saying that 'to be as it were a mediator between king and Estates is a great and parlous business. The king's rights

and the Estates' rights must be secured to each and preserved intact. Alleged also what jealousy Erik Sparre incurred when he wrote the treatise he called *Lex, rex grex*, assuring to each his *jus*: *RRP*, vi, 138; and *cf. ibid.*, 582, where Oxenstierna observed, 'We are *Senatores Regni* and ought to be as *mediatores inter Regem et subditos*, and speak not only for *jus Regium* but also for *jus regni* and *competentem libertatem patriae*, which although it may ofttimes be odious to *Regem*, is yet demanded of us by our office and calling.'

[58] *RRP*, vi, 662.

[59] Göran Rystad, 'Med råds råde eller efter konungens godtycke? Makten över ämbetstillsättningarna som politisk stridsfråga under 1600-talet', *Scandia*, xxix (1963), pp. 187–9.

[60] *Svenska riksdagsakter*, II Series, i, 73. But see the criticism of this interpretation in Hermansson, *op. cit.*, pp. 275–6.

[61] Form of Government, clauses 43 and 44: Hildebrand, *Sveriges regeringsformer*, p. 31.

[62] Folke Lindberg, 'Axel Oxenstierna som riksdagstaktiker. Ett bidrag till belysningen av riksdagsdoktrin och riksdagspraxis under förmyndartiden' (*Statsvetenskaplig Tidskrift*, xxxiv [N.s. xii], Lund, 1931). Contrast, for instance, *RRP*, vii, 101 with *AOSB*, I, viii, 233.

[63] For the divisive effects of the change, see e.g. *RRP*, iii, 34–5, 69.

[64] Lagerroth, p. 142. During the Fronde the same claim was put forward on behalf of the *parlement* of Paris: E. H. Kossmann, *La Fronde*, Leiden, 1954, p. 102.

[65] Wittrock, *Carl X Gustafs testamente. Den politiska striden i Sverige 1660*, Uppsala, 1908, pp. 255–69.

[66] *Infra*, p. 118.

[67] *Additamentum*, paragraph 14: Hildebrand, *Sveriges regeringsformer*, p. 65: my italics.

[68] Lagerroth, p. 177.

[69] *Additamentum*, paragraph 17; Hildebrand, p. 56; Sam Clason, 'Om uppkomsten af bestämda perioder för den svenska riksdagens sammanträde', *Historisk Tidskrift*, 1892.

[70] *Prästeståndets riksdagsprotokoll*, Uppsala, 1949–, iii, 227–8, 259 (and *cf. ibid.*, ii, 76); *Borgareståndets riksdagsprotokoll före Frihetstiden*, Uppsala, 1933, pp. 612–14. For earlier attempts, see Odhner, *op. cit.*, p. 11; Georg Wittrock, *Regeringen och allmogen under Kristinas förmyndare*, Uppsala, 1948, pp. 9–11.

[71] *Borgareståndets riksdagsprotokoll*, p. 190.

[72] In 1660, for instance, they are said to have threatened to 'break the diet', in Polish fashion: *Prästeståndets riksdagsprotokoll*, ii, 110 ff.

[73] *cf.* the exchanges between Erik Oxenstierna and the Nobility in 1655: *The Chancellor*: What mean you good lords by reversions?
The Nobility: Crucifige, crucifige! They should be cancelled on reasonable terms.
Col. Lars Kruus: Moved that the reversions which the counts have obtained to estates within their counties be handed over, like other reversions, to the crown: *RRP*, xiv, 108–9. And see Georg Wittrock, 'Riksskattmästaren Gustaf Bondes politiska program 1661', *Historisk Tidskrift*, xxxiii, pp. 47–50.

[74] For the special pretensions of the council, see *RRP*, iv, 22; vi, 432;

xii, 304–6; xiv, 240–1; *SRARP*, iv, 192, 216; *Prästeståndets riksdagsprotokoll*. ii, 125.

[75] *Svenska riksdagsakter*, I Series, iii, 394; II Series, i, 112.

[76] *SRARP*, iv, 345; *Dagbok, förd vid 1650 års riksdag . . . af Dr Jonas Petri* (*Handlingar rörande Skandinaviens historia*, xxi (1837)), pp. 95, 107. Christina found it necessary to issue a proclamation explaining that use of the word implied no stigma: Stiernman, Bihang, p. 333. Paulinus had protested at the use of the word *vanbördig* in the Privileges of the Nobility as early as 1634: *RRP*, iv, 183–4; and *cf. SRARP*, iii, 277.

[77] As Herman Fleming put it on 6 April 1655: 'If those who earned it did not receive their reward, no one was going to bring up his children to honour and virtue, and only the rich would have any prospects'; *RRP*, xvi, 128.

[78] *RRP*, xv, 211; *Handlingar til Konung Carl XI:tes historia*, Stockholm, 1769, x, 90; *Samtal emellan Juncker Päär, Mäster Hans* [*etc.*], in *Samling af Curieusa Samtal . . .*, Uppsala, 1768, p. 33; *Prästeståndets riksdagsprotokoll*, i, 169, 172–3, where the bishop of Linkoping commented that 'the clergy are as fond of the nobility as Caligula was of the Roman people'.

[79] Göran Rystad, 'Clas Rålambs memorial 1665 och rådsoppositionen mot Karl xi:s förmyndare' (*Karolinska Förbundets Årsbok*, 1963), *passim; id.*, *Johan Gyllenstierna, rådet och kungamakten*, Lund, 1955, p. 135; Lagerroth, p. 205; Erland Hjärne, *Från Vasatiden till Frihetstiden*, p. 80. Rålamb became a member of the council in 1664.

[80] Göran Rystad, 'Med råds råde eller efter konungens godtycke', pp. 197–236. The tone of the council's attack on the regents in 1665 resembles that in which, in the years between 1720 and 1772, ministers were wont to be censured by the Secret Committee: it is printed in *Den svenska Fatburen*, Stockholm, 1769.

[81] In 1680 the council actually discussed the possibility of appealing to the Recess of Kalmar against their citation before the Great Commission: Rystad, *Johan Gyllenstierna, rådet och kungamakten*, p. 292.

[82] For an early expression of this idea see *RRP*, ix, 16; for an early rejection of it, *ibid.*, xvi, 74.

[83] Oxenstierna in 1633 wrote of Christina's being queen 'in virtue of the unanimous *designation* of council and Estates'; *AOSB*, I, x, 12. In 1634 Gabriel Gustafsson Oxenstierna had remarked 'that just as the Estates have power to elect a king, so they ought, *interregni tempore* or *sub minorennitate regia*, to confirm the *quinque capita*': *RRP*, iv, 8; and in 1660 the Clergy, demanding the right to approve the great officers of state during a minority, argued: 'We have the power *eligendi Regem, quod majus videtur*'; *Prästeståndets riksdagsprotokoll*, ii, 93.

[84] Lennart Thanner, *Revolutionen i Sverige efter Karl XII:s död*, Uppsala, 1953, p. 313; and for the defeat of the council-party, pp. 233–73.

[85] They promised him that 'Where Your Majesty's own opinion, of your royal superior intelligence, does not agree with ours, then will and shall we set our own opinion behind us, and not put it before or alongside Your Majesty's will or opinion, which God always vouchsafes to be the best and most useful . . .': *Handlingar rörande Skandinaviens historia*, viii, 26–7: a slightly different version in *Svenska riksdagsakter*, ii, 953.

86 *RRP*, xvi, 233; and Runeby, *op. cit.*, pp. 400, 511.

87 The position was well stated in a council debate in 1635, on a question of whether to legislate by statute or by ordinance: *RRP*, v, 310. One consequence of this state of affairs was that the suspending and dispensing powers never came under serious attack. Gustav Adolf dispensed from a true statute – the Judicature Ordinance of 1614 – in one difficult case (J. E. Almquist, 'Kungl. Maj:t som revisionsrätt 1614–32' (*Svensk Jurist-Tidningen*, 1941), p. 59, n. 2); individual exceptions to the legislation against non-Lutherans were made from time to time; but on the whole, despite occasional protests from the Clergy on the religious question, no one seemed disposed to treat it as being of much constitutional importance.

88 See Nils Staf, *Marknad och möte*, Stockholm, 1935, for the use of markets as alternatives to meetings of the Estates.

89 John III seems to have levied illegal taxes: at least, his council alleged that he did: *Svenska riksdagsakter*, I Series, ii, 826; and Oxenstierna attempted to impose a tax without consent in 1642: Lindberg, 'Axel Oxenstierna som riksdagstaktiker', p. 365. But for good examples of a government's accepting defeat on a question of taxation, see *RRP*, xii, 62; xiv, 267–8. And Oxenstierna himself told the council on 23 September 1641: 'It is not advisable to lay any burden on them without a meeting of the *riksdag*, since no king has yet been so audacious as to do so, well knowing that *libertas statuum et ordinum regni* consists in a free grant': *RRP*, viii, 719.

90 *Prästeståndets riksdagsprotokoll*, iii, 234, 236. In 1655 Erik Oxenstierna, in a curious reversal of historic *rôles*, contended that the provisions of the Land Law forbidding a king to diminish the revenues of his successor were valid only for an electoral monarchy, and hence no longer had any force: Ellen Fries, *Erik Oxenstierna*, Stockholm, 1889, pp. 179–80.

91 The first statutory security for speedy trial seems to be in paragraph 23 of the Constitution of 1720: Emil Hildebrand, *Sveriges regeringsformer samt konungaförsäkringar*, p. 100.

92 In Gustaf Adolf's draft of his Articles of War (1621) he included the following passage: 'The king is God's judicial officer on earth. He is the supreme judge as well in the field as at home': Styffe, *Konung Gustaf II Adolfs skrifter*, p. 245.

93 Erik Sparre, *Pro Lege, Rege et Grege*, p. 86, quoting Justinian: 'Concessum etiam imperatori vel regi absoluto in propria causa cum de regalibus agitur judicare'.

94 In 1634 the council went so far as to arrest a bookseller who had printed Magnus Eriksson's Land Law: *RRP*, iv, 18; and most members were reluctant to allow the printing of the Form of Government of 1634: *ibid.*, v, 233: *cf.* xvi, 712.

95 The Nobility demanded it in 1649: *SRARP*, I Series, iv, 202; and the Clergy in 1660: Wittrock, *Carl X Gustafs testament*, p. 193.

96 Christina, for her own purposes, clearly enunciated the idea of liberty of debate; but only because it suited her to give free rein for the moment to the attacks of the lower Estates upon the Nobility: *RRP*, xiii, 34; xiv, 371. She seems also to have been the only public figure to advocate toleration on principle: *Prästeståndets riksdagsprotokoll*, ii, 88.

[97] *ASOB*, II, i, 457; Gustav Adolf to Axel Oxenstierna, 18 Feb. 1629; Nils Ahnlund, *Gustav Adolf inför tyska kriget*, Stockholm, 1918, p. 103.

[98] See Oxenstierna's opinion, *AOSB*, I, iv, 673 (to Gustav Adolf, 8 Nov. 1629); the discussions in 1642, in *RRP*, ix, 2, 15–17; and a view of the whole question in Nils Ahnlund, *Ståndsriksdagens utdaning 1592–1672*, Stockholm, 1933, p. 528.

[99] S. Bergh, *Karl IX och den svenska adeln*, p. 108.

[100] *Svenska riksdagsakter*, II Series, i, 73; Hildebrand, *Sveriges regeringsformer*, p. 40.

[101] Ahnlund, *Ståndsriksdagens utdaning*, pp. 300–7.

[102] *Svenska riksdagsakter*, I Series, ii, 245–6.

[103] *Ibid.*, I Series, ii, 671.

[104] But the desire to 'go to the king' remained; and Gustav Adolf, anxious not to let slip his judicial prerogative altogether, secured that the king should still be able to revise the *hovrätts* judgments. In his absence the council performed the work of revision: J. Hallenberg, *Svea Rikes Historia under konung Gustaf Adolf den stores regering*, Stockholm, 1790–6, iii, 299; Hjalmar Haralds, 'Konungsdom och konungsnämnd', *Historisk Tidskrift*, 1927, pp. 28–46; J. E. Almquist, 'Kungl. Maj:t som revisionsrätt', *Svensk Jurist-Tidningen*, 1941, pp. 52–64; Sture Petrén, 'Kring Svea Hovrätts tillblivelse', *Svensk Jurist-Tidningen*, 1945, p. 175. Petitioners to the council seem to have been carefully and fairly dealt with: see, e.g., *RRP* viii, 659.

[105] See the observations of Per Brahe and Oxenstierna, 14 Oct. 1650: *RRP*, xiv, 343. For the successful struggle against manorial codes in 1672, see *Borgareståndets riksdagsprotokoll*, pp. 114–15, and E. Hildebrand, *Svenska statsförfattningens historiska utveckling*, p. 364.

[106] *Nils Reuterholms journal* (*Historiska Handlingar*, 36:2; Stockholm, 1957), p. 45.

[107] The distinction between Hogenskild Bielke's and Erik Sparre's motives and preoccupations is made clear in Sven A. Nilsson, *Kampen om de adliga privilegierna 1526–1594*, Lund, 1952, pp. 111–21.

[108] In his Oration of 1594: *Svenska riksdagsakter*, I Series, iii, 390.

[109] *Ibid.*, iii, 386; Nilsson, *Kampen om de adliga privilegierna*, p. 128.

[110] Strömberg-Back, p. 124.

[111] Sven A. Nilsson, *På väg mot reduktionen. Studier i svenskt 1600-tal*, Stockholm, 1964, pp. 38–57.

[112] Stellan Dahlgren, 'Kansler och kungamakt vid tronskiftet 1654', *Scandia*, xxvi, (1960), *passim*, especially pp. 133–44.

[113] K. Ågren, *Karl XI:s indelningsverk för armén*, Uppsala, 1922, p. 120.

[114] Sven A. Nilsson, *Krona och frälse i Sverige, 1523–1594*, Lund, 1947, pp. 157–8, 164–5, 359–60, 379–80, 382–3.

[115] *Svenska riksdagsakter*, I Series, iii, 400 (clauses 14–16); *cf.* S. Bergh, *Karl IX och den svenska adeln*, p. 91.

[116] Hakon Swenne, *Svenska adelns ekonomiska privilegier 1612–1651*, Göteborg, 1933, pp. 296–9.

[117] *RRP*, ix, 453; he also, significantly enough, considered Christopher of Bavaria as the model Swedish king: *ibid.*, x, 20.

[118] *Cf.* Hogenskild Bielke's anxiety to get his share of donations in Estonia: S. A. Nilsson, *Krona och frälse*, p. 367.

[119] It was not really broken down until the last decade of the Age of Liberty. For an early example of this claim see *SRARP*, iii, 215.

[120] H. Munktell, *Det svenska rättsarvet*, Stockholm, 1944, p. 103; *cf.* the remarks in W. Tham, *Axel Oxenstierna. Hans ungdom och verksamhet intill år 1612*, Stockholm, 1935, p. 295.

[121] Erik Sparre, *Rättegångsinlagor i tvisten rörande Fru Görvel Abrahamsdotter Gyllenstiernas arv*, Historiska Handlingar, 27:1, Stockholm, 1927.

[122] J. Hallenberg, *Svea Rikes Historia under konung Gustaf Adolf den stores regering*, iii, 263.

[123] Jerker Rosén, *Studier kring Erik XIV:s höga nämnd*, pp. 31–2.

[124] For the agitation over this in the years around 1650, see *RRP*, xii, 342; xiii, 12; *SRARP*, iv, 171, 257.

[125] It is significant that the first threats to it seem to come in the reign of Charles XI. It was first explicitly guaranteed by express enactment in the Act of Union and Security of 1789: Emil Hildebrand, *Sveriges regeringsformer och konungaförsäkringar*, p. 148.

[126] H. Munktell, 'Till frågan om böndernas ställning vid 1600-talets mitt', *Historisk Tidskrift*, 1943. By a resolution of the *riksdag* in 1650 *forum privilegiatum* was not to apply in cases about labour services between a lord and his peasants: they were to be tried in the county court. For examples of the council's willingness to deal sternly with members of the high aristocracy who oppressed their peasants, see *RRP*, x, 563; xi, 19; Wittrock, *Carl X Gustafs testament*, pp. 125, 151. But examples might be cited on the other side: one notorious offender, though sentenced by *Svea Hovrätt*, was then promoted to the office of *landshövding*: Wittrock, *Regeringen och allmogen under Kristinas egen styrelse*, pp. 187, 227–32, 243; *id., Regeringen och allmogen under Kristinas förmyndare*, pp. 140, 299–300, 405, 415–19; *Handlingar rörande Skandinaviens historia*, xxi, 151; H. Swenne, *Svenska adelns ekonomiska privilegier*, p. 312.

[127] *Sveriges traktater med främmande magter*, iii, 376.

[128] *Svenska riksdagsakter*, I Series, iii, 396.

[129] *Ibid.*, II Series, i, 75.

[130] *Svenska riksdagsakter*, I Series, ii, 368, 375; iii, 412–14; Nilsson, *Kampen om de adliga privilegierna*, pp. 14, 19, 30, 103–4, 107. And *cf.* S. Bergh, *Karl IX och den svenska adeln*, p. 35.

[131] *Svenska riksdagsakter*, I Series, iii, 414.

[132] Nilsson, *op. cit.*, pp. 29, 78–9; Bergh, *op. cit.*, p. 18.

[133] The phrase used in the resolution of the Söderköping *riksdag*, 1595: *Svenska riksdagsakter*, I Series, iii, 617. A reminder, perhaps, that Konopczyński's confident generalization to the effect that monarchs prefer the majority-principle, aristocracies the unanimity-principle, is not universally valid: W. Konopczyński, *Le Liberum Veto*, Paris, 1930, p. 23.

[134] As Axel Oxenstierna remarked on one occasion, 'It is the highest *jus* that we have, that we are *capaces munerorum publicorum in regno*, which *jus* is *onerosum*, and it is *salus reipublicae* which draws a man to it': *RRP*, vi, 404; and *cf. ibid.*, 654.

[135] Christina and Axel Oxenstierna shared an odd admiration for Condé;

and Oxenstierna once linked him with Oldenbarneveldt as an example of a man who had suffered on account of 'virtue': *RRP*, xiv, 175.

[136] They are printed in G. O. Hyltén-Cavallius and G. Stephens, *Sveriges historiska och politiska visor*, Örebro, 1853, at p. 121. A rough translation might run (with acknowledgments to Barbour's *Bruce*, which it so curiously resembles):

> Freedom is the fairest thing
> To which a man may have liking
> In the wide world's dominions.
> Who loveth freedom more than wealth
> He tendereth his honour's health;
> For they be good companions.

3

Gustav Adolf and the Art of War[1]

Until very recent times it has been a sound generalization that no offensive action can be won by missile weapons alone. It is a generalization which may well be invalid today; but there can be no doubt that it is substantially accurate for the Middle Ages. The art of war in mediaeval Europe was essentially a hand-to-hand business, and it was no less essentially offensive, since the arms and equipment of the mediaeval knight left no other course open to him save attack. And because feudal chivalry was by its nature committed to the offensive, the defensive-offensive tactics of Crécy and Poitiers became a possibility – though even here the swords of the men-at-arms were needed to clinch a victory which the arrow-shower had only begun. But this was a method of fighting which could hardly be repeated indefinitely, since it depended for its success upon the rashness of the enemy, and upon the calculation that the opposing commander would prove incapable of tactical improvisations; and the time came when neither of these presuppositions proved true any longer. The really decisive overthrow of the heavy-armed cavalry, therefore, came not from bowmen, and still less from hand-gunners, but from the bringing to bear of a shock and mass greater and more tightly organized than that provided by a charge of men-at-arms. Such a shock, and such a mass, made its appearance first in the Swiss column, then in the *Landsknechts* and the Spanish *tercio*.

From the point of view of battle-tactics, the invention of firearms was at first of very minor importance. Indeed, it represented, for close on two centuries, a decidedly retrograde step. Firearms in battle attempted to repeat the tactics of Crécy with instruments which were ludicrously unapt for the purpose. Their weight, their unreliability, their inaccuracy, their painfully slow rate of fire, made the early hand-guns, arquebuses, and muskets inferior, in every respect save one, to the cross-bows and longbows they superseded. The arquebus possibly, the musket more probably, could claim a higher pene-trative power;[2] but this advantage could not offset the counter-vailing defects. The period of military history which extends from Charles the Bold to Tilly is marked above all by a catastrophic diminution in the firepower of the infantry arm.[3]

The commanders of the early sixteenth century seem to have cared little for this aspect of the question. The pike was now supreme; and the Swiss column, luckily for itself, never came up against massed English archers. In the first quarter of the century arquebus and musket made good their footing on the Continent,[4] and for the next hundred years or more provided military theorists with the very difficult problem of deciding how to make the best use of them. What proportion were missile weapons to bear to *l'arme blanche*? And how was the most effective combination of the two to be secured?

By about 1580, the influence of portable firearms had suc-ceeded in diverting the art of war into two exceptionally blind alleys. It had, in the first place, completed that demoralization of heavy cavalry which the English and the Swiss had begun. The man-at-arms, outweighted by the Swiss column, his lance outranged by the eighteen-foot pike, had found that the musket-eers could not be relied upon to make a practicable breach in the ranks of the enemy into which cavalry could charge. Direct assault with lance and sword became increasingly suicidal. But then came the invention (about 1520)[5] of the wheel-lock pistol; and the discomfited cavaliers were not slow to adopt it. In theory, the pistol enabled the cavalryman to blow holes in the pike-hedge, independently of infantry assistance. In fact, it provided him with a pretext for doing nothing, while seeming to do much. The effective range of the cavalry pistol being something under ten yards,[6] cavalry made use of it by advanc-ing in very deep formations to within that distance of the enemy, and discharging their weapons by successive ranks in an intricate

manœuvre known as the caracole, or *limaçon*.[7] To this evolution there could have been no objection, if the firing of the
pistols had been followed by an attack with the sword or lance.
But the pistoleers, outranged by opposing muskets, and discouraged by the bristling aspect of the *tercios* they were called
upon to attack, frequently fired at too great a distance for their
shots to be effective, and increasingly neglected to follow up
their volley with a charge. The essential of cavalry tactics – the
utilization of the impact of man and horse to disrupt the
enemy's formation – was thus wholly lost, except in Poland;[8]
and cavalry became a debilitated arm, fit only to snap its
pistols at other horsemen as debilitated as themselves.

In these circumstances, the decisive, battle-winning arm
remained the infantry: the pike was 'queen of the battlefield';
the Chevalier Bayard fought on foot.[9] And the most illustrious
exponent of the supremacy of the foot was the Spanish *tercio*.
The *tercio*, three thousand strong, with its girdle of shot wholly
surrounding a massive square of pikes and halberds, and its
four rectangular 'sleeves' of shot at each corner, represented
the first serious attempt at tactical combination of firearms with
pikes: the shot would shatter the enemy's ranks to make an
opening for the pike-thrust; the pikes would provide a rampart,
or even a hollow square behind or within which the shot could
take refuge – if it were quick enough.[10] But though this was,
indeed, a conscious effort at combination of weapons, it was a
singularly clumsy one. The great mass of the *tercio* endowed
it with inertia to resist, and momentum in attack (provided the
musketeers had got out of its way at the moment of impact);
but it was extraordinarily wasteful of manpower: the inner
ranks and files of a *tercio* contributed little beyond their weight
to the issue of the combat, and could scarcely be said to earn
their pay. And it was no less wasteful of firepower. The slowness
of the musket's rate of discharge was such that a steady fire
could be maintained only by having musketeers at least ten
deep, and training them to fire by successive ranks – an evolution known as the countermarch.[11] But in *tercio* formation this
was possible only to the 'sleeves', to the forlorn, and perhaps to
the musketeers stationed immediately to the *tercio*'s front. The
musketeers lining the *tercio*'s flanks could give only sporadic and
ineffectual fire; while those posted at its rear could not fire at

all, unless the *tercio* were actually surrounded. Thus the close attachment of shot to pikes, so far from producing a fruitful collaboration between them, succeeded only in inhibiting the characteristic qualities of each.

Moreover, the parts played by musketeers and pikemen tended by the middle of the century to become inverted. As had happened with the cavalry, there arose in the foot an increasing disposition to shrink from close action (by which alone a tactical *decision* could be secured), and an increasing preference for long-range musketry duels: the first example of the new style is perhaps to be seen in the early stages of the battle of Cerisole in 1544. The proportion of musketeers to pikes steadily rose: by the end of the century it reached approximate equality, by the 1620s it might be as two to one;[12] the 'sleeves' became stronger, and their front more extended; and the rear of the *tercio* was on occasion denuded of protecting shot.[13] At the same time the pike declined as an offensive weapon, and from being the principal battle-winner sank slowly to being a mere stiffener of the shot, a kind of barbed-wire hedge behind which fugitive musketeers might in an emergency take shelter, a weapon derided by the more advanced of contemporary theorists.[14] And as a consequence of these developments battles became more difficult to win, disillusioningly resultless when won, and unjustifiably extravagant in the expensive article of mercenaries. Commanders, therefore, turned their attention for choice to siege-warfare. Here, and here only, the coming of gunpowder had meant increased efficiency; here Tartaglia's ballistics, Italian and Dutch military architecture, and other applications of emergent sciences, could show positive results.[15] Battle became the mark of the incompetent or unfortunate commander, to be justified (if at all) only as clearing the way for further siege-operations;[16] strategy aimed at occupation of territory, rather than at annihilation; and the general preference for mercenary armies (for whom a clear-cut decision might mean unemployment) reinforced the current trend.

Thus by the last decade of the sixteenth century the natural military qualities of horse, shot, and pike had become almost totally perverted; and the art of war was stiffening into immobility. Neither cavalry nor infantry was anxious for close action; and commanders looked for victory to missile weapons whose original inefficiency had neither been overcome, nor offset, by tactical ingenuity. The sheer bulk of the *tercio*, though since the 1580s considerably diminished, made it unamenable to manœuvring and costive in action; while its organic nature made its subdivision not merely impracticable, but self-contradictory. Minor tactics, in consequence, were reduced to a primitive level; strategic thinking withered away;[17] war eternalized itself.

The reforms of Maurice of Orange and his cousins, conceived and executed in the years between 1590 and 1610, at all events offered a new approach to these problems, and a possible exit from one of the blind alleys. Maurice's inspiration was classical: it came from Vegetius, Aelian, and Leo VI, reinforced by the neo-stoicism of Justus Lipsius, and the mathematical talents of Simon Stevin.[18] In thus looking to Rome for his models Maurice was by no means singular: the tactical maxims of Vegetius and Aelian were commonplaces to the military writers of the age, from Machiavelli to Schwendi, Londoño, and de la Noue. Nor can it be said that while others merely talked of Roman principles, Maurice was the first to act on them:[19] the first commander to do this was not Maurice, but Erik XIV of Sweden, who forestalled some of Maurice's most celebrated innovations by as much as thirty years.[20] Nevertheless, Maurice's reputation as a military reformer is natural, and it is deserved. Unlike Erik, whose brief career was confined to the inner Baltic, and peripheral to the main current of European affairs, Maurice was a protagonist in the great central struggle upon which the fate of Europe hung; and in the very heat of battle he took the enormous risk of radically transforming his system of tactics, administration and training. His new infantry unit, the battalion, was consciously modelled on the cohort, and numbered only five hundred and fifty men; it was drawn up as a wide, shallow formation, only ten deep on a front of forty-nine; and the units were ranged, *quincunx*-wise, as a *duplex acies* with proper provision for a tactical reserve. By these means Maurice secured a much more efficient and economical use of manpower, a greatly increased capacity for manœuvre, and an abundant supply of tactical small change: whereas a Spanish army of twelve thousand men would have four tactical units, a Dutch army of the same size would have twenty-four.[21]

In the early decades of the seventeenth century the Dutch system was generally adopted by Protestant armies on the Continent. The Catholic powers remained sceptical; and not without reason. Battle experience could not be said to pronounce unequivocally in Maurice's favour: Turnhout was a minor engagement; Nieuwpoort came at an early stage of the reforms; while such Protestant commanders as fought battles on the Maurician system during the early years of the Thirty Years' War generally lost them. And in truth the Dutch method had very serious defects. It was a stiff and inflexible system: within the framework of the battle-line the pieces could readily be interchanged, but the framework itself was fixed and rigid. Tactically, it was essentially passive, reacting predictably to a challenge, but not apt for the offensive. The large number of small units, disposed so as to cover and support each other, the excellent scope for musketry fire, the ease with which a threatened sector of the line could be reinforced, the provision of a proper reserve, all gave to the Dutch line a respectable strength in defence; though even in defence it seems doubtful whether it was sufficiently adaptable to be able rapidly to form front to a flank. But those graceful chequers which patterned the flats of Holland or the rolling open country of Brabant, though they might make the strongest appeal to the aesthetic sense of Major-Generals, were by no means convincing as battle-winners. They had sacrificed the mass of the Spanish system without acquiring adequate compensation in hitting-power; and in the matter of the combination of arms they showed little advance upon the more modern and disencumbered type of *tercio*. And despite the claims that have been made for Maurice, it seems clear that he never really succeeded in maintaining a stable correlation between the administrative and tactical units of his armies.[22] His cavalry, moreover, was of the most vicious sort: caracoling pistoleers one and all; for Maurice formally prohibited the lance in 1597.[23] Above all, Maurice's reforms were in great measure stultified by his stolid and conventional strategy. He had no ambition whatever to fight battles; and for a quarter of a century after Nieuwpoort he contrived, with the aid of skill, geography, and the truce, to avoid them. Of an offensive tactic he had little idea; of a campaign culminating in annihilating victory, none at all. It was entirely characteristic and proper that his reputation as a commander should rest largely on his conduct of siege-operations.

The Spanish school, meanwhile, had been gradually reforming itself. It still depended for its effect upon the impact or inertia of massed infantry; but since the 'eighties the *tercio* had been fixed at sixteen hundred men, in place of the former three thousand. These new, smaller *tercios*, moreover, were increasingly coming to be arranged on the battlefield in groups of three, in arrow-head formation, or sometimes in groups of four, diamond-wise; the fourth *tercio* in such case being held in reserve. When this formation was adopted, and several battle-groups of *tercios* were ranged side by side, a Spanish order of battle might take on a delusive appearance of linear arrangement. But in one sense, at least, the new *tercios* were more adaptable than Maurice's battle-line, for the battle-group was not disturbed by attack in flank, since it could meet it by a simple left or right turn. And if the *tercio*, with all its admitted disadvantages, had been as completely outmoded as some writers have supposed, it is difficult to account for its invariable success in Germany until 1631. It would be rash to attribute its victories entirely to the ineptitude of the Protestant commanders, or the brilliance of Tilly, or the steadiness of the Spanish infantry. The tactical form itself possessed some assets, and its later exponents – Tilly and Spinola in particular – knew well how to make the most of them. It is important to recognize this fact, for it was to have some influence on the tactics of Gustav Adolf in their final phase.

Maurice's career, therefore, inaugurated a tactical controversy, but failed to decide it. And it left the great military problems still unsolved. It still remained for an enterprising commander to restore, both to horse and foot, the capacity for the battle-winning tactical offensive; it still remained for a military genius to liberate strategy from the tenacious mud of the Netherlands; and it still remained for a great administrator to fulfil and perfect those lines of development in organization, discipline, and drill, which Maurice and his cousins had been the first to chalk out. In each of these fields the career of Gustav Adolf was of decisive importance; and though as an administrator he may perhaps have been, as Delbrück called him, the

'perfecter' of Maurice's reforms,[24] in tactics he was the inno-
vator who succeeded in solving the problems which Maurice
had failed to solve, while in strategy he dealt with problems
of which Maurice had really no conception.

The military education of Gustav Adolf had fitted him to
appreciate the merits of both the Dutch and the Spanish
schools. After a firm grounding in the classical authorities on
the military art – Aelian, Frontinus, Vegetius – he had been
directed by his tutor, Johan Skytte, to the study of contemporary models. Both the Spanish and the Dutch methods were
familiar to him. Special attention was paid to the art of
'embattling' an army, so that he should know 'how to form
expeditiously some thousand men into a square, a triangle, a
circle, an arrow-head, or any other geometrical figure'.[25] The
effect of this training is perhaps to be perceived in the highly
artificial and geometrical battle-orders to which he clung in
the earlier phases of the Polish war. Circumstance and religious
sympathy, however, inclined him from the start to prefer the
methods of Maurice, and in 1608 he had the advantage of two
months' intensive training in their use from Jakob de la Gardie,
who had himself been schooled in the Netherlands tradition.
This short course was the only formal instruction in the military
art at the hands of a professional soldier that he was ever to
receive; and he was at that time not quite fifteen years old.
As a soldier, therefore, he was to be to a great extent an auto-
didact. His constant study was to improve himself; and he
expected his officers to imitate his example, for he did not
believe that the military art can be acquired simply by experience in the field. He would have agreed with Monro, that 'it
is not time, or number of yeares that makes a brave soldier, but
the continual meditation of exercise and practice'.[26] He was
never tired of insisting on the importance of theoretical knowledge, of the study of the campaigns of the great commanders,
and above all of mathematics.[27] His own military contacts were
mainly with the Netherlands school, and its influence may have
been strengthened by his discussions with John of Nassau-
Siegen at Heidelberg in 1620.[28] But he was not on that account
blind to the weaknesses of Maurice's methods, and he seems to
have studied the theorists who were concentrating upon improving and modernizing the *tercio*: at all events, the Swedish

brigade, as he eventually developed it, shows traces of the influence of that three-*tercio* battle-group which was characteristic of later Spanish practice under Tilly. And it is clear that he was never a blind imitator of Netherlands tactics – for which, indeed, the Swedish army was at first unfitted by the imperfect state of its armaments, the nature of the attacks it had to meet, and the kind of country it was condemned to fight in. Gustav Adolf's formal tactics are from the beginning a matter of free adaptation and variation, and this refusal to allow himself to set hard in a mould fashioned for other needs and in other lands is not the least of his merits as a soldier.

The foundations of Gustav Adolf's victories in Germany were laid by his work in the field of military organization and administration. He started with some advantages which were denied to Maurice, and indeed to all other military reformers of his day. First, and most important, the Swedish army was a national army: not national as the *tercios* were national (for they were mostly manned by native Spanish volunteers serving in the army as a career), but national in that military service was an almost universal obligation upon male Swedes between the ages of sixteen and sixty. This system of conscription (*utskrivning*) dated from 1544: Gustav Adolf overhauled it, reformed it, and by 1630 had established upon a permanent basis the first national standing army of conscripts in Europe.[29] Contemporary military writers, on the whole, were not in favour of militias and conscripts, until Breitenfeld modified their ideas;[30] but there is no doubt that (apart from all questions of superior morale)[31] the Swedish system had real administrative advantages. It did much to ease the difficulty of paying the troops (which so often hamstrung continental generals), for Gustav Adolf was able to pay his native levies in kind, in revenue assignments, or by allotting farms to their support.[32] And since the relationship between the general and his army was not a contractual one, but rather that of sovereign to subject, the more intractable problems of discipline were also avoided. Moreover, the king was in a position to impose some degree of uniformity and standardization in the matter of armaments, as Maurice or Henry IV were not; and he was also able to determine, on purely military grounds, the proportion which (for instance) muskets were to bear to pikes. This was an important consideration, for the commander of a mercenary army was compelled, to some extent, to acquiesce in the arms and equipment which his men were prepared to bear; and this meant, in practice, that too often there would be an undue preponderance of musketeers. Again, he was not obstructed by the antique pretensions of half-dead feudal dignitaries: no Constable or Admiral impeded logical administrative reform; for Sweden had never been a feudal country.[33] He could rely too (at least after 1630) on a native armaments industry capable of supplying most of his needs at relatively inconsiderable cost.[34] And he was able, from about the same period, to divide military finance from the ordinary budget so effectively[35] that the burden of participation in the German war was much less onerous than in any other belligerent country.

These advantages do something towards explaining the remarkable administrative reforms carried through between 1617 and 1630: the recruiting system revised and tightened; a code of discipline promulgated which, if it had many identifiable ancestors, was none the less better than any of them, and was of lasting importance abroad, not least in Brandenburg-Prussia;[36] increasing standardization of arms and equipment; organization of the pay and supply services; and finally the emergence about 1630 of a War Office (*krigsrätt*) which was not merely a council of state, but a true centre of administration using highly efficient business methods.[37] Meanwhile, throughout the twenties, there had been constant experiments designed to find the best administrative and tactical units; until at last, in 1624, the two aspects coalesced in the regiment of two squadrons or eight companies.[38] The identification of the tactical with the administrative unit, which Maurice had failed to secure, was thus for the first time achieved upon a permanent basis by Gustav Adolf: there is no need to insist on the importance of the reform. Lastly, the king proved himself fully the equal of Maurice as a drill-master and trainer of troops.[39] It is difficult to resist the impression that Gustav Adolf, if he had failed to achieve fame in other fields, might without difficulty have stolen the reputation of those possibly overrated military reformers, Le Tellier and Louvois.

The infantry squadrons of the armies of Gustav Adolf were small units – rather smaller than the Dutch battalion;[40] and they differed from the battalion also in their constitution. For they included a *higher* proportion of pikes to muskets – and not a lower, as is so often stated – than was the rule in Maurice's units.[41] The formation was also shallower than Maurice's: pikes and shot were alike only six deep, for the king held that in deeper formations the rear ranks would not hear the word of command – a consideration which, significantly enough, had not weighed with the Spanish school. The army was drawn up, as the Dutch armies were, in two distinct lines, each line having its own reserve; and cavalry was placed on the wings. Officers and NCOs were even more numerous than in the Dutch armies, and it is plain that they were trained to use their initiative. The diminished depth of all formations might have been expected, perhaps, to lead to a reduction of firepower; for it took so long to let off a musket that a steady fire could hardly be maintained by a countermarch of less than ten ranks. But in fact the change had the opposite effect. Gustav Adolf did not aim at a steady fire: he aimed at missile shock. At first the Swedish musketeers practised a form of the countermarch, in which two ranks fired simultaneously, instead of only one at a time;[42] but by the time of Breitenfeld, the king was using the salvo, a technique of which he was the inventor and first exponent. For the salvo, the musketeers doubled their ranks, so that they were but three deep; and thus (to quote Sir James Turner):

... you pour as much lead in your enemies bosom at one time as you do the other way at two severall times, and thereby you do them more mischief, you quail, daunt, and astonish them three times more, for one long and continued crack of thunder is more terrible and dreadful to mortals than ten interrupted and several ones.[43]

But if the salvo thus provided a concentration and severity of fire such as small arms had never before achieved, it entailed as a consequence the accentuation and prolongation of that critical period in which the musketeer, having discharged his piece, became both innocuous and defenceless until the tedious operation of reloading had been completed. At this moment he needed strong protection, and only pikes could give it to him. Gustav Adolf's insistence on the value of pikemen, and the increased proportion of pikemen in his infantry units, were therefore necessary corollaries of the steadily intensifying fire-discipline which was to culminate in the salvo. But they were much more than that. The pikes were not envisaged by Gustav Adolf (as they seem to have been by Maurice) mainly as a passive force, offering protection to muskets behind which they might take cover while reloading. On the contrary, he made his pikes charge the enemy. After the salvo had shattered his ranks, the pikes pushed into the ruins and increased the disorder; and when they retired, the musketeers were ready with the next salvo. Thus he devised for his infantry a method of delivering blows alternately at a distance and in close action, of attack by alternating charge and discharge; he rehabilitated the pike as a battle-winning weapon; he transformed the whole nature of infantry fighting from something essentially defensive to something essentially aggressive; and he solved the problem which had baffled all his predecessors, of how to combine shot and pike without sacrificing the essential military characteristics of each.

Before the Polish war had come to an end, experience had convinced Gustav Adolf of the need for a higher tactical unit than the infantry squadron; and in the course of the battles at Dirschau on 7 and 8 August 1627 the first attempt was made to provide such a unit. The foot was ranged in battle-groups of three squadrons; and from this innovation there developed in the following years the celebrated Swedish brigade, of four squadrons (or two field-regiments), which was to be the king's normal order of battle in Germany.[44] The new brigade tactics, which by 1630 had been perfected and standardized, resemble in some respect the grouping of three or four *tercios* under the later Spanish system. There is the same wedge-shaped or arrow-head formation, with the fourth squadron initially held in reserve. On the other hand the brigade could also be viewed as a simplification of the more formalized and extensive arrow-heads of the orders of battle of the king's middle period.[45] The brigade, in fact, represents a blending of elements of both the Spanish and the Dutch schools. With its nine or twelve light guns, its musketeers carefully disposed for an advantageous field of fire, its very numerous officers and NCOs, its precise subdivisions and articulations, it was equally effective in attack and defence. It could move as a unit; but its constituent parts were capable of acting on their own. Its numerical strength (fifteen hundred to two thousand, according to whether it comprised three or four squadrons) made it numerically fully the equal of the *tercio*; while in flexibility and mobility it was if anything superior to the Dutch battalion-group. In firepower it was greatly superior to either.

It was not so easy to find a satisfactory solution for the cavalry. Gustav Adolf did indeed deal radically with current perversions: the depth of formations was reduced to six ranks, and at Lützen to three;[46] the caracole was abandoned, at least by native Swedish horse; cavalry advanced at the trot, the front rank (and the front rank only) discharging one pistol at suitable range; and the attack was made with the sword. But the firing of one cavalry pistol was more a concession to ingrained habit than an effective preliminary to the *mêlée*: the horseman, no less than the pikemen, needed a salvo, or something like it, to open a lane in the enemy's ranks, if his attack were to make its full effect. Gustav Adolf tried to provide this missile aid by attaching platoons of musketeers to cavalry units, to act in close concert with them. Monro tells us how it was done:

> the Horsemen on both wings charged furiously one another, our Horsemen with a resolution, abiding unloosing a Pistoll, till the enemy had discharged first, and then at a neere distance our Musketiers meeting them with a *Salve*; then our horsemen discharged their Pistolls, and then charged through them with swords; and at their return the Musketiers were ready again to give the second *Salve* of Musket amongst them.[47]

It was the same system as that devised for the foot; and at Breitenfeld it was sufficiently effective to confound even Pappenheim. But inevitably it suffered from the differing pace of man and horse. The musketeer, heavily laden with musket, pouch, and fork, had no chance of keeping up with a cavalry horse at the trot; and it was therefore necessary for cavalry to advance, until the last fifty yards or so, at a pace which cannot have been much better than a walk. Thus in order to be sure of adequate firepower, Gustav Adolf was constrained to make heavy sacrifices of speed and shock. And even at the sober pace at which his horsemen proceeded, the musketeers would have had difficulty in keeping up, if Gustav Adolf had not helped them by reducing the weight of their weapon. We do not know just how, or how much, he lightened it; but we do know that he did *not* lighten it sufficiently to allow the musketeer to dispense with the fork (although historians very generally have asserted the contrary): the fork continued to be used by Swedish musketeers as late as the reign of Charles x.[48]

As to cavalry, then, it may be said that the king's attempt to develop a combination of shock and firepower entailed disadvantages which partly offset his liberation of the horsemen from the enchantments of the caracole.[49] His solution was an imperfect solution: the dilemma – speed or firepower – remained unresolved, and perhaps remains so still; but it was at all events a solution better than that which it superseded.

The last element in the new tactics was provided by a reformed artillery.[50] The king devoted much personal attention to this branch of the service, and was himself a skilled gunner.[51] As a result of his interest, what had been a semi-civilian craft or mystery was placed upon a regular basis: the first independent artillery unit dates from 1621; the first artillery regiment from 1629.[52] On the technical side, the process of simplification and standardization of calibres and types, begun long ago by Maximilian i and Henry ii, was now carried a stage further. But his main achievements in this field were, first, to have produced a really mobile field artillery; and secondly, to have introduced the light gun as a standard regimental weapon. Until his time, artillery had been virtually static in battle – as Tilly's was at Breitenfeld, for instance – and its tactical importance had been very limited. Gustav Adolf contrived to make his guns mobile: at Lützen, for instance, they were shifted more than once in the course of the battle; and thirteen years later it was the astonishing mobility of the Swedish artillery that played the major part in winning Torstensson's great victory at Jankow.[53] And it was the king's search for a satisfactory combination of mobility and firepower that produced, after numerous experiments (of which the too-famous, but quite ephemeral 'leather gun' was the best remembered) the so-called 'regiment-piece' of 1629. The regiment-piece was a three-pounder which (thanks to an improved gun-carriage) could be manhandled; it was designed for antipersonnel service at relatively short ranges, and was therefore usually charged with canister or grape; and it was relatively quick-firing, since its ammunition was provided with an attached cartridge.[54] It was designed expressly for collaboration with infantry and cavalry, and played a part similar to that played by 'commanded' musketeers in the foot: like them the light guns could be sent anywhere, and used on all occasions.[55] It was produced, after 1629, as a high-priority weapon; with such success that by the time of Breitenfeld every infantry squadron had two or three of these guns attached to it. It served much the same purpose as was served in recent times by the Lewis and Bren guns; and its effect, combined with the new fire-tactic of the salvo, was to make deep formations impossible for many years to come. The doom of the *tercio* was announced at Breitenfeld; it was accomplished – by Swedish tactics – at Rocroi.[56]

The combined effect of these administrative changes and tactical reforms was to provide Sweden by 1630 with an army far better equipped than any other of that age in the matter of firepower and shock; while at the same time the flexibility and elasticity of the battle-formations, the high degree of training and initiative in officers and men, and the effective combination of arms in defence as well as in attack, enabled its shallow formations to sustain and repel an onslaught by forces fighting in the old style, even though they might be considerably superior in numbers. But it took a full decade of constant effort before this stage was reached; and until it had been reached the king could make few important innovations in his conduct of operations. During the early twenties he was compelled to concentrate on the defensive aspect, for the weakness of his cavalry (particularly when matched against the Poles) made it impossible to take risks. The battle-plans of this period, therefore, are on the Dutch model; indeed, they are more formalized, more complex, more geometrical, less capable of rapid modification even than their exemplars, and resemble nothing so much as the fanciful structures built from a child's box of bricks.[57] After the victories at Wallhof and Mewe (1626), which had demonstrated the ability of the Swedish infantry to hold its own against the best cavalry in Europe, they became less rigid, though still mainly defensive; but with the victories at Dirschau (1627) – which proved the new Swedish horse to be equal to any that Poland could put in the field – defensive formations were gradually abandoned, and the typical Gustavian battle-line made its appearance. By 1630 the instrument was tempered for the hand of the master; and at Breitenfeld it responded to every call that he made upon it. At the climax of that battle, Horn, on his own initiative, and without delay or confusion, formed a new front to the flank exposed by the flight of the Saxons, called reserves to his assistance, and by prompt attack with all arms defeated an enemy perhaps five times as numerous as himself; while on the other wing the Swedish cavalry – which at Burgstall and Werben had already proved its superiority to any caracoling enemy – was equally successful against Pappenheim, whose cavalry tactics were strongly influenced by Koniecpolski and the Polish school.[58]

Breitenfeld marked an epoch; but contemporaries were almost more startled by the audacity of the assaults at the Lech and the Alte Feste: no other commander of that age would have taken such risks. And it is significant that the attack on the Alte Feste failed mainly because the terrain did not permit regiment-pieces to be manhandled, and because it was unfavourable to pikes, so that two essential ingredients in the Swedish tactic were not able to make their full effect.[59] So too at Lützen – which showed, incidentally, that Wallenstein was beginning to use Swedish methods – it was the shortage of pikes (and the famous November mists) which were responsible for the failure of the Swedes to clinch their tactical advantage, though it could not prevent them from winning a strategic victory.[60]

These tactical developments are reflected, at all events after Breitenfeld, in Gustav Adolf's strategy. After Breitenfeld, he does not merely seek battle on every favourable occasion; he sees a decision by battle as the logical and consciously designed end to the strategic perspective, and hence as a prime factor influencing the choice of means. In this last phase of his career his strategy was indeed (*pace* Clausewitz[61]), designed to be *Vernichtungsstrategie*. Now this was something wholly alien to the spirit of Maurice, on the one hand, and Spinola, on the other. Yet at the same time it is clear that he was equally an exponent of *Ermattungsstrategie*: the great Swedish concentration at Nuremberg in 1632 was primarily designed, not so much as a grouping for battle, but rather as an attempt to isolate the

71

Imperialists from their sources of supply.[62] Gustav Adolf, indeed, was capable both of the strategic vivacity of Banér, and the strategic canniness of Wallenstein. But his historical importance as a strategist rests on other grounds than these. It rests upon his methodical consolidation of one base-area after another, adding one to one until the whole built up to a vast strategic design; and upon a strategic vision which for magnitude and complexity has no parallel in European warfare before the age of Napoleon and mass armies.[63]

The original Swedish base in Germany was a narrow strip of Pomeranian coast between the Oder and the Peene. Gradually it was expanded; until by the time the king established his camp at Werben, a year after the landing, it had been extended to cover an area bounded by the Oder, the Spree, the Havel, and the Elbe. The victory at Breitenfeld brought a sudden leap forward to the Main and the Rhine; but Gustav Adolf took care that the new base-area in Franconia and the Rhineland was solidly integrated with the old: with Banér in Magdeburg, Horn around Bamberg, and William of Weimar in the great bastion at Erfurt, the Thuringian bottleneck was firmly secured. In the spring of 1632 came an extension of the new Rhenish-Franconian base down the Rhine towards Coblenz, and up the Rhine and the Neckar towards Heidelberg and Baden; and in the summer Gustav Adolf undertook the creation of his last main base-area in the triangle between the Lech, the Alps, and the Danube: it was from this base that the final attack on Vienna was to be launched in 1633. Throughout the whole process of expansion, there was systematic exploitation of river-lines, and a systematic establishment of strong-points and magazines (usually protected by extensive new fortifications of the most modern types) at the critical points within the areas under Swedish control: Frankfurt-on-Oder, Crossen, Spandau, Havelburg, Rathenow, Erfurt, Würzburg, Nuremberg, Augsburg, Ulm, and above all Mainz, which he transformed into a stronghold of the first order.[64] Each successive base-area was organized as an independent defensible unit; and each formed an element in a broad strategic design covering the whole of Germany. Using the Saxon bastion and the Silesian armies as a pivot, he was making a vast right-handed sweep designed to sever the Imperialists from their sources of supply and reinforcement. The advance to the Elbe isolated their forces in Mecklenburg, menaced Christian IV in rear if he should be tempted to meddle, and began the cutting-off of the Imperialist strongholds in the Lower Saxon Circle. The advance to the Rhine completed (in intention, though not, unhappily, in fact) the isolation of the Lower Saxon Circle. The Rhenish campaigns, the invasion of Alsace, the French operations against Lorraine, and the occupation of Ehrenbreitstein – these blocked the way to any help from Brussels, Nancy, or the Habsburg lands in Alsace. The final base in Suabia would prevent any assistance coming over the Alps from Italy or Spain. The whole plan – which had taken shape in the king's mind already by the close of 1630 – was conceived as one huge operation, in which seven armies acted in co-ordination on a sickle-shaped front extending from the Vistula to the Brenner, from Glogau to Lake Constance.

It was, no doubt, territorial strategy, and on a majestic scale; but it could hardly be otherwise in the conditions of the Thirty Years' War. *Bellum se ipsum alet* was a principle to which both sides perforce subscribed; and almost the first of military objectives must be to fix the *sedes belli* in hostile territory.[65] As the area of conquest expanded, the drain of troops for garrisons increased; fresh recruits had therefore to be found, for armies of unprecedented dimensions; and hence more territory must be occupied to serve as recruiting-ground, or at least to deny its manpower-resources to the enemy. Moreover, an adversary starved of recruits and supplies might well be driven by desperation to fight a battle, as Tilly is said to have been driven to invade Saxony in September 1631.[66] Thus a territorial strategy of this sort was complementary, rather than antagonistic, to a strategy of annihilation.

In the event, the design was only partially successful. In part this was because the king's grip on the Lower Saxon Circle, and on Suabia, had not been made really secure by the time of his death; but perhaps also because the still primitive logistics of that age made a prolonged and effective military occupation of so great an expanse of country almost impossible to maintain. Had Gustav Adolf survived the battle of Lützen, had he pacified the Lower Saxon Circle (as, on the eve of Lützen, he had made up his mind to do), had he made good his foothold on the Alps, it is probably still true to say that the campaign of 1633 would have needed to be short and sharp, and the victory decisive, if the vast military-administrative structure were not to crack under its own weight.

What Gustav Adolf at the height of his power had failed to make good, his successors never came near to accomplishing. Banér as a tactician was his equal, and perhaps his superior: Wittstock is one of the classic victories, to be compared with Cannae or The Wilderness;[67] but the later stages of the Thirty Years' War were not propitious to large-scale strategic designs. The exhaustion of Germany cut down the size of armies, and made a methodical and systematic conduct of operations almost impossible. Campaigns became forays, battles became encounters void of strategic significance; and of Gustav Adolf's strategic innovations little or nothing was transmitted to his immediate posterity.

It was otherwise in regard to tactics. Here the king left a great school of commanders behind him: Banér and Torstensson, Bernard of Weimar and Horn, 'those brave Heroicks',[68] were his immediate pupils, trained by him for command; and at one remove came Charles x and Rupert, and the great names of Montecuccoli and Turenne, both of whom were thoroughly permeated with his spirit. These men realized that Gustav Adolf's career had settled the question which Maurice's reforms had left still discutable: linear tactics were now acknowledged to be more effective than the old Spanish system; and no voice was raised henceforward to query that verdict, until the practice of Charles xii, and the theories of Folard, revived the doctrine of mass impact, and inaugurated a debate between line and column which outlasted the eighteenth century.[69]

Meanwhile, the Swedish discipline became the model for the training of troops; and the Swedish organization of firepower was generally adopted.[70] A light regimental artillery became universal;[71] and the mobility of the Swedish field-artillery set the standard until the improvements of Frederick the Great and Gribeauval. As for cavalry, the caracole was dead, as Wallenstein had recognized as early as the Alte Feste.[72]

But certain other innovations did not make good their footing. Despite some spirited examples from the Civil Wars, the practice of Gustav Adolf entirely failed to arrest the decline of the pike. The mercenaries of the latter years of the Thirty Years' War disliked this cumbrous weapon, and the body-armour that often went with it; and the enormous marches of Piccolomini or Banér reinforced their objections. Pikemen grew more difficult to come by; and they were also more expensive than shot, since they drew higher pay. Hence the dwindling armies of Gallas or Guébriant tended increasingly to consist mainly of cavalry and musketeers. Gustav Adolf's careful com-bination of firepower and shock became rarer; the offensive *rôle* of infantry became more difficult to sustain; battles came more and more to be decided by actions between opposing cavalry wings (as so often in the Civil Wars, or in Marl-borough's campaigns), while the mass of the foot volleyed away at murderously short range, in a style reminiscent of close action at sea, and strove to stand fast as a sort of pivot of manœuvre for the mounted arm.[73] The elasticity and dynamism of the Gustavian battle-line was lost, and linear tactics became once more rigid and unimaginative. The age of pipeclay was not far ahead. It was not until Vauban perfected the bayonet, in the last years of the century, that infantry was provided with a better means to effect what Gustav Adolf had intended by his combination of pike and musket.

Yet though in some respects the work of the great king bore little fruit after his death, it was none the less a major military revolution. Sixty years ago, a British tactical theorist wrote: 'The general who first masters the art of bringing the action of each arm into close co-operation, will initiate a new era in the art of War.'[74] Within the limits of contemporary possibility, Gustav Adolf mastered that art; and the new era was not slow to follow.

NOTES

[1] This paper was read to the second Irish Conference of Historians, May 1955 and published by Bowes & Bowes for the Irish Committee of Historical Sciences, 1958.

[2] Even this seems doubtful, in view of the astonishing prowess of the longbow.

[3] For an estimate of this development in numerical terms, see Otton Laskowski, 'Infantry Tactics and Firing Power in XVI Century', *Teki Historyczne*, London, iv, (1950), 106–15. Elsewhere Laskowski calculates that the firepower of Casimir Jagiełłon's infantry (armed with the crossbow),

compared with that of Polish infantry of the mid-sixteenth century (armed with firearms), was as forty to one: Otton Laskowski, 'Uwagi na marginesie nowego wydania Zarysu Historii Wojskowśce w Polsce Generała Mariana Kukiela,' *Teki Historyczne*, v, (1951–2), 36.

[4] Muskets were used on both sides at Pavia: Hans Delbrück, *Geschichte der Kriegskunst im Rahmen der politischen Geschichte*, Berlin, 1920, iv, 110.

[5] J. Alm, *Eldhandvapen*, Stockholm, 1933, i, 53, 80: Max Jähns, *Handbuch einer Geschichte des Kriegswesens von der Urzeit bis zur Renaissance*, Leipzig, 1880, p. 1203, gives the date as 1515.

[6] Perhaps as little as five paces: Tavannes wrote 'il faut que le bout [of the pistol] touche': J. W. Wijn, *Het Krijgswezen in den Tijd van Prins Maurits*, Utrecht, 1934, p. 164. Werner Hahlweg seems to be alone in the view that the range of the pistol was 50–80 paces: Werner Hahlweg, *Die Heeresreform der Oranier und die Antike*, Berlin, 1941, p. 101, n. 220.

[7] Deep order for cavalry is first noted at St Quentin: Wijn, *op. cit.*, p. 439; the caracole, at Dreux (1562), though the claim has also been made for Sievershausen (1553): Delbrück, iv, 148; Alm, i, 119. The caracole is well described in Generalstaben, *Sveriges Krig 1611–1632*, Stockholm, 1938, supplementary vol. ii, 149–51; but authorities are divided as to the true nature of the evolution: contrast Sir James Turner, *Pallas Armata* (1683), p. 231; O. S. F. Odenrick, *Lantkrigskonstens utveckling, sedd mot bakgrunden av den allmänna teknikens framåtskridande*, Stockholm, 1933, ii, 49; Wijn, pp. 442–3; and especially E. von Frauenholz, *Das Söldnertum in der Zeit des dreissigjährigen Krieges*, Munich, 1938, i, 60. M. Jähns (*op. cit.*, p. 1216) offers a solution which covers both views.

[8] And possibly in the native French cavalry of Henry of Navarre: General Weygand, *Histoire de l'Armée française*, Paris, 1938, p. 123; Sir Charles Oman, *A History of the Art of War in the Sixteenth Century* (1937), pp. 466–7. For the Polish cavalry, see Marjan Kukiel, *Zarys historji wojskowości w Polsce*, London, 1949, p. 54; and (for a good example at the battle of Klushino in 1610), T. Korzon, *Dzieje wojen i wojskowości w Polsce*, Kraków, 1912, ii, 164 ff.

[9] Pikes, said Londoño, 'son la fuerza de los escuadrones, y allį reinas, come se dice, de las armas': Sancho de Londoño, *Discurso sobre le forma de reducir la Disciplina Militar a mejor y antiguo estado* [new edn], Madrid, 1943, p. 26. So too he describes the nobility as 'el nervio de la infanterįa española': *ibid.*, p. 43.

[10] For the *tercio*, see Oman, *op. cit.*, pp. 58–61; R. Altamira y Crevea, *Historia de España y de la Civilización española*, Barcelona, 1927, iii, 292–5; Sancho de Londoño, *Discurso sobre la forma de reducir la Disciplina Militar a mejor y antiguo estado*, p. 34; Wijn, pp. 424–6; G. B. C:sson Barkman, *Gustaf II Adolfs regementsorganisation vid det inhemska infanteriet* (Meddelanden från Generalstabens krigshistoriska avdelning, i), Stockholm, 1931, pp. 4–6, 21–4 (with good diagram).

[11] Hahlweg (*op. cit.*, pp. 73–4) is mistaken in stating that the counter-march was first used by Maurice of Orange.

[12] H. Wertheim, *Der toller Halberstädter. Herzog Christian von Braunschweig im pfälzischen Kriege*, Berlin, 1929, i, 116.

[13] See, for instance, Verdugo's formation of 1590: Wijn, pp. 427, 432–3; Barkman, *op. cit.*, pp. 51–2.

[14] Turner, *Pallas Armata*, p. 178.

[15] A good discussion in A. R. Hall, *Ballistics in the Seventeenth Century*, Cambridge, 1952, *passim*.

[16] 'Nowadays,' wrote Henri de Rohan, 'one fights more like a fox than like a lion, and war consists far more in sieges than in battles': quoted in E. von Frauenholz, *Das Söldnertum* . . . , i, 49.

[17] Contemporary military theorists, with the possible exception of Lazarus von Schwendi, give no consideration to questions of strategy.

[18] For Maurice's reforms, see Hahlweg, *op. cit.*; Barkman, *op. cit.*, pp. 33–8; G. Oestreich, 'Der römische Stoizismus und die oranische Heeresreform', *Historische Zeitschr.*, 176 (1953); and above all J. W. Wijn, *Het Krijgswezen in den Tijd van Prins Maurits*.

[19] As a contemporary observed, 'Si discute alla romana, ma si continua combattere alla tedesca': Piero Pieri, 'La formazione dottrinale di Raimondo Montecuccoli', *Révue internationale d'histoire militaire*, 10. (1951), p. 93.

[20] Erik's achievement may be collected from Generalstabens krigshistoriska avdelning, *Axtorna. En studie i organisation och taktik* (Meddelanden från Kungl. Krigsarkivet utg. av Generalstabens krigshist. avd., iv), Stockholm, 1926; Generalstaben, *Sveriges Krig 1611–1632*, i; G. B. C:sson Barkman, *Svea livgardets historia*, Stockholm, 1938–9, ii; Ingvar Andersson, *Erik XIV: ett biografi*, Stockholm, 1948.

[21] Barkman, *Gustaf II Adolfs regementsorganisation*, p. 9.

[22] Barkman, *Regementsorganisation*, p. 38: contrast Wijn, p. 437; and Frauenholz, *Söldnertum*, i, 46.

[23] Wijn, p. 45; and see *ibid.*, pp. 42–7, 452–3, 514.

[24] Delbrück, iv, 199.

[25] Barkman, *Regementsorganisation*, p. 69. For Gustav Adolf's military education in general, see *ibid.*, pp. 69–73; Generalstaben, *Karl XII på slagfältet. Karolinsk slagledning sedd mot bakgrunden av taktikens utveckling från äldsta tider*, Stockholm, 1918, i, 75; E. Wrangel, *De Betrekkingen tusschen Zweden en die Nederlanden op het Gebied van Letteren en Wetenschap*, Leiden, 1901, p. 56. An illuminating study of the general history of military education in Sweden is W. Sjöstrand, *Grunddragen av den militära undervisningens uppkomst- och utvecklingshistoria i Sverige till år 1792*, Uppsala, 1941.

[26] Monro, ii, 175, 196; and *cf.* Sjöstrand, *op. cit.*, pp. 16–18, 78–80.

[27] See his essay, 'Om krigsmans plikter', in C. G. Styffe, *Konung Gustaf II Adolfs skrifter*, Stockholm, 1861, pp. 62 ff.

[28] Barkman, *Regementsorganisation*, pp. 92–3.

[29] Styffe, *Konung Gustaf II Adolfs skrifter*, pp. 6–25; *Sveriges Krig*, ii, 133–4.

[30] Contemporary attempts at national militia forces, and their failure, are dealt with in E. von Frauenholz, *Lazarus von Schwendi. Der erste deutscher Verkünder der allgemeinen Wehrpflicht*, Hamburg, 1939, pp. 16–21; *id.*, *Die Landesdefension in der Zeit des dreissigjährigen Krieges*, Munich, 1939, *passim*; H. Wertheim, *Der toller Halberstädter*, i, 67–75; M. Lenz, *Landgraf Moritz von Hessen*, in *Kleine historische Schriften*, Munich and Berlin, 1920,

ii, 128–31; K. C. Rockstroh, *Udviklingen af den nationale haer i Danmark i det 17. og 18. Aarhundrede*, Copenhagen, 1909, i, 4–38, 65.

[31] For Gustav's belief in the superior morale of national troops, see Styffe, pp. 4–6; *Peder Galts Depescher*, ed. Nils Ahnlund, Historiska Handlingar, 26:1, Stockholm, 1920, p. 22; *Rikskansleren Axel Oxenstiernas skrifter och brefvexling*, Stockholm, 1896, I, ii, 594 n.

[32] R. M. Klinckowström and J. Mankell, *Arkiv till upplysning om svenska krigens och krigsinrättningarnes historia, 1630–1632*, Stockholm, 1861, iii, lx–lxv, 248–54. Whitelocke gives the following description of these methods: 'The manner of maintaining their militia forces in the country was said to be this: A horseman was quartered in the house of a boor, or husbandman: if the man will work himself and his horse with the boor, to help him in his husbandry, then the boor gives the man and his horse entertainment freely, and hath their work for it, which is more worth than their meat, and the boor will give the man perhaps some small sum of money besides ... In like manner it is for the foot-soldier.' B. Whitelocke, *A Journal of the Swedish Embassy in the Years 1653 and 1654*, ed. Henry Reeve, (1855), ii, 136–7.

[33] The offices of Admiral and Marshal existed, but no prescriptive rights attached to them. The office of Constable finally lapsed in France in 1627; but Le Tellier and Louvois had difficulties with other military antiquities as late as the 'sixties and 'seventies: L. André, *Michel Le Tellier et Louvois*, pp. 317–21.

[34] For this see, in general, *Sveriges Krig*, supplementary vol. ii; E. W. Dahlgren, *Louis de Geer, 1587–1652. Hans lif och verk*, Uppsala, 1923, i–ii; E. F. Heckscher, *Sveriges ekonomiska historia från Gustav Vasa*, Stockholm, 1936, i; and for a useful summary of sources of supply, L. Hammarskiöld, 'Ur svenska artilleriets hävder', *Artilleri-Tidskrift*, 1941–4, p. 154. (Hammarskiöld's articles appeared as successive supplements to *Artilleri-Tidskrift*, with independent and consecutive pagination.)

[35] *Arkiv till upplysning om svenska krigens ... historia*, i, 147, 305–13.

[36] Text in J. Schmedeman, *Kungl. Stadgar, Förordningar, Bref och Resolutioner*, i, 39 ff.; Gustav Adolf's own draft in Styffe, pp. 243 ff. For their provenance, peculiarities, and influence, see A. Gierow, *Bidrag till det svenska militärkyrkoväsendets historia*, Uppsala, 1918, i, 21–79; O. Brusiin, 'Gustav II Adolfs krigsartiklar', *Tidskrift utgiven av Juridiska Föreningen i Finland*, 79 (1943), 373–93; K. Grönfors, 'Ur det svenska militära rättegångsväsendets historia. *Rättshistoriska studier*, II Series, i, 208–43; Wijn, p. 104; Frauenholz, *Söldnertum*, i, 5–6, 23–7.

[37] B. Steckzén, *Krigskollegii historia*, Stockholm, 1930, i. 1–51; M. Roberts, *Gustavus Adolphus. A History of Sweden, 1611–1632*, (1953), i, 276–7.

[38] Barkman, *Regementsorganisation, passim*.

[39] See, for instance, *Monro his Expedition with the Worthy Scots Regiment* (1637), ii, 141, 187, 190–1; Styffe, pp. 62 ff.; *Peder Galts Depescher*, p. 3; *Sveriges Krig*, ii, 324, 415; iv, 450; supplementary vol. ii, 99.

[40] Dutch battalion: 250 pikes, 240 shot – 490; 60 shot in forlorn – 550. Swedish squadron: 216 pikes, 192 shot – 408; 96 commanded musketeers – 504.

[41] *Cf.* the wholly erroneous comment of so recent a historian as Laskowski: 'Uwagi', p. 51. *A priori* one would expect that the thinner formations of linear tactics would require an increased proportion of pikes if they were to have adequate defensive solidity; and Maurice, like Gustav Adolf, did in fact raise the proportion: Wijn, pp. 173–80.

[42] Monro, ii, 190.

[43] Turner, *Pallas Armata*, p. 237. *The Swedish Intelligencer*, i, 124, thus describes the manœuvre on what seems to have been its first appearance at Breitenfeld: 'The Scots presently ordering themselves in seuerall small battagliaes, about 6 or 700 in a body, presently now double their ranckes, making their files then but 3 deepe . . . This done, the formost ranke falling on their knees; the second stooping forward; and the third ranke standing right vp, and all giuing fire together; they powred so much lead at one instant in amongst the enemies horse, that their ranckes were much broken by it.' For a numerical comparison of firepower as developed by Swedish, Dutch and Spanish methods, see Barkman, *Regementsorganisation*, p. 98.

[44] Lack of manpower, however, frequently necessitated the formation of brigades of only three squadrons.

[45] For this, see *infra*, p. 70.

[46] *Sveriges Krig*, vi, 433.

[47] Monro, ii, 65.

[48] Alm, *Eldhandvapen*, i, 174–5; Barkman, *Regementsorganisation*, p. 14, n. 6. The mistake may have arisen as a result of Gustav Adolf's abandonment, after 1629, of the 'swine-feather'; for the swine-feather (which was a partisan with a sharpened butt, enabling it to be fixed into a timber balk, or driven into the ground, and so serve as defence against cavalry) had a hook at its forward end which could be used to support a musket: J. Alm, *Blanka vapen och skyddsvapen*, Stockholm, 1932, pp. 136, 142. Yet if the musket still needed the fork, how did those ranks discharge it who, when a salvo was fired, were either kneeling or stooping? It may be convenient here to list some other hardy errors. Gustav Adolf did not introduce the cartridge for muskets; nor was he the first commander to put troops into uniform (it is a matter of doubt how far his troops were uniformed); nor did he reduce the length of the pike; nor were his light guns invented by Sandy Hamilton. For a representative *florilegium* of such errors, see Le Menuet de la Jugannière, *Une révolution dans la tactique au XVIIe siècle*, Le Havre, 1914, pp. 83–90.

[49] *Cf.* the comments of Laskowski ('Uwagi', p. 48): 'it was but a timid compromise between fire-tactics and the tactics of the cavalry charge'; and of Kukiel (*Zarys historji wojskowości w Polsce*, p. 65): 'This was not yet Polish tactics, but it was a step forward under their influence.'

[50] For artillery see, in general, L. Hammarskiöld, 'Ur svenska artileriets hävder'; and *Sveriges Krig*, supplementary vol. ii.

[51] Hammarskiöld, 'Ur svenska artilleriets hävder', p. 200.

[52] *Ibid.*, p. 142; *Sveriges Krig*, supplementary vol. ii, 295.

[53] For Jankow, see Försvarsstabens krigshistoriska avdelning, *Slaget vid Jankow 1645*, Stockholm, 1945, or, more succinctly, in Lars Tingsten, *Fältmarskalkarna Johan Baner och Lennart Torstensson såsom härförare*, Stockholm, 1932, pp. 267–79.

[54] For the 'leather gun' and the regiment-piece, Hammarskiöld, *op. cit.*, pp. 33–4, 147–50; *id.*, 'Om svenskt artilleri i äldre tider', *Historisk Tidskrift*, II Series, iv, (1941), 45; *Sveriges Krig*, ii, 138–9; supplementary vol. ii, 180–3, 191–207, 235–41, 253, 270–2.

[55] On 21 July 1631, for instance, the king led a reconnaissance against Tilly's forces and took with him six light guns: before his time this would hardly have been possible. *Sveriges Krig*, iv, 396.

[56] It was manhandled light artillery of the Swedish type, in conjunction with cavalry, that mowed down the *tercios* at Rocroi: Weygand, *Histoire de l'Armée française*, p. 131; J. Colin and J. Reboul, *Histoire militaire et navale* (*Histoire de la nation française*, ed. G. Hanotaux, vii), Paris, 1925, i, 316–17.

[57] Compare the orders of battle illustrated in Barkman, *op. cit.*, pp. 82–7, with that of Maurice, illustrated in Wijn, p. 478. For defensive tactics in Poland, G. Petri, *Kungl. första Livgrenadjärregementets historia*, Stockholm, 1926, ii, 105–7; C. Bennedich, *Ur det gamla Gardets öden*, Stockholm, 1926, pp. 74–5; Barkman, 'Gustaf II Adolf såsom härorganisatör och fältherre', *Kungl. Krigsvetenskaps-Akademiens Handlingar och Tidskrift*, ix, (1932), p. 25.

[58] For accounts of Breitenfeld see *Sveriges Krig*, iv, 487 ff.; *Det svenska svärdet*, ed. N. F. Holm, Stockholm, 1948 pp. 58–81; and G. Petri, *op. cit.*, ii, 127–140: for a radically dissenting view, see Sven Lundkvist, 'Slaget vid Breitenfeld 1631' (*Historisk Tidskrift* [N.S.] i, (1963)), 1 ff. For the cavalry action at Burgstall, see *Dagbok förd i det svenska fältkansliet*, ed. E. Zeeh and N. Belfrage (Historiska Handlingar, 30:3), Stockholm, 1940, p. 21. For Koniecpolski's influence on Pappenheim, see Laskowski, 'Uwagi', p. 48.

[59] *Sveriges Krig*, vi, 213–15.

[60] K. Deuticke, *Die Schlacht bei Lützen, 1632*, Giessen, 1917, can no longer be considered satisfactory: the best accounts are now *Sveriges Krig*, vi; Kungl. Liv-Rustkammaren, *Gustav II Adolf vid Lützen*, ed. R. Cederström, Stockholm, 1944; G. Nordström, *Wallensteins stridsplan vid Lützen*, in *Krigshistoriska studier tillägnade Olof Ribbing*, Stockholm, 1950; and Josef Seidler, *Untersuchungen über die Schlacht bei Lützen, 1632*, Memmingen, 1954. The lack of pikes was felt as early as June, 1631: *Schriftstücke von Gustaf Adolf, zumeist an evangelische Fürsten Deutschlands*, ed. G. Droysen, Stockholm, 1877, p. 134, which shows that it was not his rapid marches that took toll of pikemen, but rather that current military fashions were curtailing the supply of them.

[61] Clausewitz wrote: 'Ein kühner Invasions- und Schlachtfeldherr war Gustav Adolf überall nicht, . . . er liebte mehr den künstlichen manövrirenden, systematischen Krieg'; and again, 'Kurz war er ein gelehrter Feldherr voller vorsichtiger Kombinationen': C. von Clausewitz, 'Strategische Beleuchtung mehrerer Feldzüge' in *Hinterlassene Werke*, Berlin, 1837, ix, 47, 29.

[62] *Sveriges Krig*, vi, 115–16.

[63] For what follows, Lars Tingsten, 'Några data angående Gustav II Adolfs basering och operationsplaner i Tyskland 1630–1632', *Historisk Tidskrift*, I Series, xlviii, 322–338; *Sveriges Krig*, v, 282–4, 314, 330–8; vi 7, 16, 33–4, 179, 259.

[64] L. Fröhnhauser, *Gustav Adolf und die Schweden in Mainz und am Rhein*, Darmstadt, 1894, pp. 149–62.

[65] The King wrote to Oxenstierna in 1628: 'If we cannot say, *bellum se ipsum alet*, then I see no way out of what we have undertaken': Styffe, p. 520; and he told his council in May, 1630: 'the main thing is, that we should have *sedem belli sparsam per totam Germaniam*': *Svenska Riksrådets Protokoll*, ed. N. A. Kullberg, Stockholm, 1878, ii, 8.

[66] A. Ernstberger, 'Wallensteins Heeressabotage und die Breitenfelder Schlacht', *Hist. Zeitschrift*, 142 (1930), *passim*.

[67] Good accounts of Wittstock in B. Steckzén, *Johan Banér*, Stockholm, 1939; L. Tingsten, *Fältmarskalkarna Johan Banér och Lennart Torstensson såsom härförare*, pp. 63–75; *Det svenska svärdet*, pp. 106–27.

[68] Monro, ii, 180.

[69] The foot were only six deep, for instance, in the armies on both sides in the Civil Wars; Strafford's cavalry was four deep, most later cavalry three. But the French foot was still eight deep at the Dunes: C. H. Firth, *Cromwell's Army* (1905), pp. 94–5; Turner, *Pallas Armata*, pp. 215, 234; Weygand, p. 153; Colin and Reboul, p. 411.

[70] Wallenstein used salvoes as early as the Alte Feste, with powerful effect: K. Spannagel, *Konrad von Burgsdorff*, Berlin, 1907, quoting Burgsdorff's eye-witness account.

[71] Even in Britain: at Newburn fight, Leslie had 'some of his Swedish cannon' placed on the steeple of Newburn church; and a variety of 'leather gun' was also in use in the Scots army: C. S. Terry, *The Life and Campaigns of Alexander Leslie, first Earl of Leven* (1899), pp. 116, 121 n. 1.

[72] *Sveriges Krig*, vi, 216. In the later years of the war the German cavalry in Swedish service seems to have fought shy of *l'arme blanche*, but they did not revive the caracole (Alm, *Eldhandvapen*, i, 215); and Rupert and Cromwell in England, Condé and Turenne in France, used cavalry as it would have been impossible to use it, if the horsemen of Gustav Adolf had not killed the caracole for ever.

[73] Examples of this kind of battle were Breitenfeld II (1642) and Nördlingen II (1645). Breitenfeld I, indeed, has some claim to be the beginnings of this type of fight: the whole mass of the first line of Swedish foot took virtually no part in the action. But the struggle on the Swedish left, which saved the day, was no mere cavalry fight. On the general trend of tactics in the closing stages of the war, see P. Sörensson, 'Fältherrar, härorganisation och krigföring under trettioåriga krigets senare skede. En orientering.' *Scandia*, iii (1930), *passim*.

[74] G. F. R. Henderson, *The Science of War* (1906), p. 114.

4

The Political Objectives of Gustav Adolf in Germany, 1630–2[1]

The motives which impelled Gustav Adolf to invade Pomerania in June 1630, and the political objectives at which he aimed in the following two-and-a-half years, were once among the classic battlegrounds of German – and, to a less conspicuous extent, of Swedish – historiography. Since about 1920 the debate has noticeably flagged. Historians have in general been content to take their stand upon positions established by the researches of Bertil Boëthius and Nils Ahnlund. No recent book on the subject has served to keep controversy alive, as the parallel controversy about Wallenstein was reanimated during the inter-war years by the works of Srbik and Pekař; and little new material of any consequence has latterly been made available.

This paper, then, is not based on any new or unfamiliar body of evidence: it is rather an attempt to interpret evidence which has, in most cases, long been in print. And it is, perhaps, at once a disappointing and a reassuring circumstance that its conclusions do not differ greatly from the accepted judgments of modern Swedish historians.

Any investigation of Gustav Adolf's German policy must begin with an enquiry as to how far he entered upon the German war with any predetermined plan of action. There is certainly evidence to show that from as early as 1626 he was anxious to obtain a foothold on the southern Baltic shore. When Elbing was captured in that year he exacted from it an oath of fealty to the Swedish crown. So too in regard to Stralsund: in August 1628 Gustav Adolf repudiated the treaty which Filip Sadler had concluded with the town, and tried to induce the burghers to accept a Swedish *patrocinium*.[2] The attempt failed; but in the years between 1628 and 1630 Alexander Leslie, the Swedish governor, steadily strengthened his grip upon Stralsund, and in doing so certainly acted in accordance with the king's wishes.[3] And already Gustav Adolf was beginning to cast his eye on Wismar: by October 1629 he was speaking of it as a possible Swedish acquisition.[4] Moreover, although until the end of April 1630 one of the clauses common to all Swedish plans for a peace-settlement with the Emperor was the evacuation of Stralsund by Swedish troops in return for greater or lesser imperial concessions, in the instructions for Oxenstierna for the Danzig conference of 30 April 1630 this clause was modified: Gustav Adolf himself added the qualification that the evacuation was not to take place until it could be effected without risk.[5] And in the critical *råd*-debates of 4–6 May the members came round to the king's view that Stralsund must be retained, even if the Emperor accepted Sweden's terms, because 'we cannot be secure if we hand back anything which we cannot immediately retake'.[6] In this category, moreover, Gustaf Adolf now included Wismar. A week later he was reproving Oxenstierna for omitting from his draft peace terms 'the most important thing of all – *assecuratio*'; and it is clear that by this term he meant territorial security for the Imperialists' discharge of their undertakings. Such security must be provided by the retention of Stralsund 'or anything else we can annex'.[7]

How far, then, did this prospective annexation reach? And what sort of relation was contemplated between Sweden and the annexed areas? It has been argued that Gustav Adolf in fact aimed at the conquest or domination of all Germany; and certain of the king's expressions undoubtedly might be made to bear a very extended interpretation. '*Si vincimus*', he had said, '*in nostra potestate erit facere quod placuerit*';[8] and, some months later, '*Si rex victor, illi praeda erunt*'.[9] Among the motives for intervention in Germany which he urged at the *råd*-debates of October 1629, was '*ob spes plures, si in Germania possimus* advance somewhat';[10] and to Oxenstierna, after enumerating the arguments for the expedition, he added, 'To say nothing of other great hopes we may look to, if God bless the design'.[11] It has been suggested that behind these dubious phrases lay a programme of aggression. But in regard to each of them other explanations are possible. The king's remark about making the German princes his booty is now generally agreed to have been a mere debating answer, thrown out in the heat of a lively discussion in council;[12] and the same may very well be true of the somewhat similar remark that preceded it. As to the 'larger hope', the most natural explanation is surely that Gustav Adolf was referring to the prospect of liberating, not only the Baltic coastline and the two Saxon circles, but upper Germany also. It was a programme which scarcely seemed within the immediate range of practical politics; nor was its execution indispensably necessary to Sweden's immediate security. But there could be no doubt that it was desirable if opportunity should offer; and in a religious point of view the rescue of Württemberg or Baden was no less a duty than the deliverance of Pomerania and Mecklenburg. Gustav Adolf and his *råd* acknowledged that duty; but, as the king remarked in the course of discussion of this point, '*quod simul est impossibile, tempore potest fieri possibile*'.[13] And these, perhaps, were the *spes plures* to which he had earlier referred.

The motives which prompted the invasion of Germany are not in doubt. Gustav Adolf sought the security of his country; and that could be achieved only if the Imperialist forces were evicted from the Baltic shore, and the nascent Habsburg naval base at Wismar wrested from their hands.[14] But political security included as one of its main elements security from the danger of resurgent Catholicism, since in the idea of national freedom no constituent could be more important than that of religious freedom: as Oxenstierna observed to the *råd* in 1636, 'it was thus a question not so much of religion, as of *status publicus*, in which religion is comprehended'.[15] The political and religious safety of Sweden required that the Imperialists and Leaguers be pushed back as far into Germany as possible, and somehow or other be prevented from returning; that at least in the two Saxon circles the territorial arrangements revert to those of 1618; that no great power, and especially no great power of a hostile religion, be suffered to control the invasion-ports of Pomerania and Mecklenburg.[16] But if the weak

Protestant states of north Germany were thus restored, they might succumb to an Imperialist onslaught a second time as easily as they had succumbed already. It was logical, then, that Gustav Adolf should determine at least to retain Stralsund and Wismar until all danger was past, or the work might be to do all over again. Neither Gustav Adolf nor the *råd* was unmindful of the odium of making such acquisitions for Sweden. But the military situation seemed to give no choice; and the king was never prepared to compromise on military issues. His political principles remained in 1630 what they had been in 1624. Now, as then, he would not adventure his exiguous resources into Germany on any unsound bottom, and (because he could not afford to fight the battle twice over) he must take care that what he did there should be perdurable. Now, as then, he had no defined political objectives, apart from strategic considerations. There had been opportunities in the past for political adventures in Germany: he had turned his back on them, partly from a distaste for unnecessary political gambles, but partly also from a genuine unwillingness to cross other Protestant powers. The ideal of Protestant solidarity had enabled him to withstand the temptations of Wallenstein in 1627, and helped to hold him back from a preventive war with Denmark in 1629 and 1630.[17] Conscious always of the need to justify his policy to himself, his people, and the world, he was long troubled by a feeling that those grievances against the Emperor or the Emperor's servants, which he publicly proclaimed as the justification for his invasion, made but an indifferent case in international law. His qualms, his vacillations, his need for reassurance from *råd* and chancellor as to the legitimacy of his actions, accord ill with the character of ruthless adventurer sometimes attributed to him.[18]

However that may be, the conclusion which emerges from the evidence as to the king's designs up to the moment of landing at Peenemünde seems to be this: that for strategic reasons he desired to establish a semi-permanent base (including Stralsund, Wismar, and possibly other areas) along the Baltic coast; that he intended to drive the enemy out of north Germany, and keep him out; that he designed if possible to restore the *status ante bellum* in this region, and hoped that at some future date he might be able to liberate the remainder of Protestant Germany.

85

Beyond this, all was vague: '*momenta temporum* weren allezeit das fundament gewesen'.[19] And the overriding considerations determining action were, and would for long remain, not political but military. Military considerations, however, might involve political consequences. The problems of recruiting and supply could not be solved within the perimeter of a narrow beachhead; and the financial condition of Sweden made it essential that war should sustain war.[20] Already before the embarkation Gustav Adolf had announced, as a *military* objective, the establishment of '*sedem belli sparsam per totam Germaniam*'.[21]

2

On 10 July 1630 Stettin capitulated to the Swedes, and on the same day negotiations were begun for an alliance with Bogislaw XIV of Pomerania – an alliance which was intended to ensure that the duchy should not again be subject to an enemy power. And at once there appeared a complication which Gustav Adolf had partly foreseen: the claim of George William of Brandenburg, under a family compact, to the Pomeranian succession when Bogislaw should die. Experience since 1626 had given Gustav Adolf the lowest opinion of the political reliability and military strength of Brandenburg; and his contempt and suspicion emerged clearly in the audience which he gave to the Brandenburg envoy, Dr Bergman, on 11 and 12 July.[22] To Bergman he insisted that neutrality was impossible and intolerable: 'It is a fight between God and the Devil . . . *tertium non dabitur*';[23] paper guarantees were not enough – he must have 'something solid in hand' (and already he suggested that something should be Küstrin);[24] the militarily powerless princes of north Germany would do well to entrust their fortresses into his keeping, and accept him as '*tutor*'; and, finally he would defend George William's succession to Pomerania if (and only if) the elector joined him in a military alliance. In short, Gustav Adolf had realized that the security of Sweden demanded a firm alliance not merely with Pomerania, but with Brandenburg.

The treaty with Pomerania (ratified on 25 August) was designed to secure this end.[25] Though the integrity and rights of Pomerania were fully recognized and though the alliance was

86

defensive only, it was none the less 'eternal', and was to be renewed every ten years; Pomerania was not to enter into any other alliance without Sweden's consent; and the special relationship of Sweden to Stralsund was expressly reserved. A separate convention placed Pomerania's military resources wholly under Gustav Adolf's control.[26] But by a special reservation, binding Gustav Adolf only, it was declared that should George William refuse to ratify the alliance and the convention, should he fail to give military aid to Sweden, or should the Pomeranian succession be disputed (as it might well be, since Bavaria had a claim) Sweden would, upon Bogislaw's death, sequester Pomerania until the successful claimant ratified the alliance and paid Sweden's war-expenses.[27]

The object of the Pomeranian settlement was thus double: first, to ensure the permanent political reliability of Pomerania, in whatever hands; and secondly, to blackmail George William into an alliance with Sweden: one of the Swedish negotiators went so far as to say, in an unguarded moment, that this last was 'the fundamental point of the entire treaty'.[28] It is unlikely that (as some have thought)[29] Gustav Adolf already contemplated the permanent annexation of Pomerania. He was quite ready to see the Hohenzollerns installed in Stettin, as the price of George William's wholehearted collaboration. With Stralsund and Wismar in his hands, and a Pomerania linked in perpetual alliance with Sweden, he would have the *assecuratio* for which he was looking. Yet the negotiations contained the germ of future developments of a more disturbing character. In a speech to the Pomeranian council, after the conclusion of the treaty, the king brutally told them '*jure belli* you are my property!'[30] And in the special reservation to the treaty there appeared, as we have seen, a contingent claim for indemnity. From a combination of claims *jure belli*, and claims for indemnity, was to arise the notion of *satisfactio*.

In a letter of 12 January 1631, Axel Oxenstierna drew a clear distinction between alliances to be concluded with the states of the Baltic littoral, and alliances to be concluded with states of the interior.[31] The former, he held, needed the greater care; as for the latter, the main point was to secure the absolute disposal of the military resources of the ally, though only for the duration of hostilities. The Pomeranian treaty was designed as a permanent political arrangement, and was negotiated as between equals: the treaties with the states of the interior should be military conventions involving complete (but also temporary) subordination to Sweden. The type of this latter class of alliances was already in existence: it was the so-called Contingent Confederation (*Eventualkonföderation*) with Hesse-Cassel of 11 November 1630.[32] By the terms of this arrangement, Gustav Adolf took the Landgrave under his 'care and protection', an expression which the Pomeranians had successfully resisted; he was guaranteed the 'absolute directory' of the military affairs of both parties for the duration of the war; and he was styled '*caput* of this confederation'. The rights and liberties of the Landgrave were, indeed, guaranteed, and the recovery of his possessions was to be one of the objects of the alliance; but a special clause provided that lands conquered from the enemy to which Hesse had no claim should remain Swedish.

The Contingent Confederation was never ratified by William v, but it did in fact provide the pattern for a whole series of treaties extending almost to the close of 1631. Its main concern is plainly military. The demand for absolute direction, the styling Gustav Adolf '*caput*', have no far-reaching political implications: if the feeble military efforts of the riff-raff of jealous petty states were to be organized effectively, a *generalissimo* was essential. Moreover, Gustav Adolf had made precisely the same claim in earlier years against England, Denmark, and the Dutch. But the provision about lands conquered from the enemy indicates the progress of the idea of *satisfactio*: they are to be Swedish, partly by right of conquest, partly by way of indemnity. While the Pomeranian treaty had been concerned mainly with future security, the Hessian was concerned mainly with the conduct of hostilities; and while the Hessian treaty stated a frank claim for *satisfactio* at the expense of the enemy, the Pomeranian at least hinted at the possibility of *satisfactio* as a price to be paid by friends.

Gustav Adolf's relations with George William of Brandenburg, in the twelve months after the landing, illustrate the interplay of both these types of policy. He wished to incorporate Brandenburg into his permanent north-German security pact; but he also desired financial aid, facilities for recruiting, and control of strategic points within the electorate. As a long-term policy an 'eternal' alliance of the Pomeranian type was most desirable – hence the first stirring of the idea of a marriage alliance, in January 1631. As as immediate objective, the full military control of George William's lands and their resources was even more important, as the pressure applied to the elector in the autumn of 1630 shows.[33] And when, in April 1631, serious negotiations for an alliance were begun; when Gustav Adolf himself spoke hopefully of the prospects of obtaining a treaty 'of the Pomeranian sort';[34] when Götze actually offered ratification of the Pomeranian treaty;[35] it was on purely military grounds that the negotiations broke down.[36] Götze offered a 'Pomeranian' treaty within the framework of the Leipzig Resolution – that is, a treaty which would not prejudice the elector's right (and duty) to raise troops; but he did *not* offer to ratify the Pomeranian military convention; and he proposed inadequate guarantees for Swedish command of Küstrin. From this moment Gustav Adolf sought an alliance with Brandenburg not of the Pomeranian but of the Hessian type.[37] The crisis of 1–4 May, when the king was trying to force George William to join him, as a preliminary to an advance upon Magdeburg, was caused not so much by the special question of the custody of Küstrin and Spandau, as by the elector's refusal to abandon the Leipzig Resolution, and his determination at all costs to avoid a 'Hessian' treaty, with its central point of a Swedish military directory. The second crisis, a month later, was precisely similar. The matter at issue was not the Pomeranian inheritance, nor the extent of Gustav Adolf's designs upon the coastlands.[38] The final ultimatum of 9 June, and the treaties of 4 May and 10 June did not in fact mention Pomerania at all;[39] and Lars Grubbe (who certainly knew the facts) makes it plain that the crux was the question of the directory.[40]

Yet the treaty of 10 June did not in fact give Gustav Adolf the directory. It was but an emasculated version of the Hessian Contingent Confederation: George William even retained the right to raise troops on his own account. It has been suggested that this surprising abatement of the Swedish demands is to be attributed to the king's hopes of a marriage between Christina and the electoral prince.[41] The explanation is possible only on the supposition that Gustav Adolf's aims in May and June were political rather than military; and even then it is weak. The marriage at this stage had been the subject of no more than a general canvassing discussion;[42] the difficulties in the way of such a match were obvious; and at no other time did the king show any signs of compromising Swedish interests to secure it. But in fact Gustav Adolf in May and June 1631 was in an extremely critical situation, urgently needing an immediate settlement with George William; prepared indeed to raise the question of the marriage as an inducement to him to conclude, but quite unlikely to make solid concessions for what was still a mere shadow. The true reason for Gustav Adolf's willingness to accept less than he asked is much more likely to have been a fear that if he proceeded to extremities with the elector – and only violence could now extort better terms – he might alienate other princes with whom he hoped to ally.[43]

Before ever the expedition to Germany was launched, Gustav Adolf had perceived that it would be unlikely to be successful unless he could enlist the support of the more important Protestant princes. Since the collapse of the Union, the Protestant Estates of Germany had drifted on the tide of war without direction or organization. For years Gustav Adolf had been urging them to revive the Union, or something like it; for years he had been preaching unity, self-help, and *mascula consilia*. The invasion brought no alteration of his policy in this respect. The natural head of any evangelical league was John George; and in September 1630 Gustav Adolf empowered William of Weimar to make to John George a notable offer of alliance. The elector and his friends were to raise an army of 40,000 men; Gustav Adolf would provide as many; and Sweden would ally with the Protestant league on a footing of perfect equality: of a directory there was in this case no question. To this offer John George did not trouble himself to reply.[44] The elector's notorious desire to avoid a breach with the Emperor, and his scarcely-veiled hostility to a Swedish invasion of Germany (of which Gustav Adolf had received fair warning as early as January 1630)[45] provide a sufficient explanation of this rebuff, as also of his policy during the Leipzig Convention (February–April 1631).[46] John George's object at Leipzig was to frighten Ferdinand sufficiently to make further action (by Sweden or anyone else) unnecessary; while the object of the more active evangelical wing was the formation of a Protestant *bloc* which should ally with Sweden as a *bloc*, and consequently (it was hoped) on better terms than the Hessian Contingent Confederation had provided. Unfortunately for them, no such *bloc* was conceivable without John George at its head; and John George's leadership was a guarantee that no effective military action would be taken. Gustav Adolf and those around him were for a time optimistic about the Leipzig meeting;[47] and his envoys to the Convention were instructed to offer, to any evangelical league that might emerge, an alliance on terms of full equality, without any suggestion of a Swedish directory.[48] But after the king's conversations with Götze on 26 April the true nature of the Leipzig Resolution became clear.[49] It was to be a league of the loosest kind, a league in which each Circle voted money, raised troops, and appointed its own captain-general; its direction was to be in the hands of a committee which would meet only if John George chose to summon it.[50] It was not difficult to foresee squabbles about recruiting-areas and muster-places, arrears of contributions, and perhaps even (in the Lower Saxon Circle) a Danish prince as captain-general. Gustav Adolf had given the German Protestants every opportunity to organize themselves; and they had missed their chance. Gustav Adolf's reply to this situation was the *Norma futurarum actionum*.

The *Norma* was drawn up on Gustav Adolf's instructions, on or about 11 May 1631.[51] It laid down, for the first time since the landing, a definite programme for Swedish diplomacy in Germany. The first objective was defined as the establishment of 'ein neu evangelisch Haupt'; the second, as the creation of a new Protestant league under the direction of such a 'Haupt'. It is reasonable to suppose that the king intended to assume the direction of the league himself. The *corpus* was to be bound to Sweden by stringent alliances of the Hessian type; and though it was to have a council of war and state,[52] the terms of the alliances would ensure to Gustav Adolf an absolute directory in military matters for the duration of the war. It was hoped, indeed, that Saxony and Brandenburg might become members; but essentially the plan was to seize the leadership which John George had evaded, and to reconstitute something like the old Evangelical Union upon a new and militarily more effective basis. There is nothing in the *Norma* to suggest that the new arrangements were intended to persist after the end of the war;

but as early as October 1630 Gustav Adolf had indicated to Leuchtmar his view that a Protestant *corpus* would be a desirable peace-time institution.[53] At that time he had still hoped that such a body might be constituted by the efforts of the Germans themselves. But there was just as much to be said in favour of the persistence of Gustav Adolf's league after the peace, as of the persistence of a *corpus* that was purely German; and from the Swedish point of view it would provide an *assecuratio* that would make the territorial *assecuratio* doubly secure. Thus pressure of circumstance, rather than premeditated design, brought the king to contemplate a situation in which Sweden might be committed to permanent political leadership in Protestant Germany. Military necessity required the strict subordination of allies to the 'chief'; and from this it was but a short step to demanding a political subordination equally rigorous.

Gustav Adolf did not at once draw this conclusion. Under the shock of Magdeburg the new league was slow to come to birth; and in practice it was found easiest to proceed by gradual accretion: the Protestant Estates were to be bound to Sweden one by one, by separate though similar treaties of the Hessian type.[54] In this scheme the agreement with Saxony of 1 September had no place: it was concluded in haste, under the compulsion of imminent danger, between two states of (on paper) comparable military power, and it allowed to John George a considerable measure of military independence.[55] Events had forced the elector to seek Gustav Adolf's friendship; and for the rest of his life the king was prepared to go to great lengths to maintain good relations. But both his military and diplomatic operations were henceforth shaped with a view to excluding Saxon influence from north-west Germany.

The victory at Breitenfeld at first brought no great change in Swedish policy. But it entailed consequences which were to make themselves felt later on. German princes began to solicit, and obtain, appointments in the Swedish army, and thus entered into a subordinate relationship to the king which was not without difficulties; aspiring German diplomats deserted their earlier masters for the Swedish service. The area of conquest greatly increased, and with it the scope of Sweden's claims *jure belli*; and these new conquests were organized into civil governorships (sometimes, again, with German princes as governors), their towns and civil servants took oaths of obedience to the conqueror, their ecclesiastical and financial administrations were overhauled, and lavish donations made to German supporters. And as the Swedish armies approached the Rhine, the liberation of south German Protestantism, which at one time had seemed so remote, became not merely possible but probable: Swedish diplomacy, in the autumn of 1631, was already preparing the way. But the liberation of south Germany would pose another question, the echo of that which had already been asked about the north: what security could be devised to ensure that, after the war, the freedom thus regained should prove enduring? And in this question too Sweden would be doubly concerned; first, because it would be a freedom won by Swedish sacrifices, and secondly because the new 'evangelical chief' could not confine his confessional leadership to north Germany only. As Gustav Adolf descended the valley of the Main, in the idyllic progress of Monro's recollection,[56] victory itself was driving him to wider involvements than had ever been envisaged in the *råd*-debates of 1630.

3

And not to wider involvements only, but to new and more ruthless political methods. Indications of an increased sharpness of tone towards allies and possible allies had already been discernible as early as August:[57] after Breitenfeld the change is unmistakable. The victory had been won by Sweden alone, despite the caution of the princes and the shameful rout of the Saxon army. Gustav Adolf emerged from the battle with a heightened self-confidence, an increased contempt for the German states with which he was compelled to collaborate, a growing determination to exploit his advantage while the moment was propitious, and above all a nagging resentment, never really allayed, at what he considered to be the ingratitude of those princes who scrupled to comply with the demands of their deliverer. The verbal brutality with which he treated Adolf Frederick of Mecklenburg, or Einsiedel, or Vane, provides a sudden reminder that he was, after all, his father's son.

In the winter of 1631–2, then, Gustav Adolf attempted to lay the foundations of a stable order for central Europe by violent methods. The development of this tactic is well exemplified in his relations with Mecklenburg and Brunswick. At Werben, in August, he had presented to Mecklenburg a draft alliance which for the first time combined the permanence of the Pomeranian type of treaty, with the 'protection' of the Hessian[58] – a measure perhaps justified by the exceptional strategic importance of the duchies. At Halle, in September, he produced another draft which made it clear that the Swedish protection was to continue after the war.[59] But not only that: for whereas by the Werben draft Wismar and Warnemünde would have been handed over to Sweden as pledges for the reimbursement of war expenditure, by the Halle draft Sweden would have retained these places pending a settlement with the Empire[60] – which could only mean their permanent retention in return for Swedish concessions in central Germany. And when Adolf Frederick hastened to headquarters to plead his cause, he was met with a new and startling demand: that in virtue of the *jus belli* acquired by Gustav Adolf through occupation of the duchies, the dukes should recognize ('recognosciren') him and his heirs for their lands. Mecklenburg, then, would be a Swedish fief; and Gustav Adolf indicated that he would abandon this demand only if the dukes formally severed their links with the Empire, and declared themselves sovereign.[61] And this could mean only that he was confident that an independent Mecklenburg, bound by an eternal alliance, would be effectively under Swedish control.

Relations with the two main branches of the house of Brunswick developed along similar lines. Salvius's treaty with Christian of Lüneburg (which combined a 'Hessian' protectorate with the 'Pomeranian' provision that it was to be renewed every ten years)[62] was left unratified; and pressure was brought to bear instead upon Frederick Ulric of Wolfenbüttel. Frederick Ulric was without male heirs; the Lüneburg-Celle line was expected to succeed to his lands; and both lines had claims to the ecclesiastical lands of Hildesheim, which the Welfs had lost by a decision of the *Reichskammergericht* in 1629, and which were still occupied by Imperial troops.[63] Gustav Adolf now tried to exploit this situation as he had tried to exploit the claims of Brandenburg to the Pomeranian inheritance. The 'Halle compact', negotiated on the king's behalf by Louis of Anhalt (28

94

November 1631), had provided that Frederick Ulric should 'thankfully recognize' Gustav Adolf for all lands to be recovered (and especially for the Hildesheim lands) except those which would pass by hereditary right to the Lüneburg line.[64] It was indeed explained that there was no question of a vassalage, but only of recognition '*titulo protectionis vel advocatiae*', and 'from feelings of gratitude';[65] but subsequent developments were not reassuring. The Halle compact was repudiated by Gustav Adolf; and on 1 January 1632 Filip Sadler presented the Wolfenbüttel delegates with a new treaty. This made it quite clear that the ecclesiastical lands were to be held as a Swedish fief. It provided that the Lüneburg line should inherit them only if Christian and his heirs ratified the treaty and gave military aid to Sweden (compare the similar provisions in regard to Brandenburg in the Pomeranian treaty); that the Lüneburg succession even to the hereditary Wolfenbüttel lands should be subject to the same condition; and that the Estates of the various Welf lands must take resolutions not to recognize any successor who might fail to comply with the provisions of this treaty.[66]

Behind these developments in Gustav Adolf's policy lies the influence of Grotius. Grotius had laid it down that a conquest, provided it were solid and not ephemeral, conveyed not only a claim to the conquered territory, but also to the incorporeal rights of the vanquished.[67] It could therefore be argued that in conquering the lands of his enemies Gustav Adolf acquired not only ownership of the land, but the feudal rights of the Emperor as well. In virtue of this he could, and did, make large and very numerous donations in which his *jus superioritatis* was expressly acknowledged.[68] And in virtue of this also, he was entitled to grant the Hildesheim lands to the Welfs on a feudal tenure. But Grotius had also taught that the question as to whether the vanquished had really a right to the lands of which he was deprived was irrelevant to the rights of the victor.[69] Gustav Adolf could therefore claim that the lands of friends and allies, recently in enemy possession, but now liberated by him, were also at his disposal *jure belli*. And he did indeed explicitly make this claim in regard to Pomerania, Mecklenburg, Magdeburg and Halberstadt.[70] For such lands, therefore, he could also claim (if he were prepared to push matters to their logical issue) the 'recognition' which had formerly been due to the Emperor.

It seems, therefore, that Gustav Adolf, casting about for means to cement his evangelical league quickly and firmly, exacerbated by 'ingratitude' and intoxicated with victory, saw in the exploitation of these rights – not a means to destroy or undermine the old fabric of the *Reich*, which for him could scarcely be an end in itself – but a device to give added durability and cohesion to the military tie with Sweden during the war, and to the politico-military tie which (he was beginning to think) might be necessary thereafter. He was already speaking of himself, in these negotiations, as 'supreme head of the evangelical electors, princes and Estates of the German nation';[71] but the head still awaited a solid *corpus*. In the absence of Oxenstierna the king was his own foreign minister; and he notoriously lacked Oxenstierna's patience. He tried, therefore, to force the pace, selecting three particularly feeble princes, and justifying himself, perhaps, by the reflection that even alliances so unequal as those he proposed would not have been held by Grotius to infringe the liberties of the weaker party.[72] But the attempt failed. Weak as they were, Adolf Frederick and the Welfs stood fast in their refusal of such terms. Oxenstierna arrived at headquarters early in the new year, and applied, with professional dexterity, a flow of edulcorating verbiage to the ravaged feelings of the negotiators. The treaty of 29 February 1632 which he concluded with Mecklenburg was indeed onerous;[73] but at least it contained no 'recognition', and the imperial tie was expressly safeguarded. So too with Frederick Ulric: by the treaty of 5 February he recognized Gustav Adolf '*titulo protectionis vel avocatiae*' for the Hildesheim lands; but no such claim was now made for the hereditary possessions, and the subordinate relationship to Sweden was clearly stated to be a consequence of the duke's gratitude (repeatedly mentioned in the treaty) and Gustav Adolf's 'protection'.[74] The king's pointed refusal to ratify the Brunswick treaty, under various transparent pretexts, reflects his disappointment with this result;[75] but it is also an indication of a new policy, which Oxenstierna had been pressing upon him as early as December.[76] Henceforward they would avoid the conclusion of formal treaties with the German states, and content themselves with generally-phrased conventions concluded by the mere exchange of notes. It was still too early, it seemed, for a final formulation of policy: for the present Gustav Adolf would keep his hands free.

4

In October 1631 George of Hesse-Darmstadt, a Lutheran prince of Imperialist sympathies, began an attempt to mediate peace between the belligerents, and invited Gustav Adolf to assist in the attainment of this object. His invitation forced the king to define his attitude towards a settlement.[77]

Since as early as October 1630 Gustav Adolf's war-aims had included the religious emancipation of south Germany,[78] and the treaty of Bärwalde had explicitly provided for this.[79] At the close of 1631 the military prospects appeared favourable; and the king felt (as he told the delegates from Nuremberg in June 1632) that God would require a reckoning of them, if they now turned aside from the work.[80] In Sweden, the *råd* and the Secret Committee were in favour of peace only if it were buttressed by territorial guarantees; and everybody, whether at home or in Germany, was imbued with the strongest scepticism about the good faith of the Catholic party.[81] This distrust may or may not have been justified, but it was certainly one of the fundamental factors in the political situation. The king and his advisers, therefore, sought a dictated peace, a Carthaginian peace. In March 1632 Gustav Adolf proclaimed his intention of 'clipping the wings of the Imperialists so that they shall not fly again'; and in October Oxenstierna was for a peace 'with our foot on their neck and a knife at their throat':[82] had not Saul been punished by God for sparing the Amalekites?[83] The Emperor must be deprived of Bohemia; Frederick v must recover the electorate.[84] They did not want a compromise peace, or a moderate settlement. And in this the king remained consistent to the end.

It does not seem that Gustav Adolf supposed that a peace of this sort could easily be secured. Throughout the German campaign he seems to have reckoned on a long war. And this calculation, with its military consequences, governed all his policy. It implied logistical problems of increasing complexity; and it made still more disturbing the unreliability – military no less than political – of his most important ally, John George.

Some solid and enduring basis for the organization of the prolonged military effort was therefore indispensable; and Gustav
Adolf had already decided what that basis should be. The
policy of the *Norma futurarum actionum* must be maintained, and
indeed extended. In December 1631 the king was suggesting
(to William of Hesse) that he should be *protector religionis*, and
that the Protestant Estates should combine to form a standing
army, to be maintained after the peace in order to police a
Germany in which the Imperialists would have been compelled
to disband their forces. The idea was endorsed with enthusiasm
by William of Hesse and his advisers, whose own peace-terms
were if anything more stringent even than Gustav Adolf's.[85]
The project was developed in Gustav Adolf's instructions of
1 June 1632 for his envoy to John George; and again a few days
later in talks with the representatives of Nuremberg.[86] There
was to be a *corpus bellicum* – a free association of allies, to which
none should be constrained unwillingly – subordinated to a
chief who would probably be Gustav Adolf, but might still
conceivably be John George, or even William v.[87] But not a
corpus bellicum only: there must also be a *corpus politicum*, with
some central deliberative organ, some *parlamentum*. There is no
need, at least in the first instance, to make elaborate conjectures
as to what political designs lay behind this notion of a *corpus
politicum*, what its future implications for Germany would have
been, or what led Gustav Adolf to insist so carefully upon its
necessity. For it surely was, in origin, a natural and inevitable
extension of the *corpus bellicum*. Any efficient military alliance
must have machinery for dealing with the political or semi-
political issues that may arise between its members; and the
corpus politicum was designed to provide it.

Such a league, if it could be formed and made to work, might
well bring that dictated peace for which the king was striving;
but it left two large questions still open. First, what was to be
the nature and extent of Sweden's *satisfactio*? And secondly,
how far would the existing constitution of the Empire remain
undisturbed?

The question of *satisfactio* was one which Gustav Adolf seems
to have found increasing difficulty in discussing without losing
his temper. He always suspected that his allies might make
peace behind his back, and leave him in the lurch. He had no

faith in John George or George William, and the strongest sense
of the boundless ingratitude and incorrigible vacillation of the
German princes.[88] Towards Brandenburg he felt especially
bitter; and it is significant that he specifically ruled out the
possibility of George William's becoming head of his *corpus*. He
had not forgotten Küstrin; and now (as he frankly told the
Nuremberg delegates) he was at odds with him over Pomerania.[89] For Gustav Adolf, probably by the end of 1631, had
made up his mind that Sweden must retain, not the coastal strip
only,[90] but the whole of the duchy. The coastline, which at the
time of the Danzig congress had been thought of as *assecuratio*,
was now appearing in the guise of *satisfactio* too; and Gustav
Adolf was looking more and more to his politico-military
Protestant league to provide the *assecuratio* he required. At
Nuremberg in June, Gustav Adolf insisted on a territorial
satisfactio: he was no mercenary, he said, to be paid with
money.[91] In the summer of 1632, indeed, the king was pitching
his demands at the highest possible level, and explicitly grounding them upon Grotius. The German states, he proclaimed,
whether friend or foe, could be put into six categories; and
against five of these he had claims which were good in international law. As to conquered enemy lands, it was not reasonable that he should 'immediately and without more ado'[92] hand
them back at a peace. As to the four categories comprising
those not overtly his foes, it was not his intention 'solches alles
mit gewalt der waffen *mordicus* zuebeheupten', but his claims
were not therefore to be denied.[93] In short, the only German
states against which he made no claims were electoral Saxony
and Hesse-Cassel. The Nuremberg interviews make it clear
what he wanted: Magdeburg, the conquered ecclesiastical
lands, and Pomerania, 'on account of the sea'.[94] And he had
earlier made it plain that he intended to hold Pomerania as an
imperial fief.[95]

What then was Gustav Adolf's attitude towards imperial
institutions, and what relation would his *corpus* have borne to
them? There is no doubt that contemporaries considered his
candidature for the Empire as possible or even probable; and
some of his servants – especially Salvius and Sadler (though
not, apparently, Oxenstierna) – seem to have taken it almost
for granted.[96] Gustav Adolf himself referred to the matter on

99

only one occasion, and then in heat,[97] and his views are really unknown. But apart from his protestation to Bergman that he came to preserve the *Reich* and not to destroy it, and apart from similar declarations to Nuremberg,[98] his insistence that Sweden must become a member of the Empire for her future German possessions seems to show that he entertained no thought of destroying the old constitution;[99] and one explanation of the 'feudal' clauses in his donations may be that he regarded them as mediate fiefs, and himself as immediate. On the whole it seems likely that he thought of his *corpus bellicum et politicum* as a body within the Empire, as the Union and the League had been: he referred to it, for instance, as '*corpus per se subsistens in ipso corpore imperii Romani*'.[100] But he seems also to have thought that the war and the peace might considerably weaken the imperial authority: it was suggested, for instance, that members of the league might be in the same position as the Netherlands (where imperial authority was merely nominal) or Italy (where it had become virtually extinct).[101] He once compared his own relationship to the projected league with that of Henry II to the German Protestants of his day.[102] In one aspect the Thirty Years' War was a German constitutional struggle; and even so conservative a statesman as John George admitted the possibility of some modification in the constitution;[103] while a radical like William of Hesse was demanding the abolition of the votes of ecclesiastical electors, and the secularization of all church lands.[104] From the Swedish point of view imperial obligations and imperial machinery could be a nuisance – a convenient pretext for half-heartedness in the cause; and Swedish agents seem to have looked upon them with considerable impatience.[105] In so far, therefore, as such ties jeopardized Sweden's military effort, Gustav Adolf could have no compunction in severing them; but otherwise he could have no interest in constitutional innovations – and least of all, if he had really had the imperial dignity in view.

All these questions were still unsolved in the autumn of 1632. The king's attempt to enlist the two electors for his *corpus* had for the moment failed. He turned then to the south-west of Germany, and tried to launch his league there.[106] The meeting he summoned to Ulm for 2 December was intended, primarily, to inaugurate a *corpus bellicum*; and the south-west was selected for the experiment partly because the Protestants there were weak, imperilled and proportionably the more devoted to Sweden; partly because they included those great imperial cities whose assistance (on economic grounds) he had always considered of vital importance;[107] but not least because this was the area from which he proposed to deliver next year's attack on Vienna – the area, consequently, in which efficient military organization was most essential. The cardinal point in the programme for the meeting was indeed to secure a disciplined, regularly-paid standing army: much of the rest may be considered in some degree as accessory to that purpose.[108] The idea of abolishing the Imperial Chamber of Justice was a safeguard against losing the peace after winning the war; the attempt to induce members not to 'recognize' the Emperor was designed to deprive them of hampering scruples or legalistic evasions. If the meeting at Ulm went well, and if Gustav Adolf were to succeed in his expressed intention of finally reducing to order the chaos of the Lower Saxon circle,[109] the experiment might be extended to include the more jealous Protestants of north Germany.

5

Such was the situation at the time of Lützen. Gustav Adolf had arrived at it by way of successive expedients, rather than by following any precisely-determined plan. Military necessity had driven him to formulate the *Norma*, and to take upon himself the organization and leadership of the evangelical war-effort. Thereafter he had attempted, by various methods, to make the Protestant league an effective force: by separate treaties of the Hessian type; by violent pressure upon strategically important princes; by enlisting the co-operation of the Protestant electors; and lastly by a regional pact in an especially suitable area. His aim throughout remained the same as in 1630, though circumstances had driven him to plans and devices never contemplated before the landing, and though the quest for Baltic security had led him to seek it in such unlikely places as the Valtelline and Alsace. Common sense, perhaps, was on the verge of revolt; yet it was difficult to put a finger on any flaw in the chain of military logic that he had followed. Like most commanders, Gustav Adolf was an empiricist. Until Breitenfeld no plans for a peace were possible; and even afterwards (and even for a single limited issue such as *satisfactio*) the plan must alter with the fortunes of war – as became clear enough in the decade after the king's death. In short, as Oxenstierna plainly tells us, Gustav Adolf's designs varied freely with circumstances: '*momenta temporum* weren allezeit das fundamentum gewesen',[110] and the only permanent objective was to get the best peace that could be had. It seems unhistorical to attempt to distinguish between selfish 'Swedish' demands for *satisfactio*, and other, more general, perhaps more 'ideal' plans for securing the future of Protestantism or remodelling the *Reich*.[111] To the king, at least, they were all one. He saw no conflict between the interests of Sweden and the welfare of Protestant Germany. For the German princes such an identification was more difficult. The gratitude of the liberated was short-lived, though admiration proved more lasting; but it is hardly surprising if Adolf Frederick or Frederick Ulric felt that they were exchanging a Habsburg domination for a Swedish servitude.

On the eve of Lützen the future for Sweden was scarcely much clearer (and it was infinitely more complex) than at Peenemünde. Swedish popularity was on the wane; discipline was bad in the German mercenaries; John George was loyal mainly from fear, George William mainly from covetousness; only a handful of trusty allies could be reckoned on.[112] The king himself was embittered; haunted by the problem of the succession with its constitutional implications; no longer, perhaps, even invincible. For the moment, at least, Gustav Adolf seemed to have run himself into a blind alley. A victory at Lützen, a political success at Ulm, might have put all right – for a time. But it is not without significance that one of his last recorded utterances, overheard on the eve of battle, was a groaning soliloquy upon the faithlessness of allies.[113]

NOTES

[1] This paper was read to the Royal Historical Society, 11 February 1956 and published in the *Transactions of the Royal Historical Society*, Fifth Series, Vol. 7, 1957.

[2] W. Carlsson, *Gustaf II Adolf och Stralsund*, Uppsala, 1912, pp. 71–2, 102–21, 125–30: *Rikskansleren Axel Oxenstiernas Skrifter och Brefvexling*

[*AOSB*], Stockholm, 1888–, I, iv, 209 ff., 214 ff.; *cf.* Carlsson, *op. cit.*, p. 69, and *Sverges traktater med främmande magter*, Stockholm, 1890– , v. 342 ff.

[3] Carlsson, *op. cit.*, pp. 248, 250–2; Nils Ahnlund, *Gustaf Adolf inför tyska kriget*, Stockholm, 1918, p. 276. In February 1638, however, Oxenstierna told the *råd* that there was no ground for the suspicion (not unreasonably entertained by the burghers) that Sweden desired to acquire the town; 'which neither his late Majesty nor the now reigning sovereign ever thought of, since their Majesties sought nothing other than that the Emperor might not get a foot-hold in the harbour there ... Nor is it profitable to the crown of Sweden to keep Stralsund alone, but rather the garrison is a burden': *Svenska Riksrådets Protokoll* [*RRP*], Stockholm, 1878– , vii, 151.

[4] '*Si Wismaria quoque potiremur*'; *RRP*, i, 224 (27 Oct. 1629).

[5] *AOSB*, II, i, 595.

[6] And '*quia non nisi papyracea securitas*': *RRP*, ii, 1–4.

[7] *AOSB*, II, i, 603.

[8] To the *råd*: *RRP*, i, 128 (23 April 1629).

[9] *RRP*, i, 222.

[10] *Ibid.*, 224.

[11] *AOSB*, II, i, 544, Gustav Adolf to Oxenstierna, 4 December, 1629.

[12] Ahnlund, *Gustaf Adolf inför tyska kriget*, p. 260. Johannes Paul thinks it meant no more than that Protestant princes would be constrained to help him: J. Paul, *Gustaf Adolf*, Leipzig, 1932, ii, 156.

[13] *RRP*, ii, 3.

[14] 'The Imperialists in Pomerania and Mecklenburg, and their fleet in Wismar harbour, had for the Swedish diet of 1629 the same significance as had the Germans in Belgium for the English parliament of 1914': S. Arnoldsson, *Krigspropagandan i Sverige före trettioåriga kriget*, Göteborg, 1941, p. 28.

[15] 'The Chancellor retorted, that that [*sc.* religion] was not our *principalis scopus*. But his late Majesty had other large causes of war. True it is, that religion ought not to be propagated *armis*, but its *arma* are rather *spiritualia*, as *preces* and *lacrymae*; but the true *principalis scopus* is, that *regnum Sueciae* and *consortes religionis nostrae* may remain in security, and be in their *esse* preserved, *tam in statu ecclesiastico quam politico*. It is therefore in this case not so much a matter of religion, but rather of *status publicus*, within whose ambit religion also falls': *RRP*, vii, 53. Yet on 3 February 1633 Oxenstierna wrote to Salvius (whom he certainly had no motive for misleading) that the king's aim had been 'first and foremost to liberate these and all his co-religionists and relatives in the Empire from the popish yoke, shift the war from them to the papists, and keep it going until the enemy, weary of it, should himself seek peace, so that all evangelical Estates might thus with the more security and reputation come again to their former dignity, liberty and Estate': *AOSB*, I, viii, 131.

[16] '*Ita tanto erit Suecia securior, quanto illi* [the north German states] *debiliores*': *RRP*, i, 224.

[17] *RRP*, i, 229–37; J. Fridericia, *Danmarks ydre politiske Historie i Tiden fra Freden i Lybek til Freden i Prag*, Copenhagen, 1876, i, 130–5; *AOSB*, I, v, 295–8, II, i, 579–81: not for him the 'Empire of Scandinavia' which Oxenstierna seems to have believed to be within his grasp: on this see N. Ahnlund,

'Kejsardömet Skandinavien', *Historisk Tidskrift*, liv, (1934); *RRP*, vi, 394.
[18] And also with the story, told to the *råd* at third hand on 11 November 1635, that from the beginning he intended 'an *imperium Macedonicum*' in Germany, and a permanent diminution of the power of the Emperor: *RRP*, v, 298.

[19] G. Irmer, *Die Verhandlungen Schwedens und seiner Verbündeten mit Wallenstein und dem Kaiser von 1631 bis 1634*, Publicationen aus den K. Preussischen Staatsarchiven, 99, Leipzig, 1899 [Irmer, *VS*], ii, 26, Oxenstierna to the Brandenburg ministers, 30 January 1633. The preceding passage runs: 'Sei ins gemein gewesen, des feindes conatus zu brechen, dessen vorhaben, und was er durch die Ostseh thuen wollen, bekant. Haben also ihre maj. die meinung gehabt, ihr reich und die Ostsehe zu versichern und die bedrengte lande zu liberiren, hernach weiter zu gehen, oder zu stutzen, nachdem es sich schickete; *hetten anfangs so weit zu kommen, nicht vermeinet*': [my italics].

[20] 'If we cannot say, *bellum se ipsum alet*, then I see no way out of what we have undertaken': Gustav Adolf to Oxenstierna, 1 April 1628: *Konung Gustaf II Adolfs Skrifter*, ed. C. G. Styffe [Styffe], Stockholm, 1861, p. 520.
[21] *RRP*, ii, 8.

[22] G. Droysen, *Brandenburgische Audienzen bei Gustaf Adolf*, Berlin, 1878, supplants K. G. Helbig, *Gustav Adolf und die Kurfürsten von Sachsen und Brandenburg*, Leipzig, 1854, for these talks.

[23] Droysen, *Audienzen*, p. 18; *cf. RRP*, i, 231 (10 November 1629): '*Res nostrae non patiuntur neutrales in Germania*'.

[24] Droysen, *Audienzen*, p. 21.

[25] Text in *Sverges traktater*, v, 380–8; a Swedish draft in M. Bär, *Die Politik Pommerns während des dreissigjährigen Krieges*, Leipzig, 1896, pp. 263 ff.

[26] *Sverges traktater*, v, 395–404.

[27] *Ibid.*, 387–8.

[28] Bär, *op. cit.*, p. 272.

[29] J. Kretzschmar, *Gustaf Adolfs Pläne und Ziele in Deutschland und die Herzöge zu Braunschweig und Lüneburg*, Hanover, 1904, p. 161.

[30] Bär, p. 278. Compare Oxenstierna's statement in the *råd* on 9 April 1638, when he said 'we had a *jus belli* inasmuch as his late majesty recovered the country from the Emperor's armies, which *jus* his majesty transformed into a *jus foederis*, simply with the purpose of keeping the Pomeranian estates in a good humour': *RRP*, vii, 187.

[31] *AOSB*, I, vi, 44–5.

[32] *Sverges traktater*, v, 491–504; W. Struck, *Das Bündnis Wilhelms von Weimar mit Gustaf Adolf*, Stralsund, 1895, pp. 33 ff.

[33] See, e.g., Falkenberg's remarks to the Pomeranian *Rath*, 12 Aug. 1630: Bär, p. 272; Gustav Adolf's interview with Leuchtmar, 19 October 1630: Generalstaben, *Sveriges krig 1611–1632*, Stockholm, 1936, iii, 520–1.

[34] *AOSB*, II, i, 714.

[35] Kretzschmar, *Die Allianzverhandlungen Gustav Adolfs mit Kurbrandenburg* [Kretzschmar, *Allianzverhandlungen*], Berlin, 1904, pp. 3–4.

[36] *Arkiv till upplysning om svenska krigens ... historia* [*Arkiv*], Stockholm, 1860, ii, 247–8.

[37] Kretzschmar, *Allianzverhandlungen*, pp. 9–11.

[38] It is true that Gustav Adolf had on 16 February 1631 told von Pfuel, 'Ich nehme weg, was ich bekommen kann, und Pommern gebe ich ihm auch nicht wieder' (Droysen, *Audienzen*, pp. 32–3); but this was Gustav Adolf in his blackmailing mood, in the course of a heated interview, and need not be taken as an expression of serious policy – though the elector took it so (B. Boëthius, *Svenskarne i de nedersachsiska . . . kretsarna* [Boëthius, *NSK*], p. 3). And in April he had said that he would demand '*oram maritimam*' (Kretzschmar, *Gustav Adolfs Pläne und Ziele*, p. 164); in a vivid letter to the electress of 3 June he had compared himself to Jacob serving Laban, and now denied his reward (G. Droysen, *Schriftstücke von Gustaf Adolf zumeist an evangelische Fürsten Deutschlands*, Stockholm, 1877, pp. 203 ff.: *cf. Sveriges krig*, iv, 324, n. 4, for correct dating of this letter); on 5 June he had complained that he had done all the work in recovering Pomerania, while George William proposed quietly to step into the succession at the appropriate moment, without adequate acknowledgment (*Schriftstücke*, pp. 118–19); but he made it quite clear that he asked only 'reasonable' compensation and 'etzliche wenig Plätze' on the coast – and even this was not a *sine qua non* (*ibid.*, p. 119). The wording runs: 'allein gegen roial versicherung Ihrer freundtschafft vnd einer geringen vnd ganz ertreglichen abstattung ezlicher vnkosten, zu deren versicherung Sie allein etzliche wenig Plätze an der Ost See begehret (welches jedoch bei vnderhandlung veleicht noch moderirt, oder bei künftigen General tractaten mit dem Röm. Kayser, noch ganz aufgehebt hette werden können).'

[39] *Schriftstücke*, p. 128; *Sverges traktater*, v, 449–54, 457–63.

[40] *Arkiv*, i, 743–50. Arnim reported to the Brandenburg *Rath* that Gustav Adolf desired the *Direktorium*; but he also considered that he wanted Pomerania, realized this would create a bad impression in Germany, and was seeking pretexts to adduce for keeping it: Kretzschmar, *Allianzverhandlungen*, p. 34.

[41] Kretzschmar, *Allianzverhandlungen*, pp. 38–41; also Paul, *Gustaf Adolf*, ii, 198 and n. 2.

[42] For the marriage question, see in general R. Schulze, *Das Projekt der Vermählung Friedrich Wilhelms von Brandenburg mit Christina von Schweden*, Halle, 1898; R. Armstedt, *Der schwedische Heiratsplan des grossen Kurfürsten*, Königsberg, 1896; *AOSB*, II, i, 766–7; N. Ahnlund, *Axel Oxenstierna*, Stockholm, 1940, pp. 658–61; Kretzschmar, *Gustaf Adolfs Pläne und Ziele*, pp. 204–19; Kretzschmar considered that Gustav Adolf used the marriage as a mere 'bait' – a view difficult to reconcile with his contention that it was on account of the marriage that the king was prepared to make concessions in 1631.

[43] On 7 June 1631 Arnim visited Gustav Adolf's camp and told him that harsh treatment of George William would make a bad impression in Germany, and might suggest that he was himself coveting the Brandenburg electorate. Gustav Adolf admitted that this would not be an unreasonable interpretation, to those ignorant of his real intentions: Kretzschmar, *Allianzverhandlungen*, p. 32.

[44] Ahnlund, *Gustaf Adolf inför tyska kriget*, pp. 419–20; *Sveriges krig*, iii, 535–7.

⁴⁵ B. Boëthius, 'Filip Sadlers beskickning 1629–30', *Historisk Tidskrift*, I Series, xxxvii (1917), *passim*.

⁴⁶ For the Leipzig Convention, Struck, *Das Bündnis Wilhelms von Weimar mit Gustav Adolf*, pp. 61–95.

⁴⁷ *Arkiv*, i, 726, 736; Boëthius, *NSK*, pp. 127–9.

⁴⁸ W. Struck, 'Gustav Adolf und die schwedische Satisfaktion', *Historische Vierteljahrschrift*, 2 (1899), p. 357; cf. B. P. von Chemnitz, *Königlich Schwedischen in Teutschland geführten Kriegs Erster Theil*, Stettin, 1648, i, 137–8.

⁴⁹ *AOSB*, II, viii, 44, Horn to Oxenstierna, 26 April 1631; cf. Arnim's forebodings: *AOSB*, II, ix, 567, Teuffel to Oxenstierna, 29 March 1631. Text of the Resolution in Lundorp, iii, 145–7. Oxenstierna commented, 2 February 1633: 'Der Leipzische Schluss machet den kaiser gar zum tyrannen, und dass er keinen *articulum capitulationis* gehalten. Nur haben sie die conclusion ausgelassen: "Drumb bistu nicht kaiser mehr, sondern *tyrannus et hostis libertatis ac patriae*, wo du es nicht enderst!" ': Irmer, *VS*, ii, 41.

⁵⁰ Struck, *Das Bündnis Wilhelms von Weimar*, p. 93.

⁵¹ B. Boëthius, 'Norma futurarum actionum', *Historisk Tidskrift*, I Series, xxxi (1911), pp. 199 ff.

⁵² *Cf.* his offer to Brandenburg on 26 April 1631: 'Man sollte ihn ein *formatum consilium* [bei]ordnen, er wolle exequieren, was sie haben wollten; man sollte es an die andern Fürsten bringen und es machen wie die [General]-Staaten'; Brandenburg Geheimratsprotokoll, cited in Kretzschmar: *Gustaf Adolfs Pläne und Ziele*, p. 168.

⁵³ *Sveriges krig*, iii, 530–1.

⁵⁴ In May, the king concluded a draft agreement with John Albert of Mecklenburg; in June, Salvius signed a treaty with John Frederick of Bremen; in July, he was instructed to proceed to a definitive treaty with both the Mecklenburg dukes; in August, the final treaty with William v of Hesse was concluded; in December, Salvius completed an alliance with Christian of Lüneburg-Celle: *Sverges traktater*, v, 463–73, 476–90, 588–99; Boëthius, *NSK*, pp. 150 ff.

⁵⁵ *Sverges traktater*, v, 513–16.

⁵⁶ *Robert Monro His Expedition* (1637), ii, 89.

⁵⁷ E.g. In his relations with Mecklenburg: see below.

⁵⁸ Boëthius, *NSK*, pp. 171–2.

⁵⁹ *Sverges traktater*, v, 717–19.

⁶⁰ '*Donec de ijs nobis plenius cum imperio Romano convenerit*'; Boëthius, *NSK*, p. 185, n. 2.

⁶¹ The Mecklenburg negotiations are discussed in Boëthius, *NSK*, pp. 170–203; Cothmann's Relation of the negotiations in Frankfurt is printed in Kretzschmar, *Gustaf Adolfs Pläne und Ziele*, pp. 316–62. Salvius had more than once urged that Mecklenburg '*ob situm cum Svecia*' ought to be a Swedish fief; Boëthius, *NSK*, p. 54.

⁶² *Sverges traktater*, v, 588–99.

⁶³ The Wolfenbüttel line had owned all the Hildesheim lands, but in October 1631 Gustav Adolf had promised George of Lüneburg the three

Ämter of Peine, Steuerwald and Marienburg (the 'kleine Stift'): for all this, Kretzschmar, *Gustaf Adolfs Pläne und Ziele*, pp. 1–6, 18–19.

[64] The Halle compact is printed in *Sverges traktater*, v, 691 ff.; and see Kretzschmar, *op. cit.*, pp. 31 ff.; criticisms of Kretzschmar's conclusions in review by C. H. H[allendorf], in *Historisk Tidskrift*, xxiv (1904), pp. 45–8; Boëthius, *NSK*, pp. 274, n. 2.

[65] Kretzschmar, *op. cit.*, p. 32.

[66] Text of Sadler's draft, with Brunswick amendments, in Kretzschmar, *op. cit.*, pp. 247–77. The demand for ratification by the Estates had a parallel in Gustav Adolf's treaty with John Frederick of Bremen, by which a similar guarantee was to be extorted from the Chapter: *Sverges traktater*, v, 467.

[67] *Hugonis Grotii De jure Belli ac Pacis Libri Tres*, ed. W. Whewell, Cambridge, 1853, III, vi, 4§ 1, 5, 7§ 1; III, vii, 4; III, viii, 4§ 2; III, xx, 12§2. As early as the beginning of October 1631 Gustav Adolf informed Erfurt that the former rights of the elector of Mainz in the town were his by conquest: J. Bierehe, *Gustav Adolf in Erfurt*, Erfurt, 1924, p. 6.

[68] E.g., *AOSB*, I, viii, 638, 673–4, 683.

[69] Grotius, *op. cit.*, III, vi, 7 § 1. But see also Grotius's restriction in III, xiii, 1 § 1: Boëthius (*NSK*, p. 5) strains the meaning (and omits the last clause), to make this passage a basis for *satisfactio*.

[70] Gustav Adolf to Salvius, 20 December 1631: *Arkiv*, i, 530–2.

[71] Kretzschmar, *op. cit.*, p. 31.

[72] Grotius, I, iii, 21 §§ 1–3. It is noteworthy that Grotius specifically includes alliances in which one party is bound to preserve the authority and majesty of the other, 'ad quod genus referenda sunt jura quaedam eorum, quae nunc vocantur *protectionis*, *advocatiae*, mundiburdii' [my italics]; and again: 'clientes in fide sunt patronorum ... sunt sub patronicio, non sub ditione'. Indeed, the provision for arbitration, normally included in alliances of the Hessian-type, seems to Grotius one of the marks of an *equal* alliance: *op. cit.*, I, iii, 21 § 6; but see too his caution in 21 § 10.

[73] *Sverges traktater*, v, 704 ff. The treaty was to be permanent, renewable at every change of ruler, and was to take precedence over all other obligations (even to the Empire); Wismar and Warnemünde to be at Sweden's disposal for the duration of the war; Sweden to have '*absolutum foederis hujus idque comitantis belli directorium*'; the Swedish copper coinage to be current; money contributions to be made; mutual military aid was specified. Even so there was a loophole for further claims: the dukes were restored '*salva actione nobis ... regnoque Sveciae adversus singulos pluresve imperii status ex hoc bello enata competente*' – though Oxenstierna assured the dukes that this was not aimed at them. But they tried in vain to replace '*singulos pluresve*' by '*alios*'.

[74] *Sverges traktater*, v, 670 ff.; Kretzschmar, *op. cit.*, pp. 49–50.

[75] Kretzschmar, *op. cit.*, pp. 53, 101–3; Ahnlund, *Axel Oxenstierna*, p. 653. It was not ratified till 30 October 1633.

[76] Axel Oxenstierna to Gustav Adolf, 9 December 1631: *AOSB*, I, vi, 556–7.

[77] For the project of a universal peace, see the documents in Irmer, *VS*, i, 16 ff.; and G. Droysen, *Die Verhandlungen über den Universalfrieden im Winter*

1631–2 (Archiv für die sächsische Geschichte, NS., vi), Leipzig, 1880, *passim.*
[78] Gustav Adolf to Axel Oxenstierna, 8 October 1630: *AOSB*, II, i, 654.
[79] *Sverges traktater*, v, 439. Struck ('Gustaf Adolf und die schwedische Satisfaktion', p. 479) is mistaken in supposing this programme to have been adopted only after Breitenfeld.
[80] C. W. F. Breyer, *Beyträge zur Geschichte des dreissigjährigen Krieges*, Munich, 1812, p. 228.
[81] *RRP*, ii, 54; *Arkiv*, ii, 91, 94, 168; Irmer, *VS*, i, 136, 138, 289; Breyer, *op. cit.*, p. 216, where the king says of Imperial promises that one might as soon expect 'dass ein bloss papyr, wider eine halbe carthaunen helffen sollte, alss, dass man vnss dergleichen frieden vnd stattliche versprechen halten wurde'.
[82] Irmer, *VS*, i, 138, 290. Oxenstierna's words were '*In summa* der könig werde nicht mehr trauen und so lang mit ihnen fechten, bis er sie zu erden gelegt, mit seinem knie uf ihrem hals sässe und den degen an die gurgel ihnen stehen hette, so würde er alsdan sagen "so und so mache nun frieden".' And *cf.* a remark of Oxenstierna, very similar to that of the king, on 2 February 1633: *ibid.*, ii, 40.
[83] *Ibid.*, i, 139.
[84] Irmer, *VS*, i, 139–40. Arnim did not fail to point out that Ferdinand had acquired Bohemia *jure belli*, and that it was undeniably his in international law: *ibis.*, i, 93.
[85] *Ibid.*, i, 74–7, 125–33.
[86] *Ibid.*, i, 199–208; Breyer, pp. 218–31, 237–8; S. Donaubauer, *Nürnberg um die Mitte des dreissigjährigen Krieges*, Nuremberg, 1893, pp. 169–74.
[87] Irmer, *VS*, i, 207; Breyer, p. 218. The suggestion may not have been seriously meant; but it is noteworthy that Gustav Adolf told Nuremberg that they must *either* join the projected league *or* ally with Sweden (Breyer, p. 219). On the other hand, Löffler later demanded a *direktorium* for Sweden even after the war: Irmer, *VS*, i, lxxv, 216.
[88] Examples of this in *Arkiv*, i, 456, 755. He would have agreed with Monro's verdict: 'They wagge as the bush doth resolving ever to quit their best friends in adversity': Monro, ii, 44.
[89] Breyer, pp. 218, 229.
[90] Salvius's draft treaty of September 1631 would have given him '*oram maritimam donec plenius nobis cum imperio convenerit*' – the same formula as was used for Wismar and Warnemünde in the Mecklenburg treaty. George William rejected these terms: Boëthius, 'Aktstycken rörande Salvius' underhandlingar med Brandenburg', pp. 127–42.
[91] Breyer, p. 221.
[92] 'Alsobalden und schlechterdings.'
[93] Irmer, *VS*, i, 206, 215. The six classes were (i) Protestant lands formerly wholly occupied by the enemy – e.g. Mecklenburg; (ii) Protestant lands where the prince's authority had been merely nominal – e.g. Pomerania; (iii) lands hostile in spirit – e.g. Brandenburg [!]; (iv) independents, deeply indebted to Sweden – e.g. Saxony, Hesse-Cassel; (v) lands that had favoured and aided the foe [– e.g. Hesse-Darmstadt?]; (vi) open enemies.
[94] Breyer, pp. 210, 218–19; K. Spannagel, *Konrad von Burgsdorff*, Berlin,

1903, p. 382. He had earlier told George of Hesse-Darmstadt that he wanted a free hand in Mainz, Würzburg and Bamberg: Irmer, *VS*, i, 109.
⁹⁵ *Ibid.*, i, 140.
⁹⁶ Salvius to Grubbe, 12 October 1631, *ap.* Boëthius, *NSK*, p. 207. Sadler even told the Nuremberg deputies that Gustav Adolf desired to be Emperor, but would refuse to sign any *Wahlkapitulation*: Breyer, p. 239. But Sadler's language at Nuremberg by no means entirely tallied with his master's; and Gustav Adolf said nothing of it.
⁹⁷ On 2 January 1632 Gustav Adolf said to Adolf Frederick of Mecklenburg, 'Sollte ich Kaiser werden, so sind E. L. mein Fürst': Kretzschmar, *op. cit.*, p. 176 n.
⁹⁸ Droysen, *Audienzen*, p. 20; Breyer, p. 220. And *cf.* the king's indignant retort to Brézé's suggestion that they should partition the Rhineland between them: he had come, he said, 'als *protector*, nicht als *proditor Germaniae*': Paul, iii, 48.
⁹⁹ Though Arnim seems to have believed that Gustav Adolf aimed both at becoming elector of Mainz and at breaking the old constitution: G. Irmer, *Hans Georg von Arnim*, Leipzig, 1894, p. 170: and *cf.* John George's remark to the Hesse-Darmstadt envoy, 27 April 1632: '*Rex* gedächte *caesari* nit viel übrig zu lassen, welches zu einem accord sehr undienlich': Irmer, *VS*, i, 164.
¹⁰⁰ Breyer, p. 232. The League of Heilbronn, which arose out of Gustav Adolf's ideas, was expressly declared not to aim at violation of the constitution of the Empire: *AOSB*, I, viii, 445; and *cf.* the *corpus hanseaticum* for which Bremen was working in the spring of 1631: Boëthius, *NSK*, p. 117.
¹⁰¹ Breyer, p. 212. Kretzschmar missed the point of this by confusing it with another suggestion that the *corpus* might have a constitution similar to that of the United Netherlands: Kretzschmar, *op. cit.*, p. 172.
¹⁰² Irmer, *VS*, i, 137 (March 1632).
¹⁰³ *Ibid.*, i, 161: as reported by Tungel to Schwallenberg, 29 March 1632.
¹⁰⁴ Irmer, *VS*, i, 125–33.
¹⁰⁵ *Cf.* Grubbe's characteristic comment on the Brandenburg negotiations (25 May 1631): 'Objection still made on grounds of *jura imperii fundamentalia*, die Erbverbrüderung, and other such stuff, *hoc perverso Rom. imperii statu*, mighty absurd': *Arkiv*, i, 743
¹⁰⁶ Invitation to George of Hesse-Darmstadt, 20 October, 1632, in Irmer, *VS*, i, 284–6; to the nobility of the Franconian circle, 24 Oct., *Arkiv*, i, 682; instructions for Oxenstierna, 24 October, *AOSB*, II, i, 866–8; and *cf. AOSB*, I, vii, 601 ff.
¹⁰⁷ Breyer, pp. 220–1, 223, 234; Ahnlund, *Oxenstierna*, p. 667; G. Egelhaaf, 'Gustaf Adolf und die deutsche Reichsstädte', *Deutsche Rundschau*, cxi, (1902), p. 421. In particular, he was anxious to secure the permanent alliance of Ulm, Nuremberg, Strassburg and Frankfort, whose economic strength and military capabilities he much exaggerated: see Paul, iii, 62 ff.
¹⁰⁸ As Oxenstierna emphasized on 30 January 1633: Irmer, *VS*, ii, 27.
¹⁰⁹ Gustav Adolf to Steinberg, 30 October 1632: *Arkiv*, i, 687.
¹¹⁰ Or again, 'Der könig wurde sich geendert haben, nach dem, wie er gesehen, dass der feind sich gestellt, die zeiten sich angelassen und die freunde sich erwiesen haben würden ... *De futuribus casibus* sei zwar auch

wohl ehr geredet, aber *magis obiter* und das werk nicht genugsamb gefasset':
Irmer, *VS*, ii, 27.

[111] E.g. Kretzschmar, who considered *assecuratio* as the expression of the
king's 'universalen, welthistorische Pläne': *op. cit.*, p. 159.

[112] Gustav Adolf considered William of Hesse-Cassel and William of
Weimar as absolutely sure, Julius Frederick of Württemberg as reasonably
so: Breyer, p. 236.

[113] 'H.M. began to bewail and lament, saying how well he had meant in
the German business; but H.M. said that since he now understood that these
German gentry little esteemed H.M.'s favour or good will, nor would they
suffer H.M.'s direction over them, therefore (said H.M.) . . . "I will prove it,
so that every honest man shall esteem me for an honourable gentleman, let it
go afterwards as God will. But those others, that have not heeded my orders,
advice and exhortations, they shall be . . ." – what I do not venture to mention here': letter of Tönnes Langman: 'Ett par brev om slaget vid Lützen
1632', *Historisk Tidskrift*, I Series, xii (1892), p. 160. And *cf*. Ahnlund,
Oxenstierna, p. 725.

5

Queen Christina and the General Crisis of the Seventeenth Century[1]

It is usual nowadays to consider the cluster of revolutions which occurred in the 1640s and 1650s as an acute phase of a chronic disorder, more or less common to all parts of Europe, which we have become accustomed to call the General Crisis of the Seventeenth Century. There does not seem, however, to be any great measure of agreement as to what the nature of that crisis was. And, indeed, generalizations which are to fit movements as apparently dissimilar as the revolt of Portugal and the English Civil War are not, perhaps, very easy to devise; and Masaniello and Andries Bicker are certainly strange bedfellows. This paper does not purport to offer any solution to the problem: it attempts only to give some account of a crisis which seems so far to have been left out of consideration in discussions of it, and to examine how far events in Sweden square with the theories which have been put forward to explain the revolutionary movements elsewhere.

It is, of course, quite true that the Swedish crisis of 1650 did not issue in any violent upheaval. But, as Professor Trevor-Roper has remarked,[2] the revolutionary situation did not necessarily lead to revolution: revolution, to become explicit, must 'depend on events and errors'. But that it *was* a revolutionary situation seems undeniable; and Swedish observers saw it as part of the general European epidemic, which Oxenstierna, more philosophical than the rest, resignedly accepted as a seasonal fever which must run its course. The Swedish Council spent many perplexed hours debating the news from England and France; it had its eye on the troubles in Holland and Naples; it was interested in Portuguese independence; and Chmielnicki did not escape its observation. Per Brahe feared that Sweden was being infected by revolutionary doctrines imported from abroad; Jakob de la Gardie lamented that 'they want to do as they have been doing in England, and make us all as like as pig's trotters. . . . *Est res pessimi exempli*'. There was a *'spiritus vertiginis'* abroad: as Christina observed, 'neither king nor *parlement* have their proper power, but the common man, the *canaille*, rules according to his fancy'. In October 1650 Oxenstierna confessed that he was afraid to visit his country houses; and his son Erik predicted that the peasants would break their masters' necks when they got home from the Diet. The burghers, too, were affected: Schering Rosenhane, in an imaginary conversation between representatives of the four Estates, published in this year, makes the nobleman accuse the burgher of aiming at a *'populare imperium'*. And Oxenstierna, in a moment of unwonted depression, told his colleagues in Council, *'Ferrum*, that is the only *consilium'*.[3]

The fear of a social war was thus very real in 1650. It was no new thing. Throughout the Regency (1632–44) Oxenstierna had always in mind the danger of a peasant revolt, and was very apt to urge it as an argument against heavier taxes, or wider privileges for the nobility: it was not for nothing that Grotius had sent him detailed reports about the Nu-Pieds.[4] And the nervousness persisted after 1650 too: the outbreak was indeed aborted, but the threat remained. In December 1651 the elder Messenius[5] said at his trial: 'There is plenty of resolution all over the country; all they need is a leader.' In 1653 it was reported that there was a design to massacre all nobles. At the Diet of 1655 the peasants openly threatened insurrection. And in 1660 both Per Brahe and Elaus Terserus thought the country near to civil war.[6]

The crisis of 1650 was compact of many elements.[7] It was a social crisis above all; but it was a constitutional crisis too, as the Fronde and the Civil War were. It was, quite obviously, a food crisis, for the harvest was the worst Sweden had known for fifty years, or was to know for near fifty more: already in March the Stockholm bakers were fighting each other at the town gates for supplies of flour.[8] It gathered up into itself the struggles of parties and factions; but it concerned itself also with what contemporaries were pleased to call fundamental law. In one very important aspect the crisis was dynastic. And it was fought out, and the issue debated, in parliament.

The Diet which met in Stockholm in July 1650 sat for the unprecedented time of nearly four months; and it produced a concerted onslaught upon the nobility by the three lower Estates. That was unprecedented too. The lead was taken, unexpectedly, by the burghers; and all the lower clergy, with half the bishops, united with them to champion the peasants and attack the aristocracy. Preachers denounced from the pulpit nobles who allowed their horses to eat up all the corn, while the poor died of hunger. Political verses castigated the cruelties and oppressions of the landlords.[9] Respectable parsons declared passionately that there were too many nobles and too many foreigners in the country. The peasants complained that they were plagued by excessive labour services, deprived of their freeholds and their liberties, and degraded to 'a Livonian slavery'. The three lower Estates clamoured for a *reduktion* – i.e. for the resumption by the crown of lands alienated to the nobility. And on 9 October they drew up a joint *protestation*,[10] in which they demanded that henceforth there should be no alienation of crown lands in perpetuity; that all Estates should enjoy equality before the law; that offices should be open to all upon a basis of merit, should not be discharged by deputy, and should be paid by fixed salaries; that private prisons and torture should be forbidden; that the formation of manors should be restricted to the scale laid down in 1562;[11] and that no title to alienated crown lands should be considered good, once the Estates had called it in question. Hundreds of copies of the *protestation* were disseminated throughout the country, after the Diet was over; and for the next thirty years it became the great arsenal of argument of the unprivileged Estates. It is worth remarking that it challenged not only the existing social and political pattern, but also the whole imperial foreign policy of the preceding generation. 'What honour, what glory, has Your Majesty by the subjection of foreign lands, when some few only are allowed to possess them, and when on top of that they

diminish the crown's *Patrimonium* and property in the father-
land? Or what have we gained beyond the seas, if we lose our
liberty at home?'[12] It was a censure of Oxenstierna and all that
he stood for;[13] and it echoed and amplified a sentiment which
had been heard as long ago as 1634, when an anonymous
pamphleteer had asked whether Gustav Adolf had not died for
peasants, as well as for nobles?[14] And indeed the complaints of
1650 were for the most part not new. What lay behind them?

The root of the trouble undoubtedly was the massive alienations of crown lands and revenues which had taken place since
1611, and especially since 1648.[15] The alienations were of
various types. Some were sales either of crown lands or of crown
revenues, for cash, or by way of offset against indebtedness, and
such revenues might be either rents (if they came from crown
peasants) or taxes (if they came from freeholders). Others were
donations: free gifts, without any obvious *quid pro quo*. It is
tempting to see in the sales of land another instance of the
revolutionary effects of the inflated military budgets which the
Thirty Years' War brought with it. But if by this it is meant
that the wars drove Sweden to live on capital, the conclusion is
untenable. Sweden's continental armies were for the most part
meant to operate on self-balancing accounts. Up to 1654, moreover, more than twice as much went in donations as in sales;
and no less than 62 per cent. of the alienations occurred after
1648 – that is, in years of peace. No: the sales of land and
revenues were rather a deliberate change in fiscal policy, conceived originally not as a hand-to-mouth expedient, but as the
replacement of a miscellaneous income in kind by a more convenient income in cash: you cannot well pay an army of
mercenaries in ox-hides or salt herring. In exchange for a lump
sum, the crown divested itself of revenues which were trouble-
some to handle, and imposed instead indirect taxes, which
Oxenstierna pronounced to be 'pleasing to God, hurtful to no
man, and not provocative of rebellion'.[16] Hence the taunting
question of the Clergy in 1650, who enquired whether Christina
was to be crowned queen of the Swedish lands, or queen of tolls
and excises.[17] It was argued, moreover, that land alienated to
the nobility was more productively used than before, and hence
would ultimately enrich the state by way of indirect taxation.[18]
Sale of lands and revenues, in fact, was defended as a step

towards more modern methods of finance.[19] But such arguments were less easy to apply to donations. At best, donations were legitimate rewards for good service. The end of the war in 1648 saw a swarm of officers home from Germany clamouring for favours; and perhaps it was inevitable that some gratifications should be accorded. But Christina made no effort to keep them within bounds. She took pleasure in giving; she had neither interest in, nor grasp of, finance; and after 1652 seems to have been cynically indifferent to the distresses of a crown she had already decided to renounce. Donations were given faster than the land registers could record them, sometimes were given twice over; and the confusion was made worse by the activities of an exchequer official who sold forged titles to applicants.

The effects were startling. Twenty-two of the most favoured families obtained lands worth one-fifth of the ordinary revenues of the state. The area of noble land in Sweden more than doubled between 1611 and 1652; in Finland it sextupled. In the more eligible provinces of central Sweden scarcely any land was left in royal hands. Royal revenues dropped from 6·36 million silver dollars in 1644 to 3·79 million in 1653.[20] Civil servants went without wages, the peacetime maintenance of the army was disorganized, even the court was in financial straits: it was said that the queen had no money to buy firewood, and occasionally no food in her larders.[21] War taxes had to be continued in peacetime; extraordinary taxes which had been levied only after specific parliamentary grant came to be treated as ordinary revenue which needed no parliamentary sanction. The nobility was of course exempt from all ordinary taxation, for itself and its domestics; and its peasants paid taxes at half-rates, except for those attached to a manor, or living near it, who were totally exempt. The privileged position of the peasants of the nobility was a consequence of, and was balanced by, their obligation to pay dues and give services to their lords: the crown imposed taxes at only half-rates, so that the other half might go to the noble. The less the crown took, the more the lord got. It is obvious, then, that the total exemption of peasants on manors presented a strong inducement to establish as many manors as possible; and in the 'thirties and 'forties manors were indeed created by the score, to the great concern of the regents.[22] Very many of them were fraudulent, mere tax-dodging devices; but they were defended on the ground that the absence of any custom of primogeniture imposed an obligation to provide a fitting establishment for every child in the family.[23]

The social consequences of this situation began to be alarming when the alienations to the nobility took the form, not of crown lands, but of tax-revenues from freehold peasants. The nobility might then be considered to have a direct interest in increasing the burden of taxation; since it was into their pockets, not into the exchequer, that the taxes of such freeholders were now paid.[24] They fell very easily into the habit of regarding these freeholders as their tenants – to use Per Brahe's significant phrase, as mediate, and not immediate, subjects of the crown.[25] They came to think of themselves as having a right, not merely to the peasant's taxes, but ultimately to his land – a *dominium eminens*, as against the peasant's *dominium utile*. If a freeholder was three years in arrears with his taxes, the crown was entitled to declare his land forfeit; and nobles to whom taxes had been made over tried to apply the same principle. Freehold peasants found themselves threatened with degradation to the relatively rightless position of peasants of the nobility, liable to eviction without compensation, burdened with intolerable labour services, made to ride the wooden horse, imprisoned in private dungeons, harried by the lord's agents, restricted in their freedom of movement, blackmailed into obedience by the lord's power to designate them for conscription.[26] The immemorial freedom of the Swedish yeoman was menaced by German customs, imposed very often by new lords who were indeed Germans, and imitated by Swedes who had picked up German social attitudes during the wars: it was revealing that Per Brahe should have remarked that the demands of the peasants would never be tolerated in Germany. At no other moment in Swedish history would a Marshal of the Nobility have dared to say, 'It is extraordinary that persons who were formed for servitude should be deemed free.'[27] The implications were the more serious, because it was freehold revenues, rather than crown lands, that constituted a majority of all the alienations; and also because these developments threatened the *political* destruction of the peasantry as an Estate. Nowhere in Europe was an Estate of Peasants so firmly entrenched in the constitution as it was in Sweden; nowhere else had it such acknowledged constitutional rights. But the Estate represented freehold and crown peasants only, and drew its members only from them. Thus the depressing of more and more of them to the status of peasants of the nobility threatened the whole Estate with eventual (and perhaps speedy) extinction. And as more and more of the revenue from taxation was diverted into the nobles' pockets, fiscal burdens necessarily fell with increased weight on the taxpayers that remained.[28]

The burghers and the clergy felt the force of this, and had besides grievances of their own. The burghers were coming to resent the favoured position of the nobility in the competition for offices.[29] The clergy, drawn very often from the peasantry, or at least living very close to them, sympathized with their sufferings. They themselves complained of alienation of church lands to the nobility, arbitrary evictions from the glebe, illegal withholding of tithe (especially on manors), abusive extension of the right of presentation to livings: even the bishops grumbled that they were treated like the nobility's stable boys.[30] But apart from these particular grievances, Clergy and Burghers united with Peasants in 1650 because they feared that the whole social and political balance of the state was in danger of being upset. As Archbishop Lenaeus remarked: 'When the nobility have all the peasants subject to themselves, then the Estate of Peasants will no longer have a voice at the Diet; and when the Estate of Peasants goes under, Burghers and Clergy may easily go under too . . . ; and since the Estate of Nobles had all the land in the kingdom under its control, where is then the crown's power? For he who owns the land is the ruler of the land; and thereby a *servitus* introduced into the country.'[31]

The tactics which the lower Estates now adopted, and the financial problem itself, had important constitutional implications.[32] Since 1632 the Diet had made significant constitutional advances. Its monopoly of legislation had been tacitly admitted. Its consent to new taxes, and to further conscriptions – though not to the raising of loans or alienation of lands and revenues – was now recognized to be necessary;[33] and its limitation of the duration of such grants had already had the effect of ensuring regularity of summons.[34] By the 1640s it had finally surmounted the danger – so fatal to the parliaments of Germany – of being supplanted for all ordinary purposes by a committee of its own members. Its forms of business were steadily developing. On more than one occasion individual Estates had taken a firm stand on the principle of 'redress before supply'. The debates on the Form of Government in 1634 had produced the suggestion that during a minority sovereignty reverted to the Estates; and the principle of ministerial responsibility to parliament had at least been adumbrated. In 1647 an opposition pamphlet had made startling claims for the Estates to participate directly in the choice of the great officers of government.[35] The *riksdag* was indeed still far behind the English parliament – it wholly lacked the initiative, and the idea of parliamentary privilege had not even been conceived – but one would have said that it was moving, and consciously moving, in the same general direction.

In 1650 it appeared to make a sudden leap forward. The right of free speech was firmly asserted. The three lower Estates held joint committee meetings, formulated joint resolutions, and claimed (in contradiction of the *Riksdag*-Ordinance of 1617) that a majority of Estates was decisive. They carried the principle of 'redress before supply' to the point of threatening to break up the Diet. With typical constitutional antiquarianism, they clamoured for the obsolete remedy of a General Eyre (*räfste- och rättareting*). Their debates resounded with novel appeals to 'fundamental law'. Above all, they asserted their right to the initiative. Against all precedent they deferred consideration of the government's Proposition, and proceeded instead to formulate their own resolutions. To conservative statesmen, nothing in 1650 seemed more shocking, more subversive of good order, more truly revolutionary, than this.[36] Everything suggests, in fact, that the Diet of 1650 could have been a turning-point in parliamentary history, comparable, perhaps, with 1641 in England: now, one would suppose, the foundations were laid for the developments which after 1718 were to make the Swedish Diet the most advanced and most powerful representative assembly in the world. But, in fact, the constitutional struggles of 1650 were curiously unfruitful. Solid progress began only in 1660, when the nobility took over some of the constitutional principles enunciated ten years before; it was not till 1675 or so that the lower Estates resumed their

constitutional advance; and after 1680 they were content
to practise parliamentarism by the grace of an austerely
paternal sovereign. From the point of view of the Diet's
development, 1650 was a flash in the pan, almost a missed
opportunity.

The explanation lies, of course, in part in the fact that the
lower Estates were not primarily concerned with constitutional
issues. They propounded innovating doctrines only as a means
of waging the social struggle. They made no attempt to revive
the controversies of 1634: the question of the divisibility of
sovereignty, and the claim of the Estates to a share in it – which
was so important to the *Frondeurs* – was not raised in 1650. The
last thing they wanted was to curtail the power of the crown for
the benefit of parliament: it was one of their essential contentions that the crown was too weak already. Their attitude to
the prerogative was naïvely pragmatic and oddly ambivalent:
for instance, they asserted the absolute right of the queen to
resume lands alienated by her predecessors, but maintained
that she was restrained by the fundamental laws of the kingdom
from making alienations in future.[37] Their indifference to constitutional issues appears most conspicuously in regard to the
power of the purse. The alienations had put the monarchy
quite at the mercy of parliament: the government was now
dependent on parliamentary grants if it were to carry on at
all.[38] But the lower Estates had no notion of exploiting this
situation: on the contrary. Their object was to make the crown
independent of parliamentary supply – as Gustav Vasa had
been,[39] and as Charles XI was almost to be. The queen was to
live of her own.

If the Estates were thus indifferent to the constitutional
possibilities, the queen was not. And for her, in a much broader
sense, 1650 was indeed a constitutional crux. From the beginning of the fifteenth to the end of the eighteenth century,
Swedish history derives its inner dynamic from the tension
resulting from the pull of two conflicting constitutional forces:
on the one hand an aristocracy which combined the assertion
of its interests with the defence of constitutional liberties; on
the other a monarchy which could count on popular support
by seeming to protect the little man against exploitation.
Between these two extremes the pendulum had swung back and

forth, and would continue to swing, until Anckarström's bullet gave a crude and bloody retort to the bloodless revolution of a 'Patriot King'. In this perennial oscillation the Form of Government of 1634 occupied a dubious place. By those who sponsored it, it was regarded as establishing a *monarchia mixta*, a constitutional balance in which 'the king's sovereignty, the council's authority, and the reasonable rights and liberties of the Estates, are properly preserved to them'.[40] But there were many who feared that it was intended to subject the monarchy to oligarchical control, to reduce the sovereign, as Schering Rosenhane somewhat tritely remarked, to the position of a Venetian Doge, perhaps to prepare the way for a return to electoral monarchy and a crowned republic on Polish models.[41] If the Form of Government was to be considered as a permanent arrangement, and not merely as providing for a minority, it certainly seemed to make government independent of the participation of the monarch. The council, moreover, which claimed to be (as the *parlement* of Paris also did) a mediator between the crown and the nation, was an ominously close corporation of representatives of a few great families: when in 1648 a cause between the Oxenstierna and Bielke families came to the council on appeal, it was found that almost all the members were related either to one family, or to the other, or to both.[42] Christina's paternal uncle, John Casimir, and her half-uncle, Karl Karlsson Gyllenhielm, were profoundly uneasy at this situation; and Karl Karlsson certainly feared that the Vasas might be edged off the throne. They instilled their fears into Christina. Men like Johan Skytte, and, later, Johan Adler Salvius, were jealous of the Oxenstiernas, and disapproved of their policies both at home and abroad, much as Marillac disapproved of Richelieu's, and for some of the same reasons. They found support in secretaries of state such as Lars Grubbe and Lars Nilsson Tungel: a 'rule of secretaries', after all, was traditionally the monarchy's alternative to reliance on the services of the high aristocracy. From this group came the radical pamphlets of the 'forties, pamphlets which combined an advanced constitutional programme with scarcely-veiled attacks upon the chancellor – pale Nordic analogues of the *Mazarinades.*[43]

The situation – dynastic and constitutional – was made acute by Christina's decision not to marry, which became final in 1649. From that moment, the future, not only of the dynasty but of the monarchy itself, seemed to her to be bound up with her ability to obtain the acceptance by the Estates of her cousin Charles as her successor. The council debates of 1649 were remarkable for exchanges of extraordinary acerbity between the queen and her servants;[44] but by shock tactics and skilful diplomacy she carried her first objective: in 1649 Charles was recognized as heir to the throne. It remained to secure his recognition as hereditary prince, and so ensure the succession to his descendants; and it was with this objective that Christina confronted the Diet of 1650.[45]

The conflict between the Estates gave her the lever that she needed. The three lower Estates were as anxious as she was to avert the possibility of an aristocratic republic: resistance to her programme was to be expected only from the nobility. She proceeded therefore to incite the commonalty to attack the first Estate. She received their deputations with words of compassion and encouragement; she urged them to object to the nobility's privileges; she posed as the protector of the poor; and when the onslaught showed signs of flagging, she took measures to reanimate it. She had the Vasa knack of popularity; and she may even have had some vague sympathy for the victims of aristocratic oppression. She was well aware that she was playing with fire; but she judged the hazards to a nicety. By the end of August she had the nobility running to her for the protection of the crown:[46] it was a curious anticipation of the situation which made possible the revolution of 1772. Her price, of course, was the acceptance of Charles as hereditary prince; and the frightened magnates were glad enough to close the bargain. She then coolly threw over her parliamentary allies. She had never intended agreeing to a *reduktion*, which she regarded as an intolerable infringement of her prerogative; and she now forced the lower Estates to drop it from their programme. The popular front thereupon collapsed. The Clergy were given a sop in the shape of a long-sought grant of privileges; the peasants were offered an ordinance limiting labour services; the leaders of the burghers were given official promotion to posts at a reassuring distance from Stockholm. The trial and execution of Messenius and his son, in December 1651, emphasized the queen's dissociation of herself from the tribunes of 1650, and gave a severe fright to the court-faction which had been intriguing with them; and in the euphoric atmosphere of total victory she could in 1652 even reconcile herself with Oxenstierna.

Such was the crisis of 1650. How does it accord with the explanations that have been propounded for the general European crisis?

It is not easy, certainly, to regard it as a 'crisis of production', induced by the failure of a still-feudal society to provide an elastically-expanding market for mass-produced goods.[47] Sweden at this period was only beginning to be an industrial country. Production of copper reached a peak just in 1650 and the ensuing decade, and the later decline was not due to the limited capacity of the market; while iron production shows a fairly steady expansion throughout the century. Swedish trade was increasing, not decreasing; and in the 1650s and 1660s Swedish shipping began to get an appreciable share of Baltic commerce. And it is not until the 1670s, perhaps, that any signs are visible that Sweden was becoming a less attractive field for foreign investment. In short, there seem to be few signs of that 'slackening of spontaneous economic development and of the development of capitalism' which M. Mousnier sees as typical of the period.[48]

On the other hand, there are obvious parallels between the predicament of the Swedish freeholders and the fate of the peasantry of eastern Europe; and it is plain that the crisis of 1650 in one aspect represents resistance to what in Germany was termed *Bauernlegen*. But the resemblance does not go very deep. The 1640s and 1650s no doubt saw the beginnings of the large compact domain based on consolidation of strips, evictions, and perhaps enclosure; and the creation of a manor was often the first stage in this process. But it was still only beginnings, affecting only a small percentage of noble land; and most landowners still preferred to secure themselves against harvest failures by having isolated farms well scattered over the country. In any case, the Swedish landlords were innocent of the economic motives which lay behind *Bauernlegen*. They had little idea of large-scale agriculture for a market, or for export; they lived on the rents and taxes and services their peasants rendered them: a *Grundherrschaft*, in fact, not a *Gutsherrschaft*.[49] Many of them spent a good deal more than their fathers had spent; and to meet the drain they tried, of course, to extract more from their peasants, who naturally complained. But in fact the margin for exploitation was small. Ordinary taxes, or rents, were already deliberately fixed at a level which, for the peasant who paid them, left enough (but not much more than enough) to maintain himself and his family; and war taxes probably took most of what remained. Yet at least the tax-collector and the lord's bailiff were not competitors for the peasant's resources, as they were in France. The share of the crown and the share of the lord were fixed; and the nobility were under no temptation to incite the peasantry to refuse taxes in order that they might pay the rent.[50] And although dreadful cases of noble cruelty did occur, most landlords realized that to ruin their peasantry was shortsighted policy: as Gustav Bonde remarked, 'it is better to milk the cow than to hit it over the head'.[51] Oppressed peasants could and would go elsewhere, when their short leases were up; and the ordinary courts could and did protect the poor man and punish the oppressor.[52] In 1650 the peasants at the Diet told horrific stories of landlords who exacted 500 or 600 days' labour service in the year from each farm; but in 1652 the Estate of Nobility was ready enough to accept an ordinance fixing the maximum for extraordinary labour services at eighteen.[53] What spurred on the peasants in 1650 was not so much actual oppression (which was probably not usual), as the fear of oppression, and above all the fear that they might lose security of tenure, personal liberty, and political rights.

Nevertheless, the alienations of crown lands and revenues did result in both the absolute and relative enrichment of a small class. It was not that the crown conferred a gratification by selling below the market price, as in some other countries:[54] a price of thirty-three and a third years' purchase was attractive only because prospective, unspecified and non-material advantages entered into the reckoning.[55] It is true, of course, that the nobility's increased wealth was relatively quickly dissipated by massive prestige-spending,[56] and also by the rapid dispersal of estates which followed from the absence of primogeniture or entail. But still the great landlords undoubtedly did very well.

They had not been weakened by the price-revolution, since their incomes were mostly in services and in kind; nor were they affected by the recession in prices after about 1640 – a recession which was in any case somewhat masked in Sweden.[57] The alienations were the most comprehensive change in the ownership of land since the Reformation, and indeed were of even greater social significance; for they created, as the Reformation had not, a *new* landed nobility. Thus Sweden *is* an example of 'a shift in social forces arising from changes in the ownership of land' – which Vicens Vives held to be one of the constituent elements in the general crisis.[58] And the concentration of wealth in the hands of one class coincided with an absolute decline in the standard of living of the peasantry.[59] The aristocracy grew richer at the expense of the rest of society. Not least, at the expense of the crown.

It is one of the peculiarities of the Swedish crisis, that it was not an attack upon the crown. In Sweden the burdens imposed by the state were never so intolerable as to provoke serious insurrection, though unjust bailiffs now and then might come to violent ends; and after 1613 the peasant had no need (as he had in France) to seek the protection of a lord against the depredations of a royal army. Since the later 1630s taxes had ceased to be farmed; and a comparatively high percentage of the taxes actually paid seems in fact to have reached the treasury.[60] The reduction of taxation was in 1650 only a subordinate objective; and that objective, it was believed, could be attained, in alliance with the crown, by measures of social reform rather than by the assertion of constitutional rights. The attack was rather upon the class which had appropriated the apparatus of government, and seemed likely as a consequence to push the crown into the background. The reign of Gustav Adolf had seen the reconciliation of the high nobility with the monarchy: for twenty years the secular struggle of the two great forces in Swedish constitutional history was pretermitted; the pendulum, it seemed, had ceased to swing. It was not Oxenstierna's fault that the struggle was now resumed. From 1632 to the day of his death, Oxenstierna pressed upon his colleagues a policy of moderation which would permit the reconciliation to be maintained. Gustav Adolf, he came to think, had had the better of the bargain between them, and after 1632 the balance was tipped a little the other way; but the oligarchical implications of 1634 were never fully exploited. Oxenstierna insisted that the nobility must be ready to make voluntary contributions, and be willing to waive its exemption from taxation on occasion; it must be careful to give no opening to its enemies by abusing its privileges, or making unwarrantable demands for their extension; it must give visible evidence of responsibility and patriotism; and above all must avoid committing itself to the defence of indefensible positions.[61] Erik Oxenstierna inherited this policy from his father, and made it the basis of the partial *reduktion* of 1655; and Clas Rålamb and Gustav Bonde would try to maintain it in the 1660s. The aristocracy had, on the whole, a high sense of public duty. Clientelage never developed into a political danger. Sweden could show no analogue to Korfitz Ulfeld, Condé, or Radziejowski – except for Patkul, and he was a Balt – and anything like a Fronde of the princes was unthinkable. It was a slander to accuse Oxenstierna of seeking to weaken the crown by alienations, and so force it to depend on a *riksdag* in which the first Estate would have the preponderant voice.

Nevertheless, Christina's suspicions were natural enough; and it was she who broke the alliance that had bound her father and Oxenstierna together. But the movement of 1650 might just as well have been directed against the crown as against the nobility; for the crisis was produced quite as much by Christina's folly and extravagance as by the greed of a rapacious aristocracy. From this point of view, indeed, the crisis is classifiable in Professor Trevor-Roper's terms, as a protest against the waste and profusion of an extravagant Renaissance court.[62] But the court, and the appendages to the court, were far too small for this to be a complete or satisfactory explanation, and only by juggling with words can we view the problem in terms of 'Court' against 'Country'.[63] The element of parasitism in Swedish society was inconsiderable; monopolists were rare birds; the Church was free of pluralism and absenteeism, and no churchman had held ministerial office for a century. What was amiss was the high aristocracy's near-monopoly of power; and one could, no doubt, describe this situation as a 'refeudalization' of society.[64] But the term sounds strange and jarring in a Swedish context. For historically the rule of Oxenstierna is to be seen as the realization of those plans of administrative reform which had been propounded by the aristocracy half a century before; as the defeat of the casual and *ad hoc* methods associated with the 'rule of secretaries'; as the placing of the task of government in the hands of the class best fitted by education and legal training to discharge it. By 1650, however, experience was showing that this involved social evils which made the price too high. Nor, perhaps, was it the most modern solution any longer. A new secretary-class, bigger, better and more respectable than the old, and reinforced by a newly-aspiring and newly-importunate lesser nobility, stood ready as an alternative government. And from this angle it *is* possible to describe 1650 as the clash of rival oligarchies,[65] the first skirmish in a battle which would not be fought out for another thirty years. In Gustav Adolf's reign the central administration 'went out of court'; in 1634, Oxenstierna endowed the state with modern bureaucratic machinery; and in 1680 the new bureaucrats wrested the state from the control of his successors – not so much because they were more efficient than the old aristocracy (Oxenstierna, after all, was the prince of administrators) as by sheer weight of numbers, and above all by union with the arch-bureaucrat who now occupied the throne. The alliance of Charles XI and Erik Lindschöld, considered in this light, meant much the same as the alliance of Gustav Adolf and Oxenstierna – it meant that the monarchy harnessed the forces of progress. In 1611 those forces lay in the high aristocracy, in 1680 in the petty nobility. And 1650 is the date when the monarchy begins to swap horses. Christina quite missed the significance of what was happening. But Charles XI was perhaps the only really successful example of what Professor Trevor-Roper has called the 'Puritanism of the Right';[66] and it was that cause (among others) that triumphed in 1680. He stood for austerity, order, devotion to duty, balanced accounts, and, as a necessary consequence, peace: in 1680 the opposition of the 1640s and 1650s has become the Government.[67] The crown really does turn back the clock; finance in Oxenstierna's style is abandoned; the king really does try to live of his own: an odd programme, we may think, for the forces of progress; but at least it realized some of the objectives of 1650. It was a solution born of necessity and defeat; but it was based on popular support. And indeed, without that support the establishment of absolutism would have been impossible in Sweden, for there was no state in Europe where a standing army was so little fitted to be an instrument for suppressing popular liberties. The break which some have discerned in the history of the seventeenth century[68] comes in Sweden in 1680, not in 1650; and only then is the ideal of mixed monarchy finally overthrown. And the differing outcome of the two crises depends not only on the differing personalities of Christina and Charles XI, but equally on the fact that in 1650 the political alliance of the lesser nobility with the unprivileged Estates had not yet had time to mature.

The common objective which drew them together was the attainment of office. And in this matter the position in Sweden was very different from that in most European countries. For there never was a time, in all Sweden's history, when offices were sold by the crown – though there came to be a time when they were sold by their possessors.[69] A few offices – that of county court judge (*häradshövding*) for instance – were in practice hereditary in great noble families, and were often executed by deputy;[70] and in Christina's reign we hear of the gift (but not the sale) of offices in reversion (a practice condemned by the Clergy in 1655 as conducing to a breach of the Tenth Commandment);[71] but venality of offices in the French sense simply did not exist, and the absence of it does not seem to have entailed a greater degree of corruption than elsewhere – at least, in Oxenstierna's time – although some historians will no doubt feel that it ought to have done so.[72] It might therefore appear superfluous to touch on the controversy as to whether the revolutionary movements of the mid-century were directed against office-holders, or engineered by them.[73] But in fact this matter of office-holding was important in Sweden too; and it certainly helped to range Burghers and Clergy on the Peasants' side in 1650.

For both Estates wanted offices, and both saw the nobility blocking their way. The representatives of the burghers at the Diet were no longer mainly merchants or traders; they were professional municipal officials, 'royal burgomasters' paid by the crown, civil servants, men learned in the law, very often with a degree from Uppsala. As Schering Rosenhane's parson put it: 'in former times we had good old merchants for burgo-masters, who understood trade and commerce, and thought not beyond their own concerns, but drove their trade as best they could; but now, since burgomasters have begun to speak French and Italian, and have a book or two under their arm when they come to the office, it is become vulgar to speak of salt and cloth, for they must be telling us what Tacitus says, and how things stand at court'.[74] Such men wanted a career open at the top; and at the Diet of 1650 they threw up leaders in the persons of Nils Nilsson and Nils Skunk – the first pro-fessional political lawyers in Swedish history. So too with the clergy, who desired official appointments for their sons. It happened that in the 1650s Sweden was suffering from a glut of priests; and in the absence of vacant livings the sons of the manse were looking to a career in the civil service, with the result that the university was turning out far too many gradu-ates in the contemporary equivalent of PPE: as Magnus Gabriel de la Gardie said in 1655, 'there are more *literati* and learned fellows, especially *in politicis*, than means or jobs available to provide for them, and they grow desperate and impatient'.[75] Sweden was acquiring a learned proletariat of unemployed academics; and de la Gardie, as Chancellor of Uppsala, was driven to the heroic remedy of making the examinations harder, and cutting down the number of bursaries. In 1650 the pros-pects for such persons were poor. For the nobility claimed a preference for all the better jobs; and though the bureaucracy was increasing slowly, the nobility was increasing so fast that there was no keeping track of it.

During the reign of Christina the process which Mr Stone has called the inflation of honours[76] reached heights that would have staggered James I. In ten years she doubled the number of noble families, and sextupled the number of counts and barons. She ennobled army contractors, chancery secretaries, impor-tunate creditors, land-agents of the aristocracy, customs inspec-tors, her court tailor, a round dozen of court physicians, droves of army officers, Germans, Dutchmen, Scots – there was no end to them.[77] The flood of new peers was so great that there was not enough land in the market for all of them to acquire estates; and we hear of counts for whom the crown found it impossible to provide counties.[78] And this meant that they were shut out from the essential financial advantage of noble status. The war was over; the prospects in the army were poor; and the new nobility was therefore driven back on the civil service, only to be confronted with equally hungry competitors, of better blood than they. These were the old petty nobility, whose lineage was longer than its purse; men who had backed the abortive sumptuary ordinances of the 1640s because they could not afford to keep up with French fashions, men who demanded to be allowed to club together in twos or threes to provide one collaborative cavalryman by way of knight-service, men with only two or four horses, who complained loudly of the expense of Christina's coronation.[79]

It was against the pre-emptive claims of such persons that the lower Estates in 1650 advanced the demand for appointments to be made on merit alone. They failed; for on this occasion the nobility was united against them, and the queen in the end let them down. But their cry for a *reduktion* was destined five years later to split the apparently solid front of the first Estate. By 1655 the latent tensions and antagonisms within the peerage had risen to the surface.[80] The refusal of members of the historic families to enter the civil service at the bottom of the ladder; the pretensions of counts and barons to a superiority over the untitled nobility; the divergent interests of those who had, and those who had not, great estates; the contempt of the old aristocracy for *parvenus*; the lack of any common interest between the Brahes and Bondes and Bielkes on the one hand, and the poor rustic squires on the other – all these things destroyed the ability of the aristocracy to resist a *reduktion*, for they made many nobles its most fervent advocates.[81] For from the point of view of the office-holding noble, the clinching argument for a *reduktion* was, that it would enable the crown to be regular in the payment of wages. It was this argument which led them to ally with the lower Estates, and which turned them into supporters of the revolution of 1680 and the new bureaucratic absolutism of Charles xi. Thus the struggle of the peasants against deteriorating conditions becomes potentially revolutionary (in 1650) only when it receives the support of the other non-noble Estates; and is successful (in 1680) only when that support is reinforced by a section of the nobility, and by the alliance of the crown. And even then success comes only incidentally, as a by-product of quite other conflicts. For the events of 1680, in fact, registered first the emancipation of the monarchy from oligarchical control, and secondly the victory of the petty nobility over the high aristocracy. And the bureaucracy of which that nobility was the backbone can plausibly be equated with the high *bourgeoisie* in other countries.[82] They were hard-working, respectable, and of solid but (as a rule) not immoderate means, and to most of them their salaries were important. Some of them were nobles, some not; but all might hope to be, when they reached the appropriate grade in the service.[83] It is not easy to contend, as Porshnev argued in regard to the office-holding class in France, that their very success feudalized them, converted them into defenders of the aristocratic exploiting classes, and deprived them of their *bourgeois* characteristics.[84] The charter of their liberties, the tangible evidence of their victory, was the Table of Ranks of 1680, which laid it down that in civil life, as well as military, status in the social hierarchy should henceforth depend not on birth, but on rank, and rank itself upon service and merit.[85] After 1718 the high aristocracy made a brief attempt to recover political power, as they did in France in 1715. They were unsuccessful, in the one instance as in the other; and in 1739 the triumph of 'democracy' within the first Estate once more revealed the alienation of the bureaucracy from the old families. The Age of Liberty, despite constitutional appearances, is the true successor to the absolutism of Charles XI; for it is the age of bureaucratic rule in alliance with the quasi-sovereign Estates, who have stepped into the vacuum of power left by the overthrow of unlimited monarchy. And the deliverance – or the catastrophe – of 1772 was possible only because, as so often happens, the bureaucratic class in course of time developed an exclusiveness which made it vulnerable. It may seem a far cry from 1650 to 1769; but the two situations are in many ways not dissimilar;[86] and it is not altogether fanciful to trace the political ancestry of Kepplerus to Nils Skunk.[87]

The example of Sweden, then, does little to make easier the provision of a plain answer to the enigma of the general crisis; for it is pretty clear that Sweden does not exactly fit any of the generalizations which have been put forward to explain it. No doubt we are not entitled to demand of a historical explanation that it should explain everything, or be true for all cases. Yet the case of Sweden may reasonably be held to present features of more than local interest: the country resembled a western European state a good deal more closely than did (for example) the Ukraine; and in 1650 Stockholm looks much nearer to the centre of the revolutionary movement than (for instance) Naples or Amsterdam. If we are really determined to bring the Cossacks and the Ironsides within the scope of a single explanation, it does not seem legitimate to leave Sweden out of the reckoning. Is it too much to hope for an explanation which will accommodate Nils Nilsson as well as John Pym, embrace Oxenstierna no less than Zuidpolsbroek,[88] and find room for Archbishop Lenaeus side by side with Cardinal de Retz?

NOTES

[1] This paper is an expansion of the A. L. Smith Lecture for 1962, delivered in the Hall of Balliol College, Oxford, on 9 March 1962. It was originally published in *Past and Present*, no. 22, July 1962, and was included in *Crisis in Europe 1560–1660*, ed. Trevor Aston (Routledge & Kegan Paul, London 1965). It is reprinted by kind permission of the Past and Present Society and Routledge & Kegan Paul.

[2] H. R. Trevor-Roper, 'The General Crisis of the Seventeenth Century', *Past and Present*, no. 16 (1959), p. 51.

[3] [*Svenska*] R[*iks*] R[*ådets*] P[*rotokoll*] xiii, 17, 103, 117, 163, 165, 182, 214, 282–3, 298; xiv, 9, 16, 81, 175, 358; xv, 128: S[*veriges*] R[*idderskaps och*] A[*dels*] R[*iksdags*] P[*rotokoll*] iv, 420, 433; H[*andlingar rörande*] S[*kandinaviens*] H[*istoria*] xxi, 123, 137; A[*xel*] O[*xenstiernas*] S[*krifter och*] B[*refvexling*] 2nd ser., iii, 544, 553; [Schering Rosenhane], *Samtal emellan Juncker Päär, Mäster Hans, Niels Andersson Borgare och Joen i Bergha Danneman*, in *Samling af Curieusa Samtal . . .*, Uppsala, 1768. Rosenhane, it is interesting to note, in 1650 also published a book on the Fronde, entitled *Observationes Politicae super Galliae Motibus*: 'Riks-Rådet och Öfverståthållaren Friherre Schering Rosenhanes Lefverne, af honom sielf beskrifvit', *Nya svenska biblioteket*, ii, Stockholm, 1763, p. 610.

[4] G. Wittrock, *Regering och allmoge under Kristinas förmyndare*, Uppsala, 1948, pp. 76–7, 156, 216, 239, 371; C. T. Odhner, *Sveriges inre historia under Drottning Kristinas förmyndare*, Stockholm, 1865, p. 71; S. Lundgren, *Johan Adler Salvius*, Lund, 1945, p. 62; for Grotius' letters on the Nu-Pieds, *AOSB*, 2nd ser., ii, 637, 639–40, 642, 648, 656, 670, 672, 674.

[5] Arnold Messenius was arrested for sending an anonymous letter of seditious tendency to the future Charles x. On interrogation he involved his father, Arnold Johan Messenius, who then vainly tried to shield his son by taking all the blame himself. Both were executed in December 1651.

Arnold Messenius was undoubtedly playing on prevailing discontents to try to tempt the heir to the throne into something like treason; and he probably hoped to enlist the faction that was hostile to the Oxenstiernas. At his trial he reported compromising remarks by such prominent persons as the burgomaster of Stockholm, Nils Nilsson, and a member of the Council, Bengt Skytte (later emphatically denied by both of them). But there never seems to have been anything more than loose and dangerous talk in the affair: it was certainly not the 'widely-ramifying conspiracy' of the textbooks. See Verner Söderberg, *Historieskrifvaren Arnold Johan Messenius*, Uppsala, 1902, and the report of the interrogation in *RRP* xv, 209 ff., 353–63.

⁶ *RRP* xv., 243; S. Bonnesen, *Karl X Gustav*, Lund, 1958, p. 48; G. Wittrock, *Regering och allmoge under Kristinas egen styrelse*, Uppsala, 1953, p. 35: *cf.* Johan Ekeblad's disagreeable experience in 1652: *Johan Ekeblads bref*, Stockholm, 1911, i, 110; G. Wittrock, *Carl X Gustafs testamente*, Uppsala, 1908, pp. 128, 238.

⁷ The crisis is well documented; besides *RRP*, *SRARP*, and *HSH* xxi (which has the parliamentary diary of a member of the Clergy, Jonas Petri) we have now *P[räste-] S[tåndets] R[iksdags] P[rotokoll]* i, Stockholm, 1949. Unfortunately *Borgarståndets riksdagsprotokoll före Frihetstiden*, Uppsala, 1933, begins only in 1654. The literature includes Wittrock, *Regering och allmogen under Kristinas egen styrelse*; B. Lövgren, *Ståndsstridens uppkomst*, Stockholm, 1915; N. Ahnlund, *Ståndsriksdagens utdaning*, Stockholm, 1933; S. I. Olofsson, *Drottning Christinas tronavsägelse och trosförändring*, Uppsala, 1953; R. Holm, *Joannes Elai Terserus*, Lund, 1906. Hj. Holmquist's *D. Johannes Matthiae Gothus*, Uppsala, 1903, unfortunately stops at 1648.

⁸ *RRP* xiv, 78; *cf. SRARP*, iv, 307, 561.

⁹ See, e.g. G. O. Hyltén-Cavallius and G. Stephens, *Sveriges historiska och politiska visor*, Örebro, 1853, i, 343–55; Axel Strindberg, *Bondenöd och Stormaktsdröm*, Stockholm, 1937, pp. 95–100.

¹⁰ Printed in *Handlingar til Konung Carl XI:tes Historia*, Stockholm, 1769, x, 70–98.

¹¹ For the creation of manors, see M. Roberts, *Gustavus Adolphus, A History of Sweden, 1611–1632* (1953–8), ii, 54–5, and *cf. ibid.*, p. 12 and n. 1.

¹² *Handlingar til Konung Carl XI:tes historia*, x, 84–5.

¹³ On 9 July 1650 the clergy censured 'him who had brought the crown to many needless expenses ... (thereby understanding a particularly high personage among the lords)': *HSH* xxi, 70.

¹⁴ Wittrock, *Regering och allmoge under Kristinas förmyndare*, pp. 57–8.

¹⁵ For a discussion of the alienations and their implications, see Eli Heckscher, *Sveriges ekonomiska historia från Gustav Vasa*, i, Stockholm, 1936, 301–55; S. Clason, *Till reduktionens förhistoria*, Uppsala, 1895; Sven A. Nilsson, 'Reduktion eller kontribution?', *Scandia*, xxiv (1958); Robert Swedlund, *Grev- och friherreskapen i Sverige och Finland*, Uppsala, 1936; E. Ingers, *Bonden i svensk historia*, i, Stockholm, 1943.

¹⁶ Odhner, *op. cit.*, p. 227. Hence Oxenstierna's insistence, as early as 1633, that the nobility must waive their exemption from customs dues: *HSH* xxvi, 265–6: *cf. AOSB* 2nd ser., iii, 337. They did surrender it in 1644,

but only in exchange for improved privileges in other respects. See F. Lagerroth, *Statsreglering och finansförvaltning i Sverige till och med frihetstidens ingång*, Lund, 1928, pp. 59–61.

[17] *HSH* xxi, 75, 82. The archbishop reported that the Nobility received the question '*risu*'. Oxenstierna had no opinion of the clergy as economists: see *SRARP* v, 207.

[18] A good summary of these arguments in *Samtal* . . ., pp. 55–7.

[19] And on other grounds too: in 1660 Per Brahe remarked that 'a king's income ought not to consist in hens, eggs, butter, flax and such small gear as peasants give . . . but in tolls, *régales* on mining, and revenues of that sort': Wittrock, *Carl X Gustafs testamente*, p. 128. In 1654 M. G. de la Gardie attributed a very similar remark to Axel Oxenstierna: R. Fåhraeus, *Magnus Gabriel de la Gardie*, Stockholm, 1936, p. 63.

[20] Bonnesen, *op. cit.*, p. 32.

[21] 'Nils Skunks självbiografi' (*Tidningar utg. i Uppsala* [1777]), p. 36.

[22] For the question of the limitation of manors, and the effects of their creation, see *RRP* x, 319, 366; *PSRP* i, 151; *SRARP* iii, 125–7; iv, 353; v, 14, 102; Wittrock, *Regering och allmoge under Kristinas förmyndare*, pp. 258, 437, 441.

[23] See Christina's approving comments on the social effects of primogeniture in England, in *RRP* xiv, 48; and *cf.* Oxenstierna in *SRARP* iii, 47.

[24] Their interest seems obvious, as the Clergy pointed out in 1650 (*PSRP* i, 203; and see *Handlingar til Carl IX:tes historia*, x, 91); but they do not seem in fact to have pursued it very vigorously. The question is complex and controversial: see e.g. H. Swenne, *Svenska adelns ekonomiska privilegier 1612–1651*, Göteborg, 1933, especially p. 311; E. Brännman, *Frälseköpen under Gustav II Adolfs regering*, Lund, 1950, and Sven A. Nilsson's review of Brännman in *Historisk Tidskrift*, 2nd ser., xv (1952), 404–15.

[25] 'We are all *subditi regni*, the peasants *mediate subditi*, but we *immediate*': *RRP* xiv, 343.

[26] For a defence of the nobility (which, however, largely ignores the crucial question of the freehold peasants) see Swenne, *op. cit.* His argument on conscription (pp. 229, 232) is controverted by Christer Bonde's remark in 1655: 'It is certain that the only means to keep the peasant under discipline is conscription': *SRARP* v, 54 (*cf. ibid.*, iii, 95); and by Christina herself (*HSH* xxi, 87).

[27] *RRP* xiv, 333, for Per Brahe's remark; *SRARP* v, 86, for Christer Bonde's. He was sharply rebuked by Oxenstierna, who had earlier observed, 'though they be *glebae addicti*, yet they are not slaves': *ibid.*, iv, 345.

[28] And, equally, as the number of crown peasants diminished the burden of labour services fell more heavily on them. Swenne found instances of peasants who had to travel 150 km. to get to the place where their services were to be performed: *op. cit.*, p. 146.

[29] See pp. 127–8. They had other grievances against the nobility too: *RRP* xiii, 11; xv, 198.

[30] *RRP* xiv, 331. For the Clergy's grievances, see *PSRP* i, 64, 89, 127, 164, 189, 269 ff.; *SRARP* iii, 46, 75; v. 75; *HSH* xxi, 76, 272. For a vivid

explanation of the effects of manor-creation on the economic position of the clergy, see *AOSB* 2nd ser., xii, 590, (Baazius to Oxenstierna, 19 Aug. 1637).

[31] *HSH* xxi, 145; *cf.* the bishop of Växjö's remarks, *PSRP* i, 172.

[32] For a discussion of the constitutional problem, see Ahnlund, *op. cit.*; F. Lagerroth, *Frihetstidens författning*, Stockholm, 1915: Erland Hjärne, *Från Vasatiden till frihetstiden*, Uppsala, 1929.

[33] As Oxenstierna remarked in 1643: 'If it were here as in other countries, that one could call the Estates together and say: so much is required. . . . But here it is not so': *RRP* x, 301.

[34] Sam Clason, 'Om uppkomsten af bestämde perioder för den svenska riksdagens sammanträde', *Historisk Tidskrift*, 1st ser., xii (1892).

[35] *Mestadeles ständernas och goda patrioters betänkande om regementsformen* (printed in *SRARP* iii, 409–14). See L. Stavenow, *Om riksrådsvalen under Frihetstiden*, Uppsala, 1890, pp. 1–11, for the constitutional background to this claim.

[36] *RRP* xiv, 370, *SRARP* iv, 328; *Samtal*, pp. 14, 18, where Juncker Päär says: 'to begin on *gravamina*, and prefer them before the government's Proposition, I hold to be *praeposterum*, untimely, and not to be practised in our constitution. For though the German Estates have begun to usurp the Emperor's place at the Diet, that it is a different kind of state, and by doing so they have brought the Emperor to that condition, that his power consists only in grand titles, and more in a seeming than in realities; and how it has gone in England since the Estates began upon the same fashion, is sufficiently manifest to us'; *cf.* Oxenstierna's remarks to Whitelocke in 1654: Bulstrode Whitelocke, *A Journal of the Swedish Embassy* (1855), ii, 278–81.

[37] The Nobility took the opposite line – that Christina was entitled to alienate freely because Sweden was now a hereditary and not an elective monarchy; a curious inversion of their historic *rôle*: *HSH* xxi, 155.

[38] Lövgren, *op. cit.*, p. 32. It is of course true that the lower Estates resented having to pay the heavier indirect taxation which the crown's loss of direct revenues made necessary; and they also objected to the uncertainty and variability of the yield of customs and excises: Lagerroth, *Statsreglering och finansförvaltning*, p. 63.

[39] As Christina herself remarked: *RRP* xiv, 345; *cf.* Oxenstierna's comment, *ibid.*, 353.

[40] Printed in E. Hildebrand, *Sveriges regeringsformer 1634–1809*, Stockholm, 1891, p. 2.

[41] See Christina's comments, *RRP* xiv, 309; and *cf.* xiii, 344, 362. It was not without significance that Per Brahe in 1660 should have said that nowhere was '*senatoris officium* so noble' as in Sweden, Poland, Denmark and Russia: Wittrock, *Carl X Gustafs testamente*, p. 206.

[42] *RRP* xii, 312.

[43] Lövgren, *op. cit.*, pp. 18–27, 31–7; Ahnlund, *op. cit.*, pp. 229–30; Lundgren, *Salvius*, pp. 194–6, 242–4. Oxenstierna notoriously sided with parliament against Charles I, and often expressed the view that Charles (and Laud) had only themselves to thank for their troubles. In December 1651 the younger Messenius, at his trial, recalled that his father had told him

how Oxenstierna had one day remarked, 'I think, Messenius, that you are in too much of a hurry to be chancellor here in Sweden', and had been answered, 'And I think that you are in too much of a hurry to be king here in Sweden': *RRP* xv, 211; but *cf.* p. 239.

[44] See especially *RRP* xiii, 343–6.

[45] For the succession-question, see Olofsson, *op. cit.*; N. Ahnlund, *Drottning Kristinas tronavsägelse*, in *Från Medeltid och Vasatid*, Stockholm, 1933; C. Weibull, *Drottning Christina*, Stockholm, 1934, H. Rosengren, *Karl X Gustaf före tronbestigningen*, Uppsala, 1913.

[46] *HSH* xxi, 140; *cf. SRARP* iv, 420, 422.

[47] E. J. Hobsbawm, 'The General Crisis of the European Economy in the Seventeenth Century', *Past and Present*, no. 5 (1954), especially pp. 39–42.

[48] R. Mousnier, *Les XVIe et XVIIe siècles*, Paris, 1954, pp. 150–1.

[49] See Arthur Montgomery, 'Tjänstehjonsstadgan och äldre svensk arbetarpolitiken', *Historisk Tidskrift*, 1st ser., liii (1933), 246–7; Heckscher, *op. cit.*, i, 323–8.

[50] Contrast B. Porshnev, *Die Volksaufstände in Frankreich vor der Fronde*, Leipzig, 1954, pp. 90, 440; *cf. RRP* x, 414.

[51] G. Wittrock, 'Riksskattmästaren Gustaf Bondes politiska program 1661', *Historisk Tidskrift*, 1st ser., xxxiii (1913), 53.

[52] See H. Munktell, 'Till frågan om böndernas ställning vid 1600–talets mitt', *Historisk Tidskrift*, 2nd ser., vi (1943); and *cf.* Christer Bonde's complaint, *SRARP* v, 43.

[53] Swenne, *op. cit.*, p. 151; Wittrock, *Regering och allmoge under Kristinas egen styrelse*, p. 188.

[54] Contrast Trevor-Roper, *op. cit.*, p. 45.

[55] This seems to have been a price based on the yield to the crown of the so-called 'determinate revenues', and it was high probably because there was a tacit agreement that the buyer should also be entitled to the 'indeterminate revenues': in instances where the price was based on a figure which excluded the 'indeterminate revenues' it tended to be about twenty-two years' purchase: Heckscher, *op. cit.*, i, 309–13. For 'determinate' and 'indeterminate revenues', see M. Roberts, *Gustavus Adolphus*, i, 311.

[56] For standards of aristocratic luxury, see W. Karlsson, *Ebba Brahes hem*, Lund, 1943; Claes Annerstedt, *Om samhällsklasser och levnadssätt under förra hälften af 1600-talet*, Stockholm, 1896; and Ellen Fries, *Ur svenska adelns familjeliv i gamla tider*, Stockholm, 1910.

[57] Heckscher, *op. cit.*, i, 646–51.

[58] J. Vicens Vives, 'Estructura administrative estatal en los siglos XVI y XVII', *XIe Congrès International de Sciences Historiques*, 1960: Rapports, iv, 8.

[59] Heckscher, *op. cit.*, i, 420–2.

[60] The situation in this regard seems to have changed for the worse after 1660.

[61] *SRARP* iii, 44; v, 22–3; *RRP* x, 315, 319, 366; and *cf. ibid.*, x, 562; xiii, 258.

[62] *Cf.* Trevor-Roper, *op. cit.* In 1644 court expenses came to 3·1 per cent. of the total budget; in 1653 to 12·3 per cent., or, if Maria Eleonora's and Prince Charles's be included, 20 per cent.: Olofsson, *op. cit.*, p. 75. Court

etiquette became more elaborate under Christina: Odhner, *op. cit.*, pp. 355–6; Rosengren, *op. cit.*, p. 189.

[63] *Cf.* the suggestive remarks of E. H. Kossmann in 'Trevor-Roper's "General Crisis": a Symposium', *Past and Present*, no. 18 (1960), p. 11. Nor was there any question (before the annexation of Skåne) of a clash between regionalism and centralism, or of any serious collision between the traditional power and prestige of provincial magnates and the administrative encroachments of bureaucracy.

[64] Vicens Vives, *op. cit.*, p. 16.

[65] *Cf.* D. H. Pennington and L. Stone, in 'Seventeenth Century Revolutions', *Past and Present*, no. 13 (1958).

[66] Trevor-Roper, *op. cit.*, p. 49.

[67] Contemporaries did not fail to remark that Johan Gyllenstierna was Johan Skytte's grandson.

[68] Trevor-Roper, *op. cit.*, pp. 33–4.

[69] The so-called *ackord* system, by which an office-holder provided himself with a lump sum on retirement by the sale of his office to his successor, seems to have arisen in the generation after 1680, when Charles XI, by prohibiting any further donations, made some such expedient necessary.

[70] Around the mid-century the absenteeism of these *häradshövdingar* was heavily attacked: *SRARP* iv, 216, 417; *HSH* xxi, 237; *RRP* xii, 342; xv, 509.

[71] *PSRP* i, 342.

[72] Vicens Vives, *op. cit.*, pp. 20–1; Jacob van Klaveren: 'Die historische Erscheinung der Korruption, in ihrem Zusammenhang mit der Staats- und Gesellschaftsstruktur betrachtet', *Vierteljahrschrift für Sozial- und Wirtschaftsgeschichte*, xliv (1957), 289–324. Klaveren would no doubt attempt to explain the comparative purity of Swedish official life either as a consequence of the absolutism of Charles XI (since it is his thesis that absolutism inhibits corruption), or perhaps as evidence of the weakness of the 'Zwischengruppen' in Swedish society: 'Die Mittelschichten waren die Brutstätten der Korruption. Dies gilt allgemein sowohl für die traditionellen Zwischengruppen wie für die vom Fürsten geschaffene Beamtenschaft'; *op. cit.*, p. 312. But the change from oligarchy to absolutism made, if anything, for greater rather than less corruption: see E. Ingers, *Erik Lindschöld*, Lund, 1908, i, 212–15; Alf Åberg, *Karl XI*, Stockholm, 1958, pp. 67, 112–13, 121; and the sale of offices by their owners was systematized only after the victory of parliamentarism in 1720: contrast K. W. Swart, *Sale of Offices in the Seventeenth Century*, The Hague, 1949, p. 116.

[73] *Cf.* R. Mousnier, in 'Trevor-Roper's "General Crisis": a symposium', *Past and Present*, no. 18, pp. 18–25.

[74] *Samtal*, p. 29. From the short autobiographical notes made by Nils Skunk in 1668 it is pretty clear that it was to him that Rosenhane was referring: 'Nils Skunks självbiografi', in *Tidningar utg. i Uppsala* (1777), pp. 33–9. And *cf. SRARP* iv, 427; and Tom Söderberg, *Den namnlösa medelklassen*, Stockholm, 1956, pp. 118, 121–2.

[75] Sven Edlund, *M. G. de la Gardies inrikespolitiska program 1655*, Lund, 1954, pp. 40–1, 51–2, 64; *cf. SRARP* iv, 625. This well bears out Trevor-Roper, *op cit.*, pp. 52–3.

[76] Lawrence Stone, 'The Inflation of Honours, 1558–1641', *Past and Present*, no. 14 (1958).

[77] *Samtal*, p. 5, where *Juncker Päär* says: 'You see yourself by daily experience, that he who anyways addresses himself to ensue honour and virtue, and does any good service, can without difficulty come into the Estate of Nobility, whether his origins be in the Estate of Clergy, Burghers, or Peasants . . . and when he is come thereto, he has a like right and access to high office with any other . . . But that any should leap into the highest posts straight from his pepper-bags or his dung-cart is a thing whose consequence you may well imagine.' Johan Ekeblad commented: 'We have now arms and escutcheons by the hundred. Herr Carl Krusse (*sc.* Kruus) has now joined the mob they call counts': *Johan Ekeblads bref*, i, 195. For the bad quality of some of the new nobility, see *SRARP* iii, 238; iv, 433; v, 301; *Riksrådets memorial till K.M:tt, 1665* (printed in *Den svenska Fatburen*, 1769), p. 113; R. Swedlund, 'Krister Bonde och reduktionsbeslutet 1655', *Karolinska Förbundets Årsbok* (1937). And for the whole question, Tom Söderberg, *op. cit.*, pp. 94–9, 105, 112.

[78] Swedlund, *Grev- och friherreskapen i Sverige och Finland*, pp. 134–5.

[79] *SRARP* v, 55, 260; iv, 431; iii, 24, 41; *RRP* xiv, 339, 383.

[80] For the tensions within the Nobility, see *SRARP* iii, 215, 219; iv, 181, 192, 217, 362, 454, 584; v, 237, 241; Swedlund, 'Krister Bonde och reduktionsbeslutet' *passim*; Edlund, *op. cit.*, pp. 45, 239; Wittrock, 'Riksskattmästaren Gustaf Bondes politiska program', pp. 48–9.

[81] *Riksrådets memorial . . . 1665*, pp. 110–11, 115; Wittrock, *op. cit.*, pp. 44–7; *SRARP* iv, 267; Sven A. Nilsson, 'Reduktion eller Kontribution?', *passim*, and p. 106.

[82] See, in general, Tom Söderberg, *Den namnlösa medelklassen* (which, however, dissents from the view taken above); and Sten Carlsson, *Svensk ståndscirkulation, 1680–1960*, Stockholm, 1950.

[83] Sten Carlsson, *op. cit.*, pp. 21–2.

[84] Porshnev, *op. cit.*, p. 479; and Vicens Vives, *op cit.*, pp. 15–16. As M. Mousnier remarks: 'tous les officers aspirent à devenir juridiquement nobles. Ils ne deviennent pas de ce fait des féodaux ni des gentilshommes'. And again, 'Une noblesse de service, une noblesse dans laquelle on est classé par le service envers le Prince, incarnant l'Etat, est-ce la même chose qu'une féodalité?': R. Mousnier, in ' "Serviteurs du Roi". Quelques aspects de la fonction publique dans la société française du XVIe siècle', *XVIIe Siècle*, nos. 41–3 (1959), pp. 5, 6.

[85] S. Bergh, 'Rangstriderna inom adeln under 1600-talet', *Historisk Tidskrift*, 1st ser., xvi (1896), *passim*, and p. 149.

[86] It was scarcely by accident that some of the more important documents on the crisis were printed for the first time in 1768–9. And it is no less significant that Anders Schönberg, in his *Historiska bref om det svenska regeringssättet* (1773) should have taken the line that the social struggles of 1650 were now (after Gustav III's *coup*) better forgotten: *op. cit.* (new edn 1850), ii, 149–60.

[87] For Kepplerus, see *infra*, p. 280.

[88] For Zuidpolsbroek, see J. E. Elias, *Geschiedenis van het Amsterdamsche Regentenpatriciaat*, 's Gravenhage, 1923, pp. 145–9.

6

Cromwell and the Baltic[1]

I

The purpose of this paper is to discuss Cromwell's relations with some of the Protestant powers during the period of the Protectorate; and in particular to try to arrive at some estimate of his handling of the crisis in the Baltic which followed the invasion of Prussia by Charles x in 1655. And, since the Dutch were more directly interested in that crisis than was any other power outside the Baltic itself, it will be necessary to give particular attention to the vexed question of Cromwell's relations with the United Provinces.

The weight of historical opinion seems clearly adverse to Cromwell in these matters. Gardiner, for instance, says roundly that 'it is in his Baltic policy that the defects of his method were most clearly revealed'.[2] Firth, though more qualified in his judgment, seems to regard the Protector's Baltic policy as essentially a failure.[3] Abbott wavers between a confessional and an economic interpretation; and perhaps it would not be altogether unfair to suggest that he found Cromwell's policy not only confused, but confusing. When in 1950 Mrs Prestwich published her important article – the first serious attempt for many years to review the foreign policy of the Protectorate as a whole – she could find little good to say of Cromwell's dealing with the Baltic.[4] And quite recently Professor Trevor-Roper, in what was admittedly no more than an aside in a paper devoted to other matters – but an aside which nevertheless perhaps fairly represented the prevailing climate of opinion –

alluded to Cromwell's 'cultivation of the robber-empire in the Baltic to which he would have sacrificed English commercial interests'.[5] It is clear, in fact, that a main count in the indictment against Cromwell is that he subordinated English trade to the pursuit of the antiquated illusion of a general Protestant league against the Roman Catholic powers. Thus Mrs Prestwich argues with some force that he ought to have recognized the Dutch as the natural enemy, and ought to have used the Baltic crisis to undermine or destroy their dominant commercial position in the Eastland trade. This is a line of argument which would have appealed to those Commonwealthsmen who blamed him for making peace with the Dutch, while he was alive, and bitterly attacked his predilection for Sweden, after he was dead. Yet it is remarkable that when John Thurloe, soon after the Restoration, sat down to draw up an account of Cromwell's foreign policy for the guidance of his successors, he laid great emphasis, not on the Protector's friendship for the Dutch, but upon his opposition to them, 'being always jealous of that people'; on his scheme for getting Dunkirk in order to establish a staple for English trade there and so dish the Dutch; on his ambition to conquer the whole of the Flanders coast in order to 'put a bridle upon the Dutch'; and he crystallized this view of the matter into a well-remembered sentence, when he wrote 'that there were no greater considerations in England, in reference to forraigne objects, than how to obviate the growing greatness of the Dutch'.[6] It is perhaps no wonder that G.L. Beer, reading this passage nearly sixty years ago, should have based upon it the generalization that 'economic opposition to the Dutch is the fundamental note of Cromwell's policy after the conclusion of the West Indian expedition'.[7] It was a conclusion which found a distinguished supporter in Professor Wolfgang Michael; who in his elegant biography of Cromwell, published in 1907, maintained that trade rivalry, rather than confessional solidarity, was the predominant strand in Cromwell's statesmanship.[8] And the viability of Thurloe's thesis appears from its endorsement by Mr Hinton, in his recent book on the Eastland trade.[9]

Sir Charles Firth, however, had in his day decisively rejected Thurloe's version. 'Cromwell's desire to keep the peace between England and Holland', he wrote, 'was the corner-stone of his diplomacy.'[10] But this did not lead him to the corollaries adopted by some later writers. Firth felt that though the determinant of the Protector's policy was his concern for religion, that did not preclude him from 'a constant care for the nation's economic and political interests'.[11] And this view has been reaffirmed in recent years by Mr Paul,[12] and, most persuasively, by Professor Wilson, who considers Cromwell's policy to have been 'a curious mixture of religious idealism and judicious economic interest', and is inclined to give him the credit for realizing (as Clarendon also was to do) that a trade war against the Dutch was neither necessary nor desirable.[13]

It is difficult, after a careful examination of Cromwell's actions in the years after 1655 (whatever he himself may have said from time to time) to escape the conclusion that Firth was right about Thurloe.[14] Thurloe no doubt wished to represent his foreign policy in as favourable a light as possible; and he may either have sought to depict it as anti-Dutch because he felt that after the Restoration this was a popular policy; or he may have hoped to put upon it a gloss of *Realpolitik*, and free it from association with a 'Protestant Cause' in which the new men did not believe, and which to them was something of a joke; or he may simply have unconsciously projected the anti-Dutch feelings of 1657–9 back to the events of 1655–7. But, whether pro-Dutch or anti-Dutch, whether careful of economic interest or not, whether essentially religious or half-hypocritical, Cromwell's Baltic policy has not been popular with historians. Until Professor Wilson's book made its appearance, only one historian of eminence had shown much inclination to bestow upon it anything more than the most tepid approval, and that was Wolfgang Michael; whose biography contained so cogent a justification of Cromwell's statesmanship as for a moment almost to convince Firth himself.[15]

It is perhaps permissible to think that the difficulty and complexity of the issues that confronted the Protector have been a little underrated. Certainly – and despite Firth's full and careful narrative – there has been little attempt to analyse his policy from the point of view, not of economics or religion, but of politics: to enquire what was politically possible and desirable for England in the context of the times, and how far Cromwell's actions squared with that. Material is now available to which Firth had no access; and there are some other sources (notably much of De Witt's voluminous correspondence) which, though they have long been in print, Firth does not seem to have used. The vast accumulation on which Professor Abbott lavished his scholarship puts us in a position which Firth never enjoyed.[16] But the story of Cromwell's foreign policy (or any other topic, for that matter) is not to be disengaged from Abbott's volumes without much trouble; and the plan upon which he worked really precluded Abbott from the synoptic views which he was so well placed to command. And even a survey based only on the sources which Firth used could lead to conclusions rather different from those which Firth in fact drew from them. For those sources, though extensive, are fragmentary; the evidence they present is often conflicting; and it is not always easy to interpret. What follows, then, is an interpretation: an interpretation partly differing from Firth's, partly complementary to it. It will be contended that Cromwell's policy in the Baltic – after the attack on Hispaniola – was sound in its objectives, appropriate in its choice of means and (by and large) correctly calculated; and it will be argued that even if that policy was strongly influenced by religious motives, it was in point of fact right, and reasonably successful, from a strictly secular point of view.

It is, of course, futile to attempt to minimize the religious element. Every diplomat in Europe knew of the Protector's enthusiasm for Protestant solidarity. Roman Catholic statesmen credited him with the most sinister ambitions;[17] Protestants such as Christer Bonde or Nieupoort played upon his religious passions in order to forward their cause.[18] The notion of a general Protestant league was one of Cromwell's favourite pipe-dreams; and the example of the negotiations with France showed that he was prepared to put religion before expediency for the sake of the Huguenots or the Vaudois. Oppressed Protestants in Silesia looked to him for aid; fast-days and public subscriptions reinforced diplomacy; consignments of Bibles were sent to the more far-flung members of the reformed community;[19] and the supposed machinations of Alexander VII gave the Protector *frissons* which (it may not be uncharitable to think) were not wholly disagreeable.[20]

No doubt it is true that the decade after the conclusion of the peace of Westphalia saw a marked decline of religious motives in politics;[21] but it is easy to overrate this development, and probably wrong to look upon Cromwell's religious attitude to politics as something already outmoded. The 'fifties saw an astonishing recrudescence of apocalyptic speculation, converging on Charles x as a revived Lion of the North; and Comenius in Poland, Drabik in Transylvania, Matthiae Gothus in Sweden, Durie and Hartlib in England, looked to the speedy overthrow of Habsburg and of Rome at the hands of a grand alliance of Cromwell, Charles x and George Rákóczy.[22] Christer Bonde found notions of this sort common in London: he informed his master that 'the common folk speak openly, on 'Change and in the street, that all learned men have shown from the prophecies of Daniel and by other reasons, that a King of Sweden, with England, shall overturn the seat of the Pope, and give to the service of God its right prosperity and use again, which time is now at hand, and the occasion fit to be embraced'.[23] And William Lilly's almanack for 1656 was sent home to Sweden by Barkman because it contained 'astronomic *prophetia* of Y.M.'s incomparable successes and heroick enterprises'.[24] There is, perhaps, little trace of this apocalyptic daydreaming to be found in Cromwell or Thurloe, or any responsible English minister. Cromwell held the Fifth Monarchy to be a mere 'notion', and latterly came to think of it as an exception to his useful *dictum* that 'notions hurt none but them that have them'; and we are perhaps entitled to infer Thurloe's attitude from the fact that Pell could write him a letter making fun of apocalyptic numerology and its professors.[25] And even in regard to Durie's projects for reunion of the churches, Cromwell, though warmly sympathetic, had a clearer eye than Durie for the practical difficulties, as appears from his sceptical letter to William of Hesse.[26] But although by the standards of Hartlib and Comenius they are to be reckoned Laodiceans, they did to a great degree make religion the rule of their policy; and in this they were neither singular nor old-fashioned. It is true that Bonde told Thurloe that he thought a war simply for the sake of religion was unjustified, and refused to base an Anglo-Swedish alliance on that ground alone, as being too *éclatant*;[27] and it is true too that Nieupoort warned Thurloe that other motives than religion must be taken into account when estimating Dutch policy.[28] But it was Bonde himself who told the Swedish council in 1657 that 'when one considers the intention of the treaties that were to be entered into with Denmark, Holland and England, it was to the end that our religion be preserved against the Catholic league';[29] it was Nieupoort who propounded to De Witt a scheme for a great Protestant league against the Catholics, to be headed by Charles x;[30] while De Witt for his part hoped to cement the friendship between England and Holland by a tight confessional union of the churches of each: he even thought of sending over Dutch divines to help Cromwell to draw up a church settlement.[31] Boreel in Paris reacted precisely as Cromwell did to the news of the Vaudois massacres, and had the same nightmares about popish plots.[32] Charles x was as suspicious of Alexander vii's supposed pan-Catholic projects as ever the Protector was, and Mazarin tried vainly to persuade him that there was nothing to be afraid of.[33] As late as November 1661, a memorial which the Swedish regency drew up for Bengt Horn was based on the assumption that there existed a general Roman Catholic conspiracy, fomented by the pope.[35] And many statesmen – Sagredo and Bonde among them – thought that a general religious war was certainly coming.[35] Cromwell had not, as Charles x to some degree had, freed himself from the attitudes of mind of the previous generation, for the good reason that those attitudes had very generally persisted. Charles x was a young man; Cromwell an ageing one; and middle-aged or elderly statesmen have not always been abreast of their times, still less ahead of them. To dismiss Cromwell's foreign policy as 'Elizabethan' – as Abbott, for instance, does[36] – is perhaps no more useful or valid than if one were to stigmatize a contemporary foreign policy based upon the championship of liberty as 'Gladstonian'.

Yet it may still be worth while to try to see how far Cromwell's policy, apart from all these religious considerations, made sense politically. And it may be helpful, as a preliminary, to take a look at the methods by which foreign policy was managed under the Protectorate; since an examination of this may shed some light on the Protector's procedures.

In the time of the Little Parliament, foreign affairs were dealt with by a standing committee of varying size, meeting at stated times and reporting to the council.[37] But with the coming of the Protectorate this system seems for a time to have been dropped in favour of *ad hoc* sub-committees of council, appointed to consider specific questions: thus in November 1655 Strickland, Lambert, Fiennes and Lawrence acted as a special sub-committee for Swedish affairs:[38] or (to take another example) in July 1657 Fiennes, Fleetwood, Lisle, Thurloe, Strickland and Rous were appointed to consider 'what may be offered to Council concerning Denmark, according to to-day's debate'.[39] Major decisions were taken by the council as a whole; and on at least one occasion Cromwell excused a delay in answering Nieupoort by saying that 'he himself without the council did not use to dispose of such affairs'.[40] Nevertheless, there was a natural tendency for important matters to be concentrated in the hands of Thurloe; and foreign ministers complained bitterly of the difficulty of doing business when there was only one secretary of state who deliberately tried to monopolize foreign policy.[41] For the purpose of negotiating treaties, of course, England followed the general practice of appointing commissioners to treat with the foreign minister concerned; but in 1656, at all events, Cromwell was pursuing something like a private foreign policy of his own in regard to Sweden: he told Bonde that he attached little importance to the matters transacted between the ambassador and the commissioners; the really important business would be dealt with directly between Bonde and himself, through the intermediary of Charles Fleetwood. One might almost speak, in eighteenth-century terms, of a *secret du Protecteur*.[42] This phase passed, however; and perhaps it was possible only in the case of Bonde, who happened to speak English (it will be recalled that Cromwell's Latin, in Burnet's phrase, was 'very vicious and scanty'): certainly towards the end of the Protectorate there seems to be a return to the system of *ad hoc* committees of council.[43]

But whatever the methods employed, foreign ministers found negotiation in England a grievous trial of their patience. There was universal complaint of the intolerable slowness of the government in despatching business: diplomats from unpopular countries such as Poland or Denmark, or from unimportant ones such as Courland or Gelders, might wait literally months before they were so much as granted an audience;[44] and even

the favoured Swedes and Dutch were not much better treated.[45]
The more touchy of them were disposed to think that the delays
were deliberate: another symptom of that overweening arrogance which had produced a situation in which there were half a
dozen ministers waiting cap in hand on Cromwell's good
pleasure, while there was not a single English minister at a
foreign court.[46] The more penetrating rightly attributed the
situation to the crushing weight of business which the Protector
and his secretary had to handle, and to their constant preoccupation with the difficult problems of domestic affairs.[47]
But all agreed on the ignorance and inexperience of the men
with whom they had to deal: ignorance of vital facts (such as
the terms of the treaty of Osnabrück);[48] ignorance of protocol
(which often led them into blunders and apologies);[49] ignorance
of Latin: 'it is a great scandal', wrote Bonde angrily, 'that since
Mr Meadowe went to Portugal they have not anybody that can
write a decent line of Latin; but the blind Miltonius has to
translate from English anything they want done, and you can
easily imagine how slowly it goes.'[50] Moreover, the most
important channels of business – those which led through
Thurloe, and through the Protector himself – were often
blocked by illness. It is remarkable how often Cromwell was
indisposed; and Thurloe was almost as frequently laid up with
what appears to have been a chronic sore throat – a sympathetic affection, perhaps, induced by listening to Cromwell's
speeches. Cromwell, moreover, developed the habit of retiring
to Hampton Court on Friday afternoons, and returning to
London on Monday mornings – he has thus some claim to be
regarded as the inventor of the English weekend – and though
Nieupoort and Bonde were occasionally invited to go down
with him, this was an exceptional favour which does not seem
to have been extended to other diplomats.[51] He had, besides,
an infuriating habit of giving audiences of major importance on
the late afternoon of post-days, so that ambassadors were unable
to get off their accounts of them until a week later. And lastly
there was the extraordinary state of social quarantine in which
ambassadors were supposed to live. It was strictly forbidden for
any servant of the state to communicate with the minister of a
foreign power, or to receive visits from him.[52] 'I must say',
wrote Bonde, 'that what annoys me most is that I sit in my

house like a prisoner, and can get no one to come to me, nor may I go to them.'[53] The rule was indeed at times evaded;[54] but it was there, and it was felt to be galling. And this, perhaps, is one reason why so much important business was transacted at apparently casual encounters in St James's Park.

Two things, however, impressed all diplomats about England's conduct of foreign affairs. The first was its secrecy: 'I do not believe', wrote Sagredo to the Doge, 'that any government on earth conducts its affairs with greater secrecy than this one'; and Schlezer found its intentions 'almost impenetrable.'[55] The other thing was its extraordinarily efficient intelligence service; and to this the state papers of John Thurloe bear impressive witness. Nevertheless, Thurloe's intelligence was patchy – it was fullest and most accurate about Dutch affairs – and, as will appear presently, the information he had at his disposal was sometimes dangerously tendentious.

But the strongest impression that remains about foreign policy in the period of the Protectorate is that it was conducted by amateurs. Highly intelligent amateurs, some of them; but amateurs. And certainly amateurs grossly overworked: we hear more than once of Cromwell's giving audience in the afternoon after having sat from early morning in council without anything to eat; of his being 'weary'; of his being 'too busy' to eat.[56] It was no wonder if they made mistakes: the wonder was rather that they made so few.

2

What, then, were the main political considerations which must sway this ignorant (but shrewd) government? Let us place ourselves about the beginning of the year 1655: the Dutch war is over; the fleet is on its way to attack Hispaniola; Cromwell, though he does not as yet realize it, has virtually made his option between France and Spain; and negotiations, of infinite tedium, have already for some months been under way for a treaty with Louis xiv. Some clear consequences for English foreign policy flowed from this situation. First, if Cromwell were to be friends with France, that friendship would probably also imply good relations with the Dutch. Mazarin had latterly been on cordial terms with the States-General, and had looked to them (though in vain) to contrive his admission to the treaty of Westminster. The Dutch, on their side, had every reason to desire more normal relations between France and the Commonwealth: in the event of an Anglo-French war, the States party must fear that French support of the Stuarts might lead also to support of the house of Orange.[57] They could not so soon forget William II's intrigue with Mazarin. This was one reason why De Witt worked so hard to bring France and England together; why Nieupoort was so tireless in good offices; and why a great deal of the credit for the Anglo-French treaty of 1655 must be given to him.[58] A triple alliance between England, France and the Dutch was always at the end of De Witt's political perspectives in the 'fifties. Secondly, the interests of the revolution in England, and the personal interests of Cromwell himself, prescribed friendship with the enemies of the house of Stuart, and enmity to its friends. This accorded well with De Witt's hostility to the house of Orange; it had already bound England and Holland together in the dark deed of the Act of Seclusion.[59] It was so clear a thing that the exclusion of the leading royalists from France was accepted by Mazarin as early as the spring of 1654 as a necessary consequence of any English alliance.[60] It was at least as powerful in influencing Cromwell's attitudes in foreign policy as was the criterion of common religious faith. Even the Protestant Cause could not override the law of self-preservation. And that law drove Cromwell and De Witt together.[61]

But Cromwell was no more England than De Witt was the United Netherlands; and though each of them took Anglo-Dutch friendship as the basis of his foreign policy (because each of them saw in that friendship the security of his party) there were serious sources of friction between the two countries. There was a long score unsettled between them in the East Indies; a long-standing fisheries dispute; irreconcilable attitude to maritime law; and a growing trade-rivalry which had found its expression in England in the first Act of Navigation (1651). These factors produced three Dutch wars; they produced the constant diplomatic oscillation between friendship and hostility which is typical of the relations between the two countries in this century – an oscillation which could be so delicate that at times only a hair's-breadth separates close alliance from open war, and a featherweight decides which it shall be:[62] as, conspicuously, in 1652. But during the Protectorate the influence of Cromwell and De Witt is constantly exerted to depress the scale in favour of alliance. And this is explained, on Cromwell's part, not only by religion, not only by the bond of parallel fears and common enmities (for the clamour for a trade war might have submerged these as it submerged them in 1652); but also in part by consideration of the question of naval stores.

Except for the English oak used for the hull of a ship, almost all naval stores in 1652 came from the Baltic area. But when at the end of that year Denmark entered the war as Holland's ally, Frederick III closed the Sound to all English ships; and the Dutch-Danish alliance of 1653 bound him to keep it closed for as long as the war should last. The main consideration which led the Dutch thus to seduce Frederick from the neutrality which he was so anxious to preserve, was the hope of ruining the English Baltic trade;[63] but one effect of the alliance was to deal a severe blow – or at least, to level a serious threat – at English naval power. The result was a naval emergency, which for the first time sent the Admiralty to the American colonies in search of masts.[64] The war ended with stocks in the dockyards depleted.[65] Thereafter, the vast naval efforts of the Protectorate would probably have kept them low in any case; but the situation was made much worse by the chronic financial stringency under which the government laboured. It seems clear that Cromwell was not able to afford the money to build up any reserves which would tide him over a crisis;[66] and when Montagu's fleet was sent to the Sound in 1659 it was plain that this was the last fleet which the yards could fit out: if it were lost or damaged, there could be no replacements; they had scraped the barrel to the bottom.[67] It followed from all this that Cromwell, who (as he told Bonde on one occasion)[68] had to maintain one fleet in the West Indies, another in the western approaches, and a third off the Straits or in the Mediterranean, must not risk, if it could at all be avoided, another naval war with the Dutch, nor another closure of the Sound by a Danish-Dutch combination. Nor could he tolerate any arrangement which gave to a single power the sole control of the areas from which naval stores were exported.[69] These plain facts were to be of vital importance for his relations to Sweden, to Denmark, and to the Dutch.

3

In the summer of 1655, Charles X, after long hesitation as to whether to attack Poland, Russia or Denmark, finally decided to make Poland his victim. Like Gustavus Adolphus before him, he landed in Polish Prussia, and proceeded to try to conquer the mouths of the Vistula. He blockaded Danzig, since he could not take it; and it was feared, by all who were interested in the Baltic trade, that he would emulate Gustavus in another particular also – in the imposition of tolls upon merchants trading to Prussian ports. And in fact, within a few months of the landing, these fears proved to be justified.

The Dutch were immediately concerned, for the Baltic trade was the most important branch of their commerce – 'the mother-trade', they called it – more important to them even than the trade of the Indies. They feared, with reason, a Swedish conquest of Prussia, which would put Charles X in control of virtually the entire southern shore of the Baltic – in control, therefore, of the great trade routes whereby the produce of Poland and Muscovy reached the West. It was inevitable that they should seek to oppose Charles's progress, and highly probable that their opposition might lead to open hostilities between Sweden and the States-General.

In this situation the Dutch and the Swedes both made great efforts to enlist Cromwell on their side. Although there were already two Swedish envoys in England,[70] Charles X now sent two more: Christer Bonde as a special ambassador, and George Fleetwood (brother of the milk-sop) on a semi-private recruiting mission.[71] Between them and the Dutch ambassador Nieupoort there developed a protracted diplomatic struggle; Nieupoort endeavouring to draw Cromwell into a project for an alliance with Denmark, Brandenburg, the Dutch, and possibly France, to be directed to the preservation of liberty of trade in the Baltic;[72] the Swedes trying to cajole him into the conversion of Whitelocke's treaty of 1654 into a close political alliance.

Cromwell found himself in an embarrassing position. Despite

his clear realization that good relations with the Dutch were imperatively necessary to him, he felt a strong inclination towards Sweden. As a young man, he had shared the enthusiasm of his contemporaries for Gustavus Adolphus, and he once vividly described to Bonde the emotion with which he had heard the news of Lützen.[73] He regarded Sweden as the champion of continental Protestantism; and at a time when the peace of Westphalia was less than ten years old it is hardly surprising that he should have done so. It seemed to him now that Charles was stepping forward to complete the work which Gustavus had been cut off too soon to finish; and though he knew little or nothing of Charles, he developed what can only be described as a sentimental admiration for him. To Bonde he always spoke of Charles as 'your great and noble king';[74] he publicly rejoiced at Charles's victories; declared that he hoped his conquests might reach to Constantinople and the Caspian;[75] and in a burst of enthusiasm remarked that England and Sweden were the 'two columns' upon which the Protestant cause reposed, who between them 'might hold Europe in subjection ... since Your Majesty on land, and he at sea, were mighty considerable'.[76] Of Charles's real political motives and aims he was imperfectly informed. He regarded him, not without reason, as the destined adversary of the house of Habsburg and of the pope; but would have been surprised if he had known how careful Charles was to cultivate Roman Catholics in Poland.[77] He was, indeed, disagreeably affected when the Dutch maliciously took care to inform him of the rigour with which Charles was forced by his Lutheran subjects to treat Calvinists in Sweden;[78] but the bad impression seems to have been only transient.

Apart from these religious considerations, there were good secular reasons why Cromwell should look benevolently on Charles's enterprises in Prussia. The Commonwealth could have no sympathy for Poland, for John Casimir had contributed money to the Stuart cause; and the English and Scottish merchants in Poland were believed to have been victimized by the Polish government.[79] In 1653 England had given an honourable reception to the Polish vice-chancellor Radziejowski – a traitor who had come to England looking for support against his king;[80] and when early in 1655 John

Casimir sent an emissary to seek English aid against the Muscovites, he was kept waiting, snubbed, and (when at last he obtained audience) put out of countenance by the Protector's vehement reproaches.[81] Nor could Cromwell feel any concern for beleaguered Danzig; for Danzig was levying discriminatory taxation on English merchants,[82] and was in any case a hotbed of royalist activity: 'No place', wrote Middleton to Nicholas, 'has more kindness for the king than this.'[83] As to the Russians, with whom it seemed very likely that Charles would also come into conflict, the Muscovy Company had a long account of grievances against them; diplomatic relations had been broken off in 1649; and the Tsar's letters to the Protector were deemed unsatisfactory in matters of style and title.[84] Finally, there remained Brandenburg – a Protestant power which in the autumn of 1655 seemed almost certain to clash with Sweden. But the Great Elector was deeply suspect in England. He was the guardian of young William of Orange, and his court was regarded as the centre of the Orange faction. He was believed to have offered Charles Stuart 3,000 men; and Thurloe's agents told him (and Thurloe believed it) that Frederick William was 'more Orange party and royalist than anyone in the world'.[85] When in the summer of 1655 the Dutch, who were more afraid of Charles x's interference with their trade than of Frederick William's interference with their constitution, made an alliance with Brandenburg, in hopes of stiffening the elector to resist Sweden, Thurloe regarded the treaty with consternation, as an Orange triumph.[86]

There were thus sound political, as well as religious and sentimental, grounds for the sympathy with which Charles's campaigns were watched in England; and Cromwell's hope of diverting him to an attack on the Habsburgs was intelligible enough, at a moment when the formal rupture with Spain was imminent. In this respect Cromwell's policy coincides almost exactly with Mazarin's;[87] and it does not seem so far to have been suggested that Mazarin was motivated by zeal for the Protestant cause.

These circumstances, and Cromwell's personal predilection for Charles, no doubt do much to explain the special favour with which the Swedish diplomats were treated: Bonde and Coyet both received the Garter; the penurious Commonwealth

treated Bonde to public entertainment of unexampled lavish-
ness; and both Bonde and Fleetwood were given an ease
of access to the Protector's person such as no other foreign
minister enjoyed.[88] Cromwell even so far compromised with his
principles as to drink a furtive health to Charles x.[89] But in
view of all this it becomes all the more significant that in 1655
and 1656 Cromwell should in fact have eluded all Bonde's
efforts to inveigle him into a Swedish alliance. After infinite
delays and some acerbities, a trade treaty, expanding and
making precise the Whitelocke treaty of 1654, was indeed
signed in July 1656.[90] The Protector also permitted a limited
amount of recruiting for the Swedish armies by Lord Cranston,
and later by Sir William Vavasour – not without some qualms
lest the Scottish recruits might find their way to Charles
Stuart.[91] But the negotiations for an alliance were for the
present a complete failure. Cromwell refused to give Charles x
a subsidy, saying, quite truly, that he had no money to spare.[92]
He refused to give or lend naval assistance, on the equally
irrefutable ground that his fleets were fully extended by the war
against Spain.[93] He refused decisively the bait of special commercial privileges in the Baltic region, which Bonde at first
held out, as being too provocative of the Dutch: was not Danzig
(he asked Bonde) the Dutchman's breadbasket?[94] He refused
to enter any alliance directed *contra quoscunque*, because, as he
explicitly stated, he did not wish to offend Frederick III or the
States-General, who might think that such a provision was
directed against them.[95] And, finally, he wrecked the whole
negotiation by insisting that the Dutch should be included in
any treaty that was made between England and Sweden.[96]
The treaty of peace between England and the United Netherlands in 1654 had contained an article (art. 15) which bound
either side not to conclude any treaty with a third power without including a clause providing for each other's accession to it.
It is true that England had been slack about observing this
article; but Thurloe was always rather shamefaced and apolo-
getic when he was reminded of his omissions, and it is noteworthy that the treaty with France of October–November
1655 did make provision, in its final paragraph, for the inclusion
of the Dutch.[97] The Dutch, on their side, scrupulously complied
with article 15, at least for a time: so in regard to their treaty

with Brandenburg,[98] and also (which was much more important) in regard to the treaty of Elbing with Sweden in 1656.[99] Certainly they would have viewed as a provocation any Anglo-Swedish alliance which left them out.

Now it may well be true that Cromwell's refusal of the Swedish alliance in 1656 arose in part from a desire not to deepen existing cleavages in the Protestant Front.[100] His policy certainly was to reconcile Charles x and the Dutch; and he rightly thought that an Anglo-Swedish treaty would have the opposite effect. But it is no less true that such a splitting of the Protestant powers would have political and economic consequences quite as objectionable as the religious implications, and would involve England in serious dangers.[101] And these political considerations seem to have been decisive for him. He showed a really statesmanlike grasp of the fact that whereas for England the Baltic trade, as an economic asset, was of only moderate importance, for the Dutch it was the very nerve of the state; and that any attack upon it by way of an agreement for special privileges for English merchants would be a challenge to vital interests which even De Witt must resist, if need be to the point of war. And even when the proposed alliance had been divested of these dangerous and provocative economic lures, Cromwell refused it for two weighty political reasons: first, because he feared it might drive the Dutch to the 'desperate consilia' of seeking the friendship of Spain; and secondly, because he feared that it might be followed by a renewal of political collaboration between the Dutch and Denmark.[102] To act in such a way as to produce either of these consequences would be to play the game of Orange and Stuart.[103] It is not easy to say how far there was a firm basis for Cromwell's fear of a Dutch-Spanish *rapprochement*: Dutch economic interests were certainly closely tied up with Spain, and there was a good deal of underhand collaboration between them on a private and unofficial level, with a powerful pro-Spanish pressure-group in Amsterdam.[104] But there could be no doubt of the other danger: an Anglo-Swedish alliance, in the existing circumstances, might well have been followed by a Dutch-Danish league. Hostilities between Sweden and Denmark had been probable at any time since 1653, and were not rendered less likely by the prolonged negotiations for an alliance between them.[105] If Charles x were successful in conquering Prussia, Denmark might feel driven to attack him in self-defence, before he overran the whole Baltic; if he failed, Denmark would probably not let slip the chance of recovering the losses of Brömsebro. The Dutch could not help supporting Denmark, to maintain a Baltic balance which an Anglo-Swedish alliance would upset. Thus the conclusion of a political treaty between Cromwell and Charles x would involve the hazard of a major explosion. And the first thing to happen thereafter would be the loss of parity in regard to the Sound dues which England had gained in 1654, the restoration of the Dutch to a position of special privilege, and the closing of the Sound, as in 1653. Could England, with her navy heavily committed against Spain, and her stocks of naval stores run down, risk this? Had the Protectorate the financial resources to shoulder another war?[106] Could Cromwell, or any other rational statesman (which excludes the Commonwealthsmen) contemplate another naval war with the Dutch, while the Spanish war was in progress? The questions answer themselves.

Cromwell in 1656 was prepared for alliance with Sweden only in two cases: first, in the case that the alliance was explicitly and solely directed against the Habsburgs. This would have meant that Charles x left Poland for Germany; consequently, that the anxieties of Denmark and the Dutch were allayed, and that England obtained the benefit of a real diversion. In this case he was ready for an offensive alliance.[107] Or secondly, he was ready for a defensive alliance with Sweden as part of a general league of Protestants, including the Dutch, and, if need be, that traditional political Protestant, France. Such a league would, he hoped, ease the tension in the Baltic, reconcile Charles x with the States-General, and isolate Spain.[108] That it would also have religious attractions is for our present purposes (though not for his) immaterial. For indeed, the idea of a comprehensive alliance of this sort was by no means an aberration personal to Cromwell. It hung in the air of contemporary politics, and was from time to time grasped at by statesmen who were certainly not greatly concerned about the outlook for a Protestant Front. In 1655, for instance, Denmark met Swedish offers of a treaty with a proposal for a league to include the Dutch;[109] and Frederick

III would at any time have been happy to add England to his alliance with the United Provinces – hence Petkum's melancholy haunting of the purlieus of Whitehall. In March 1656, again, the Dutch ambassadors to Denmark were ordered to propose a quadruple alliance, with Denmark, England and Sweden as members.[110] In the autumn of 1656 Charles X himself was insisting that any alliance with Denmark must embrace England and France; and a few months later he was thinking of a combination which should include both England and the Dutch.[111] In every case the object was the same: to minimize the risk of a clash in the Baltic; or, if that were too much to hope for, to try to ensure that the two great maritime powers should not be dragged into it on opposite sides.

It is worth noting how strong were the forces which Cromwell resisted when he formulated this policy; how formidable the anti-Dutch pressures with which he successfully contended. Not only was the mercantile community bitterly hostile to the Dutch; but an important section of those who stood nearest to the Protector seems to have been hostile too.[112] The Commonwealthsmen and all that party had never forgiven Cromwell for making peace before the union of the two republics had been attained. Nieupoort's Marine Treaty was now hard aground on differences over maritime law. There was growing suspicion that Dunkirk privateers were financed with Dutch money, that Spanish ships and goods were sailing under the protection of the Dutch flag, that private persons in Holland were making fortunes out of unofficial aid to Spain.[113] And, not least, there was the poison-pen of Leeuw van Aitzema, Thurloe's main informant on Dutch affairs.[114] Week after week Aitzema poured into Thurloe's ears the most insidious and malignant attacks upon De Witt and his policies, twisting every Dutch action to make it appear unfriendly to England, exaggerating the Orange influence in the Netherlands, inciting English statesmen to courses which led straight to a Dutch war. The information was the more dangerous since – however misleading the glosses which Aitzema put on it – it tapped the most secret Dutch sources, and was in substance usually extremely accurate. It does infinite credit to the common sense and courage of Cromwell and Thurloe that they resisted Aitzema's insinuations for so long.

4

It became much less easy to resist them in 1657. Throughout the first half of this year, Frederick III of Denmark was steadily preparing – and was known by Cromwell to be preparing – for the attack on Sweden which he eventually launched on 1 June.[115] And it became increasingly likely (though on this point the information was for long distractingly contradictory) that this act of aggression was deliberately incited by the Dutch.[116] The Swedes, for their part, had no doubt of it.[117] Aitzema accused De Witt – or, more plausibly, van Beuningen – of being at the bottom of it, and alleged that the States-General were intriguing with Austria and Spain; and Thurloe was carefully reminded by his agents of the crisis of 1652, of the risk of another Dutch-Danish closure of the Sound, and of the consequences of a stoppage of the supply of naval stores.[118] At the end of July Nieupoort frankly told Cromwell that his government considered that the peace of Westphalia had absolved them from the obligation to maintain the treaty of Brömsebro.[119] It is not altogether surprising that the Protector and his secretary came to be convinced that the new conflict had been engineered by the Dutch.[120]

In this, as it happened, they were mistaken. Among the Dutch ambassadors to Denmark, van Beuningen, who had become fanatically hostile to Sweden since his unsuccessful mission to Stockholm in 1653–4, no doubt did his best to encourage Frederick III to plunge into war.[121] But the policy of De Witt was certainly pacific: Danish historians, indeed, find it weak and wavering.[122] De Witt, like Cromwell, would have been glad enough to be friends with Denmark and Sweden simultaneously; and Frederick III was deeply chagrined at what he considered to be Dutch duplicity in concluding the treaty of Elbing behind his back.[123] He seems to have made up his mind for a war of revenge upon Sweden some months before van Beuningen's arrival; and certainly there was nothing in the embassy's instructions to encourage such an adventure: the furthest that De Witt was prepared to go – until Denmark was actually *in extremis* – was to urge Frederick to put his forces (and especially his navy) into a state of preparedness sufficient to make Denmark *bündnisfähig,* and to conclude a strictly defensive alliance.[124] The Danes probably made too much of De Witt's encouragement; and they certainly seem to have been misled by the reports of their agents in Holland, who depicted the Dutch as strongly hostile to Sweden, and anxious for war.[125] But on this point Frederick III was undeceived before the final decision for war was taken.[126] And as to van Beuningen, it seems probable that his influence has been exaggerated: if Frederick needed any urging, a more important impulse probably came from the Spanish and Imperial courts; for Joachim Gersdorff, Frederick's influential Lord Chamberlain, was closely linked with the Spanish ambassador, Rebolledo, and was a convinced partisan of Habsburg.[127]

Of much of this, however, Cromwell was ill-informed, or ignorant.[128] He saw that the attempts of himself and Mazarin to dissuade Frederick from war met with no success; and he ascribed their failure to Dutch machinations.[129] The real link between Denmark and the Habsburgs, the supposed connection between Denmark and the Dutch, lent plausibility to his growing suspicion that the Dutch were already secretly in league with Spain. In the first half of 1657 evidence for this seemed to be piling up on all hands.[130] And it was reinforced by the impression produced by Dutch policy towards Portugal, Sweden, and France. The recovery of Brazil by the Portuguese raised such a storm in Zeeland (whose West India Company was the chief sufferer) that the States-General were forced to take vigorous retaliatory measures. A Dutch fleet was sent to cruise off Lisbon; a Dutch-Portuguese war in Europe (it had long been raging unofficially beyond the seas) appeared imminent.[131] At the same time, the dangerous tension between the United Provinces and Sweden, which had seemed to be satisfactorily removed by the treaty of Elbing, again became acute when the Dutch unexpectedly refused to ratify that treaty unless Charles X accepted certain 'Elucidations' which they propounded; and this he was not prepared to do.[132] As if this were not enough, De Ruyter's capture of two French privateers in the Mediterranean in April led to a sharp crisis in Franco-Dutch relations, which was not resolved – by a Dutch surrender on the essential points – until July. In the early summer a conflict between France and the Dutch looked extremely probable.[133]

Cromwell was in a difficult position. Since 23 March he had been the ally of Louis xiv; and already preparations were under way for the sending of English troops to France. But he was also bound by articles vii and viii of the treaty of Westminster to aid the Dutch against their enemies, and to forbear aiding their enemies against them. Yet Mazarin certainly counted on being able to borrow from England 'more than thirty warships', if war with the Dutch broke out:[134] the hope of being able to do so had been one of the considerations which predisposed him to an English alliance from the beginning.[135] And it seems that a *projet de traité* was drawn up, providing for Anglo-French collaboration against the United Provinces and Denmark, if it should come to a general war.[136] But such a war was the last thing that Cromwell wanted. A conflict in the North would be of no advantage to England, but might well assist Philip iv by distracting his adversaries: indeed, there was some evidence that this was just what Philip desired. The same was certainly true of a Franco-Dutch war. Despite all real and imagined provocations, despite too the strong tide of anti-Dutch passion in some sections of the nation, Cromwell had no ambition to fight the Dutch again. On the contrary, Lockhart well knew the mind of his master when he told Mazarin that he was 'persuaded, that a rupture with Holland in this juncture of tyme would not prove very reasonable'.[137] The good offices which Cromwell offered to France and the Dutch were undoubtedly made in all sincerity; and the suspicion, entertained by Mazarin for a moment, that the Protector was fomenting the crisis underhand with a view to appropriating the Dutch carrying-trade in the course of a war in which England would be no more than an auxiliary[138] – this suspicion had probably no basis in fact.[139] There was to be no return, if the Protector could help it, to the anti-Dutch policy of the Rump. If Cromwell (as Giavarina remarked) had really wanted a war with Holland in 1657, he would hardly have neglected so obvious an opportunity of bringing it on.[140] And this was true of De Witt also. Indeed, De Witt's first action after the crisis was over was to press forward, more urgently than before, with his favourite scheme for a triple alliance with England and France.[141]

For this neither Cromwell nor Mazarin was immediately ready. Cromwell played for time, alleging his preoccupation

with domestic affairs;[142] in reality, it seems clear, waiting to
see how far the Dutch were going to commit themselves in the
Baltic struggle. And in fact, tension between England and the
United Provinces continued throughout the autumn and winter.
Nieupoort's long-pursued Marine Treaty made no progress, to
De Witt's annoyance.[143] The crisis in Dutch-Portuguese
relations grew, if anything, more acute. The Swedes had some
idea of offering mediation between the disputants, foreseeing
with malicious satisfaction that such an offer would be highly
objectionable to the Dutch; while the Portuguese sent a
special mission to England to ensure the admission of their
country to the league between England, France and Sweden,
which they mistakenly believed to be preparing.[144] On 8
October, it is true, Nieupoort made a formal declaration that
the Dutch sought only reparation from the King of Portugal,
and had no design of aiding, directly or indirectly, the enemies
of England.[145] But within a month the two countries were at
war. The French did their best to stiffen Cromwell against the
Dutch on this issue.[146] And in the meantime the progress of
Anglo-French arms in Flanders had already begun to cause
serious alarm in the United Provinces.[147]

The clash between Cromwell's new suspiciousness of Dutch
good-will, on the one hand, and his old (and still-standing)
determination not to quarrel with them again, on the other,
appears very plainly in the history of his relations with Charles x
in 1657 and 1658. On Bonde's departure in August 1656,
George Fleetwood had remained in England to represent
Charles's interests, and to take care of the levying of recruits.
As the signs of an impending attack from Denmark grew more
alarming, Charles x became more anxious to extract from
Cromwell immediate financial aid, and, if possible, the despatch
of an English squadron to the Sound. In the early months of
1657 there were moments when Fleetwood was almost sure
that the ships would be sent;[148] but in the end he had to reconcile himself to the fact that the Protector was not prepared to
sanction a step so provocative of the Dutch: 'such a move'
(wrote Barkman) 'was esteemed impolitic: Holland would
thereby be driven to side with Spain, and no real help given to
Sweden, but rather perchance the contrary'.[149] The Protector
was prepared to look the other way while Fleetwood enlisted

English privateers for his master's service,[150] for that was but a reasonable offset to the marauders of Dunkirk; but he had no mind to risk a head-on clash with the Dutch fleet in Baltic waters.

Charles x's request for monetary assistance was not so easily disposed of. Towards the end of 1656 he had asked Cromwell to make Sweden a loan of 'some hundred thousand pounds sterling'.[151] The Protector did not reply until 13 January 1657. It was a moment when he was already alarmed at the prospective aggression of Denmark, and when there still seemed a reasonable prospect of a satisfactory parliamentary supply. His reply was therefore favourable. He indicated that he was prepared to consider making the loan; but in return he asked a reasonable security. And the security he demanded was the temporary transfer into his hands of the Swedish duchy of Bremen.[152]

The suggestion of taking Bremen as pledge was less remarkable and less eccentric than might at first sight appear. Nobody familiar with the financial position of Charles x (or of Cromwell) could be surprised that some security should be demanded for the repayment of so large a sum; the most convenient form of security was undoubtedly the revenue of some portion of the Swedish dominions; and of those dominions Bremen was the most accessible to England, the most recently-acquired by Sweden, and certainly the least contented with Swedish rule. It was only a few months, after all, since the States-General, in a similar situation, had asked for Pillau as security for advances to the Great Elector.[153] By what was possibly no more than an odd coincidence, there had been rumours in circulation at the *Reichsdeputationstag* at Frankfurt, in September 1656, that Charles was intending to pawn Bremen and Verden to Cromwell.[154] The Protector had, no doubt, a general disposition towards the acquisition of continental bases which he believed would strengthen his hand in dealing with his neighbours; and he may well have thought (as he told Fleetwood) that his occupation of Bremen would animate the Protestants of Germany. But Bremen at this juncture had special political attractions for him. Apart from the possibility of using it as a staple for English exports (and the suggestion seems to have been in the air about this time)[155] it offered very considerable strategic and diplomatic advantages. If the Dutch were indeed hatching plots with Denmark against Sweden, an English force in Bremen, and an English flotilla in the Weser, might perhaps make them think better of it; for Bremen was excellently placed to cut the landward communications between Holland and Denmark, and to threaten each of them with invasion from the rear.[156]

Moreover, a loan against Bremen had other advantages. It suited Cromwell's policy in that it was a *substitute* for an alliance with Sweden; and also because it chimed in with his ripening friendship with France, at a time when Mazarin was urging him to give Charles financial support.[157] Above all, it was a measure of insurance against being involved in a northern war in opposition to the Dutch. In this respect it accorded well with Cromwell's attempt (which had to be abandoned) to get the Dutch and the Scandinavian powers included in the alliance which he signed with France in March.[158] He hoped, indeed, that war in the Baltic might be averted by the diplomatic pressure of himself and Mazarin in Copenhagen.[159] If that hope proved vain, and if the Dutch were to send naval assistance to Denmark, then indeed he knew that he must face the prospect of sending an English fleet after them, to hold the balance even; and he seems to have given Charles x a clear promise of naval aid, if the Dutch should interfere.[160] But in the meanwhile, until that worst should happen, his terms for a Swedish alliance were the same as in 1656: an alliance directed primarily against Habsburg, and comprehending the Dutch.

Charles x was not in the least inclined to purchase a loan by the temporary hypothecation of Bremen. An alliance *contra quoscunque*, and effective aid (naval, for choice) was what he wanted. And it was perhaps in order to defer any such positive commitment that the Protector, apparently on his own initiative, in May renewed his offer of a loan and his suggestion about Bremen.[161] It is not easy to believe that he made it in good faith; for his financial position (as he confessed to Schlezer on three separate occasions about this time)[162] was now such that it was only with difficulty that he could carry on the war against Spain. Charles's reply was to suggest that Oldenburg or East Friesland might serve instead of Bremen;[163] though since neither of these territories was in Swedish ownership they could scarcely be considered to afford very attractive security for a loan, however plausible in a strategic point of view. It seems, indeed, difficult to resist the conclusion that neither side was very serious about Bremen in the summer of 1657. For Cromwell, in particular, demands for the duchy may well have been mainly a convenient device for keeping the talks with Sweden alive, until it should be clear whether the Dutch were prepared to commit themselves in the Baltic. Seen in this light, the controversy over Bremen was a useful diplomatic asset. If the Dutch were really the accomplices of Frederick III, if therefore Cromwell were forced into that narrow and exclusive alliance with Sweden which he had always sought to avoid, then Bremen might be of great importance in a military, and still more, in a naval, sense. But if the Dutch should confine their aid to Denmark to semi-official financial support, he would be glad enough to keep Charles quiet, and the balance trimmed, by the grant of permission to levy recruits; and the dispute over Bremen would give him the pretext he needed for refusing more than token aid. Meanwhile, he stood uncommitted.

But on 13 August came the news of Denmark's attack, and with it the realization that the crisis was upon him. And a little later Charles x's new emissary, Friesendorff, arrived in England with offers of a very remarkable nature. He proposed, in return for active assistance against Denmark, nothing less than the partition of the Danish dominions; England's share to be a great part of Jutland (together with East Friesland and Münster), with Oldenburg as a personal principality for Cromwell, most-favoured nation treatment for English traders in all Swedish harbours, and in the middle distance (when Denmark was finished with) a joint campaign against the Habsburgs. Charles was even prepared to hand over to Cromwell a port and a strong place in the Vistula delta, with a view to facilitating operations against Silesia.[164] This astonishing project was followed in rapid succession by others: suggestions for a four-year alliance against Austria as well as Denmark; proposals for a joint landing in Sjaelland; offers of Iceland and Greenland;[165] and these inducements were accompanied from time to time by more or less explicit threats that if they were not quickly accepted, Charles would seek a reconciliation with Austria.[166] Reduced to its basic constituents, what Charles was proposing was this: *either* an alliance against Denmark, to be rewarded by more or less extravagant territorial cessions; *or* a cash contribution against a modest security – for instance, the estuary of the river Stör, or Buxtehude and Lehe fort, or the harbour (but not the town) of Glückstadt.

Cromwell received these advances with a profusion of good words and an apparent irresolution in action which alternately encouraged and exasperated Charles and his envoys. But in reality he did not in the least desire to ally with Sweden against Denmark; and Charles's magnificent offers do not seem to have tempted him very much. Even when Charles so far improved his bid as to offer the whole of the duchy of Bremen, as well as all Jutland, in return for a declaration of war on Denmark, the Protector did not rise to the bait.[167] As to the alternative of financial assistance, Charles was told that England had no money to spare;[168] and even if the exchequer had been full it is hard to think that Buxtehude and the rest afforded proper security for a loan. Their value was military and naval; and only a very optimistic financier would look for much revenue from the estuary of the river Stör. If Charles were prepared to make peace quickly with Denmark, if he would turn his arms away from the Baltic and against the Habsburgs, then Cromwell might be ready enough to assist him with a contingent of troops; but only if he had a firm assurance that they would have a defensible base and port of embarkation on the continent. Aid in money might be difficult or impossible; but of troops the Protector had enough and to spare – provided Charles would promise to refund his war expenses![169] He did not, as it happened, think much of Buxtehude or the Stör: he would have preferred Stade[170] (which would have had economic as well as military possibilities), and Charles seems to have been nervous lest he should ask for the city of Bremen.[171] But in any event there was no longer any question, in the autumn, of Charles's pawning the whole duchy against a large loan; and the possibility of military aid to Sweden against the Emperor was a possibility only, a matter of secondary importance. Cromwell might make difficulties about Buxtehude or Stade to amuse Friesendorff, but his attention was really concentrated on the immediate and urgent problem of Denmark. And on this his line was already determined, and determined in a sense adverse to Sweden. Mediation was his policy, if mediation were at all possible. The despatch on 3 September of Meadowe to Copenhagen, and Jephson to Charles's camp, makes this plain; and Jephson's instructions of 22 August suggest that the Protector was not too anxious to be taken at his word about Bremen.[172] Peace in the north was his object (as it was Mazarin's also), even before it was clear to which side the balance was likely to incline. To the Swedish envoys he and Thurloe used that blend of procrastination and naïve duplicity upon which they so often fell back when in a difficulty: early in September, at the very moment when Meadowe was hurrying to Copenhagen with precise instructions to mediate a peace, Thurloe was professing that the Protector could not make up his mind whether to treat Denmark as an enemy, or not.[173]

The success of this policy, however, depended upon whether the Dutch would sit still. Cromwell was still very much in the dark as to the extent of the States-General's commitments to Frederick III; and Thurloe at the beginning of October was speculating uneasily about their motives and intentions.[174] Then suddenly there came news which seemed to put an end to all such speculation – and seemed to suggest, too, that the policy of mediation had become impossible. In the first week of October it was reported that eighteen Dutch warships were lying off the Dogger, and that they were bound for the Sound. The English government's reaction was immediate: on 3 October the Protector issued a warrant for equipping the fleet; on 9 October came a secret order for Montagu to take the Channel fleet to the Sound in order to 'give countenance to Sweden, whose affairs are in a most dangerous condition'.[175] At the same time the Swedish ambassadors were given an explicit promise of an alliance: so explicit that they wrote home jubilantly to their government announcing that Cromwell was committed to intervention on their side.[176] But the sequel was significant. When the news about the Dutch fleet turned out to be false, the Protector did not hesitate to wriggle out of these undertakings. At the end of the month his promised assistance had diminished to an offer to pay Charles X £30,000 in three monthly instalments when parliament should meet – a benefit which even the most benevolent commentator could scarcely qualify as other than speculative. And he followed this up on 29 November, after a rather lengthy interval, by a project for an alliance which would have pledged Charles to a campaign against Austria (assisted by contingents from other Protestant powers, the contingents to be paid by Sweden), while Cromwell in return would have done no more than bind himself to go on fighting Spain at sea (the fleet to be fitted out at Sweden's expense). The Dutch and France were to be invited to join. And 'if it were necessary' England would send a fleet to the Baltic.[177] It can hardly be supposed that Cromwell imagined his hero to be simple-minded enough to accept a proposal such as this; nor is it altogether surprising that the Swedish envoys should have described it to their government as 'an impertinence'.[178]

From the moment Meadowe was sent to Copenhagen, in fact, Cromwell was playing a double game with Charles X. If van Beuningen's story be true, that Meadowe on Cromwell's secret orders tried to open discussions with Frederick III with a view to an alliance,[179] his policy was, first, to counteract Dutch influence in Denmark by making a better bid. Failing that, mediation. Only in the last resort a clearly anti-Dutch attitude: as Thurloe wrote to Henry Cromwell: 'without they [the Dutch] doe provoke this state above measure, little notice will be taken of their injuries, but endeavours will be used to continue in peace with them'.[180] Meadowe's instructions, indeed, had ordered him to assure Frederick III that it was not in England's interest that he should be overwhelmed or plundered.[181] Already, in fact, Cromwell had begun to discern that there was some danger that the Baltic balance might be upset, not in Denmark's favour, but in Sweden's.[182] And from that thought it was an easy transition to the recognition of the community of interest between England and Holland in this question. The sending of Downing as ambassador to the Hague in December (which repaired the regrettable gap left by the absence of Nieupoort on leave) was perhaps a sign of this.[183] De Witt on his side was more than ready to welcome co-operation in the North. He believed that Cromwell would realize that he could not afford to witness the extinction of Denmark;[184] but he was clear too that the time had passed for the 'pernicious *consilia*' and 'owl-screeches' of van Beuningen.[185] On 12/22

December Cromwell's restraint was justified by a resolution of the States of Holland recommending a settlement in the North on the Brömsebro terms – a basis which meant in fact the renunciation of a Danish *revanche*, the disavowal of van Beuningen, and the acceptance of Cromwell's solution.[186] On 8 February [N.S.] 1658 the States-General reaffirmed this policy.[187] And when Downing explicitly renounced any trading preferences for England in Eastland, unless assented to by the Dutch, De Witt saw to it that this notable offer was met by a reciprocal pledge from the States-General.[188] Downing and de Thou were now collaborating closely together; and were pressing for tripartite mediation by England, France and Holland – an anticipation of the Hague Concerts of 1659 – as the best means of bringing peace to the North.[189] Their success was still uncertain, when their efforts were rendered useless by the news of the signing of the peace of Roskilde on 26 February.

The situation in the Baltic had now been turned upside down. As recently as 1 January Cromwell had lavished professions of goodwill on Fleetwood and Friesendorff, assuring them that he had no objection in principle to Sweden's attainment of her natural frontiers on the Sound, and replying to Charles x's complaints of Meadowe's diplomatic activities by bland regrets that the ambassador had exceeded his instructions.[190] And on 25 January he had uttered that famous panegyric on Charles x which has misled so many historians as to his attitude to these problems.[191] It was a characteristic effusion of Protestant sentiment; it vented the Protector's accumulated irritation with the Dutch; and it was (perhaps above all) a speech designed to rally support in parliament; but it was not a statement of policy. It may be, indeed, that the prick of conscience led him to paint a dark picture of the tribulations of the Protestant Hero grappling with false friends and inveterate foes, in the faint hope that parliament would enable him to make good that light-hearted promise of £30,000. But not even Cromwell could have persuaded himself that at that date Charles x was 'a poor prince . . . now reduced into a corner': if a poor prince were to be exhibited for compassion the obvious candidate was Frederick III. Ever since the fall of Fredriksodde on 24 October it had been apparent to everybody that the question was not whether Charles would be able to resist the Danish attack, but rather how severe the terms which he would be able to extort from his enemy. In December it had been strongly rumoured in London that Charles had taken Fyn, was perhaps already on Sjaelland, and that Frederick had fled to Skåne – intelligence which, as Fleetwood and Friesendorff noted with satisfaction, provoked 'much gladness, and not least in the Protector himself'.[192] Jephson, no doubt, swallowed Charles as the Protestant Hero without blinking: he was a simple soul who looked at politics very much as Cromwell is supposed by his critics to have done; and he took quite seriously the idea of active naval aid to Sweden, or exclusive trading privileges for England, or the acquisition of Bremen, or massive English annexations in Jutland which (as he told Bengt Skytte) would have made England and Sweden *neighbours*.[193] But Meadowe's mediation had for months been directed primarily to maintaining the Baltic balance; which in the context of the times meant securing the best possible terms for Denmark: 'unless I make peace', he wrote, 'adieu Denmark'.[194] He succeeded, in fact, in extracting some important concessions from the Swedes; and was duly rewarded by Frederick III with the Order of the Elephant.[195] Even so, Meadowe is reported to have said that he feared the Protector would think the peace-terms too severe.[196]

5

Thus the great crisis of 1657–8 was surmounted, as that of 1655–6 had been surmounted, with the basic principles of Cromwell's foreign policy intact. The grand Protestant coalition against the house of Habsburg was, indeed, at least as far off as ever; but the Protector had contrived to earn the gratitude of Denmark without sacrificing the friendship of Sweden; and by a statesmanlike forbearance he had avoided precipitating Holland into the arms of Spain. He showed no disposition to enrol himself among the clients of the victor. The terms he had propounded to Charles on 26 February, at a moment when he knew Denmark to be already prostrate, and a dictated peace a matter of days – and when, therefore, it might appear that the prospect of a Swedish campaign against Austria was more hopeful than for some time past – had been, if anything, more exigent than ever: the proposed alliance must comprehend not only the Dutch, but Denmark and Danzig – a suggestion at which the Swedes are said to have laughed outright. And not only that: Charles was informed that the Protector was reluctant to send any troops to the continent; and was even advised not to involve Sweden in war with Austria unless it were absolutely unavoidable.[197]

The Swedes might well laugh; and Charles might have been forgiven if he had washed his hands of a friend so demanding, and now, it appeared, so capricious. But the explanation of this astonishing abandonment of the old plan to engage Sweden against the Emperor was intelligible enough; and one aspect of it, at least, Charles was well placed to comprehend. Cromwell had dissolved his last parliament on 4 February; and henceforward the financial outlook was bleak indeed. So bleak, that he could no longer afford to pay for the luxury of a diversion, even if that diversion were the long-desired Swedish attack on the Habsburg hereditary lands. Thurloe was later to make the position clear: there could be no question of armed assistance, nor even of cash aid – the £30,000 still rankled with Charles x – until another parliament should meet.[198]

There were perhaps other considerations that helped to confirm this new line. One was a growing nervousness lest France and Spain should make peace behind England's back: in such a case, if England were left to fight on single-handed against Spain, there could be nothing to spare for adventures in Germany.[199] Another was implicit in the curious position in which Charles x found himself after Roskilde. He was still faced with a coalition of Austria, Poland and Brandenburg; and though by this time he was ready for peace, it was clear that a general settlement would take some months to negotiate. In the meantime, his armies must be paid and maintained, since he dared not disband them before peace was secure. And the only resource at his disposal for this purpose was to employ them in war, and supply them from enemy country. Thus Charles's only safe road to peace lay through continued war.[200] There is some sign that Cromwell appreciated this.[201] But he made a mistake of assuming that the necessary consequence would be a Swedish attack on Austria: it was a mistake which Charles naturally did everything to encourage. If then Charles's own necessities would drive him to attack the Habsburgs, what need was there from England's side for more than good words, good will, and diplomatic aid?

And there was one other circumstance, in the closing months of the Protector's life, which must have altered his views about the need for a Swedish diversionary attack upon Austria. This was the inclusion in Leopold's election capitulation of a clause prohibiting him from giving aid to Spain against France *or France's allies*. Mazarin's diplomacy thus provided Cromwell with one of the main objectives of his foreign policy, at no cost to himself;[202] and when on 14 August the League of the Rhine was constituted (with Charles x as a member), with the object, among other things, of ensuring the observance by the Emperor of his pledges, these events may indeed have 'knocked the bottom out of'[203] the plan for a Protestant League, but they gave England most of the political advantages which such a league would have produced.

Cromwell therefore confined himself to diplomatic aid to Charles. He did his best to get Swedish troops out of Denmark by using English good offices to smooth out remaining differences between Charles and Frederick:[204] Denmark was too combustible an area for a Swedish army to stay in; the sooner it departed to batten on some remoter (preferably popish) country, the better. He made a valiant attempt to win back Brandenburg from Austria, and even sought to persuade Frederick William that an arrangement was possible which would leave West Prussia in Swedish hands – though only (it was a characteristic touch) if the Dutch were given security against fiscal discrimination.[205] But Charles x, by refusing to receive the Brandenburg envoys, made sure of having at least one hostile country conveniently placed for support of his armies, if or when he must withdraw them from Denmark; and when Cromwell appealed to him not to attack the Great Elector, he was able to reply with some cogency that he could no more invade Silesia without marching through Brandenburg and Polish territory, than Cromwell could attack Burgundy without marching through Brabant.[206] It was not surprising, perhaps, that Charles, on the eve of his onslaught upon Denmark, should have confided to Terlon that he was uncertain of England's attitude; nor was it remarkable that he should have lied to Meadowe about his objective.[207]

More hopeful was the attempt to reconcile Sweden with the Dutch. For some time after Roskilde the Protector treated the Dutch with considerable reserve. The experience of 1657 had done much to inspire Thurloe, at all events, with that distrust of the Dutch which so strongly colours his memoranda of 1660–1. The war with Portugal was still raging, despite Anglo-French efforts to end it; and Thurloe was almost inclined to think that it was better to have the Dutch fleet off Lisbon than in dangerous proximity to the Sound.[208] In Copenhagen, van Beuningen – 'the veriest *boutefeu* in ye world' – after failing to prevent the peace of Roskilde, was trying to subvert it, and was artfully ensnaring Meadowe into unseasonable and misquotable utterances.[209] It was by no means clear that Holland would be content to make no effort to rehabilitate Denmark. The Roskilde settlement, from England's point of view, had had the enormous merit that it divided the control of the Sound, and so made impossible a recurrence of the situation of 1652–3; and if the Dutch tried to overturn that arrangement, Cromwell, however reluctantly, must fight to maintain it. His policy in the spring of 1658, therefore, was non-committal, since he was waiting to see what the Dutch would do. It was for that reason that he made no haste to accept a proposal for a triple alliance with France, put forward by De Witt in March; though in principle, as Thurloe explained, he was rather predisposed in its favour.[210]

And, as it turned out, Anglo-Dutch relations became more strained in the summer of this year than at any time since the peace of 1654. Cromwell's conquest of Dunkirk alarmed and infuriated the States-General;[211] while the English mercantile community on their side were incensed by the capture of three East Indiamen off Bantam.[212] But De Witt, like Cromwell, was in no mood for adventures, and Thurloe's suspicions of him were unjustified. He had no intention of trying to overturn the Roskilde settlement.[213] Despite some stormy scenes between them, Downing – even Downing, who suspected all Dutchmen – at last came to the conclusion that De Witt was perfectly sincere in his desire to keep on good terms with the Protector.[214] The negotiations which he was conducting to persuade the Dutch to ratify the treaty of Elbing without the 'Elucidations' began to assume a quite hopeful aspect.[215] De Witt asserted his authority to secure restitution of the captured English ships.[216] And in August the Grand Pensionary was writing that, come what might, the Dutch must inevitably align themselves with France and England, rather than with Brandenburg and the Habsburgs;[217] and he even admitted that Dutch insistence on the 'Elucidations', and the consequent alienation of Sweden, had been a grave mistake.[218] As the Protectorate approached its end, the enemies of Orange and of Stuart recognized once again, and for almost the last time, their community of interest.[219] Could Cromwell have known of De Witt's utterances, he might well have claimed them as the justification and endorsement of his policy.

But in that same month of August Charles x, by his sudden attack upon Denmark, plunged the Baltic once more into confusion. The news reached London on the day when the Swedish envoys hoped and believed that the council would come to a decision upon the long-deferred question of the alliance.[220] And it was typical, perhaps, that while Thurloe received the news with consternation, the City greeted it 'with unspeakable joy', as a blow against their hated rivals the Dutch.[221]

Cromwell did not live long enough to formulate a policy for this new emergency.[222] It has been said that Charles's aggression announced the ruin of the Protector's foreign policy.[223] That was not its necessary consequence; nor was it even its consequence in fact. Oliver's successors fell back upon Oliver's policy, despite occasional temptations to divagate into bargain-hunting in Stockholm;[224] and it was Oliver's policy that eventually disposed of the imbroglio. The Hague Concerts of 1659 were already implicit in the diplomacy of Downing, de Thou and De Witt in the opening months of 1658; the divided control of the Sound, reaffirmed in 1660, had been Meadowe's great achievement at Roskilde; the improved balance of power which emerged from the peace of Copenhagen was a better result for England – and a result more in accordance with Oliver's wishes – than an unchallenged Swedish predominance. And though the Dutch and Swedish fleets actually came to blows this time, Richard's government faithfully followed his father's example in refusing to be stampeded into precipitate partisanship. The determination not to fight the Dutch, if it could be avoided, survived not only Oliver, but the return of Scot to power – an historic *amende* which must have given the Cromwellians some satisfaction.[225] For this line was, indeed, the best line, if only because it was the safest; and in the Baltic, at all events, the safe line was what the old Protector had always preferred.

6

To sum up, then. After the attack on Hispaniola, it seems that Cromwell's foreign policy towards the Protestant powers was self-consistent, logical and conservative. The anti-Dutch attitudes of Thurloe's memorandum are exaggerated, possibly mythical, or at least ante-dated. In regard to the Dutch, as in regard to Sweden, the Protector's policy was marked throughout by caution and restraint. He turned his back on the prospect of adventure; he consistently abjured any attempt to garner short-range gains. The idea that some diplomatic deal with Sweden could at a stroke put the Eastland trade into English hands, and destroy the position which the Dutch had built up for themselves on the basis of long connection, fly-boats, low freights, cheap money and easy credit – this is a proposition which at least is not self-evident: as susceptible of doubt, perhaps, as is the corresponding notion of the Commonwealthsmen, that the same result could be achieved overnight by victorious war.[226] Cromwell may indeed, as Schlezer reported,[227] have been ignorant of the complexities of the Baltic situation, and he may have had but an imperfect idea of the motives that animated Charles x and his adversaries. Thurloe on occasion may have written about Baltic affairs of high import in an oddly casual and perfunctory style. But each of them had enough common sense to perceive where England's real interests lay; and Cromwell, at least, seems to have made up his mind that a speculative policy based upon possible and prospective economic advantages was a gamble too risky to engage in. Equality of privilege and parity of opportunity was all he asked for English commerce to the Baltic: it is clear that he felt that here, as in the wider field of imperial expansion, there was room enough, and trade enough, for two.[228] As he said on one occasion to Bonde, his policy was for 'freedom of religion and trade'.[229] And this was a line the more easy to adhere to, since it was exactly De Witt's line also:[230] hence the willingness of each of them, on more than one occasion, to renounce special privileges to the prejudice of the other.[231] And indeed, any particular favours for England in the Baltic must have been purchased at an exorbitant price: Dutch enmity would have more than counterbalanced the advantage of a Swedish attack on Austria. Nor would the gains have been secure. For if an English alliance had helped Charles to victory, England's privileges would have been precariously dependent upon the continued goodwill of the unchallenged master of the Baltic. And if, despite English aid, Charles had been beaten, his grants would have been worthless. Either way, that Baltic balance would have been destroyed which it was the common interest of all trading nations to preserve.

Cromwell's Baltic policy, then, does not represent the sacrifice of trade to religion, nor the subordination of the interests of England to the dream of a Protestant Front. Nor did it aim (conversely) at the maintenance of the *status quo* simply for the sake of the country's economic interests.[232] It is not even to be dismissed as an unintelligible muddle. The struggle with Spain, the fear of the Stuarts, the dangers of another Dutch war – these were quite as much the determinants of his action as was any feeling of confessional solidarity. And in the Baltic, at all events, the chronic financial stringency entailed the consequence that the Protector cut his coat according to his cloth. As to the attempt to divert Charles x's superabundant energies into an attack upon the Austrian Habsburgs, this was so far from being the private fantasy of a naïve enthusiast, that it may almost be said to have been a commonplace of contemporary politics.

It would certainly be difficult, and it would probably be dangerous, to attempt to provide any unified and self-consistent interpretation of Cromwell's foreign policy as a whole. His treatment of Spain, his early bullying of France, cannot comfortably be compressed within the limits of a formula which fits his dealings with the Protestant powers. In the one case the irrational and emotional elements, though they are present, are kept subordinate; in the other they are habitually in the ascendant. The huge and menacing power of England, the aggressiveness and violence of her foreign policy, understandably impressed Roman Catholic statesmen; and even so shrewd an observer as the Venetian envoy could in August 1658 write to the Doge:

The designs of this government are so vast that they aim at taking possession of any part of the world . . . while in the matter of religion they aim at nothing less than one day infecting the whole Catholic world with Lutheranism.[233]

To Christer Bonde, on the other hand, such an interpretation would have appeared as wild in its politics as in its theology. Two years earlier, Bonde had made his own comment:

To be sure things go on here rather slowly; but this is a state which stands in great uncertainty, and they act therefore with very considerable timidity, fearful of every thing that can turn to their disadvantage . . .

. . . their affairs are in so bad a state that they scarcely venture to proceed to any real decision, which is why they are so extraordinarily slow . . .

they are so anxious that they hardly know what to do.[234]

The difference between Giavarina's view and Bonde's does seem to reflect a real difference between the Protector's policy in the one area and in the other. As Cromwell and Thurloe groped and fumbled their way through the alien intricacies of Baltic diplomacy, they sought, no doubt, to set their course – in the east, as in the west – by the guiding star of religion; but Providence, or good luck, or their own innate shrewdness, contrived almost always that the cause of God should here accord with England's interests; and if they themselves believed that 'Protestantism' was their watchword, we are not thereby debarred from observing that from another angle that watchword might be made to read 'Prudence'. For, in the Baltic, at all events, the key to their policy was not fanaticism, but fear.

NOTES

[1] A summary of this paper was read as a communication to the XIth International Congress of Historical Sciences, 1960 and published in *The English Historical Review*, Vol. 76, 1961.

[2] S. R. Gardiner, *Oliver Cromwell* (1901), p. 298.

[3] Sir Charles H. Firth, *The Last Years of the Protectorate* (1909), ii, 224; and *id.*, *Oliver Cromwell and the Rule of the Puritans in England* (new edn, 1935), pp. 387–9.

[4] Menna Prestwich, 'Diplomacy and Trade under the Protectorate', *The Journal of Modern History*, (1950), pp. 103–21. Mrs Prestwich remarks, for instance, that 'an alliance with Sweden to deprive the Dutch of their trade in the Baltic did not appeal to Cromwell's Protestant sensibilities' (p. 114), and writes of 'a muddled and ineffective policy in the Baltic, from which English trade derived little benefit' (p. 116).

[5] H. R. Trevor-Roper, 'Cromwell and his Parliaments', in *Essays presented to Sir Lewis Namier* (1956), p. 7. Note, however, the irreconcilability of this view with Mrs Prestwich's.

[6] See Thurloe's memorandum 'Concerning the Forraigne Affairs in the Protector's Time', printed in *Somers Tracts* (2nd edn, 1811), vi, 330, 331, 335; and Sir C. H. Firth, 'Secretary Thurloe on the relations of England and Holland', *EHR*, xxi (1906), especially p. 327, where Thurloe's talent for obscuring the truth with the half-truth is particularly evident.

[7] G. L. Beer, 'Cromwell's Policy in its Economic Aspects', *Political Science Quarterly*, xlvii (1902), 47.

[8] Wolfgang Michael, *Cromwell*, Berlin, 1907, ii, 151, where he writes: 'So klar und einfach erscheint dieses [Cromwell's anti-Dutch policy], so sehr dem praktischen englischen Interesse entsprechend, dass daneben das angebliche Streben nach einem protestantischen Bündnisse wenigstens nicht als die Hauptsache genommen werden dürfte. . . .'

[9] R. W. K. Hinton, *The Eastland Trade and the Common Weal in the Seventeenth Century*, Cambridge, 1959, p. 124.

[10] Sir C. H. Firth, *The Last Years of the Protectorate* (1909), i, 337.

[11] *Ibid.*, 340.

[12] Robert S. Paul, *The Lord Protector. Religion and Politics in the Life of Cromwell* (1955), pp. 341, 374.

[13] Charles Wilson, *Profit and Power* (1958), pp. 85, 156–7.

[14] Even before Firth, Guernsey Jones had been cautious about taking Thurloe too literally: Guernsey Jones, *The Diplomatic Relations between Cromwell and Charles X*, Lincoln, Neb., 1898, p. 73, n. 1.

[15] Firth's review of Michael's book contained the following sentence: 'Considered in this way it is clear that Cromwell pursued a thoroughly practical national policy, but that he constantly endeavoured to combine with the pursuit of national ends the common interests of Protestantism', *EHR*, xxv, (1910), 776–7.

[16] Wilbur Cortez Abbott, *The Writings and Speeches of Oliver Cromwell*, Cambridge, Mass., 1945, vols. iii–iv. Abbott was very unfortunate in his translator from the Swedish. Almost all excerpts from Swedish sources in vols. iii and iv of his work, as far as I have been able to check them, are marred by numerous and often very serious mistranslations. It would be pleasant to suggest that these excerpts should be used with caution; but indeed they should not be used at all.

[17] See, e.g. C[alendar of] S[tate] P[apers,] Ven[etian] (*1655–1656*), p. 80 (Paulucci to Sagredo, 11 July 1655); *ibid.*, pp. 141, 143 (Sagredo to Doge,

19 and 26 November 1655); *ibid.*, (*1657–1659*), p. 128 (Giavarina to Doge, 16 November 1657); Guizot, *History of Oliver Cromwell and the English Commonwealth* (trans. A. R. Scoble) (1854), ii, 427–35, Lamilletière's memorandum, 21 July 1654.

[18] Brit. Mus., Add. MS. 38100, fo. 238 (Bonde to Charles x, 23 August 1655); *ibid.*, fos. 258v–9; *Brieven geschreven ende gewisselt tusschen de Heer Johan de Witt . . . ende de gevolmaghtigden van de Staet der Verenigde Nederlanden* [cited, De Witt, *Brieven*], 's Gravenhage, 1724, iii, 78–9 (Nieupoort to De Witt, 9 July 1655).

[19] *CSP. Dom[estic]* (*1657–1658*), pp. 256, 343, 344; *ibid.*, (*1658–1659*), pp. 76, 89, 132; *The State Papers of John Thurloe* (1742), v, 705, and *cf.* *ibid.*, iii, 422–3; and Sven Göransson, *Den europeiska konfessionspolitikens upplösning 1654–1660*, Stockholm, 1955, pp. 44–5, 59 ff., 76–84, &c.

[20] For reactions to the election of Alexander, Brit. Mus., Add. MS. 38100, fo. 98 (Coyet to Charles x, 18 May 1655); *CSP. Ven.* (*1655–1656*), p. 53 (Paulucci to Sagredo, 17 May 1655); Cromwell's speech of 25 January 1658, in T. Carlyle, *The Letters and Speeches of Oliver Cromwell* (ed. S. C. Lomas), iii, 167: 'A Pope fitted – I hope indeed born not in but out of due time – to accomplish this bloody work'. And see *CSP. Ven.* (*1657–1659*), p. 183 (Giustinian to Doge, 9 April 1658), for an outburst by Thurloe against Alexander.

[21] For this see Göransson, *op. cit. passim.*

[22] Abbott quite missed the significance of the Transylvanian connection: *op. cit.* iii, 709–10.

[23] Brit. Mus. Add. MS. 38100, fo. 259 (Bonde to Charles x, 23 August, 1655).

[24] *Ibid.*, fo. 45v (Barkman to Charles x, December 1656). For the political implications of astrology, see Folke Dahl, 'King Charles Gustavus of Sweden and the English astrologers William Lilly and John Gadbury', *Lychnos*, ii, Uppsala, 1937, 161–86.

[25] Robert Vaughan, *The Protectorate of Oliver Cromwell* (1839), i, 156–7.

[26] David Masson, *The Life of John Milton, narrated in connection with the . . . History of his Time* (1877), v, 291.

[27] Add. MS. 38100, fos. 289v–90, 361v–2 (Bonde to Charles x, 18 April, 1656): Bonde insisted that the treaty of Osnabrück must be the basis of any Anglo-Swedish alliance, 'since *nomen religionis* is too *éclatant*'.

[28] De Witt, *Brieven*, iii, 108 (Nieupoort to De Witt, 20 August 1656); Nieupoort told Thurloe 'dat wy het werk van de Religie wel behertighden, maer ook op onse behoudenisse ende tydelycke welvaeren schuldigh waeren te letten'. Frederick iii of Denmark, too, like his father before him, was anything but accessible to appeals to 'the Protestant Cause'; J. A. Fridericia, *Adelsvaeldens sidste Dage. Danmarks Historia fra Christian IVs Død til Enevaeldens Indførelse*, Copenhagen, 1894, p. 230.

[29] *Svenska riksrådets protokoll*, Handlingar rörande Sveriges historia, 3rd ser., Stockholm, 1929, xvii, 13 (6 February 1657).

[30] De Witt, *Brieven*, iii, 69 (Nieupoort to De Witt, 11 June 1655): 'Het soude myns bedunckens al een groot werck wesen omme de Koningh [Charles x], siende de animositeyt van 't Pausdom in Savoyen, ende ook

hoe de Roomsche Geestelyckheyt gestadigh woelt in de Erflanden van den Keyser, bewogen werden, al waere het met een geldt-subsidie, als voor desen *Gustavus*, omme syne Wapenen in plaetse van tegens Protestantse Steden in Pruyssen, in de voornoemde Erflanden tot afweringe van de voorgeroerde Oppression te willen gebruycken, ende vernieuwen met onsen Staet ofte alleen, of gemeen met desen Staet [England] ende Denemarcken een defensieve Alliance.' This is just what Cromwell was after.

[31] *Ibid.* iii, 35 (De Witt to Nieupoort, 2 April 1655), and *cf. ibid.*, pp. 43, 45, 93, 96; *Brieven van Johan de Witt . . . bewerkt door Robert Fruin*, edd. G. W. Kernkamp, N. Japikse (Werken uitgegeven door het Historisch Genootschap . . . te Utrecht, 3rd ser., nos. 18, 25, Amsterdam 1906, 1909) [cited: *Brieven van de Witt*], i, 224-5.

[32] De Witt, *Brieven*, i, 224-5, &c.; and *cf.* Coyet, in Brit. Mus., Add. MS. 38100, fo. 98 (to Charles x, 18 May 1655).

[33] *Lettres du Cardinal Mazarin* (edd. A. Chéruel, G. D'Avenel), Paris, 1890-4, [cited: *Mazarin*] vii, 118-19, 188 (Mazarin to d'Avaugour, 29 October, 1655, 25 February, 1656).

[34] Birger Fahlborg, *Sveriges yttre politik 1660-1664*, Stockholm, 1932, p. 103, n. 1. And Fahlborg comments (*loc. cit.*): 'In a word, it was Austria that had formed the great coalition [of 1658-60], and in the long run maintained it. And in Charles x's last years his policy had in the last resort been directed against Austria, whether it operated by way of war or of diplomacy.' Which is precisely what Cromwell had always maintained. On 27 March 1656, in the course of a general discussion on foreign affairs in the Swedish council, Per Brahe observed: 'As regards France, it seems best that (provided the Muscovite will but sit still) H.M. conclude an alliance with that crown also, *since it is apparent that H.M.'s design is against the House of Austria*, by reason that what was promised and granted in the treaty of Osnabrück has not yet come to any execution': *Svenska riksrådets protokoll*, Stockholm, 1923, xvi, 425; my italics. If this was the view of Per Brahe, is it so very remarkable that it should have been Cromwell's view too? – or that he should have based his policy upon it?

[35] *CSP. Ven.* (*1655-1656*), p. 130 (Sagredo to Doge, 29 Oct. 1655); Brit. Mus., Add. MS. 38100, fos. 283, 297ᵛ (Bonde to Charles x, 12 October and 2 November 1655); *Urkunden und Actenstücke zur Geschichte des Kurfürsten Friedrich Wilhelm von Brandenburg. Politische Verhandlungen*, Berlin, 1877, [cited: *Urk. u. Act.*], vii, 741 (Schlezer to Elector, 16 March 1656); *cf.* Thurloe, vi, 99; De Witt, *Brieven*, i, 224-5 (Boreel to De Witt, 22 October 1655); and *cf.* Cromwell's speech to Stocker, 15/25 January 1654, in Abbott, iii, 159-60.

[36] 'He was harking back to the days of Elizabeth, not looking forward to the days of Anne'; 'The Protector was engaged in the politics of the past – in the Spanish Armada, the Gunpowder Plot, and the Thirty Years' War'; Abbott, *op. cit.* iii, 861, 893.

[37] *CSP. Dom.* (*1653-1654*), pp. 53, 90, 237, for the appointment of these committees; *ibid.*, pp. 73, 78, 105, 198, 254, for examples of their work.

[38] De Witt, *Brieven*, iii, 146 (Nieupoort to De Witt, 26 November 1655): *cf. CSP. Dom.* (*1654*), p. 156.

³⁹ *CSP. Dom.* (*1657–1658*), p. 27.
⁴⁰ Thurloe, iv, 683 (Nieupoort to De Witt, 26 November 1655); *cf.* Brit. Mus. Add. MS. 38100, fo. 20 (Barkman to Charles x, 26 September 1656: 'In these days, when all foreign affairs are at a stand, since *Concilium* does not sit').
⁴¹ Brit. Mus., Add. MS. 38100, fo. 372ᵛ (Bonde to Charles x, 9 May 1656: 'Thurloe monopolizes everything into his own hands'), *CSP. Ven.* (*1655–1656*), p. 26 (Paulucci to Sagredo, 1 March 1655: 'foreign ministers here find themselves condemned to exercise extraordinary patience and have to apply to a single new secretary of state, most difficult of access'). Schlezer writes of Thurloe as the man 'die hie fast alles vermag', and 'auf welchem fast alles liegt'; *Urk. u. Act.*, vii, 781, 785.
⁴² Brit. Mus., Add. MS. 38100, fo. 343, 360 (Bonde to Charles x, 1 February, 11 April 1656); *CSP. Ven.* (*1655–1656*), pp. 270, 286 (Giavarina to Doge, 6 October, 1 December 1656). It is clear, for instance, that the commissioners appointed to negotiate with Bonde did not know the course of the private negotiations with the Protector, still less the details of them, although two of them, at least, were members of the council: B. Whitelocke: *Memorials of the English Affairs* (1732), pp. 638, 641. There are some signs, too, that Cromwell may have been conducting a private foreign policy at the end of 1657, if van Beuningen's report that Meadowe offered an alliance to Denmark be true, see above, p. 165 and n. 3.
⁴³ See, e.g. *CSP. Dom.* (*1656–1657*), pp. 77, 140. Cromwell did speak Latin to Schlezer on one occasion; but Schlezer found it advisable when talking to the Protector to make his points twice over, 'und damit ichs desto verständlicher mache, mit noch schlechterem Latein, mengte zu desto klärer Expression hie und da etwas Engeländisch mit hinein', *Urk. u. Act.* vii, 745.
⁴⁴ Brit. Mus., Add. MS. 38100, fos. 106ᵛ–7 (Coyet to Charles x, 1 June 1655, for de Bye); Thurloe, iv, 698 (Petkum to Rosenvinge, 25 April 1656: 'I have sent continually for these three weeks to speak with the secretary of state, but he will never be at home'); And *cf.* Abbott, iii, 255, 286, 494, 679.
⁴⁵ Whitelocke, *Memorials*, p. 636: *cf.* the Swedish complaint of 19 June 1657, in Thurloe, vi, 361; or Nieupoort's appeal, *ibid.*, iv, 283.
⁴⁶ 'The court of England, by sheer force, has made itself the most dreaded and the most conspicuous in the world. Six ambassadors from crowned heads are now resident here, and others are expected', *CSP. Ven.* (*1655–1656*), p. 77 (Sagredo to Doge, 6 July 1655); 'As regards any idea of reciprocity, it is enough to state that there is not at present any English ambassador at any court in the world'; *ibid.*, p. 153 (same to same, 10 December 1655). 'I can come to no other conclusion than that those who rule this country have never transacted business before, especially foreign business, and that they therefore err much from lack of knowlege; a contributory factor being that they are much puffed up, rely on their advantageous situation and great power at sea . . . and are therefore somewhat slow', Brit. Mus., Add. MS. 38100, fo. 313 (Bonde to Charles x, 30 November 1655).
⁴⁷ *CSP. Ven.* (*1653–1654*) p.274 (Paulucci to Sagredo, 2 November 1654).
⁴⁸ Brit. Mus., Add. MS. 38100, fo. 361ᵛ (Bonde to Charles x, 18 April 1656). Whitelocke even got the name wrong, and habitually refers to it as

the treaty of Augsburg. For Thurloe's ignorance, see the complaint of van Beverningh (to De Witt, 6 February 1654), *Brieven aan Johan de Witt . . . bewerkt door Robert Fruin* (ed. N. Japikse) (Werken uitgeg. door het Hist. Genootschap . . . te Utrecht), 3rd ser., no. 42, Amsterdam, 1919, [cited: Japikse, *Brieven aan de Witt*], i, 86; or the curious lapse recorded by Friesendorff, 30 October 1657, in Samuel von Pufendorf, *Sju böcker om Konung Carl X Gustafs bragder* (trans. Adolf Hillman), Stockholm, 1913, iv, c. 84 (p. 390). Cromwell once ingenuously confessed to Schlezer that he was a little vague as to what was at stake in the Baltic, for 'die Oerter wären etwas weit abgelegen; hätte keine eigentliche Gemeinschaft mit diesen Landen; die Interesse, die jura, die privilegia wären etwas verwickelt und hieselbst nicht so gar wol bekant' – and Schlezer obligingly gave him a short lecture on the subject, illustrated by maps, *Urk. u. Act.*, vii, 734 (11 January 1655).

[49] E.g. Whitelocke, pp. 636, 640. As Paulucci wrote to Sagredo on 2 November, 1654: 'the English are so impressed with their own importance and their own usages that they expect any form of negotiation adopted by them to be admitted', *CSP. Ven.* (*1653–1654*), p. 274. The ceremonial at Cromwell's court is said to have been modelled (by Sir Oliver Fleming) on that used in the Swiss cantons: Alfred Stern, 'Oliver Cromwell und die evangelische Kantone der Schweiz', *Sybels Historische Zeitschrift*, xl (1878), p. 58.

[50] Brit. Mus., Add. MS. 38100, fo. 367 (Bonde to Charles x, 25 April 1656): *cf.* the confirmatory account in Whitelocke, p. 644. Masson was mistaken in suggesting that Whitelocke exaggerated Bonde's indignation in order that his own command of Latin might appear to advantage: Masson, *Life of Milton*, v, 256.

[51] 'He commonly goes to Hampton Court every Friday, and comes back again on Monday', Brit. Mus., Add. MS. 38100, fo. 224 (Bonde to Charles x, 27 July 1655). Bonde had the advantage over Nieupoort: he could play bowls; Nieupoort could not. For an account of one such week-end visit by the Swedes, see *Johan Ekeblads bref* (ed. N. Sjöberg), Stockholm, 1911, i, 414; and *Christer Bondes Diarium*, in *43rd Annual Report of the Deputy Keeper of the Public Records* (1882), App. II, p. 50.

[52] Brit. Mus., Add. MS. 38100, fo. 90 (Coyet to Charles x, 11/21 May 1656).

[53] Brit. Mus., Add. MS. 38100, fo. 372 (Bonde to Charles x, 9 May 1656). Whitelocke confirms this detail: the rule originated in an order of the Long Parliament: *Commons Journals*, iii, 384. On an earlier occasion Bonde wrote: 'I can scarcely believe that there is any place which can be worse for a great minister to act in than here, since he is cut off from all intercourse with all those who have any say in the conduct of affairs. To go and wait upon Thurloe in his own house, as the Dutch ambassador does, like any private suitor, I hold to be *indignum* for Your Majesty's great honour and reputation', *ibid.* fo. 188ᵛ (7 September 1655).

[54] For instance, Coyet arranged a secret meeting with Lord Lisle at his country house at Richmond (*ibid.*, fo. 90); and Charles Fleetwood, probably at Cromwell's instigation, called on Bonde at his house more than once, *ibid.*, fos. 199ᵛ, 293, 339.

[55] *CSP. Ven.* (*1655–1656*), p. 122; *Urk. u. Act.* vii, 741; and *cf.* Mazarin's opinion, A. Chéruel, *Histoire de France sous le Ministère de Mazarin,* Paris, 1882, ii, 352.

[56] Brit. Mus., Add. MS. 38100, fo. 363 (Bonde to Charles x, 18 April, 1656); *ibid.,* fo. 381v (same to same, 6 June 1656).

[57] *Cf.* the letter from Jane to Nicholas, 21 June 1655, where this possibility is discussed, *The Nicholas Papers* (The Camden Society), n.s. l (1892), ii, 349.

[58] De Witt realized that until the differences between France and England were settled there could be no Marine Treaty, since England used those differences as a pretext for privateering. For De Witt's anxiety for an Anglo-French settlement, see *Brieven van de Witt,* i, 169; Thurloe, iii, 2, 528; De Witt, *Brieven,* i, 173, 186, 188, 191. For Nieupoort's contribution to the treaty, *ibid.,* iii, 5, 22, 31, 36, 49–50, 59, 138–9; Brit. Mus., Add. MS. 38100, fos. 54, 64, 93.

[59] As Nicholas put it (to Hyde, 14/24 April 1653): '. . . the now ruling party among the States of the Province of Holland had much rather that the present government of the Rebels in England were well established than that the K. were restored, and would much rather contribute to that than to this, so as the Pride and insolency of the rebels would suffer them but to live and traffic quietly on any tolerable conditions', *Nicholas Papers,* ii, 8.

[60] *Mazarin,* vi, 111, 135.

[61] A striking and unfamiliar example of this is afforded by the unofficial soundings to the Dutch ambassadors as to the reactions of the 'well-intentioned' in Holland to the forthcoming attack on Spain – this at a time when everybody else in Europe was trying to guess where the blow was to fall; Japikse, *Brieven aan de Witt,* i, 95 (Beverningh and Nieupoort to De Witt, 8 August, n.s. 1654). For a general discussion of the political effects of the Orange-Stuart alignment, see P. Geyl, *Oranje en Stuart,* Utrecht, 1939, *passim,* and p. 149, where he writes that for Cromwell the Republic (as against the stadhouderate) 'de spil van heel zijn systeem moest sijn'. In March 1655 the Brandenburg minister in Holland wrote to the Elector that the Regents in Holland 'fast auf nichts gedenken dürfen, welches demselben [Cromwell] auch von weitem unangenehm sein möchte', Michael, *Cromwell,* ii, 156.

[62] For an important examination of this question of 'alliance or war?' as applied to Swedish-Danish relations in this century, see Georg Landberg, *Johan Gyllenstiernas nordiska förbundspolitik,* Uppsala, 1935, pp. 14–44. Professor Landberg's analysis could very well be applied to Anglo-Dutch relations.

[63] Fridericia, *Adelsvaeldens sidste Dage,* pp. 208–12.

[64] R. G. Albion, *Forests and Sea Power,* Cambridge, Mass., 1925, pp. 200 ff.

[65] For naval stores in 1653, see *CSP. Dom.* (*1653–1654*), pp. 2, 9, 125, 313; for attempts to organize alternative sources of supply, *ibid.,* pp. 22, 31; *CSP. Ven.* (*1653–1654*), pp. 5, 51–2.

[66] For the shortages and financial stringency, see *CSP. Dom.* (*1654*), p. 388; *ibid.,* (*1656–1657*), pp. 7, 15–16, 121, 138, 165, 241, 250; *ibid.,* (*1657–1658*), p. 316; *ibid.,* (*1658–1659*), p. 85; Thurloe, iv, 79–80; De Witt, *Brieven,* iii, 337–8, 340–1.

[67] *CSP. Dom.* (*1658–1659*), pp. 280, 290, 293, 298, and especially p. 305.
[68] Brit. Mus. Add. MS. 38100, fo. 393ᵛ (Bonde to Charles x, 4 July 1656).
[69] This was to be a main consideration in the mediation of the peace of Roskilde: Philip Meadowe, *Narrative of the principal Actions occurring in the wars betwixt Sweden and Denmark* (1677), pp. 16–19. The Dutch, of course, viewed the question similarly. It was because they feared that England might crush Denmark and gain control of the Sound that they were so anxious to secure the inclusion of Frederick III in the peace of Westminster: Fridericia, pp. 217–18. But the situation as regards naval stores was probably less serious for them than for England. It is true that during the war England was able to organize some sort of alternative source of supply by way of Hamburg; but the transit thence to an English port necessitated a naval convoy if the cargoes were to come safe home; while the Dutch ran their cargoes in shallow-draught craft sailing inshore, out of reach of the English navy. And during the first war they were able to bring home at least one large fleet direct from the Sound: Whitelocke, *Memorials*, pp. 563, 648. It seems, therefore, that Mr Hinton (*op. cit.*, p. 123) may be mistaken in suggesting that the closure of the Sound affected both sides equally.

[70] Benjamin Bonnel and Peter Coyet. They were not recalled on Bonde's arrival, but were left without either instructions or money, so that Bonnel, especially, was in great distress. Jokes were made about Charles's having four ministers simultaneously in one place: the Swedes became rather sensitive about it; Brit. Mus., Add. MS. 38100, fos. 159ᵛ, 176, 189ᵛ, 236ᵛ–7. Bonnel in the end had to ask Thurloe for money to get him home, Thurloe, iii, 655.

[71] For Bonde's embassy, see Pufendorf, ii, c. 88; P. Kalling, *Riksrådet Christer Bondes Ambassad till England 1655*, Uppsala, 1851; J. Levin Carlbom, *Sverige och England 1655–1657*, Göteborg, 1900; Ellen Fries, *Erik Oxenstierna*, Stockholm, 1889; *Johan Ekeblads bref*, i, 405–43; and, in English, the admirably clear and judicious summary in J. N. Bowman, *The Protestant Interest in Cromwell's foreign Relations*, Heidelberg, 1900. For Dutch policy, W. J. Kolkert, *Nederland en het Zweedsche Imperialisme*, Deventer, 1908, N. F. Noordam, *De Republiek en de Noordse Oorlog*, Assen, 1940, and N. Japikse, *Johan de Witt*, Amsterdam, 1915, pp. 132–45.

[72] De Witt, *Brieven*, iii, 47 (Nieupoort to De Witt, 23 April 1655).
[73] Brit. Mus., Add. MS. 38100, fo. 117 (Coyet to Charles x, 22 June 1655); *ibid.*, fo. 326ᵛ (Bonde to Charles x, 21 December 1655).
[74] Brit. Mus., Add. MS. 38100, fo. 224 (Bonde to Charles x, 27 July 1655).
[75] *Ibid.* fo. 276 (Bonde to Charles x, 28 September 1655).
[76] *Ibid.*, fo. 110ᵛ, 95–8ᵛ (Coyet to Charles x, 8 June, 18 May 1655).
[77] On this see Sven Göransson, *op. cit.*, p. 112.
[78] Pressure from the Swedish church forced Charles to issue a stringent Statute on Religion in 1655: Göransson, p. 105. For Dutch attempts to make political capital out of this, Brit. Mus., Add. MS. 38100, fo. 189, 267ᵛ (Bonde to Charles x, 7, 13 September 1655); De Witt, *Brieven*, iii, 107. The Great Elector employed similar tactics to alienate English sympathy from Sweden, *Urk. u. Act.*, vii, 797, 801. The Swedish council, foreseeing the

possible prejudice to Anglo-Swedish relations, had in September 1655 taken the bold step of suspending, on their own authority, and in the king's absence, the promulgation of the statute, *Svenska riksrådets protokoll*, xvi, 278.

[79] Brit. Mus., Add. MS. 38100, fos. 77–8 (Coyet to Charles x, 20 April 1656); *CSP. Ven. (1655–1656)*, p. 40 (Paulucci to Sagredo, 3 April 1655); Thurloe, iii, 50.

[80] *CSP. Ven. (1653–1654)* pp. 103, 116, 134, 147.

[81] *Ibid.*, p. 46 (Paulucci to Sagredo, 17 April 1655).

[82] Thurloe, iv, 369–70; v, 88; Brit. Mus., Add. MS. 38100, fo. 349 (Bonde to Charles x, 8 February 1656); Cromwell's letter of protest, 1 February 1656, printed in Abbott, iv, 91.

[83] *CSP. Dom. (1656–1657)*, p. 345; *cf.* Thurloe, vi, 101.

[84] *CSP. Dom. (1653–1654)*, p. 340; *ibid.*, (1654), pp. 202–3; Brit. Mus., Add. MS. 38100, fo. 212 (Bonde to Charles x, 2 May 1656).

[85] Thurloe, iii, 525–6; *State Papers collected by Edward, Earl of Clarendon*, Oxford, 1786, iii, 201, 220; *cf.* Brit. Mus., Add. MS. 38100, fo. 229 (Bonde to Charles x, 27 July 1655); '... in this place [London], where the Elector of Brandenburg, as guardian of the young prince in Holland, is considered as chief of the Royalists'; *ibid.* fo. 298ᵛ (Bonde to Charles x, 2 November 1655), for the malign influence of Amalia von Solms, and *cf. The Nicholas Papers*, iii, 103. See too De Witt, *Brieven*, iii, 47 (De Witt to Nieupoort, 23 April 1655) where he writes of the Elector that 'hy gepassioneert was in het interest van den Prince van Orange'. For the 3,000 men, Thurloe's remarks quoted in *ibid.*, iii, 112 (Nieupoort to De Witt, 27 August 1655). The Brandenburg envoy, Schlezer, was always struggling against suspicion on this account; and the alleged pro-Stuart sympathies of the Elector were made one of the pretexts for neglecting to inform Schlezer of Richard's accession; *Urk. u. Act.*, vii, 710–13, 732, 750, 752, 798. When Baillie wrote: 'I wish Brandenburgh may returne to his old postour, and not draw on himself next the Suedish armies, which the Lord forbid; *for, after Sweden, we love Brandenburgh next best* ...' (my italics), he was expressing a personal opinion, which was scarcely shared by his government. *The Letters and Journals of Robert Baillie*, ed. D. Laing, Edinburgh, 1842, iii, 371.

[86] De Witt, *Brieven*, iii, 96–9 (Nieupoort to De Witt, 6 August 1655).

[87] See e.g. *Mazarin*, vi, 423 (to d'Avaugour, 8 January 1655); De Witt, *Brieven*, i, 269 (Boreel to De Witt, 15 March 1656), or *ibid.*, 251–2, where Boreel writes to De Witt (14 January 1656): 'De grootste progressen insgelycks van den Koningh van Sweden, doen hopen, dat daer uyt volgen sal eene generaele rupture he van de Sweden met 't Huys van Oostenryck.' And see Thurloe, iii, 473, for similar intelligence from The Hague, 29 May 1655.

[88] *CSP. Dom. (1656–1657)*, pp. 50, 79, 95, 115; *CSP. Ven. (1655–1656)*, pp. 250, 260, for the presents to Bonde, and his knighthood; *ibid.*, pp. 215, 218, for the presents to Coyet, and his knighthood; Brit. Mus., Add. MS. 38100, fo. 30 (Barkman to Charles x, 24 October 1656) for ease of access to Protector. Nieupoort was given a rather smaller present on his taking leave at the end of 1657: *CSP. Dom. (1657–1658)*, p. 142. And *cf. ibid.* (1655), p. 315 (Nicholas to Jos. Jane, 4/14 September 1655).

[89] 'Bibit mihi sed secrete adeo Dñus Prot. in memoriam Regiae Maie-
statis, quod adeo contra morem ipsorum, sed nunc maximam amicitiam
annuebat', *Bondes Diarium*, p. 52.

[90] Brit. Mus., Add. MS. 38100, fo. 397.

[91] Brit. Mus., Add. MS. 38100, fo. 151ᵛ (Coyet to Charles x, 28 September 1655), 204ᵛ (Bonde to Charles x, 29 February 1656); *CSP. Dom.*
(*1655–1656*), pp. 221, 375 (for the desequestering of Cranston's estates);
ibid. (*1656–1657*), p. 71 (leave to enlist malignants); *CSP. Ven.* (*1655–1656*),
p. 106; Thurloe, v. 372 (Barkstead to Thurloe, 1 September 1656) for fear
of desertion to the enemy.

[92] Brit. Mus., Add. MS. 38100, fos. 200ᵛ–1, 207ᵛ, 357 (Bonde to Charles x,
15 February 1656, 7 March, 1656, 4 April 1656); *CSP. Ven.* (*1655–1656*),
pp. 221–2 (Giavarina to Doge, 26 March 1656), for story of Cromwell's
bursting into tears in council over the financial situation. Pufendorf (ii,
c. 92 (p. 137)) thought lack of money the main reason for the failure of the
negotiations. *Cf.* Thurloe to Pell, 19 June 1656: 'Our want of money to
support our own engagements is more than theirs [the Protestant cantons]
can be', Vaughan, i, 428.

[93] Brit. Mus., Add. MS. 38100, fo. 393ᵛ (Bonde to Charles x, 4 July 1656).

[94] *Ibid.* fos. 302ᵛ, 304 (same to same, 9 November 1655), where Bonde
narrates that Cromwell 'began to expound the Hollanders' interest in the
Prussian trade, that it was not wonderful if they were now a little troubled';
and later 'he repeated once more how necessary it was for the Dutch that
Danzig, which is their bread-basket, remain open to them'. *Ibid.* fos. 192ᵛ–
3ᵛ, 241, 263ᵛ (Bonde to Charles x, 4 Jan. 1656, 23 August 1655, 31 August
1655), 174ᵛ–5 (Coyet to Charles x, 7 December 1655); Thurloe, iv, 389.
De Witt was ready to give a reciprocal renunciation of particular commercial advantages in the Baltic: *Brieven*, iii, 110 (De Witt to Nieupoort, 27
August 1655); and the Dutch diplomats sent to negotiate the treaty of
Elbing with Charles x were instructed to make it plain that any alliance with
Sweden must provide for Charles' according equal advantages to England;
ibid., v, 423. The Eastland merchants were understandably anxious for the
specially favoured position which Bonde seemed to offer, and he incited
them to bring pressure to bear on Cromwell; Brit. Mus., Add. MS. 38100,
fo. 280ᵛ, 295ᵛ, (Bonde to Charles x, 5, 26 October 1655). The offer was
later withdrawn; *ibid.*, fos. 174ᵛ–5 (Coyet to Charles x, 7 December 1655).

[95] *Ibid.*, fos. 365, 370ᵛ, 388ᵛ, 396 (Bonde to Charles x, 25 April, 9 May,
20 June, 11 July 1656).

[96] *Ibid.*, fos. 365–6ᵛ, 370ᵛ.

[97] Text in Abbott, iii, 937. For Thurloe's embarrassment, see e.g. De Witt,
Brieven, iii, 143, 272 (Nieupoort to De Witt, 19 November 1655, 1 September
1656).

[98] In the hope of thereby making the treaty acceptable to England, *Urk.
u. Act.*, vii, 713–14. For the difficulties about making this treaty, see Kolkert,
Nederland en het Zweedsche Imperialisme, pp. 81–154.

[99] Thurloe, v, 285, 309–10; De Witt, *Brieven*, v, 435–6 (van Slingelandt to
De Witt, 5 September 1656).

[100] The mixture of motives which animated the Protector is well shown in

his remarks to Bonde on 4 February 1656. Bonde reports that he said that 'his intention had only been to do the Dutch a service [by insisting on their inclusion] if he could, or at least to show them that he was doing what he could for them, especially since he thought that that would be a means whereby unity between Protestants might be achieved and built up, and so that that state, which exists only by trade, might not be driven to adopt any adverse *consilia* – they had still many Papists among them', Brit. Mus., Add. MS. 38100, fo. 346 (Bonde to Charles x, 8 February 1656).

[101] Which was why Bonde believed that Charles x's treaty with Brandenburg would make his task in England easier, since it could be represented as a step towards more amicable relations between Sweden and Brandenburg's ally, the Dutch. Abbott (iv, 109) however, writes that the Swedish-Brandenburg treaty 'automatically eliminated any close alliance between Sweden and the United Provinces'. But if that were so, Bonde would hardly have regarded it as a help to his negotiation. And in fact Whitelocke (who is Abbott's authority at this point) contradicts Abbott's remark: Whitelocke wrote 'there was no Likelihood but there would also be a good Understanding between the King of Sweden and the United Provinces', *Memorials*, p. 634.

[102] Brit. Mus., Add. MS. 38100, fos. 193^v, 207^v–8 (Bonde to Charles x, 4 January 1656, 7 March 1656). Bonde early formed the view that fear of offending the Dutch was the main obstacle, 'since they are the nearest at hand to them, and if, from desperation, or because of the danger which they [the Dutch] fear in the Baltic, or that they perceive that they may look for no good from England – if then the Dutch should once more take up seriously the King of Scots' cause, then they [Cromwell's government] fear that the country, which is not well content with this government, may assist them, and thereby once more new and great troubles arising' (fo. 269^v, 14 September 1655). Or again: England will not offend the Dutch 'since their rupture with Spain and also *res angusta Domi* do not permit it, besides that *status Regiminis* itself, as far as I can ascertain, is very sick and in an ill condition, so that it is scarcely to be remedied without some serious resolution of my Lord Protector' (fo. 282, 12 October 1655).

[103] As Aitzema took care to point out: '. . . they [the Dutch] believe that the design of Sweden is to give all commerce to England; and their belief or unbelief is incurable, and they do not perceive, that the Orange party do studiously cast oyl into this fire, instigating the States of Holland and Amsterdam to irritate and offend the Swede more . . .', Thurloe, iv, 312–13.

[104] *Cf.* Schlezer's comment, *Urk. u. Act*, vii, 744; *CSP. Ven. (1655–1656)* p. 166 (Quirini to Doge, 19 January 1656), p. 184 (Sagredo to Doge, 3 March 1656); Thurloe, iv, 588–9; *Mazarin*, vii, 435 (to Bordeaux, 16 December 1656). Amsterdam's inclination to Spain came out very clearly in 1657; see E. C. Molsbergen, *Frankrijk en de Republiek der Vereenigde Nederlanden, 1648–1662*, Rotterdam, 1902, pp. 157, 160.

[105] See Birgit Grabe, 'Den nordiska allianstanken under holländsk-engelska kriget', *Historisk Tidskrift*, 2nd ser., i (1938), 272–87.

[106] Nieupoort certainly thought not; De Witt, *Brieven*, iii, 114 (to De Witt, 3 September 1655).

[107] The English draft treaty is in Thurloe, iv, 486–7; Bonde's disgusted comments in Brit. Mus., Add. MS. 38100, fos. 339 ff. (to Charles x, 1 February 1656).

[108] Brit. Mus., Add. MS. 38100, fo. 333^v (Bonde to Charles x, 11 January 1656); cf. De Witt, Brieven, iii, 170–3 (Nieupoort to De Witt, 14 January 1656).

[109] J. Levin Carlbom, Magnus Dureels negotiation i Köpenhamn. 1655–1657 Göteborg, 1910, pp. 40, 57.

[110] Ibid., p. 70 n. 2; cf. Thurloe, iv, 610.

[111] Svenska riksrådets protokoll, xvi, 744–5 (and cf. ibid., p. 747, where Erik Oxenstierna remarks 'It would be a good thing to keep England and Holland together'); Carlbom, Magnus Dureel, p. 252.

[112] For instance, Fleetwood, Lambert, Fiennes, Fleming, Monck, Whitelocke. The main supports of the Dutch interest in the council seem to have been Lawrence and Strickland: Strickland – like Cromwell himself – had relatives in the Dutch forces whose promotion was a matter of concern to him.

[113] Thurloe, v, 94, 226; CSP. Dom. (1655–1656), p. 207.

[114] Aitzema was not merely an English but a Swedish agent: Charles x paid him a pension of 1,200 riksdaler a year, and he supplied Appelboom with secret information: Kolkert, p. 111 and n. 1; Memoriën van den Zweedschen Resident Harald Appelboom (ed. G. W. Kernkamp) (Bijdr. en Mededeelingen van het Hist. Genootschap te Utrecht, vol. 26), Amsterdam, 1905, p. 317, n. 1. He seems also to have had Orange sympathies; Brieven van de Witt, i, 242.

[115] Thurloe, v, 748, 783 (Dutch ambassadors in Denmark to Ruysch, 11 January, n.s., 21 January, n.s. 1657); vi, 36 (Frederick iii to States-General, 1/11 February 1657). For a day-to-day account of the perplexing vacillations of Danish policy in the months before the outbreak, see the letters of Magnus Dureel, the Swedish minister in Copenhagen, printed (partly in précis) in a Danish translation in P. M. Becker, Samlinger til Danmarks Historie under Kong Fredrik den Tredies Regiering af udenlandske Archiver, Copenhagen, 1847, i; and the detailed study by J. Levin Carlbom, Magnus Dureels negotiation i Köpenhamn.

[116] For reports tending to show Dutch complicity, Thurloe, v, 287–8; vi, 9, 27, 60, 113, 227, 269, 359–60: and cf. CSP. Ven. (1657–1659), p. 28; for reports of a contrary tendency, Thurloe, v, 290–1; vi, 41, 309, 353–4 (this last a motion in the Estates of Holland deploring the Danish attack and urging prevention of any extension of the war).

[117] See, e.g. Becker, op. cit.. i, 107, 156; Svenska riksrådets protokoll, xvi, 429; xvii, 142.

[118] Thurloe, vi, 322, 370–1.

[119] De Witt, Brieven, iii, 391–2 (Nieupoort to De Witt, 29 July 1657).

[120] 'This warre is of greate consequence, especially because it is fomented by the Dutch, who favour the Dane, hopeing by his meanes to get the trade and comerce of the East-Sea' (Thurloe to Henry Cromwell, 28 July 1657: Thurloe, vi, 425).

[121] For van Beuningen's mission, see his despatches in Japikse, Brieven aan de Witt. C. Roldanus, Coenraad van Beuningen, Staatsman en Libertijn

('s Gravenhage, 1931), is thin on this episode. Appelboom was able to buy, at high prices, copies of van Beuningen's letters from Denmark, which proved that he was inciting Frederick III – 'with or without orders', as Appelboom remarked; *Memoriën van Harald Appelboom*, p. 324.

122 See, e.g. Fridericia, *Adelsvaeldens sidste Dage*, pp. 222–3; E. Gigas, *Grev Bernardino de Rebolledo, spansk Gesandt i Kjøbenhavn*, Copenhagen, 1883, p. 271; and *cf.* L. Beins, *Jan de Witt en zijne buitelandsche politiek tijdens den Vrede van Westminster en de Noordsche Kwestie*, Groningen, 1871, p. 18. For evidence of De Witt's attitude, see *Brieven van de Witt*, i, 386–7, 409–12; De Witt, *Brieven*, iii, 344–5; v, 497.

123 Japikse, *Brieven aan de Witt*, i, 357.

124 The so-called 'Amplification-Treaty'; see *Brieven van de Witt*, i, 416 (De Witt to van Beuningen, 16 March 1657); Thurloe, v, 243–4. It was eventually signed on 17 June.

125 *Ibid.*, i, 390; Fridericia, p. 244.

126 Carlbom, *Magnus Dureel*, pp. 191, 193.

127 For all this see Fridericia, *op. cit.*, pp. 222–4, 229, 232–3, 244, 248–9, 252–3, 290; E. Gigas, *Grev Bernardino de Rebolledo*, pp. 258–9, 267, 269–70, 274–5, 280. The Tsar was also inciting Frederick to attack Sweden: Becker, i, 136; *Svenska riksrådets protokoll*, xvii, 210; Gigas, p. 274.

128 But both he and Mazarin knew about Frederick III's intrigue with Vienna: *Clarendon State Papers*, iii, 337 (Lockhart to Thurloe, 21 April 1657), *cf.* Thurloe, vi, 259–60, 412; *Mazarin*, viii, 73 (Memorial for Gramont and Lionne, 29 July 1657).

129 By 1660 Thurloe was certain of Dutch complicity: the Dutch, he writes, 'engaged that King [of Denmark] contrary to his own interests, to invade the King of Sweden in his duchy of Bremen': *Somers Tracts*, vi, 332. Frederick III had been levying mercenaries in the expectation of being able to attack Sweden with the backing of a Habsburg alliance; and when the Emperor held off it seems that war was decided on as the only means of providing for these troops – a curiously similar situation to that in which Charles X had found himself two years earlier; Fridericia, p. 251; Sten Bonnesen, *Karl X Gustav*, Malmö, 1958, p. 255, quoting Frederick III's letter to his council of 17 April 1657, and their reply of 22 April, giving him a free hand to declare war.

130 E.g. *CSP. Dom.* (*1656–1657*) pp. 249, 340; Thurloe, vi, 60, 87, 113, 205; and *cf. CSP. Ven.* (*1657–1659*), pp. 5, 57, 73, which suggests that Giavarina believed it. On 3 February 1657 Thurloe wrote to Henry Cromwell: 'I feare the Dutch have noe very good intentions towards us; they are prepareinge a fleet, and are alsoe upon a private treatie with Spayne, and its more than probable they may be engaged by Spayne to become our enemies', Thurloe, vi, 38. For Dutch denials, De Witt, *Brieven*, iii, 313, 332.

131 De Witt, *Brieven*, iii, 357 (Nieupoort to De Witt, 27 April 1657), for Thurloe's anxiety about Portugal.

132 For the question of the 'Elucidations', see Ellen Fries, *Bidrag till kännedomen om Sveriges och Nederländernas diplomatiska förbindelser under Karl X Gustafs regering*, Uppsala, 1883, pp. 53–62, 69–72, 77–80, 86–8; Noordam, *De Republiek en de Noordse Oorlog*, pp. 25–40.

[133] De Witt, *Brieven*, 346, 349; Thurloe, vi, 148, 214, 243; Molsbergen, *op. cit.*, pp. 154–74; Beins, pp. 15–16. Other causes of friction were the seizure of two English ships by four Dutch in the Gulf of Guinea; and the failure of Bradshaw's mission to the Tsar, which seems to have been due to the machinations of Dutch and Danish agents; Pufendorf, iv, c. 50 (p. 344).

[134] *Mazarin*, vii, 467 (to Bordeaux, 18 May 1657); *cf. ibid.*, 463.

[135] *Ibid.*, vi, 141 (to de Baas, 27 March 1654).

[136] The *projet* is printed in J. Du Mont, *Corps universel diplomatique*, Amsterdam, 1728, vi, 178–9. And see Chéruel, *op. cit.*, iii, 60, n. 1. Rumours of the existence of this treaty, and of its nature, soon leaked out: at the end of June van Beuningen was relaying them to De Witt – no doubt on the strength of information from Rebolledo, since he added that a copy of the treaty was said to have fallen into Spanish hands; Japikse, *Brieven aan de Witt.*, i, 396.

[137] Thurloe, vi, 149 (Lockhart to Thurloe, 28 March 1657).

[138] *Mazarin*, vii, 452 (to Bordeaux, 28 April 1657); and *cf. ibid.*, 465 (to de Thou, 17 May); De Witt, *Brieven*, iii, 365 (Nieupoort to De Witt, 11 May 1657).

[139] Though Chéruel accepted Mazarin's mere assertion of it as 'proof': Chéruel, *Histoire de France sous ... Mazarin*, iii, 59. *Cf.* Lockhart's letter to Thurloe of 27 May 1657 (misdated 27 March by Vaughan), where he writes: 'I hope the business shall come to an accommodation'; Vaughan, ii, 135.

[140] *CSP. Ven.* (*1657–1659*), p. 79 (Giavarina to Doge, 6 July, n.s. 1657).

[141] De Witt, *Brieven*, iii, 389–90 (De Witt to Nieupoort, 20 June 1657), 396 (Nieupoort to De Witt, 13 July), 398–9 (same to same, 20 July), 401 (De Witt to Nieupoort, 27 July); Thurloe, vi, 380 (de Thou to Bordeaux, 13 July, n.s.); *Mazarin*, viii, 82 (to Brienne, 31 July).

[142] De Witt, *Brieven*, iii, 398, 401.

[143] De Witt, *Brieven*, iii, 425–6; Thurloe, vi, 477–8 (Nieupoort to Ruysch, 31 August, n.s.); *CSP Ven.* (*1657–1659*), p. 131–2.

[144] Karl Mellander, 'Svensk-portugesiska förbindelser under Sveriges stormaktstid', *Historisk Tidskrift*, 1st ser., xlvii (1927), 387–8; Edgar Prestage, *The Diplomatic Relations of Portugal with France, England and Holland from 1640 to 1688*, Watford, 1925, pp. 136, 139.

[145] Thurloe, vi, 559.

[146] De Witt, *Brieven*, iii, 439 (Nieupoort to De Witt, 2 November 1657); *Mazarin*, viii, 236 (to Bordeaux, 13 December 1657). For the Portuguese question see also De Witt, *Brieven*, iii, 442 (De Witt to Nieupoort, 16 November), 418–20, 425–7, 439; Thurloe, vi, 493; *CSP. Ven.* (*1657–1659*), pp. 110, 146.

[147] De Witt, *Brieven*, iii, 431 (Nieupoort to De Witt, 5 October 1657); *cf.* Thurloe, vi, 620 (Thurloe to Lockhart, 19–29 November 1657); Japikse, *Brieven aan de Witt*, i, 418–19 (van Beuningen to De Witt, 13–23 December 1657).

[148] On 10 March 1657 the Swedish council read a letter from Fleetwood to Dureel in which he reported that Cromwell had agreed to write again to Frederick III, and 'will send a squadron of twenty ships into the Baltic to

aid Sweden, if need be, and he presumes that the King of Denmark, in regard that the Dutch fleet last year went through the Sound, will have no ground for hindering him, the Protector, from passage through it', *Svenska riksrådets protokoll*, xvii, 52.

[149] Becker, i, 166; Carlbom, *Magnus Dureel*, pp. 208, n. 3, 252, n. 2.

[150] Carlbom, *Magnus Dureel*, p. 314, *cf. CSP. Ven.* (*1657–1659*), p. 116.

[151] He was simultaneously trying (in vain) to induce Mazarin to pay him nearly a million *riksdaler*, alleged to be still owing on account of France's old war-subsidy: Bonnesen, pp. 400–1.

[152] Pufendorf, iv, c. 79 ff. (pp. 380 ff.), for what follows. Guernsey Jones, *The diplomatic Relations between Cromwell and Charles X*, is based mainly on Pufendorf. A more modern, and better, account (which does something to disentangle Pufendorf's difficult chronology) is in C. G. Weibull, *Freden i Roskilde*, Malmö, 1958. Best of all (though in other respects now superseded) is J. Levin Carlbom. *Karl X från Weichseln till Bält 1657: Tåget över Bält och freden i Roskilde 1658*, Stockholm, 1910. Fleetwood's letter of 13 January is printed in translation in Abbott, iv, 383, and in the original German in Michael, ii, 223–4.

[153] *Brieven van de Witt*, i, 381; Brit. Mus., Add. MS. 38100, fo. 302, where Bonde reports mentioning the report of this proposal to Cromwell.

[154] Michael, ii, 168–9.

[155] Public Record Office, State Papers, Foreign, Sweden, SP. 95/5B/152 has a 'Proposition in order to a Treaty with Sweden', of which the final clause runs: 'That Prouision be made for the English to enioy their former priuileges in state [*sc.* Stade] or other Cittyes in the Dukedome of Bremen if they think fitt to fix there the residence of any incorporated society of English merchants'. Mr Hinton makes it probable that the proposition may have been drawn up by the Eastland merchants; but he appears to prefer a date some time in 1658, *op. cit.*, p. 135.

[156] Pufendorf, iv, c. 79 (p. 380). *Cf.* Per Brahe's remark that Bremen would be 'a bridle for the Jute', and would cut his line of communications: Yngve Lorents, *Efter Brömsebrofreden. Svenska och danska förbindelser med Frankrike och Holland, 1645–1649*, Uppsala, 1916, p. 100. It was generally assumed by Denmark's backers that the forthcoming attack on Sweden would be directed, not against Småland, but southward against Bremen, which had indeed until 1645 been in Frederick III's possession: Gigas, *Rebolledo*, p. 301; and this is in fact what the Danes did; Pufendorf, iv, c. 71 (p. 369).

[157] Weibull, p. 16.

[158] Abbott, iv, 410.

[159] *Cf. Mazarin*, vii, 451, 490 (to Bordeaux, 14 April, 2 June 1657); Abbott, iv, 352–4; Pufendorf, iv, c. 65 (p. 364); Gigas, p. 290.

[160] Pufendorf, iv, c. 79 (p. 381); Weibull, p. 23.

[161] Weibull, p. 17.

[162] *Urk. u. Act.* vii, 767 (15 May o.s.), 771 (5 June o.s.), 774 (19 June o.s.), when Cromwell told him that 'er denn ziemlich erschöpft wäre, und müsste er dasjenige gegen mir repetiren, was er dem Königl. Schwedischen Ambassadeur zum öftern remonstriret hätte, dass er nämlich gnug zu thun hätte,

die Flotte im Gang und *esse* zu halten.' It is true that Cromwell was at this time trying to dodge an inconvenient request from the Great Elector for a subsidy of £50,000, but he was none the less telling the truth; Michael, ii, 159–60.

[163] Weibull, p. 17.

[164] Pufendorf, iv, cc. 81–2 (pp. 382, 384–5); Weibull, pp. 24–6; Carlbom, *Karl X Gustav från Weichseln till Bält*, pp. 141–2. Friesendorff's instructions were dated 3 August, o.s. A copy fell into Danish hands, and its production caused a sensation at the congress of Oliva in 1660; Carlbom, *Magnus Dureel*, pp. 316, n. 3; 317, n. 2.

[165] Carlbom, *Karl X Gustav från Weichseln till Bält*, pp. 142, 345, 349.

[166] *Ibid.*, pp. 142, 346.

[167] Carlbom, *op. cit.*, pp. 345–6.

[168] *Ibid.*, p. 341; Thurloe, vi, 478–9.

[169] Carlbom, *op. cit.*, p. 337; Thurloe, vi, 674.

[170] Pufendorf, iv, c. 81 (p. 383).

[171] Carlbom, *Magnus Dureel*, p. 318.

[172] Jephson was ordered not to mention Bremen unless Charles did so, and if the cession of the duchy were offered he was to find out what the possibilities of defence were before committing himself: Thurloe, vi, 478–9. But the matter was in fact raised in the course of his discussions with Charles, though it is not clear by whom. On 16 November the Swedish council considered a letter from the king, dated 27 September, 'concerning the duchy of Bremen, whether H.M. can give it to the Protector as a pledge for the money subsidy which the English envoy on his principal's behalf *has promised H.M.* [my italics], or otherwise gratify him in the trade to the Baltic, etc.', *Svenska riksrådets protokoll*, xvii, 277. It looks as though Jephson had exceeded his instructions.

[173] J. Levin Carlbom, *Karl X Gustav från Weichseln till Bält*, p. 337.

[174] E.g. two letters of Thurloe written on 2 October, immediately before the crisis blew up (Thurloe, vi. 545–7).

[175] Thurloe, vi, 582 (Thurloe to Montagu, draft, 9 October 1657). It may be noted that when a Dutch fleet was sent to Danzig in 1656, Cromwell took it calmly enough: circumstances had altered. In 1656, indeed, Thurloe had been relieved to have the Dutch out of the way: there had been too many uncomfortable scuffles in home waters between hot-tempered commanders: Thomas Carte, *A Collection of Original Letters and Papers concerning the Affairs of England* (1739), ii, 113. (Thurloe to Montagu, 26 August 1657).

[176] Their letters to Charles x are printed in *Handlingar rörande Skandinaviens Historia*, Stockholm, 1818, v, 205–20. Bonnesen (*op. cit.*, p. 404), suggests that Cromwell was spurred to action by bad news from Europe: the fall of Cracow, the failure of Rákóczy, the desertion of Brandenburg. If so, it is difficult to see why he changed his mind again so soon.

[177] Pufendorf, iv, c. 84 (p. 377); Weibull, p. 43; Carlbom, *Karl X Gustav från Weichseln till Bält*, pp. 355–6. Thurloe told Jephson that this unhopeful project was 'but an essay, and is intended only as a foundation to begin upon'; E. Jenks, 'Some Correspondence of Thurloe and Meadowe', *EHR*,

vii (1892), 726–7, and added: 'his [Charles x's] ministers here propound things almost impossible for us to doe as that his Highness should land an army in Westphalia and pay hym a certayne sum of money every year for his carrying on a warre against the King of Hungary in Germany with some other things as hard as these without being *instructed* for ought I perceive to agree to anything yt hath a *reciprocation in it* or may be for the interests of this state either in trade or otherwise. . . .'

[178] Bonnesen, p. 408, where a different explanation of Cromwell's possible motives is suggested.

[179] There is no suggestion of the sort in Meadowe's Proposition to Frederick iii, which is printed in Joseph Weiss 'Zur Vermittlungspolitik Cromwells zwischen Dänemark und Schweden im Jahre 1657', *Historisches Jahrbuch*, xiv, 612–13. Van Beuningen had the story from Gersdorf, who was in a position to know; but both of them had ample motives for distorting the truth: *Brieven van de Witt*, i, 441–2; Japikse, *Brieven aan de Witt*, i, 412, 414–15. Denmark accepted English mediation in principle on 25 September, n.s.: Thurloe, vi, 515; Meadowe, p. 20.

[180] Thurloe, vi, 609, 10 November 1657.

[181] They are printed in Abbott, iv, 605–6.

[182] *Cf.* De Witt, *Brieven*, iii, 438 (Nieupoort to De Witt, 26 October), v, 522 (van Dorp to De Witt, 15 November). 'The envoy extraordinary of England [Jephson] recently allowed us to see from his conversation that his master has a jealousy of the design of Sweden, and would be unwilling to see her make herself mistress of *Dominium Maris Baltici*, but was of opinion that the Kings must be kept in balance against each other', and *cf.* De Witt's reply, *ibid.*, p. 538. Giavarina realized this very early; *CSP. Ven. (1657–1658)*, p. 107 (Giavarina to Doge, 7 September n.s. 1657).

[183] *CSP Dom. (1657–1658)*, 169, 222; Thurloe, vi, 676; J. Beresford, *The Godfather of Downing Street* (1925), p. 79. The departure of Nieupoort, at the height of an international crisis, is said to have made a bad impression; De Witt, *Brieven*, v, 528 (van Dorp to De Witt, 13 December 1657).

[184] *Brieven van de Witt*, i, 445 (De Witt to van Beuningen, 30 November 1657).

[185] *Memoriën van . . . Harald Appelboom*, p. 324, n. 1, where Appelboom reports (14 December 1657) De Witt as saying of van Beuningen that 'hij is au bout de son latin, en zit daar in Denemarken te schreeuwen als een uil'.

[186] Thurloe, vi, 672–3.

[187] *Ibid.*, vi, 766.

[188] *Ibid.*, vi, 790–1. This at a moment when Thurloe was being urged by correspondents (not least by Aitzema) to exploit the Swedish victory to collar the Baltic trade from the Dutch: *ibid.*, pp. 796, 815.

[189] *CSP. Dom. (1658–1659)*, p. 244; *Mazarin*, viii, 311–12 (to Bordeaux, 15 February 1658); Thurloe, vi, 788 (de Thou to States-General, 18 February n.s. 1658), 811 (Downing to Lockhart, 28 February n.s.), 818–19 (Downing to Lockhart, 28 February n.s.), 818–19 (Downing's Memorial to States-General [5 March n.s. 1658]); Molsbergen, pp. 178–9.

[190] Carlbom, *op. cit.*, p. 358.

CROMWELL AND THE BALTIC

¹⁹¹ T. Carlyle, *Letters and Speeches of Oliver Cromwell* (ed. S. C. Lomas), iii, 168. Even Firth could write: 'The Protector's conclusion was that England must intervene to prevent the King of Sweden from being crushed, and be ready to back him, not only with its fleet, but by landing a force on the continent', Firth, *Oliver Cromwell*, p. 386.

¹⁹² Carlbom, *op. cit.*, p. 354. *Mercurius Politicus*, 26 November 1657, p. 128.

¹⁹³ *Ibid.*, pp. 342, 356; Thurloe, vi, 629.

¹⁹⁴ Thurloe, vi, 802 (Meadowe to Thurloe, 14 February 1658).

¹⁹⁵ Jenks, pp. 732, 734. Meadowe seems also to have taken bribes from Charles x: Weibull, p. 89. The most important concession that he secured was the insertion of the word 'hostile' in the clause prohibiting the entry of foreign warships into the Baltic: this addition made possible the entry of the Dutch or English fleets as auxiliaries, Weibull, p. 141. For other efforts of Meadowe to soften the terms, see *ibid.*, pp. 102, 123, 125 ff.; and Meadowe's own *Narrative*, pp. 58–62. The Swedes 'accidentally' omitted 'hostile' from their copy of the treaty, but later put it in again, Japikse, *Brieven aan de Witt*, i, 447 (van Beuningen to De Witt [3/13 August 1658]).

¹⁹⁶ Thurloe, vi, 875 (van Beuningen Ruysch, 24 March n.s. 1658).

¹⁹⁷ Pufendorf, v, cc. 74–5 (pp. 501–3). On 4 March the Swedish envoys were told that Cromwell, though he would not advise Charles to attack Austria, was prepared if he did so to 'assist him as far as their circumstances allowed, adding that they had not the slightest ambition to appear with an army in Germany, which (moreover) would be contrary to their interest and beyond their powers', *ibid.*, p. 505.

¹⁹⁸ Pufendorf, v, cc. 76–9 (pp. 505–9), c. 81 (p. 512); Jenks, pp. 733–4 (Meadowe to Thurloe, 8 June 1658), 737–8 (same to same, 29 June 1658). At a meeting of the Swedish council on 29 March 1658, Charles was still hopeful of financial aid: he told them (according to one version of the minutes) that 'England had incited H.M. to engage himself against Austria, as also against Spain, and offered to advance the means': Lennart Thanner, 'Rådsprotokollen år 1658: Några källkritiska bidrag', *Karolinska förbundets årsbok* (1959), 30. Charles x's later comment to Meadowe on the Protector's financial straits was to the effect that he ought to have accepted the crown: Jenks, pp. 739–40 (Meadowe to Thurloe, 12 July).

¹⁹⁹ Lockhart wrote to Thurloe on 27 February 1658: 'The propositions for the general peace are pressed here very hotly, the Cardinal's last answer was, that France and its allies (amongst which England is the first) were ready to treat . . .', *Clarendon State Papers*, iii, 389. But he had been afraid of such a peace since 1656, Chéruel, *Histoire de France sous . . . Mazarin*, iii, 25–7.

²⁰⁰ See T. Gihl, *Sverige och Västmakterna under Karl X Gustafs andra krig med Danmark*, Uppsala, 1913, pp. 42–3; Bonnesen, pp. 473–5.

²⁰¹ Pufendorf, v, c. 78 (p. 508). Meadowe certainly did, *Narrative*, pp. 79–80.

²⁰² See Chéruel, *Histoire de France sous . . . Mazarin*, iii, 114, n. 5, 119. It is perhaps significant that Mazarin had now abandoned the policy of inciting Charles to attack Austria, on the ground that Spain desired a conflagration in Germany as the best hope of keeping her war against France alive,

Mazarin, viii, 251–61, 286–7. It was important, moreover, that France should not seem to be contributing to a breach of the peace in the Empire, which it was the object of the League of the Rhine to preserve.

²⁰³ This is Firth's phrase: Firth, *Last Years*, ii, 254–6.

²⁰⁴ Meadowe, *Narrative*, pp. 67–8.

²⁰⁵ 'An insane proposal' writes Gardiner, with unwonted asperity: Gardiner, *Oliver Cromwell*, p. 305. Meadowe's instructions in S.P. 95/5A/73, 9 April 1658; *cf.* Jenks, p. 728 (Thurloe to Meadowe, 26 March 1658); De Witt, *Brieven*, v, 551–2 (van Dorp to De Witt, 17 June 1658); Japikse, *Brieven aan de Witt*, i, 437, for van Beuningen's sour comment to De Witt. It may be that Cromwell was really alarmed by the prospect of a Baltic dominated by the Habsburgs and Poland, and in which English and Dutch traders would be discriminated against: it is at all events certain that Charles x's agents in England had done their best to alarm him on this account, Carlbom, *Karl Gustav från Weichseln till Bält*, p. 404.

²⁰⁶ Pufendorf, v, c. 82 (p. 513).

²⁰⁷ Lauritz Weibull, 'Från Kiel till København i augusti 1658', *Scandia*, ii (1929), 296, 301, 313. Meadowe professed to have expected it, all the same: Jenks, pp. 741–2.

²⁰⁸ Thurloe, vii, 31, 49.

²⁰⁹ Jenks, pp. 729–30 (Meadowe to Thurloe, 21 April 1658), 735–6 (same to same, 22 June); Thurloe, vi, 838 (same to same, 2 March); Japikse, *Brieven aan de Witt*, i, 423 and n. 2, 425, for other examples of van Beuningen's stories. And see Fries, *Bidrag*, p. 87, n. 7, and C. Weibull, *Freden i Roskilde*, pp. 149–50, for his intrigues with Habsburg diplomats.

²¹⁰ Thurloe, vi, 851 (Downing to Thurloe, 17 March n.s.), 873 (Thurloe to Downing, 12 March): 'you may carry it as if this state were enclyned to it; and so it may be upon the matter, if considered: but surely our present business is to pause a little, to see how they will serve us in the matters of the East-Sea'.

²¹¹ *Brieven van de Witt*, ii, 46–53 (De Witt to Cornelis de Graaff, 29 July 1658); *CSP. Ven.* (*1657–1658*), p. 223 (Giustinian to Doge, 14 July 1658); and see Fries, *Bidrag*, p. 85.

²¹² De Witt, *Brieven*, iii, 448 (Nieupoort to De Witt, 9 August 1658); *CSP. Ven.* (*1657–1659*), pp. 235–7 (Giavarina to Doge, 23 August 1658). See also *CSP. Dom.* (*1658–1659*), p. 8: petition of commanders of ships in and about London for full enforcement of Navigation Act against the Dutch. Mazarin may have been making mischief too; *Clarendon State Papers*, iii, 399 (Lockhart to Thurloe, 10 April).

²¹³ *Brieven van de Witt*, i, 458–9 (De Witt to van Beuningen, 12 July 1658). For a discussion of De Witt's policy at this period, see Noordam, *De Republiek en de Noordse Oorlog*, pp. 56–63; Gihl, pp. 35–41, 51–3.

²¹⁴ Thurloe, vii, 333 (Downing to Thurloe, 3–13 August 1658).

²¹⁵ De Witt, *Brieven*, iii, 451 (De Witt to Nieupoort, 23 August), 455 (Nieupoort to De Witt, 30 August n.s. 1658).

²¹⁶ Thurloe, vii, 293, 296. Cromwell had made a similar gesture with reference to Dutch ships detained by Montagu in the Channel: *CSP. Ven.* (*1657–1659*), p. 224.

[217] *Brieven van de Witt*, ii, 59–62 (De Witt to Cornelis de Graaff, 18 August 1658).

[218] *Ibid.*, *loc. cit.*; De Witt, *Brieven*, iii, 451 (De Witt to Nieupoort, 23 August 1658). *Cf.* the letter of De Witt to De Graaff of 8 January 1658, where he suggests that it would be cheaper to buy off Charles x's claims by paying his war expenses, rather than run into the incalculable cost of themselves fighting a war: *Brieven van de Witt*, ii, 40–3. According to Appelboom, the suggestion originated with van Beverningh, who coupled it with the proposal that it should be stipulated that Charles should use the money to fight Austria, and so advance 'the Protestant cause', Fries, *Bidrag*, p. 83; Bonnesen, pp. 399–400.

[219] Even van Beuningen could write (to De Witt, 10/20 July 1658): 'Maer ik bedriegh my seer, indien *Protector* niet immers soo sorgvuldigh is, om met *Haer Hoog Mog.* in geen verwyderingh te komen, als wy niet behoeven te sijn; ook soude den *Coning van Vranckrijck* niet noders sien als dat, soolangh hy nogh niet volkomen meester is in *overheerde provinciën* [*sc.* Belgium]; Japikse, *Brieven aan de Witt*, i, 444.

[220] Gihl, p. 62.

[221] De Witt, *Brieven*, iii, 458 (Nieupoort to De Witt, 9 September n.s. 1658), *CSP. Ven.* (*1657–1659*), p. 241; *cf.* Nieupoort's comment: 'ontbrak het haer niet meer aen de maght, als de wille, wij souden al over lange geruïneert wesen', De Witt, *Brieven*, iii, 459 (Nieupoort to De Witt, 13 September n.s., 1658).

[222] Unless the obscure wording and chronology of Thurloe's memorandum at this point (*Somers Tracts*, vi, 333) apply to Oliver rather than to Richard.

[223] Firth, *Last Years*, ii, 290.

[224] Meadowe, p. 120.

[225] *Ibid.*, pp. 122–3.

[226] As Sir Dudley North wrote: 'no people ever yet grew rich by policies; it is peace, industry and freedom that brings trade and wealth and nothing else', quoted in Hinton, p. 112; and *cf. ibid.*, pp. 19, 62. As Mr Hinton elsewhere points out, the decisive expansion of English trade to the Baltic came only with the opportunities presented by English neutrality in the years 1675–8; and would have been impossible without a large native-owned and -built mercantile marine, suited to the trade – which does not seem to have existed in Cromwell's time, *ibid.*, p. 108–11. Grauers makes the same point, Sven Grauers, 'Sverige och den första engelska navigations-akten', in *Historiska studier tillägnade Ludvig Stavenow*, Stockholm, 1924, p. 215; and Appelboom made it in regard to Sweden, in the memorandum which he drew up for Gustav Bonde in 1664, *Memoriën van Harald Appelboom*, pp. 343–67.

[227] Above, p. 179, n. 48. *Cf.* Gardiner's judgment, 'Oliver's whole scheme [for the Baltic] can only be described as the product of consummate ignorance', *Oliver Cromwell*, p. 298.

[228] As Clarendon also did, Wilson, *op. cit.*, p. 108. As Cromwell said to the Dutch commissioners in July 1653: 'He knew well that the industry of the Dutch ought not to be prevented. . . . The world was wide enough for both', translation in Abbott, iii, 73.

[229] Brit. Mus., Add. MS. 38100, fo. 275 (Bonde to Charles x, 28 September 1655): 'he then expounded, as in great confidence, *fundamenta* of all his designs, which looked to nothing other than *libertatem religionis* and freedom of trade.'

[230] Wilson, pp. 16–17.

[231] Pufendorf attributes to Downing, in September 1658, the remark that Cromwell had no idea of obtaining special privileges for England in the Baltic, since the Baltic trade 'was for England of subordinate importance, since they could obtain all the commodities which hitherto they had been wont to fetch from the Baltic (including masts) from New England': Pufendorf, v. c. 102 (p. 541). This no doubt was a characteristic swagger, put on to impress the foreigner; but what Downing said of Cromwell was true.

[232] As Guernsey Jones maintained, *op. cit.*, p. 69.

[233] *CSP. Ven.* (*1657–1659*), p. 234 (Giavarina to Doge, 23 August 1658).

[234] Brit. Mus., Add. MS. 38100, fos. 210ᵛ, 213ᵛ, 382ᵛ (Bonde to Charles x, 14 March, 2 May, 6 June 1656).

7

The Military Revolution, 1560–1660[1]

It is a historical commonplace that major revolutions in military techniques have usually been attended with widely ramifying consequences. The coming of the mounted warrior, and of the sword, in the middle of the second millennium B C; the triumph of the heavy cavalryman, consolidated by the adoption of the stirrup, in the sixth century of the Christian era; the scientific revolution in warfare in our own day – these are all recognized as major turning-points in the history of mankind. The period in the history of the art of war with which I shall try to deal in this lecture may seem from this point of view to be of inferior importance. But it brought changes which may not improperly be called a military revolution; and that revolution, when it was accomplished, exercised a profound influence upon the future course of European history. It stands like a great divide separating mediaeval society from the modern world. Yet it is a revolution which has been curiously neglected by historians. The experts in military history have mostly been content to describe what happened, without being overmuch concerned to trace out broader effects; while social historians have not been very apt to believe that the new fashions in tactics, or improvements in weapon-design, were likely to prove of much significance for their purposes. Some few sociologists, indeed, have realized the importance of the problem; but historians tend to find their expositions a trifle opaque, and their conclusions sometimes insecurely grounded. Yet it remains true that purely military developments, of a strictly technical kind, did exert a lasting influence upon society at large. They were the agents and auxiliaries of constitutional and social change; and they bore a main share of responsibility for the coming of that new world which was to be so very unlike the old.[2]

The military revolution which fills the century between 1560 and 1660 was in essence the result of just one more attempt to solve the perennial problem of tactics: the problem of how to combine missile weapons with close action; how to unite hitting-power, mobility, and defensive strength. And the solution offered by the reforms of Maurice of Orange and Gustav Adolf was a return, under the inspiration of Vegetius, Aelian, and Leo the Isaurian, to linear formations.[3] In place of the massive, deep, unwieldy squares of the Spanish *tercio*, or the still larger but more irregular blocks of the Swiss column, they relied upon a multiplicity of small units ranged in two or three lines, and so disposed and armed as to permit the full exploitation of all types of weapon. Maurice used these new formations wholly for defence; but it was the great achievement of Gustav Adolf to apply them with brilliant success in offensive actions too. Moreover, he restored to cavalry its proper function, by for-bidding the caracole; he made it charge home with the sword; and he insisted that it rely for its effect upon the impact of the weight of man and horse. And lastly, as a result of his experi-ments in gunfounding, he was able to arm his units with a light and transportable field-piece designed to supply close artillery support for infantry and cavalry alike.

These were fundamental changes; and they were essentially tactical in nature. But they entailed others of much larger implication. They entailed, for instance, a new standard in the training and discipline of the ordinary soldier. The soldier of the Middle Ages had been, on the whole, an individualist; and he (and his horse) had been highly trained over a prolonged period. The coming, first of firearms, then of the Swiss column, put an end to this state of affairs. The mercenary in the middle of a pike-square needed little training and less skill: if he inclined his pike in correct alignment and leaned heavily on the man in front of him, he had done almost all that could be required of him.[4] So too with the musketeer: a certain dexterity in loading – it could take as many as ninety-eight words of command to fire a musket – a certain steadiness in the ranks, sufficed to execute the countermarch, since no one could reasonably demand of a musket that it should be aimed with accuracy. The training of a bowman, schooled to be a dead shot at a distance, would be wasted on so imperfect an instrument as an arquebus or a wheel-lock pistol; and the pike, unlike the lance, was not an individual weapon at all. One reason why firearms drove out the bow and the lance was precisely this, that they economized on training.[5] Moreover, deep formations, whether of horse or foot, dispensed with the need for a large trained corps of officers, and required a less high morale, since it is difficult to run away with fifteen ranks behind you.

The reforms of Maurice inaugurated a real, and a lasting, revolution in these matters. Maurice's small units had to be highly trained in manœuvre; they needed many more officers and NCOs to lead them. The tactics of Gustav Adolf postulated a vastly improved fire-discipline, and long practice in the combination of arms. The sergeant-major of the *tercio* had been well content if he mastered the art of 'embattling by the square-root';[6] the sergeant-major of Maurice's army must be capable of executing a great number of intricate parade-ground evolutions, based on Roman models,[7] besides a number of battle-movements of more strictly practical value. For Londoño drill and exercises had been designed primarily to promote physical fitness; for Lipsius they were a method of inculcating Stoic virtues in the soldier; for Maurice they were the fundamental postulates of tactics. From Aelian Maurice borrowed the whole vocabulary of military command, transmitting it almost unaltered to our own day.[8] Contemporaries found in the new drill which he introduced a strange and powerful fascination: it was an 'invention', a 'science',[9] indeed, a revelation; and a large literature appeared, designed to explain to the aspiring soldier, in two pages of close print, the precise significance of the order 'right turn' – a service the more necessary, since it sometimes meant, in fact, turn left.[10] And so officers became not merely leaders, but trainers, or men; diligent practice in peacetime, and in winter, became essential; and drill, for the first time in modern history, became the precondition of military success. The decline in the size of the basic infantry unit from about three thousand to about thirty meant that individual initiative was now expected at a far lower level of command than before. The slowly-increasing technical complexity of firearms was already beginning the process of forcing the soldier to be a primitive technician. If the revolution in drill implied a more absolute subordination of the soldier's will to the command of a superior, it implied also an intelligent subordination. Henceforth it might not be the soldier's business to think, but he would at least be expected to possess a certain minimal capacity for thinking. The army was no longer to be a brute mass, in the Swiss style, nor a collection of bellicose individuals, in the feudal style; it was to be an articulated organism of which each part responded to impulses from above. The demand for unanimity and precision of movement led naturally to the innovation of marching in step, which appears at some date impossible to establish about the middle of the seventeenth century.[11] And the principle of mass-subordination, of the solution of the individual will in the will of the commander, received a last reinforcement with the slow adoption of uniforms: 'without uniforms', said Frederick the Great, 'there can be no discipline.' The process was already observable in the 1620s; but it was scarcely complete by the end of the century. The long delay is easily explained. As long as body-armour remained general, uniforms were scarcely practical; and even when armour was abandoned, the common use of the sword-resisting buff-coat prevented for a time a general change.[12] Moreover, the habit of using mercenary armies, and the notorious readiness of mercenaries to change sides, induced men to prefer the 'token' – a kerchief round the arm, a green branch in the hat – which could be discarded easily as the occasion for it passed. Nevertheless, by the time Louvois was well in the saddle it was sufficiently plain that the general adoption of uniforms would not long be delayed.[13] Their mass-psychological effect will be readily appreciated by anyone who has ever worn one. The way was clear for the armies of the nineteenth century: it remained only for the twentieth to complete the process by replacing dolmans, busbies, eagle's wings, and all the flaunting *panache* of Cossack and Hussar, by the flat uniformity of field-grey and khaki.

The new emphasis on training and drill seemed to contemporaries to reinforce their already established convictions about the best way to recruit an army. The armies which carried through the military revolution – or upon which that revolution impinged – were nearly all mercenary armies. It has indeed been argued, with some plausibility, that the great military innovations throughout history have generally coincided with the predominance of mercenaries;[14] and it has been asserted, more specifically, that the reforms of Maurice were possible only in a mercenary force, since the prolonged drilling and high degree of professional skill which they demanded would have been impossible to obtain from a citizen militia.[15] But though this last contention (as we shall see in a moment) cannot be sustained, there is no doubt that the use of mercenaries was attended with certain obvious advantages. The mercenary had no local attachments, was indifferent to national sentiment; and this made him an invaluable agent in the suppression of popular disturbances. A mercenary army cared not at all if the war were prolonged, or fought far from home; it economized the state's own manpower, and hence its wealth; the system of recruiting through captains relieved the government of a good deal of administrative work. There were, of course, many countervailing disadvantages: the mercenary was undisciplined, unreliable, and averse to battle; his arms and equipment were unstandardized and often bad;[16] the employer was invariably swindled by the captains; and the whole system was ruinously expensive. So expensive, indeed, that the smaller and poorer states were forced to look for alternatives. Around the turn of the century many of the lesser German states – and even some quite big ones such as Saxony, Brandenburg and Bavaria – began to experiment with local militias.[17] Military writers such as Machiavelli and Lazarus von Schwendi had urged the superiority of the citizen army, with many a backward glance at the military virtues of republican Rome.[18] But it was forgotten that the classical authors whose military teachings formed the basis of the Maurician reforms all dated from times when the Roman forces were citizen-armies no longer. The event proved that the half-trained militias were incapable of mastering the modern art of war. Their failure in Germany was universal, ignominious and complete; and it seemed that those were right who contended that in the new conditions only mercenary armies could be effective. The Swedish victories, however, were a warning against too hasty a conclusion; for the Swedish army was a conscript national militia – the first truly national European army – and it proved capable of mastering military techniques much more complex than had been seen before. The second and more important stage of the military revolution, which Gustav Adolf carried through, was in fact launched, not by highly-skilled professionals, but by conscript peasants; and experienced mercenary soldiers such as Robert Monro had to go to school again to learn the new Swedish methods.[19] And not only were the Swedish armies better than any mercenaries; they were also incomparably cheaper. There was no peculation by captains; and payment could be made in land-grants, revenue-assignments, tax-remissions, or in kind.

But conditions in Sweden were exceptional, and other European countries felt unable to follow the Swedish example. The Spanish army under Philip II did indeed contain some conscripts, as well as international mercenaries and Spanish 'gentlemen-rankers', and the Prussian army of Frederick William I was a mixed army too;[20] but on the whole the rulers found no feasible alternative to a mercenary force, drawn, often enough, from the more impoverished and mountainous regions of Europe such as Scotland, Albania, or Switzerland.[21] Few monarchs of the sixteenth and seventeenth centuries were prepared to establish national armies; for most of them agreed with Christian IV of Denmark and John George of Saxony in being unwilling to put arms into the hands of the lower orders:[22] only where the peasantry had been reduced to a real serfdom was it esteemed safe to proceed upon the basis of conscription. This stage was not reached in Prussia before the end of the century; nor even in Russia before the reforms of Peter the Great. Except in Sweden, therefore, and to some extent in Spain, the armies continued to be mercenary armies throughout the century. The difference was that they became standing armies too. And this change arose mainly from the obvious need to make them less burdensome to the state. Already before the end of the sixteenth century it was realized that the practice of disbanding and paying-off regiments at the end of each campaigning season, and re-enlisting them in the following spring, was an expensive way of doing business. Large sums were payable on enlistment and mustering, and (in theory at least)

all arrears were paid up on disbandment. But between mustering and disbandment pay was irregular and never full, despite
the so-called 'full-pays' which occurred from time to time.[23] If
then a mercenary force were not disbanded in the autumn, but
continued from year to year, the calls upon the exchequer were
likely to be considerably lessened, and the general nuisance of
mutinous soldiery would be abated. Moreover, if the army
remained embodied throughout the winter, the close season
could be used for drilling and exercising, of which since the
tactical revolution there was much more need than ever before.
There were, moreover, special areas where winter was the best
season for campaigning: it was so in the marshy regions of
Poland and north-west Russia; and it was so in Hungary, for
the Turkish camels could not stand the cold of the Hungarian
plain, and their annual retirement provided the Habsburgs
with the chance to recoup the losses of the preceding summer.[24]
Considerations such as these led one prince after another to
retain his mercenaries on the strength throughout the winter
months: Rudolf II was perhaps the earliest to do so; but Maurice
of Orange was not far behind. From this practice arose the
modern standing army; and it is worth while emphasizing the
fact that it was the result of considerations of a military and
financial, and not of a political or constitutional nature. Writers
such as de la Noue, Duplessis-Mornay, Wallhausen and
Montecuccoli all advocated standing armies on purely military
grounds.[25] There seems little basis for the suggestion that standing armies were called into being by artful princes in order to
provide employment for their turbulent nobility;[26] or that they
were a sign of the inherent *Drang nach Machtentfaltung* of the
monarchs;[27] or that they were designed to enable the rulers to
establish a sovereignty unrestrained by law and custom and
free from constitutional limitations – though they did, no doubt,
prove very serviceable instruments of despotism. Where absolutism triumphed in this century, it did so because it provided the
response to a genuine need; and though an army might be
useful for curbing aristocratic licence, it was but an accessory
factor in the general political situation which produced the
eclipse of the Estates. Essentially the standing armies were the
product of military logic rather than of political design. And
the same is true of the permanent navies: greater obligations

in the way of commerce-protection, increased need for making blockades effective, the demand for trained crews and officers constantly at call, economy of administration – these were some of the factors that produced permanent navies; and it was a constitutional accident that the first two attempts in this direction – the *Compagnie van Assurantie* of Frederick Henry, and the Shipmoney fleets of Charles I – should both have acquired a sinister significance in the minds of their opponents.[28]

But it was not only that armies were tending to become permanent; it was also that they were rapidly becoming much larger. And this I take to be the result of a revolution in strategy, made possible by the revolution in tactics, and made necessary by the circumstances of the Thirty Years' War. The sixteenth century had already seen a notable broadening of strategic horizons: in the long duel between Valois and Habsburg, simultaneous operations on two or more fronts had been the rule, and it would have been difficult at times to decide which was the encircler, and which the encircled. The same was true, on a vaster scale, of the struggle against the Turks: Portuguese attacks on Eritrea, Persian assaults upon Asia Minor, were balanced by Turkish alliances with France and England. At the same time the discovery of the New World, and the penetration of the East Indies, extended the possible area of European conflict until it covered most of the globe, and inaugurated a new age of amphibious warfare. But these developments were for long unsystematic, the realm of the project-maker and the armchair strategist: the day had not yet arrived when the military and naval administrations of Europe were equal to the coordination of effort over distances so formidable. The sterility of warfare in Europe, in the time of Prince Maurice, is the accurate measure of the strategic thinking of the age.

The Thirty Years' War brought a change. Battle came again into favour, perhaps under the influence of confessional ferocity, and with it a strategy aiming at battle; and as hostilities ranged back and forth over Germany, and along the borders of Germany from Poland and Transylvania to Italy, Lorraine and the Netherlands, commanders were driven to look at the whole of central Europe as one great theatre of war. When Gustav Adolf wrote that 'all the wars of Europe are now blended into one',[29] he was thinking in terms of politics; but the remark was equally true in regard to strategy. Wallenstein sends Arnim to fight on the Vistula; Pappenheim rushes to the relief of Maestricht; Olivares dreams of seizing Göteborg, and of a Spanish naval base at Wismar, to be made accessible by a Kiel canal;[30] Piccolomini makes a famous march from Flanders to Bohemia;[31] Savoy, Venice, Transylvania and even the Tatars of the Crimea become elements in ever-wider and more unified plans of operations. Above all, Gustav Adolf's strategic thinking seems a whole dimension bigger than any that had preceded it. He successfully combines two types of strategy: on the one hand a resolute offensive strategy designed to annihilate the enemy in battle – the product of confidence in the superiority of the new Swedish tactics; on the other a wholly new gradualist strategy, designed to conquer Germany by the occupation and methodical consolidation of successive base-areas. The two blend in his plan for the destruction of the Austrian Habsburgs by the simultaneous and effectively co-ordinated operations of five or seven armies moving under the king's direction on an enormous curving front extending from the middle Oder to the Alpine passes.[32] It was a strategic concept more complex, vaster, than any one commander had ever previously attempted. His death prevented its being carried out; but the closing years of the war saw other developments of interest. The strategy of devastation began to be employed with a new thoroughness and logic; and, as its consequence, the war became pre-eminently a war of movement, best exemplified in the campaigns of Baner, Torstensson and Gallas.[33] Not all of these developments were to be pursued in the years that followed: an age of reason and mathematical logic would try to bring war itself within the scope of its calculations, to the detriment of that offensive spirit without which wars cannot be won; but the effects of the strategic revolution of which Gustav Adolf was the most illustrious exponent were not to be effaced.

The most important of them was the great increase in the scope of warfare, reflected in a corresponding increase in the normal size of the armies of the major powers. Philip II had dominated Europe in his day with the aid of an army which probably did not exceed 40,000 men: a century later, 400,000 were esteemed necessary to maintain the ascendancy of Louis XIV.[34] In 1627, under the Elector George William, Brandenburg possessed a defence force totalling 900:[35] under Frederick William I, the normal establishment was about 80,000. The previous millennium could show nothing to compare with this sudden rise in the size of western European armies. Great agglomerations of troops for a particular occasion had indeed occurred in the past, and the Turks had brought vast hosts to bear upon their enemies; but in the West, at least, the seventeenth century saw the permanent establishment of some armies at levels which earlier ages had rarely, if ever, known. With Louvois, indeed, the passion for mere numbers had something of a megalomaniac quality: an aspect, perhaps, of that 'pursuit of the quantitative' which has been considered as an essential characteristic of the new industrialism.[36] It may perhaps be legitimately objected that the instances I have chosen to illustrate the growth of armies are hand-picked: the Spanish armies of 1690 were certainly no bigger than those of 1590; and the army with which Charles XII won the battle of Narva was slightly smaller than that with which Charles IX lost the battle of Kirkholm:[37] that Gustav Adolf had 175,000 men under arms in 1632 was for Sweden a quite exceptional circumstance, never repeated. But this does not alter the fact that the scale of European warfare was throughout the century prodigiously increasing: the great armies of Louis XIV had to be met by armies of comparable size; and if one state could not manage it, there must be a Grand Alliance. Moreover, in the seventeenth century numbers had acquired a precise meaning: when Charles V is credited with assembling an army of 120,000 men to repel the Turkish attack, we are perhaps entitled to decline to take the figure too literally; but when Louvois states the French army at 300,000, it is safe to assume that there was just that number on the muster-rolls, even though not all of them may have appeared in the ranks. And so it happened that (as Montecuccoli observed) men, no less than money, became in the seventeenth century the sinews of war:[38] hence the concern of the earliest demographical investigations to make sure that population was not declining; hence the insistence of the mercantilists, with their eyes ever upon the contingency of war, that a copious population is among the chief riches of the state.

The transformation in the scale of war led inevitably to an

increase in the authority of the state. The days when war partook of the nature of feud were now for ever gone, and the change is reflected in (among other things) the development of international law, of which I shall speak in a moment. Only the state, now, could supply the administrative, technical and financial resources required for large-scale hostilities. And the state was concerned to make its military monopoly absolute. It declared its hostility to irregular and private armies, to ambiguous and semi-piratical naval ventures. Backward countries such as Scotland were the exceptions that proved the rule: the failure of Scottish parliaments to disarm Highland clans was a sign of weakness in the body politic. Navies become state navies, royal navies: the old compromise of the armed merchantman falls into disuse; the Dutch West India Company goes bankrupt. Effective control of the armed forces by a centralized authority becomes a sign of modernity: it is no accident that the destruction of the *streltsi* by Peter the Great preceded by a century and a quarter the destruction of the Janissaries by Mahmud II.

This development, and the new style of warfare itself, called for new administrative methods and standards; and the new administration was from the beginning centralized and royal. Secretaries of state for war are born; war offices proliferate. The Austrian Habsburgs had possessed a *Hofkriegsrat* since the mid-sixteenth century; but in the seventeenth the rising military powers – Sweden, France, Brandenburg, Russia – all equipped themselves with new and better machinery for the conduct of war. Inevitably these new officials spent a good deal of their time in grappling with problems of supply – supply of arms and armaments, supply of goods, clothing, transport and the rest. Experience showed that it was bad for discipline, as well as inefficient, to permit the mercenary armies to equip themselves:[39] it was better to have standardized weapons, a limited number of recognised calibres, an agreed maximum of windage, a consistently-compounded gunpowder, and, in the end, uniform clothing, and boots in three standard sizes. Hence the state was driven to attempt the supervision of supply; in many cases, to production on its own account; sometimes, to monopoly: the Spanish Netherlands had a state monopoly of the manufacture of gunpowder, the Swedish Trading Company was created to facilitate control of a strategic material – copper. Military needs drove the monarchs into ever-increasing interference in the lives of their subjects: in Sweden, as in England, there were bitter complaints at the grisly perquisitions of the saltpetre-collector. The developments in the science of fortification, of which Vauban was to be the most eminent exponent, meant new fortresses for the *pré carré*, and this in turn meant heavier *corvées*, the subversion of municipal liberties, and the increased power of the sovereign: 'fortresses', says Montecuccoli, 'are the buttresses of the crown'; and he added that the fact that 'licentious' nations such as the English disliked them merely proved their utility.[40] The stricter discipline, the elaborately mechanical drilling, required by the new linear tactics, matched the tendency of the age towards absolute government, and may well have reinforced it: it was tempting to think that the discipline which had succeeded so well in the field might yield equally satisfactory results if applied to civil society. The ruler was increasingly identified with the commander-in-chief, and from the new discipline and drill would be born not merely the autocrat, but that particular type of autocrat which delighted in the name of *Kriegsherr*. It was not the least of England's good luck, that for the whole of the critical century from 1547 to 1649 she was ruled by monarchs with neither interest nor capacity for military affairs. It was certainly no accident that Louis XIII should have been 'passionately fond' of drill;[41] nor was it a mere personal quirk that led Louis XIV to cause a medal to be struck, of which the reverse displays him in the act of taking a parade, and correcting, with a sharp poke of his cane, the imperfect dressing of a feckless private in the rear rank.[42] The newly-acquired symmetry and order of the parade-ground provided, for Louis XIV and his contemporaries, the model to which life and art must alike conform; and the *pas cadencé* of Martinet – whose name is in itself a programme – echoed again in the majestic monotony of interminable alexandrines.[43] By the close of the century there was already a tendency in monarchs of an absolutist cast to consider military uniform as their normal attire – as Charles XII did, for instance, and Frederick William I. It was not a fashion that would have commended itself to Henry VIII, or Gustav Vasa, or Philip II.

One very important effect of all these developments was in

the sphere of finance. The ever-increasing cost of war – the result of larger armies and navies, more expensive armaments, longer periods of training, bigger administrative staffs, in an age when prices were still rising – embarrassed the finances of every state in Europe. Kings were presented with new problems of paying large and distant armies, which posed new difficulties of remittance; and the solutions they found to these difficulties contributed a good deal to the development of financial instruments and a structure of credit: Wallenstein's ties with the great German financiers were an essential element in his success.[44] Everywhere kings found that though they might still – with care – live of their own in peacetime, they plunged into debt in wartime. And in this period it was almost always wartime. They fell back on *affaires extraordinaires*, on *ad hoc* financial devices, some of them sufficiently remarkable: this is the age of Peter the Great's *pribylshtiki*, or tax-inventors, and of the analogous officials employed after Colbert's death by Le Pelletier at the *Contrôle Générale*.[45] They had recourse to currency debasement, sale of monopolies, sale of crown lands, inflation of honours, and above all to the sale of offices, which in this century for the first time becomes a general European phenomenon.[46] But sooner or later financial stringency, in country after country, involved the authorities in constitutional crises: the monarchs found themselves forced to parley with their Estates, or to violate the ancient constitutional liberties. Behind all the great insurrectionary movements of the age – the Thirty Years' War, the English rebellion, the Fronde, the revolts in the Spanish realms – there lay, as one major element in the situation (though of course not the only one) the crown's need for money; and that need was usually produced by military commitments whose dimensions were in part the result of the military revolution. On the whole, the monarchs prevailed; the income for maintaining standing armies was taken out of the control of the Estates; sometimes military finance – as in Brandenburg – was wholly separated from the ordinary revenues. And in Germany this issue of the conflict resulted, in part, from the fact that in the last resort the Estates had rather sacrifice a constitutional principle, and retain the security afforded by a standing army, than risk the appalling sufferings and crushing financial exactions which, as the experience of the

Thirty Years' War had shown, awaited the militarily impotent or old-fashioned.[47] Nevertheless, though the standing army thus came to be accepted as the lesser of two evils, it was a grievous burden to the smaller and financially weaker states. They had discarded the alternative of a militia; a standing army seemed inescapable; but many of them could scarcely finance it from their own resources. It was this situation which presented such opportunities to that subsidy-diplomacy upon which the aggressive policies of Louis XIV were to thrive.

If liberty, then, were thus to be sacrificed to the army, it ought at least to be an army that was really the property of the king, and not a mere agglomeration of recruiting speculators. The free bargaining between recruiting captain and employing prince, the Articles of War which partook more of the nature of an industrial agreement than of a code of military discipline,[48] – these things were repugnant to the orderliness and efficiency of the new military ideal. The larger the army, the greater the need for disciplining it from above.[49] The monarch must take over the business of recruiting and paying men, as he was already beginning to take over the business of supplying material and supervising war-industries. And the monarchs, in fact, did so. The Articles of War of Gustav Adolf set a new standard of royal control, and were imitated even in countries which employed a predominantly mercenary army. Wallenstein made a start in curbing the independence of the recruiting captains;[50] and a generation later Louvois and the Great Elector were to profit from his example.[51] By the end of the century the monarchs had mostly gained effective control of their armies. It was a significant development; for once the armies became royal (as the navies already were) the way was open for their eventually becoming national.

The social consequences of the military revolution were scarcely less important than the constitutional. In the Middle Ages war had been almost the privilege of a class; by the seventeenth century it had become almost the livelihood of the masses. The Military Participation Ratio (to borrow the language of the sociologists)[52] rose sharply. Men flocked to the swollen mercenary armies. In part they did so, no doubt, because in the Germany of the 1630s and 1640s the army was the safest place to be;[53] but also, and more generally, because the new warfare offered fresh prospects of a career. Never before had commanders required so many subalterns and NCOs. It was no wonder that impoverished Scots and Irish made all haste to the wars of Low Germanie: 'He who is down on his luck', ran the contemporary Gaelic proverb, 'can always earn a dollar of Mackay'.[54] Even the cavalry, which had once been the close preserve of the nobility, was now open to all who could sit a horse and fire a pistol; for with the abolition of the lance the European nobility tended to abandon heavy cavalry to the professionals, while light cavalry had long appeared to them almost as socially subversive, since it eliminated the difference, in mount, arms and equipment, between the noble and his esquire. The decline of expensive heavy armour, which was a consequence of the growing realization that no armour could stop a musket ball, and that in any case few musket balls hit their mark, had obvious social implications too. The obliteration of the old distinction between cavalry and foot, gentlemen and others, is a matter of common remark in the seventeenth century: as Sir James Turner put it, 'the ancient distinction between the Cavalry and Infantry, as to their birth and breeding, is wholly taken away, men's qualities and extractions being little or rather just nothing either regarded or enquired after; the most of the Horsemen, as well as of the Foot, being composed of the Scum of the Commons'.[55] The new armies, in fact, served as the social escalators of the age; the eternal wars favoured interstratic mobility; and for a young man with some capital behind him a regiment could be a brilliant investment: Wallhausen lamented that war was ceasing to be an honourable profession, and was becoming a mere traffic.[56] But even for the youth who had no other assets than a native pugnacity and the habit of survival, advancement was now probable, and the impecunious commoner whose wits were sharp might certainly hope for a commission. He could not, indeed, feel that he carried a baton in his knapsack. Very few of the leading commanders on the Continent were of humble origin: Aldringen had been a lackey, Derfflinger was a tailor's apprentice, Jean de Werth rose from absolute obscurity; but the great names are still noble names: even Catinat came from the *noblesse de robe*.[57] Nevertheless though the highest positions might in practice remain unattainable, the

army had become an attractive career, and in France three
generations of military service would enable a family to claim
reception into the *noblesse de race*.[58] As the old custom of con-
ferring knighthood on the battlefield declined, the new custom
of ennoblement came to take its place. Nor were the possibilities
of advancement restricted to the army in the field. A host of
clerks and secretaries was now required to keep the muster- and
pay-rolls, and conduct the correspondence of semi-literate
commanders:[59] Grimmelshausen makes Herzbruder's father a
muster-clerk in the Saxon army, and the merchant's son,
Oliver, becomes secretary to a Swedish general. Administrators
were in brisk demand for the new war offices;[60] business heads
were needed to solve the ever-widening problems of logistics:
such careers as those of Michel Le Tellier, Johan Adler Salvius,
and Louis de Geer, tell their own tale. The importance of the
civilian, bourgeois, administrators in bringing order and
method into the management of the fighting services has often
been remarked, and Colbert and Louvois are the most famous
representatives of this development. But it has less often been
pointed out that it was the purely military changes of the late
sixteenth and early seventeenth centuries that opened to the
middle classes a quite new field of activity, and tempting prospects of social advancement. How good those prospects could
be may best be seen from a glance at the peerages conferred by
successive Swedish monarchs upon persons of this sort.

It is true that the enhanced opportunities provided by the
new style of army tended, before the century was out, to be
somewhat restricted. The decay of heavy cavalry, the decline
of individualist warfare, was accompanied by the gradual
withering away of such remnant of the old noble obligation of
military service as had survived from the middle ages. In
France, in Sweden, in Brandenburg, knight-service had
vanished for all practical purposes by the third quarter of the
century.[61] It was outmoded and inefficient, disorderly and
unreliable, and subversive of the new principle of concentrating
military power under the absolute control of the sovereign.
But the nobility found, in the new standing armies, an opening
which more than compensated them for the loss of their own
special military organization; and the monarchs, indeed, took
care that it should be so. The more impoverished of them – the

hoberaux, Junkers, *knapar* – were delighted to be relieved of the burden of supplying the expensive equipment of the heavy cavalryman, and glad to be able to find a full-time career in the king's service. It was not long before they attempted to claim, as a privilege of birth, an excessive share of the new opportunities. By the beginning of the eighteenth century, though the social escalator was still on the move, there was a widespread tendency to label it 'Nobles Only', and this tendency was not wholly counteracted by the practice (prevalent in some countries) of ennobling non-noble officers who might attain to a certain grade.

Meanwhile, the arm which presented the aspiring soldier with the fewest social barriers was undoubtedly the artillery.[62] Empirical in method, generously approximate in effect, the artillery was nevertheless ceasing to be a 'mystery', and was on the way to becoming a regular arm of the services, with a normal military organization: the first purely artillery regiment seems to have been that established by Gustav Adolf in 1629.[63] And behind the artillery lay a fringe of scientific laymen and minor mathematicians – those 'mathematical practitioners' whose part in educating the seamen, gunners and surveyors of the age has now been made clear.[64] Indeed, one main element in the military revolution was the harnessing, for the first time and on a large scale, of science to war. The invention of corned powder towards the end of the sixteenth century gave to firearms a new effectiveness, and would have been still more important if the techniques of metallurgy had been able to take full advantage of this advance.[65] A century of notable technical progress, nevertheless, lay behind the Swedish light artillery. Very soon after the invention of a satisfactory portable telescope it was being used in the field by Maurice and Gustav Adolf. The importance for military purposes of advances in cartography seems first to have been recognized by Stefan Batory, who caused military maps to be drawn for him in the 1580s.[66] Technicians and theoreticians vied with each other in devising new and more terrible weapons: multiple-barrelled guns were invented upon all hands; Napier, the father of logarithms, was more favourably known to his contemporaries as the man who built a submarine, suggested the use of gas-shells, and designed an armoured fighting vehicle; Gilius

Packet invented the first hand-grenade for Erik xiv in 1567;[67] Jan Bouvy in his *Pyrotechnie militaire* (1591) described the first practicable torpedo.[68] Maurice of Orange dallied with *saucisses de guerre*, with saws fitted with silencer attachment (for nocturnal attacks upon fortresses), and with other contrivances more curious than effective.[69] In 1650 the Venetians resorted to biological warfare in the defence of Crete, despatching Dr Michael Angelo Salomon thither to infect the Turkish armies with 'the quintessence of the pest'.[70] It comes as no surprise that when Colbert founded his *Académie royale des Sciences*, one of its main objects should have been the application of science to war.

These developments brought to an end the period in which the art of war could still be learned by mere experience or the efflux of time. The commander of the new age must be something of a mathematician; he must be capable of using the tools with which the scientists were supplying him. Gustav Adolf consistently preached the importance of mathematics; Monro and Turner spoke slightingly of illiterate old soldiers.[71] And since war must be learned – even by nobles – institutions must be created to teach it: the first military academy of modern times was founded by Johan of Nassau at Siegen in 1617. The need for military education was especially felt by the nobility, whose former supremacy in arms was beginning to be challenged; and the century saw the foundation of noble academies or cadet-schools, which sought to combine the now-gentlemanly acquirement of fortification with the Italian tradition of courtly education: such were Christian iv's Sorø, Louvois' short-lived cadet-school, and the similar Austrian establishment, founded in 1648 by the ominously-named Baron de Chaos.[72]

Side by side with the older stratification of society based upon birth or tenure, there now appeared a parallel and to some extent a rival stratification based on military and civil rank. The first half of the seventeenth century sees the real emergence of the concept of rank. In the armies of the *Landsknechts*, for instance, the distinction between officers and men had been faint, and their bands had at times something of the aspect of a self-governing democracy.[73] All that was now changed. After captains came colonels; then (in the Thirty Years' War) majors; then a regular hierarchy of generals and field-marshals.

Soon after 1660 Louvois regulated precedence in the French army.[74] And this hierarchization was the more necessary, since very soon military ranks were drawn into that general sale of offices which was one of the characteristics of the age. On the whole, the parallel hierarchies of rank and birth avoided conflict; the nobility contrived to evade non-commissioned service, except in special regiments (such as Charles xii's guards) where it was recognized to be no derogation; and the locution 'an officer and a gentleman' became a pleonasm rather than a nice distinction. But in some countries at least (Russia and Sweden, in particular) the state found it expedient to promulgate Tables of Rank, in order to adjust delicate questions of precedence as between (for instance) a second lieutenant and a university professor, or an ensign and a college registrar. By the close of the century, the officer-corps had been born: a European, supranational entity, with its own ethos, its own international code of honour, its own corporate spirit. The *duellum* of a dying chivalry is transformed into the affair of honour of a military caste. And the military revolution is seen to have given birth, not only to modern warfare, but also to modern militarism.

The effect of war upon the economic development of Europe in this period is one of the classic battlefields of historians – a 'dark and bloody ground' whereon Professor Nef still grapples valiantly with the shade of Werner Sombart, much as Jacob wrestled with the Angel – and it would be rash for one who is not an economic historian to intrude upon this argument. But this at least may be said: that war was a fundamental presupposition of mercantilist thought, and by many mercantilists was considered to be necessary to the health of the state; and implicit in all their theories was the new concept of war-potential.[75] The mercantilists held that the economic activities of the state must be so directed as to ensure that it be not at the mercy of a foreign power for those commodities – whether men, money, or goods – without which wars cannot be waged: Thomas Mun, for instance, urged the stockpiling of strategic raw materials.[76] And when mercantilist writers in France and England and Austria – and even in Sweden – boasted that their respective countries excelled all others in fertility of soil and mineral wealth, they were in fact proclaiming their preparedness for war, and warning off an aggressor. But since few states could be truly autarkic, there arose, more clearly than ever before, the idea of economic warfare; the more so, since the needs of armies were now greater and more varied. There had, of course, been conscious economic warfare before: repeated attempts had been made to cut off the Turks from supplies of war-materials; similar attempts were made in the 1560s and 1570s to deny them to Muscovy; Sweden had been hard hit in the Seven Years' War of the North by the Danes' stoppage of her imports of salt. But in the seventeenth century economic warfare became wider in range, sharper, and more effective than before. This increased efficacy is a consequence (but also a cause) of larger navies, and of the building of ships with a greater sea-endurance. It was a sign of the new scope of economic warfare that the Dutch in 1599 not only declared a total blockade of the entire coasts of Italy, Portugal and Spain, but also proceeded to a serious attempt to make that blockade effective.[77] At the same time, the notion of contraband of war underwent a considerable extension: by the mid-century it could be made to cover even such commodities as corn, specie, cloth and horses.[78] It was to meet this situation that the legists of Europe began the attempt to formulate an international law of contraband and blockade. Before the middle of the century the Dutch had already induced at least three nations to recognize the principle 'free ships make free goods';[79] and it was partly because of the serious military implications that there had arisen the classic controversy between the advocates of *mare liberum* and *mare clausum*. The military revolution, indeed, had important effects upon international relations and international law. There can be no doubt that the strengthening of the state's control of military matters did something to regularize international relations. The mediaeval concept of war as an extension of feud grows faint; military activities by irresponsible individuals are frowned on; the states embark on the suppression of piracy; the heyday of the Algerines and the Uscocchi is drawing to a close. The century witnessed a steady advance towards restriction of the old rights of looting and booty, and before the end of it cartels governing the exchange of prisoners had become usual. This was a necessary consequence of the decline of individual warfare; for looting and booty had been juridically based on the idea of feud, and the apportionment of booty had been generally linked to the amount of capital invested by the soldier in his arms and equipment, so that the cavalryman received more than the footsoldier: hence when the state provided the capital it reasonably claimed the disposition of the loot.[80] Nevertheless, before this stage had been arrived at, Europe had endured a period – the period of the Thirty Years' War – when war-making seems to have been only intermittently under the state's control, and when ordinary conduct was of exceptional savagery. The explanation of this state of affairs lies, it seems to me, in the technical changes which I have been considering. The increased size of armies, the new complexity of their needs, at first confronted the states with problems of supply which they were incapable of solving – hence the bland indifference of most generals during the Thirty Years' War to any threat to their line of communications. Armies must live off the country; looting and booty were necessary if the soldier were to survive.[80a] The occupation of territory thus became a legitimate strategic object in itself; and conversely, the commander who could not deny to the enemy the territory he desired must take care so to devastate it that it became useless to him. Thus, as Piero Pieri observes, frightfulness became a logistical necessity,[81] a move in a struggle for supply which was itself the result of the increased size of armies and the low level of administrative techniques. Already, however, there were signs of better things. Gustav Adolf, despite his dictum that *bellum se ipsum alet*,[82] was not content to plunder Germany haphazard; and among other innovations he introduced a system of magazines, by which supplies and war material were concentrated at strategic points such as Erfurt, Nuremberg, Ulm, and Mainz:[83] it was a development that looked forward to the eighteenth century. Nevertheless, the menace of the self-supporting army, wandering at large over central Europe, lasted sufficiently long to induce in Germany's neighbours a sharpened consciousness of frontiers, and a new determination to make them defensible. Richelieu put the point clearly when he wrote in his *Testament politique* that a well-fortified frontier was necessary to prevent the raids of a marauding enemy. A generation later the idea of a frontier as one or more lines of fortified places was well developed, and from it there followed the rather new notion that frontiers must be 'rectified' to meet strategic requirements. The age of Vauban, of the *pré carré*, of the *Réunions*, is not far ahead.[84]

Before that stage was reached, the administrative nihilism which had been one of the early consequences of the military revolution made it urgent to draw up afresh some code for the conduct of war. This was the situation in which Hugo Grotius wrote his *De Jure Belli ac Pacis*. It bears on every page the impression of the military revolution; for it was the hopelessness of maintaining the old standards in the face of the new situation that forced Grotius to go so far in the condonation of evil. It seemed to Grotius that the old restraints – moral, conventional or religious – had ceased to be effective, and that man in his war-making had sunk to the level of the beasts. The last vestige of chivalry had perished in the French civil wars; and the antagonism of Catholic and Protestant had made religion the pretext for ferocity, rather than a check upon it. To these factors were now added the growing predominance of missile weapons, which were dehumanizing war into an affair of undiscriminating slaughter at a distance,[85] and also the new strategy of devastation. It was an age when the soldiery came near to asserting a prescriptive right to massacre a recalcitrant civilian population;[86] and the armies of the Thirty Years' War had latterly to contend, not only with their official enemies, but with the bloodthirsty vengeance of peasant guerillas: Simplicissimus might well comment on 'the enmity which there ever is between soldiers and peasants'.[87] In this situation, Grotius sought to set limits to what was legitimate in war. But the importance of his attempt has obscured the fact that the limits he did set were appallingly wide: wider, for instance, than in Suárez and Gentili; and far wider than in Vitoria.[88] Grotius taught that it is lawful to kill prisoners of war; that assassination is legitimate, if not accompanied by perfidy; that unrestricted devastation of the lands and cities of the enemy is permissible, even if they have surrendered; that the civilian has no right to special consideration; and that 'the slaughter of women and children is allowed to have impunity, as comprehended in the right of war' – a position which he buttressed, according to his habit, with an apposite quotation from the 137th Psalm: 'Blessed shall he be that taketh thy children and dasheth them against the stones.'[89] It is true that he proceeded to urge moral considerations which must deter the good man from making use of these rights; but they remain rights none the less. Grotius, in fact, reflects the logistical devastation of the age of the Thirty Years' War;[90] though it was to the same classical authorities which had given Maurice the inspiration for his disciplinary reforms, that he turned for his repertory of convenient instances. The absolute, feral warfare of the epoch, with which Grotius thus felt obliged to come to terms, gave a peculiar incisiveness to the logic of Leviathan.

The continued use of mercenary armies, with their professional codes and traditions, and the rise of an international officer-class, did indeed provide mitigations before many decades had passed: new military conventions grew up, to regulate the relations of armies to one another. But it was long before these restrictions were applied to civilians: not until the most civilized state in Europe, impelled by military logic, had twice devastated the Palatinate, did public opinion begin to turn against the type of warfare which Grotius had been compelled to legitimize. Grotius, indeed, represents a transitional stage at which the military revolution had not yet worked out its full effects. A completer control by the state of its armies, better administrative devices – and the fear of reprisals – were required before there could be any real alleviation. If the military revolution must be given the responsibility for the peculiar horrors of the Thirty Years' War, it did at last evolve the antidote to them. The eighteenth century would bring to Europe a long period in which a limitation of the scope of war was successfully maintained. But it is a long way still, in 1660, to the humane rationalism of Vattel.

Such were some of the effects of the military revolution: I have no doubt that others could be distinguished. I hope, at least, to have persuaded you that these tactical innovations were indeed the efficient causes of changes which were really revolutionary. Between 1560 and 1660 a great and permanent transformation came over the European world. The armies of Maximilian II, in tactics, strategy, constitution and spirit, belong to a world of ideas which would have seemed quite foreign to Benedek and Radetzky. The armies of the Great Elector are linked infrangibly with those of Moltke and Schlieffen. By 1660 the modern art of war had come to birth. Mass armies, strict discipline, the control of the state, the submergence of the individual, had already arrived; the conjoint ascendancy of financial power and applied science was already established in all its malignity; the use of propaganda, psychological warfare, and terrorism as military weapons was already familiar to theorists, as well as to commanders in the field. The last remaining qualms as to the religious and ethical legitimacy of war seemed to have been stilled. The road lay open, broad and straight, to the abyss of the twentieth century.

NOTES

[1] This paper is a revision of an inaugural lecture delivered before The Queen's University of Belfast on 21 January 1955.

[2] For a general treatment of the period Hans Delbrück, *Geschichte der Kriegskunst im Rahmen der politischen Geschichte*, Berlin, 1920. iv, is the best authority, though this volume is on a slighter scale than its predecessors. Paul Schmitthenner, *Krieg und Kriegführung im Wandel der Weltgeschichte*, Potsdam, 1930, is a stimulating and suggestive survey. Sir Charles Oman's *A History of the Art of War in the Sixteenth Century* (1937) necessarily ends with Maurice of Orange. The best discussions in English are the chapter in Sir George Clark, *The Seventeenth Century*, Oxford, 1929, and the same author's *War and Society in the Seventeenth Century*, Cambridge, 1958.

[3] For a fuller consideration of the changes in the art of war in Europe, and the reforms of Maurice and Gustav Adolf, see chapter 3, *supra*.

[4] 'Non bisogna credere che l'addestramento dei combattanti richieda tempo e spese: non ci sono esercizi d'armi nel senso moderno. Una sia pur rudimentale istruzione permette agli Svizzeri di formare dei corpi tattici . . .': Piero Pieri, *Il Rinascimento e la Crisi militare italiano*, Turin, 1952, p. 236.

[5] There were many reasons for the decline of the lance, but this was certainly one of them: see Raimondo Montecuccoli, *Mémoires*, Strasbourg, 1735, p. 16; and *cf.* J. J. Wallhausen, *Art militaire à cheval*, Frankfurt, 1616, pp. 3–22.

[6] I.e., the art of drawing up a given number of men into a perfect square. There is a description in Sir James Turner, *Pallas Armata* (1683), pp. 266–8.

[7] E.g. 'The Quadrate or Square, the Wedg, the *Tenaille* or Tongs, the Saw, and the Globe': Turner, *op. cit.*, pp. 112–14.

[8] Werner Hahlweg, *Die Heeresreform der Oranier und die Antike*, Berlin, 1941, pp. 25–93, 110–16; J. W. Wijn, *Het Krijgswezen in den Tijd van Prins Maurits*, Utrecht, 1934, pp. 74, 138–40, 430; H. Wertheim, *Der toller Halberstädter. Herzog Christian von Braunschweig im pfälzischen Kriege*, Berlin,

1929, i, 116. Jähns suggested that Maurice's reforms may have been forced on him by the great wastage of trained soldiers during protracted hostilities in a small area, and the consequent need to use untrained men. But the old style would have suited untrained men much better. Max Jähns, *Handbuch einer Geschichte des Kriegswesens von der Urzeit bis zur Renaissance*, Leipzig, 1880, p. 1207.

[9] J. J. Wallhausen, *L'Art militaire pour l'Infanterie*, Oppenheim, 1615, p. 65.

[10] Jähns, *op. cit.*, p. 1208.

[11] The matter of marching in step needs investigation. The only discussion appears to be E. Sander, 'Zur Geschichte des Gleichschrittes', *Zeitschrift für Heeres- und Uniformkunde* (1935), who as a result of a misreading of Francis Grose, *The Military Antiquities of Great Britain* (1812), i, 345, attributes the credit for the idea to the Earl of Essex, on the strength of a sentence which he believes to be contained in *A Worthy Speech spoken by his Excellence the Earl of Essex* (1642). But the quotation is in fact (as Grose plainly states) from the Regulations of 1686; and confidence in Sander's views is not much restored by his suggestion that marching in step was the 'gegebene Form' for armies of the Nordic Race. It has been said that it was Leopold of Dessau who made it the rule in the Prussian army (W. Sombart, *Der moderner Kapitalismus*, i, 345); but it seems probable that it was used much earlier. The Swiss columns and the *tercios*, though they marched to tap of drum, do not seem to have kept step; and such reproductions of Callot's etchings as I have seen suggest that the armies of the Thirty Years' War did not keep step either. Wallhausen says nothing of it in his chapter on marching (Wallhausen, *L'Art militaire pour l'Infanterie*, pp. 121–4); nor does Monro (*Monro his Expedition* [London, 1637], ii, 190). But whatever may have been the case on the march, it seems quite certain that the infantry of the early seventeenth century kept step for drill. Thus Wallhausen writes (*op. cit.*, p. 73): 'Tenez le pied gauche coy, conversez vous en reculant le pied droict'; and E. D. Davies, in *The Art of War and Englands Traynings* (1619), is even more explicit: 'The Captaine commands, *Files to the right hand Counter march*, and then the Leaders of the Files advancing with their right legge, turn to the right hand, and march downe towards the Reare . . .' (p. 194). Indeed, it might be possible to argue from Davies that English soldiers already kept step on the march: 'Let him march then with a good grace, holding vp his head gallantly, his pace full of grauities and state . . . and that which most imports, is that they haue alwaies their eies vpon their companions which are in ranke with them, and before them going iust one with the other, and keeping perfit distance without committing error in the least pace *or step* [my italics]' (p. 76). This may be to attach too much importance to a mere flower of Davies' exuberant style; but it seems very likely that pikemen, at least, could not afford to be out of step when marching in close order, for the position of the pike when held at the trail, and its extreme length, would otherwise have been liable to imperil the haunches of the man in front: see Davies' description, *loc. cit.*

[12] 'Il n'y a pas un Cavalier dans les trouppes de France, qui n'ait un habillement de Bufle, depuis que l'on s'est deffait de ceux de fer': Gaya, *Traité des Armes*, Paris, 1678, p. 56.

¹³ R. Knötel, H. Knötel, J. Sieg: *Handbuch der Uniformkunde. Die militärische Tracht in ihrer Entwicklung bis zur Gegenwart*, Hamburg, 1937, is a standard history. The authors consider that there were no true uniforms before about the middle of the century; but it is possible to dispute this view: see, e.g., Wertheim, *op. cit.*, i, 94; E. von Frauenholz, *Das Söldnertum in der Zeit des dreissigjährigen Krieges*, Munich, 1938, i, 41–2; K. C. Rockstroh, *Udviklingen af den nationale haer i Danmark i det 17. og 18. Aarhundrede*, Copenhagen, 1909, i, 18, 52–3.

¹⁴ Paul Schmitthenner, *Europäische Geschichte und Söldnertum*, Berlin, 1933.

¹⁵ *Ibid.*, p. 26; Piero Pieri, 'La formazione dottrinale di Raimondo Montecuccoli', *Revue internationale d'histoire militaire*, x, (1951), p. 94: 'le esigenze della nuova tattica esigono insomma degli eserciti mercenari permanenti'.

¹⁶ See on this Eugen Heischmann, *Die Anfänge des stehenden Heeres in Österreich*, Vienna, 1925, pp. 199–200.

¹⁷ For these attempts see E. von Frauenholz, *Die Landesdefension in der Zeit des dreissigjährigen Krieges*, Munich, 1939; H. Wertheim, *Der toller Halberstädter*, i, 68–75; Max Lenz, *Landgraf Moritz von Hessen*, in *Kleine historische Schriften*, Munich and Berlin, 1920, ii, 128–31; C. Jany, *Geschichte der Königlich Preussischen Armee*, Berlin, 1928, i, 26–9, 61; Otton Laskowski, 'Uwagi na marginesie nowego wydania Zarysu Historii Wojskowośce w Polsce Generała Mariana Kukiela' *Teki Historyczne*, v (1951–2), p. 39; Rockstroh, i, 4–38, 65; H. Kretzschmar, *Sächsische Geschichte*, Dresden, 1935, ii, 39.

¹⁸ For Lazarus von Schwendi, see E. von Frauenholz, *Lazarus von Schwendi. Der erste deutsche Verkünder der allgemeinen Wehrpflicht*.

¹⁹ As Gustav Adolf put it to Adolf Frederick of Mecklenburg; 'Es möchtte E. L. imandt einbilden wollen, als wen das lands volck nicht zum krige tauget, lasen sich solches ja von den grossprecheren nicht einbilden, glauben mihr (der ich tegelich die probe da von nehmen muss) das wen sihe wol gefürret vnd gecommendiret werden, mit ihnen mehr, dan mit der irregularen soldatesce, auss zu richtten': C. G. Styffe, *Konung Gustaf II Adolfs skrifter*, Stockholm, 1861, p. 414. Sweden did indeed employ mercenaries in time of war to supplement her standing army of conscripts; but the permanent force, as provided for in the Form of Government of 1634, was a militia.

²⁰ R. Altamira y Crevea, *Historia de España y de la Civilizaciòn española*, Barcelona, 1927, iii, 289–93; P. Schmitthenner, *Krieg und Kriegführung im Wandel der Weltgeschichte*, p. 196.

²¹ V. K. Kiernan, 'Foreign Mercenaries and Absolute Monarchy', *Crisis in Europe 1560–1660*, ed. T. Aston (1965), pp. 122–3.

²² Rockstroh, i, 4, 6, 31, 65; Irmer, *Die Verhandlungen Schwedens und seiner Verbündeten mit Wallenstein und dem Kaiser von 1631 bis 1634*, Leipzig, 1899, i, 259: in August 1632 John George told Lars Nilsson Tungel, 'Ich will die bauren nicht bewehren, solte auch das land unter sich, über sich gehen'.

²³ For all this E. von Frauenholz, *Das Söldnertum in der Zeit des dreissigjährigen Krieges* is now the best authority.

[24] Heischmann, pp. 105–6.

[25] Wallhausen also made the point that a standing army eased the burdens of the civil population, since it avoided the excesses which usually accompanied disbandment: Wallhausen, *L'Art militaire pour l'Infanterie*, pp. 19–20; Montecuccoli, p. 64. In the last months of his life, Gustav Adolf was driven to attempt to form a standing army for the whole of Protestant Germany, in the interests of *discipline*.

[26] As suggested by A. Vagts, *A History of Militarism* (1938), p. 46.

[27] As suggested by Werner Sombart, *Der moderne Kapitalismus*, i, 345, though he did add, 'Die Waffentechniek mag dabei mitgesprochen haben'.

[28] J. E. Elias, *Het Voorspel van den eersten Engelschen Oorlog*, 's Gravenhage, 1920, i, 150–1, for a suggestive comparison of the two cases.

[29] *Axel Oxenstiernas skrifter och brefvexling*, Stockholm, 1888–, II, i, 396.

[30] The Kiel canal was Wallenstein's idea. It is noteworthy that the biggest canal enterprise of the century – the Canal des Deux Mers, linking Bordeaux with the Mediterranean – was essentially a strategic work.

[31] In 1639: one of the great military feats of the war: see Birger Steckzén. *Johan Baner*, Stockholm, 1939, p. 330.

[32] Lars Tingsten, 'Några data angående Gustaf II Adolfs basering och operationsplaner i Tyskland 1630–1632', *Historisk tidskrift*, I Series, xlviii (1938); *Sveriges krig 1611–1632*, v, 282–4, 314, 330–8; vi, 7, 33–4, 179, 259. For a fuller discussion of Gustav Adolf's strategy, *supra*, pp. 71–3.

[33] B. Steckzén, *Baner*, pp. 208, 332, 342; Piero Pieri, 'La formazione dottrinale di Raimondo Montecuccoli', pp. 100, 110: 'La guerra cessa per sfinimento, attraverso una strategica logoratrice sempre più crudele e implacabile'; and *cf.* Per Sörensson, 'Fältherrar, härorganisation och krigföring under trettioåriga krigets senare skede' *Scandia*, iii (1930), *passim*.

[34] Altamira, iii, 295; J. Colin and J. Reboul, *Histoire militaire et navale* (= *Histoire de la nation française*, ed. G. Hanotaux, vii), Paris, 1925, i, 428, 432, 433; General Weygand, *Turenne*, Paris, 1934, p. 98.

[35] C. Jany, *op. cit.*, i, 53.

[36] J. U. Nef, *La Naissance de la Civilisation industrielle*, Paris, 1955, *passim*.

[37] The Swedes had 10,800 at Kirkholm; 'at most 10,000' at Narva: G. B. C:sson Barkman, *Svea Livgardets historia*, Stockholm, 1938–9, ii, 537; Rudolf Fåhraeus, *Karl XI och Karl XII*, Stockholm, 1932, p. 338.

[38] Pieri, 'Formazione dottrinale di . . . Montecuccoli', p. 114.

[39] 'Self-equipment is conducive to the relaxation of discipline – that is, to the flattening of the pyramid of subordination': Stanislaw Andrzejewski, *Military Organization and Society* (1954), p. 99. But I cannot agree with his view that arms monopolies were 'the expression of [the rulers'] desire to assert their control, and not dictated by technical necessities': *ibid.*, p. 88.

[40] Montecuccoli, pp. 110–11.

[41] Colin and Reboul, p. 368.

[42] Weygand, *Histoire de l'Armée française*, p. 144, reproduces this medal.

[43] For a discussion of related problems, see James E. King, *Science and Rationalism in the Government of Louis XIV*, Baltimore, 1949.

[44] A. Ernstberger, *Hans de Witte, Finanzmann Wallensteins*, Wiesbaden, 1954.

[45] J. Saint-Germain, *Les financiers sous Louis XIV*, Paris, 1950, p. 17. V. Klutchevski, *Pierre le Grand et son oeuvre*, Paris, 1953, pp. 162–6.

[46] K. R. Swart, *The Sale of Offices in the Seventeenth Century*, The Hague, 1949, *passim*.

[47] The point is well made in M. Ritter, 'Das Kontributionssystem Wallensteins', *Historische Zeitschrift*, 90 [N.F. 54] (1930), pp. 248–9.

[48] G. Droysen, *Beiträge zur Geschichte des Militärwesens in Deutschland während der Epoche des dreissigjährigen Krieges*, Hanover, 1875, pp. 28–31, for the resemblances between a mercenary company and a gild.

[49] Andrzejewski, *op. cit.*, p. 96.

[50] V. Loewe, *Die Organisation und Verwaltung der Wallensteinischen Heere*, Freiburg i.B., 1895, pp. 22–4.

[51] L. André, *Michel Le Tellier et Louvois*, Paris, 1942, pp. 327–40; Gordon A. Craig, *The Politics of the Prussian Army 1640–1945*, Oxford 1955, pp. 5–6.

[52] The term is Andrzejewski's.

[53] Especially for those who lived on a main traffic artery: one major cause of the decline in the population of Coburg during the period was enlistment. G. Franz, *Der dreissigjährige Krieg und das deutsche Volk*, Jena, 1943, p. 41.

[54] T. A. Fischer, *The Scots in Germany: being a contribution towards the History of the Scots abroad*, Edinburgh, 1902, p. 74, gives the proverb in the original. *Cf.* the Scots ballad:

> First they took my brethren twain, Then wiled my love from me,
> O, woe unto the cruel wars In Low Germanie!

See B. Hoenig, *Memoiren Englischer Officiere im Heere Gustaf Adolfs und ihr Fortleben in der Literatur*, in *Beitr. z. neueren Philologie J. Schipper dargebracht*, Leipzig, 1902, pp. 324–50.

[55] Turner, *Pallas Armata*, p. 166. Or as Wallhausen put it, when lamenting the decline of the lance, 'on est contraint de se servir de gens basses et vils': *Art militaire à cheval*, p. 3; and *cf.* similar remarks in Richelieu, *Testament politique*, p. 476.

[56] Wallhausen, *L'Art militaire pour l'Infanterie*, pp. 9–10.

[57] There is a good discussion of the question in H. J. C. von Grimmelshausen, *Simplicissimus the Vagabond* [trans. A. T. S. Goodrick] (1912), in chapters xvi–xvii: 'Who was the Imperialist John de Werth? Who was the Swede Stalhans [i.e. Stålhandske]? Who were the Hessians, Little Jakob and St André? Of their kind there were many yet well known, whom ... I forbear to mention'. He argues that this is no new state of affairs; but when he comes to give a list of earlier examples he can think of no instance between Hugh Capet and Pizzaro except Tamerlane. Simplicissimus was mistaken about Stålhandske, moreover: his father had been *kammarjunkare* to Erik xiv.

[58] Roland Mousnier, *La Vénalité des Offices sous Henri IV et Louis XIII*, Rouen, n.d., p. 506; *cf.* Frauenholz, *Söldnertum*, i, 27: 'vom Ritterschlag hört man nichts mehr, an denen Stelle tritt die Nobilitierung'. For conditions in Sweden, E. Ingers, *Bonden i svensk historia*, Stockholm, 1943, i, 234; B. Steckzén, *John Baner*, p. 57: 'Their [sc. Swedish infantry officers]'

coats of arms are often of recent origin, and many of them are not easily distinguishable from the young peasant lads that serve as NCOs, or fill the ranks as privates'.

[59] It was said of the *Feldschreiber* that 'er muss fast des Hauptmanns Meister sein, der selber oftmals nicht schreiben und rechnen kann': Loewe, *op. cit.*, p. 20.

[60] As for instance in the Great Elector's *Generalkriegskommissariat*: 'From the beginning its civilian officials interfered with military affairs and acted very independently of the army command': F. L. Carsten, *The Origins of Prussia*, Oxford, 1954, p. 263.

[61] Richelieu, *Testament*, pp. 393–4, condemns *ban* and *arrière-ban*; and see, for Sweden, P. Sörensson, 'Adelns rusttjänst och adelsfanans organisation', *Historisk tidskrift*, 42 (1922), 145–50, 221–3; and for Brandenburg, Jany, *op. cit.*, i, 10–12.

[62] In the armies of the Great Elector, for instance, 'the officers of the artillery and the engineers were almost exclusively commoners': Carsten, *op. cit.*, p. 271.

[63] *Sveriges krig 1611–1632*, supplementary vol. ii, 295.

[64] E. G. R. Taylor, *The Mathematical Practitioners of Tudor and Stuart England*, Cambridge, 1954, *passim.*

[65] A. R. Hall, *Ballistics in the Seventeenth Century*, Cambridge, 1952, p. 16: 'The standard of engineering technology was not merely insufficient to make scientific gunnery possible, it deprived ballistics of all experimental foundation, and almost of the status of an applied science, since there was no technique to which it could, in fact, be applied'.

[66] M. Kukiel, *Zarys historji wojskowośce w Polsce*, London, 1949, p. 46. For Gustav Adolf's interest in cartography, see Försvarsstabens krigshistoriska avdelning, *Vägar och vägkunskap i Mellaneuropa under trettioåriga krigets sista skede*, Stockholm, 1948, pp. 41–2.

[67] L. Hammarskiöld, 'Ur svenska artilleriets hävder', *Artilleri-Tidskrift*, 1941–4, p. 93.

[68] *Krijgskundige Aantekening van Johan van Nassau*, ed. J. W. Wijn, p. xii.

[69] *Saucisses de guerre* are described by Johan of Nassau as 'korbe welche langerlich und geflochten sint . . . mit eisernde schroten kugel oder kleinen steinen auffollet', and as 'wurste welche voll pulvers gefullet und in die rustlöcher [of a fortress] so viel man dun kan, gesteckt, und die mauer also gesprengt werden'. They are said to have been sacks an ell thick and ten to twelve feet long: *Krijgskundige Aantekening – van Johan van Nassau*, pp. 50, 94 and note 2. They are possibly to be distinguished from the *saucissons* described in a note to Montecuccoli (*Mémoires*, p. 137, note) as 'grosses fascines liées en trois endroits'.

[70] Sir G. N. Clark, 'The History of the Medical Profession', *Medical History*, x, (1966), p. 218.

[71] Styffe, *Gustaf Adolfs skrifter*, pp. 65, 67; *Monro His Expedition*, II, 175, 196; and in general for military education W. Sjöstrand, *Grunddragen av den militära undervisningens uppkomst- och utvecklingshistoria i Sverige till år 1792*, Uppsala, 1941. The concluding section of Wallhausen's *Art militaire à cheval* (pp. 97–134) is 'a discourse of two persons . . . on the excellence of

the Military Art, maintaining that (except Theology) it excels all the other arts and sciences, as well liberal as mechanical', and insisting that 'the Military Art ought to be taught in Academies, as Letters are'. And Davies writes (*The Art of War and Englands Traynings*, p. 29) that the military profession 'being then more perfect and aboue all other Arts, consequently it is necessarie we vse in the same greater Studie, and more continuall exercise then is to be vsed in any other Art'.

⁷² Sjöstrand, pp. 177–83; Wijn, pp. 74–80; Heischmann, pp. 211–13.
⁷³ Loewe, pp. 18–25.
⁷⁴ André, *Le Tellier et Louvois*, pp. 317–21; and (on the emergence of rank) Wijn, pp. 62–73; Frauenholz, *Söldnertum*, i, 28–9; Sjöstrand, p. 71.
⁷⁵ Edmond Silberner, *La Guerre dans la Pensée économique du XVIe au XVIIIe siècle*, Paris, 1939.
⁷⁶ *Ibid.*, p. 99.
⁷⁷ J. E. Elias, *Het Voorspel van den eersten Engelschen oorlog*, i, 141–2.
⁷⁸ Bulstrode Whitelocke, *Memorials of the English Affairs* (1732), pp. 633 ff.
⁷⁹ Elias, *op. cit.*, i, 134–177, especially pp. 157, 167–8; Charles E. Hill, *The Danish Sound Dues and the Command of the Baltic*, Chapel Hill, 1926, p. 155.
⁸⁰ For all this see F. Redlich, *De praeda militari. Looting and Booty 1500–1815*, Wiesbaden, 1956.
⁸⁰ᵃ See, e.g., M. Ritter, 'Das Kontributionssystem Wallensteins', *passim*.
⁸¹ Pieri, 'Formazione dottrinale', p. 100.
⁸² Styffe, *Gustaf II Adolfs skrifter*, p. 520.
⁸³ *Axel Oxenstiernas skrifter och brefvexling*, I, vii, 126.
⁸⁴ For Vauban and the notion of the *pré carré*, see *Makers of Modern Strategy*, ed. E. M. Earle, Princeton, 1944, pp. 40–6.
⁸⁵ The best early example of this is perhaps the close-action broadside; but the new linear tactics were not far behind.
⁸⁶ 'Les maisons n'étoient que de bois, comme dans la pluspart de l'Allemagne, et en moins de six heures tout fut reduit en cendre: exemple terrible mais nécessaire contre des bourgeois insolents qui ne sachent ce que c'est que de faire la guerre, osent insulter de braves gens et les défier d'entrer dans leurs murs, lors-qu'ils n'ont ni l'adresse ni le courage de s'y défendre': G. Gualdo-Priorato, *L'Historie des dernières campagnes et negociations de Gustave Adolphe en Allemagne. Avec des notes . . . par M. l'Abbé de Francheville*, Berlin, 1772, p. 185. It is difficult to agree with Professor Nef (*War and Human Progress* [1950], pp. 138) that Spinola's courteous treatment of the enemy at the surrender of Breda (1625), as against the horrors of Magdeburg (1631), marks the beginning of a new chivalrousness and the age of limited warfare, though Oestrich (*op. cit.*, p. 31) endorses Nef's comment. Breda capitulated; Magdeburg was stormed: the two cases are not comparable.
⁸⁷ Grimmelshausen, *Simplicissimus*, p. 32.
⁸⁸ Francisco Suárez, *De Triplici virtute theologica, fide, spe, et charitate* (1621) (new edn, Oxford, 1944), especially vii, p. 13–16; Alberico Gentili, *De Jure Belli Libri Tres* (1612) (new edn, Oxford, 1933), II, iv, viii, xxi, xxiii; James Brown Scott, *The Spanish Origin of International Law: Francisco de Vitoria and his Law of Nations*, Oxford, 1934, especially p. 285.

[89] *Hugonis Grotii De Jure Belli ac Pacis Libri Tres,* ed. W. Whewell, Cambridge, 1853, III, iv, 9 § 1, for this passage; and see *ibid.,* III, iv, 8–10, 15, 16; III, v, 1; III, viii, 1–4.

[90] Bynkershoek is said to have remarked 'dat de Groot zich steeds aan de bestaande gewoonten en gebruiken houdt, zoodat hij bij gebreke daarvan nauwelijks eenigen regel van jus gentium durft te stellen': J. Kosters, 'Het Jus gentium van Hugo de Groot en diens voorgangers', *Mededeelingen der Koninklijke Akademie van Wetenschappen,* Afd. Letterkunde, 58 (1924). Series B., p. 13.

8

Charles XI[1]

It may well seem that I have chosen as the subject of this lecture
a monarch whose lineaments are unmemorable, and whose
achievement is obscure. It is certainly true that the visitor to
Stockholm will find no statue of Charles XI among the public
monuments of that city. Charles XII stands in Kungsträd-
gården, with gull-whitened pate and rigid finger pointing
towards Pultava, in silent rebuke of the diners on Opera-
källarens *terrass*; a hundred yards to the rear Charles XIII leans
upon a property anchor; across the water, outside Skansen,
Charles XV sits trimly on his charger; but for Charles XI you
will look in vain. One remembers him (if at all) from a large
canvas of David Klöcker Ehrenstrahl; which shows him, not
altogether at his ease, in company with a Swedish lion *dormant*;
and it is not Ehrenstrahl's fault if the lion steals the picture. For
Charles was, indeed, ill-equipped for the representative side of
royalty: personally unprepossessing, invincibly shy, and of no
general conversation. Of the native demagogic eloquence of
the Vasas he had no share. He suffered, moreover, from word-
blindness, which caused him to spell like a mishandled type-
writer;[2] and to the end of his days he was a slow and reluctant
reader. Hot-tempered, obstinate, narrow-minded, bigoted, he
was almost equally deficient in imagination and in the capacity
for abstract thought; and of his virtues too many were unen-
dearing virtues of the barrack-square or the Inland Revenue.
His sense of duty was overpowering; and it is recorded of him
that he rose at four o'clock on his wedding night to make a

routine inspection of his troops.[3] Yet in spite of it all he was of critical importance in the history of his country: the hinge upon which the whole of modern Swedish history swings; the link between the world of Axel Oxenstierna and the world of Arvid Horn.

When he came to the throne at the age of four in 1660, the strange destiny of Sweden had touched its zenith. The empire of the Baltic was still intact, and the peace of Copenhagen had for the first time given Sweden her natural limits within the Scandinavian peninsula. As a guarantor of the peace of Westphalia, she had both a right and a duty to interfere in the great questions of the European mainland. Charles x had contemplated the conquest and annexation of Denmark; he had made what proved to be the last serious attempt to achieve total control of the great trade between Muscovy and the West; and he had barely missed success.[4] After sixty years of strife, the peace of Oliva had ended the dynastic quarrel with Poland: henceforward there would be nothing to fear on that side.[5] The peace of Kardis in 1661 registered the failure of Russia to gain a foothold on the Baltic.[6] Territorially, Sweden was a satisfied power: her problem now would be to hold what she had, against Frederick III's plan to recover Skåne, or the Great Elector's designs upon Pomerania. With a long regency in prospect, Swedish policy must therefore aim at standing still, at keeping the peace, at preserving the armed forces in good shape (especially the navy, on which all else hung), and at building up the mercantile marine in order to free her exports from dependence on the Dutch.

But in politics it is never easy to stand still; in the circumstances in which Sweden found herself after 1660 it was almost impossible. The great territorial gains of the last three reigns had been the product of military victory, made possible only because Gustav Adolf and his successors had had at their disposal large and well-trained armies. After 1660 it was no longer feasible to maintain forces on the old scale. Gustav Adolf, and even Charles x, had been able to do it only because their armies in war-time had been nearly self-supporting. Upon the domestic revenues they had borne relatively lightly. The longer the Thirty Years' War continued, the less the burden upon Sweden. But these were conditions never to be repeated, and in any case irrelevant to times of peace. The plain truth was, that in peace-time Sweden was too poor to be able to keep large armies on foot for very long. If a sudden emergency compelled her to raise troops as a precautionary measure, the only escape from the financial strain seemed to be to move them with all speed into foreign territory. On purely financial grounds, mobilization probably entailed war: Charles x had found it so, in 1655 and 1658; Charles xi was to find it so in 1674. The Swedish empire, moreover, was exceptionally vulnerable: it was widely scattered, sundered by the sea, and dependent for survival on long communications which might be cut by enemy action, or blocked for months on end by ice.[7] In these conditions the most that could be done was to give the overseas territories a nucleus of troops which could perhaps hold out until help should arrive from home; but even this was a strain upon available resources.[8] If, then, Sweden was now to find the task of defending her empire almost beyond her capacity, what hope had she of maintaining herself in the position of a great power? What claim to be treated as the equal of France, and Austria, and the Dutch? Was it conceivable that she should fill the leading part which the Westphalian settlement had assigned to her?

The ink was hardly dry upon the treaties of 1660 before these questions pressed upon the Regents. They were soon forced to halve the size of the army.[9] And they found themselves driven to base their foreign policy on the maintenance of the balance of power, and the preservation of the *status quo* as it had been established in 1648 and 1659. If this could be done, if peace could be preserved, Sweden's inability to compete with the great powers might perhaps go unobserved. But if it could not, national pride would compel participation: as Admiral Stenbock remarked, 'when others arm, Sweden cannot sit still'.[10] In either event, they were forced to face the fact that even in peacetime they must look for foreign subsidies in order to be able to maintain the army and navy in a condition sufficiently respectable to render Sweden safe from attack.[11] But from the beginning it was a delusion to suppose that a policy of balance could be successfully pursued by a country already coming to be notorious as a subsidy-hunter. The financial carelessness and incompetence of the Regents, the chronic exhaustion of the treasury, put Sweden very much at the mercy of her paymasters. Balance was indeed (*pace* Fahlborg!) a chimera, when pursued by a power as weak as Sweden already was: her pretensions, as has been well said, were contradicted by her impotence.[12] She could no longer tip the scales in Europe, still less impose her arbitrament. The experience of 1672–4 afforded no justification for the naïve expectation that Louis xiv and the Emperor would meekly regulate their conduct in conformity with Magnus de la Gardie's view of the correct interpretation of the guarantee clause of the Peace of Westphalia. Only very sanguine statesmen, bemused by past glories, would have thought so. Had they so soon forgotten their own resentment at the proceedings of the Hague Concerts?[13] It may be freely admitted that those older historians were mistaken who condemned the French alliance of 1672 as simply a financial gamble by a government at its wits' end for money; it may even be conceded that it was possible for men to believe that the European balance had tipped so plainly towards the Emperor that Sweden's alignment with France had some transient justification. But the policy of redressing the balance in France's favour by the formation of a neutral block in Germany had already been condemned in advance by its author: as recently as October 1671 de la Gardie had told the *råd* that 'he who opts for neutrality usually enjoys *beneficium Polyphemi*'.[14] Georg Landberg has rightly stigmatized their 'lack of that grip upon reality without which even the most refined argumentation is vitiated'.[15] By 1674, in fact, they had contrived to put themselves into a position where they could neither afford to be neutral, nor not to be neutral. In the end French blackmail, made easy by de la Gardie's laxness or incompetence in drawing the terms of the subsidy-treaty, was able to drive them into just the sort of preparatory military movement which, in the existing financial stringency, was almost certain to escalate into war, however little they might desire it.[16] Such a foreign policy is hardly susceptible of rehabilitation. The best that can be said for the Regents is that they did no more than make the worst of a situation which was admittedly beset with formidable difficulties. Yet throughout the period since 1661 it had been the height of their political ambition to play the part of mediator in Europe: in 1673 a member of the *råd* even described that function as 'among the most precious jewels in H.M. diadem'.[17] But this was itself a sign of their weakness: they grasped at prestige in default of power. Even in the desperate financial circumstances of 1674, de la Gardie tried to impose on Europe by vast dispendious embassies.[18] Charles x would never have used such tactics, nor held such language. Already Swedish statesmen are beginning to speak in the accents of Höpken and Tessin.

By 1679, then, the power which thirty years before had terrified and astonished Europe had been reduced to a position of considerable ignominy. Peace with security necessitated subsidies; subsidies entangled her in war; war, if recent experience went for anything, led to defeats which cast doubt on the long-unquestioned quality of the Swedish army. And when a peace at last extricated Sweden from these embarrassments, she owed her salvation to a settlement dictated, almost behind her back, by Louis xiv. The heirs of Gustav Adolf had become the vassals of France: French and Dutch diplomats debated the fate of Swedish territories in the same tone as they discussed the possessions of Spain, as pieces of booty or objects of exchange.[19] In 1672 Sir William Temple could still write of Sweden as a great and potentially aggressive power;[20] but the unrivalled French diplomatic service knew better. Already Mazarin in his day had opined that 'la balance penche plutôt du côté de sa chute';[21] a decade or so later Lionne treated the Swedes as clients whom he could reduce to order at the crack of the whip.[22] Pomponne and Courtin were contemptuous of the enervation of Sweden's energies and venality of her politicians.[23] And as late as 1689 Bidal (a bad observer, however) classed Sweden with Hanover among the minor powers.[24]

Meanwhile, in 1672, the regency had come to an end, and Charles xi had assumed (at least nominally) the government of his dominions. It was not until the outbreak of war in 1674 that he began to develop a mind and a policy of his own, and to permit himself for the first time to think that his magnificent uncle de la Gardie might possibly be less wise and less deserving than he had been taught to believe. The disasters of the war, the administrative and financial weaknesses which it laid bare, the insinuations of de la Gardie's political enemies, convinced him of the incompetence and self-seeking of the Regents; and his own vigorous performances in the field gave him self-confidence. Charles XI had none of his father's military genius: his solution to all tactical problems was to attack with the sword;[25] he was quite destitute of any strategic insight. It was as quartermaster and adjutant, rather than as commander-in-chief, that he made his indispensable contribution to Swedish military history. At the battle of Lund, nevertheless, his reckless bravery turned the tide and saved his country; and his success as a soldier set a permanent mark on his reign. The army became his passion; the comrades in arms of the dark days of 1676 and 1677 – Rutger von Ascheberg[26] and Nils Bielke, in particular – always held a special place in his esteem. To them he turned with confidence, in preference to the civilians who had let the country down. By 1679 this tendency had become so marked that the central government in Stockholm had been virtually superseded or thrust aside by a camarilla of king's friends at headquarters.[27] Already before the war ended events had made Charles something like a military dictator.

The most intelligent, influential and unscrupulous of the new advisers was Johan Gyllenstierna; and it was he, more than any other man, who laid the foundations upon which absolutism was to be erected in the next decade. In the few months of life which remained to him after the war (he died prematurely in 1680) Gyllenstierna also tried a new venture in foreign policy. Its basis was reconciliation with Denmark; and historians long considered it to be the forerunner of the 'Scandinavianism' of a later age. The researches of Georg Landberg have pricked that bubble;[28] and we now know that Gyllenstierna was really an expansionist of the traditional type, essentially a man of the Age of Greatness. His friendship for Denmark was purely opportunist and tactical; and he saw the solution to Sweden's problems in renewed aggression in Germany, or perhaps in the conquest of Norway.[29] His foreign policy was really a blind alley: the way forward was to be indicated by his successor, Bengt Oxenstierna, and above all by Charles XI himself.

It would be idle to pretend that Charles's views on foreign affairs were either subtle or profound. On the contrary, they were simple to the point of being simple-minded. To preserve his freedom of action; not to allow Sweden to be bullied; above all, to keep the country out of another war – this, really, was the sum of his policy. 'A war is soon begun,' he wrote on one occasion, 'but as to its ending – that is in God's hands.'[30] Every effort, then, must be made to take the heat out of Sweden's relations with other powers: Swedish historians who referred contumeliously to the Danes as 'Jutes', or called the Russians barbarians, would find their works censored in the interests of international good feeling.[31] The ideal was still, as before, a European balance; but Charles and Oxenstierna, reacting against de la Gardie's gallophil propensities, sought to achieve it through friendship with the maritime powers.[32] The political conflicts of a later age are already taking shape; Nils Bielke's contest with Bengt Oxenstierna foreshadows the clash of Hats and Caps. But the new alignment after 1680 did not affect the king's resolve to keep out of the European struggle. It was not only that like Frederick William I of Prussia, a generation later, he could not bear to spoil his beautiful army by using it;[33] it was also that the work of domestic reform and rehabilitation was so important to him that he was not willing to jeopardize it by war unless Sweden's vital interests were involved. If his alliances committed him as an auxiliary, it could usually be contrived that his contribution was too late.[34] The Anglo-Dutch blockade of France stung him for a moment into joining Denmark in a still-born armed neutrality which looks forward to the agreement of 1756;[35] and he did not hesitate to mobilize on behalf of Holstein-Gottorp, the geographical situation of which made it the strategic linchpin of the Swedish position in Germany.[36] But it is significant that in the end it was *international* action, at the congress of Altona, that restored the duke of Holstein-Gottorp to his dominions; and no less significant that this time Sweden was able to mobilize without mobilization's entailing war. Twenty years before, the Regents would have held it to be axiomatic that a peace policy of this kind could not possibly be pursued in safety without the aid of foreign subsidies. It was Charles XI's achievement to prove that this idea was erroneous, to demonstrate that Sweden could live without a paymaster, maintain a first-class army in peacetime, and remain neutral at will, not only without danger, but with increased international prestige. He thus solved perhaps the greatest political problem which his country had to confront in his time: the problem of how to abdicate gracefully from the status of a great power, without becoming either a puppet in the hands of the strong, or a mere carcase for the international vultures. For a generation Sweden had been drunk with victory and bloated with booty: Charles XI led her back into the grey light of everyday existence, gave her policies appropriate to her resources and her real interests, equipped her to carry them out, and prepared for her a future of weight and dignity as a second-class power. He could not foresee that his son's inflexible logic would shake the foundations he had laid, nor that domestic faction afterwards would compromise the freedom of action which he had won; but in the interval between those two aberrations we can recognize, in Arvid Horn, a statesman who in this respect has some claim to be considered his political legatee; and in a longer view it may not be fantastic to see in him the ancestor of Östen Undén. No doubt he underestimated the danger that threatened Sweden from the east: preoccupied with the threat of a Danish revenge, he postponed too long defensive measures against the Muscovite. But at least his policy was based upon recognition of the truth that the age of expansion was over; and if it had been followed by his successor it might well have made possible an adjustment to international realities less violent and less painful than the experience which Sweden was to undergo in the next generation.

How, then, did Charles XI accomplish the feat which had baffled the political sagacity of the Regents? How was he able to afford a first-class army in peacetime? By what financial conjuring did he contrive to exist without subsidies, and still balance his budget? The short answer is that the financial resources were provided mainly by that vast and ruthless resumption of alienated crown lands and revenues which goes by the name of the *reduktion*, and which effected a revolution in the power of the monarchy comparable with that which had resulted from the Reformation. Its full consequences, admittedly, were not felt for a decade or so after 1680. Those who had advocated a *reduktion* in the expectation that it would make taxation unnecessary – and especially taxation of the nobility – soon found themselves disappointed.[37] The reform of army and navy, the heavy expenditure on fortification, did indeed necessitate increases of taxation at the Diets of the 'eighties. But by the beginning of the 'nineties ordinary revenue was more than adequate to ordinary expenditure: for the first time since the reign of Gustav Vasa the king could live of his own.

Hand in hand with the *reduktion* went the new system of army maintenance, famous in Swedish history as the allotment system (*indelningsverket*).[38] This meant, in effect, the settling of the native conscript army upon the land. To each soldier and officer was assigned a farm, or a portion of the rent or taxes due to the crown from a farm; and all the men from one unit received their allocations in the area from which the unit was recruited. They were mustered at regular intervals for training and manœuvres; but between times they were farmers, or cottiers, or labourers, according to their rank and the pay that was due to them. While small mercenary forces held the bastions of empire beyond the sea, in Sweden and Finland the army in peacetime became territorial, self-recruiting (by the system known as *ständigt knektehåll*)[39] and above all self-supporting. The estates which the nobility lost by the *reduktion* provided lands and revenues which henceforward could be for ever reserved to the maintenance of the native troops.[40] Those troops were thus for the most part paid in kind. It was a deliberate return to the methods of the sixteenth century, to decentralized finance, to a natural rather than a cash economy; a reversal, in short, of all the financial reforms associated with the names of Gustav Adolf and Axel Oxenstierna.[41] There was an obvious danger that the army under such a system might degenerate into a half-trained militia, slow to muster and ineffective in a sudden emergency. As long as Charles xi lived his personal supervision made it certain that this would not happen. When Charles xii was attacked by his neighbours in 1700, the Swedish citizen army mobilized with a precision and a speed which no contemporary state could emulate, moving by routes determined long before, to prearranged halts ready supplied with necessities according to a standard schedule. Everything, to the last detail, had been planned by Charles xi and his military coadjutors; and in 1700 everything went according to plan.[42] Charles xi bequeathed to his son perhaps the best-trained and best-equipped army ever to leave the shores of Sweden.

After 1721, no doubt, it was a different story. In the decades
after the peace of Nystad the agricultural side of the soldier's
life tended to obscure the military; the officer grew too attached
to his *boställe*, the soldier to his *torp*; the old martial spirit was
lost;[43] faction played havoc with the officer-class; army administration sank into inefficiency. Hence the lamentable performances of the Swedish armies in the wars of the mid-
eighteenth century. And there was one other disadvantage in
indelningsverket: a system devised for maintaining an army at
home in peacetime could not work well if that army were fighting overseas. It was precisely this consideration that had led
Gustav Adolf and Axel Oxenstierna to try to turn as much of
their revenue as possible into cash. To Eli Heckscher, of course,
Charles xi's work looked like a barbarization, a reversion to
pre-mercantilist practice, an attempt by a man of narrow
views and limited intelligence to turn back the current of
economic history.[44] But at least it preserved Sweden from the
possibility of anything resembling the Great Elector's *Generalkriegskommissariat*, with all the social and constitutional consequences that flowed from it. And in fact it was entirely logical
and appropriate, given Charles's principles of foreign policy.
Gustav Adolf wanted cash because he had to pay his troops in
Germany; Charles xi paid in kind because he had no intention
of fighting abroad if he could help it. His political and military
system was neither designed for, nor suited to, protracted
campaigns beyond the seas, and this was recognized both by his
supporters and his critics. The author of *Les Anecdotes de Suède*,
writing shortly before Charles's death, remarked that 'la
Suède ne peut faire aucun entreprise considérable sans l'argent
d'autruy'.[45] Charles xii's ministers were of the same mind.
After the battle of Narva, they insisted that foreign aid was a
necessary precondition for carrying the war against Augustus ii
into Poland; and they felt that large explosive questions such
as that of Holstein-Gottorp must be settled by international
action, since Sweden could no longer tackle them alone. It was
Sweden's misfortune that Charles xii was of the contrary
opinion.[46] The days were gone, moreover, when foreign war
offered attractions to the nobility. Nowhere did the *reduktion*
make a cleaner sweep of noble donations than in the Baltic
provinces.[47] The aristocracy could expect no repetition of the

grants which former sovereigns had made of lands in newly-conquered territories, for Charles XI was resolved to make no such donations in future; and even if he were to change his mind they could not forget how he had revoked his pledged word, overridden considerations of equity and charity, changed the terms of tenure *ex post facto*, and declared the crown's right untrammelled by any statute of limitations.[48] No one now was anxious to engage in a speculation of which the terms were so uncertain. As the *reduktion* signified the crown's renunciation of adventure, so for the nobility it deprived adventure of all its savour.[49]

Charles XI's resolve to rehabilitate the finances and to rebuild the army on a sounder basis, his determination to tolerate no opposition to reforms which he considered essential to the safety of Sweden, go far to explain his gradual assumption of absolute power in the years after 1680. It was a constitutional upheaval which left an ineffaceable impression upon the history of his country. Within a few decades, no doubt, war and revolution had swept the *régime* away, for the structure which he set up could not survive the strain which the distortions of his son placed upon it; but still it is true to say that after 1680 things were never quite the same again. To contemporaries, certainly, the changes of the 'eighties appeared as a sudden and violent revolution. Yet there can be no doubt that it was less sudden than it seemed: the preconditions for absolutism existed in abundance, and some of them had been present for many years. At a moment of national defeat and demoralization Charles XI had emerged as the leader and saviour of the state; and just as Frederick III of Denmark's defence of Copenhagen in 1658–9 prepared the way for the *coup* of 1660, so Charles's valour at Lund helped to establish his reputation in the popular imagination. Military necessity sapped the capacity for resistance of the ordinary organs of constitutional control, much as it had done in Brandenburg twenty years earlier; and when the war was over the argument from security made men more ready to accept the need for a concentration of authority in a single hand: as the Danish *Kongelov* (*lex regia*) put it: 'The more power and authority a lord and king possesses, the safer are he and his subjects from the attacks of external foes.'[50]

Certainly there had been no such security under the rule of the Regents and the *råd*. After fourteen years of peace and prosperity the national finances were in disorder, the armed forces run down, the administration discredited. The diplomacy of de la Gardie had landed Sweden in a war which the Diet of 1672 had explicitly asked him to avoid. The Regents had been slack in pursuing Charles x's partial *reduktion*, and they were accused with some justice of having feathered their own nests and neglected their duty. It was a period when more and more men were seeking a career in the service of the state, and such persons were sharply critical of a *régime* which so mismanaged its affairs that public servants could not be certain that the crown would be able to pay their wages: this was one main reason why the demand for a *reduktion* was so strong and so widespread. In 1677 a ruined member of the *råd* was trying to obtain six years' arrears of the salary due to him, to supply his essential living-expenses; and three years earlier it had been noted as an extraordinary instance of favour that two of the king's secretaries should have been paid their wages in full.[51] Feeling was especially bitter among the lower nobility – men whose estates did not permit them to live as expensively as their social status required, men who in the past had supplemented their resources by service in the army, by booty taken in war, by donations from a grateful sovereign. Where now could they look for donations, when the crown lands were mostly alienated, and Charles x's *reduktion* seemed to have stuck fast? Where for booty, when the crown could no longer afford great continental wars? What prospects had they, if not in the civil service? But here they found themselves competing against incomers who had done well out of the wars, against sons of the clergy who had entered the royal service rather than engage in the rat-race for benefices, against ambitious academics, against a new generation of purely Swedish financiers; and their chances were further diminished by the pre-emptive claim to the best posts put forward by the high nobility, and particularly by members of the *råd*. Already by 1660 the grip of the great magnates upon the better posts had become so tight that one of them, at least, feared that the frustrations and discouragement of the lower nobility might lead to a diversion of their interests into other fields, and a mass flight from the

king's service.[52] All through the first twenty years of Charles
XI's reign the lower nobility waged a grim battle against the
magnates. They were enraged by the pretensions of the titled
nobility (i.e. the counts and barons) to a *votum decisivum* in the
Estate of Nobles; they refused to concede the *pas* to counts and
barons who were their inferiors in the hierarchy of service.
Johan Gyllenstierna (himself of the high nobility, though at
that time untitled, and with family connections trending
downwards rather than upwards)[53] expressed the feeling with
his usual crudeness when he said 'If I'm senior, no count is
walking before me'.[54] The demand for a Precedence Ordinance,
which should lay down a Table of Ranks based strictly on
service and not on birth, was one of the main points in the
programme of the lower nobility during the minority. They
obtained it at last, in 1680. And the deep division in the first
Estate crippled its powers of resistance to the monarchy. If
that division had not existed, absolutism might not have been
possible: certainly it would not have come as easily.[55]

But the social strains which the monarchy was able to exploit
extended far beyond the internal tensions within the aristocracy.
The non-noble Estates were clamouring against the nobility's
fiscal and social privileges. Clergy and Burghers looked to a
reduktion to alleviate the burden of taxation. Above all, the
peasants feared lest the passing of crown lands into noble
hands might expose them to the oppression of aristocratic
landlords, and perhaps degrade them to 'a Livonian servitude'.[56] These fears and resentments had lain at the heart of the
aborted revolutionary situation of 1650, when for the first time
since the 1590s the non-noble Estates had found in the crown a
temporary ally against the aristocracy. And though Christina
had then played them false, and though the partial *reduktion*
of Charles X, the so-called *fjärdepartsräfst*, had for the moment
plastered over the social ulcer, the fundamental strife of
Estates had not been ended. In the twenty years that followed,
it was never far below the surface of politics. On occasion, as at
the Diet of 1672, it blazed furiously in the open.[57] A monarch
who was really serious about a *reduktion* would always find
enthusiastic allies in the three lower Estates. To strengthen his
hand they would not hesitate to make constitutional sacrifices, and
were willing enough to shut their eyes to political implications

if they could realize their social programme. And if at the Diet of 1680 it was the lesser nobles who first pushed on the plan for a *reduktion*, the lower Estates soon turned the occasion into a massive demonstration of hostility to the high aristocracy and loyalty to the throne.[58] In Olof Thegner they produced a great parliamentarian, who took up the struggle where Nils Skunk had dropped it thirty years before. It was not altogether extravagant for a cantankerous Whig in the reign of Queen Anne to describe Thegner and his allies as a set of 'monarchical levellers'.[59]

Absolutism in Sweden was certainly not (to borrow Geijer's famous phrase) 'an accident that looked like an idea': on the contrary, it was an idea which had long been gaining ground in the minds of clerics, lawyers and political theorists. The researches of Dr Nils Runeby have made it possible for us to follow step by step the trends of Swedish political thought in the first three-quarters of the seventeenth century; and it is now plain that already in the 'fifties there had been a marked change in the intellectual climate.[60] Althusius was out, Arnisaeus was in, as far as the dons at Uppsala were concerned. Precisely the same change of fashion in political thought – with, once again, Arnisaeus as the modish textbook – had occurred in Denmark in the two decades before 1660.[61] In both countries the absolutist revolution had been prepared in men's minds before it became a political reality. If Charles x had lived longer he might well have anticipated the work of his son.[62] The revolution which Frederick iii carried through in Copenhagen was not unremarked on the other side of the Sound, and the Swedish aristocracy were intermittently afraid that something of the sort might happen in Stockholm:[63] at the Diet of 1672 a member of the Estate of Burghers pointedly alluded to it.[64] Some idea of the nature of *Kongeloven* must have reached Sweden, especially when, after the accession of Christian v, its existence became generally known. But indeed, the whole current of the age seemed setting strongly against constitutionalism and in favour of monarchy. The victory of the Great Elector over the Estates of Brandenburg and of Prussia was necessarily an event of concern to Sweden, if only for its military implications. The magnificent beginnings of Louis xiv's personal rule were circumstantially reported by Swedish diplomats and travellers; the fall of Fouquet, Colbert's harrying of delinquent nobles and administrators, were useful examples to those who wished to bring the Regents to book.[65] And though there cannot be much in the suggestion that Charles II's dissolution of his last parliament had some influence on Swedish events, there seems to be rather more substance in the charge that Oxford doctrines of Divine Right had infected the clergy, both in Sweden and in Denmark.[66]

Despite all these considerations, the relatively easy triumph of the crown was, and is, surprising. For in Sweden it was not, as in Denmark, a matter of the defeat of a class which stood for privilege alone, divorced from any intelligible constitutional cause; nor was it, as in Brandenburg, the overthrow of constitutionalism by a bargain between monarchy and aristocracy. In Sweden Charles XI struck down simultaneously a privileged order and a constitutional tradition; and that tradition was not, as in France, a tattered remnant from a bygone age. On the contrary, it appeared living and strong, rooted in centuries of history, never forgotten, and (if the past were any guide) surely not to be abandoned without a major struggle. It was perhaps natural enough that the country should cry out against the Regents, that the Diet of 1675 should insist on an investigation of their conduct, and that the Diet of 1680 should allow itself to be manœuvred by the king into undertaking their trial. But it was another thing that their fall should involve the end of the political power of the *råd*. From mediaeval times the *råd* had been the watchdog of the constitution, the custodian of the country's liberties, the undying authority to whom sovereignty reverted in an interregnum. It stood as mediator between king and people; it had the duty of making sure that each fulfilled the pledges and discharged the duties owed to the other. The change from elective to hereditary monarchy in 1544 had not permanently obscured these duties and functions, and in the second half of the sixteenth century the *råd* had stood forward again as the opponent of the absolutist tendencies of John III and Sigismund. At Linköping, in 1600, the demagogic tyranny of Charles IX had brought some of its boldest spokesmen to the block. But the tradition of aristocratic constitutionalism as it had been propounded by Erik Sparre and Hogenskild Bielke,[67] firmly grounded in history and law, looking back to Magnus Eriksson's Land Law (*ca.* 1350) as its fundamental charter, and to the Recess of Kalmar (1483) as its ideal for the monarchy – was too vital to be uprooted by a few executions. The Charter of 1611, the Form of Government of 1634, represented its engrafting upon the stock of monarchy. After 1611, the *råd* stood, as always, for limited monarchy and constitutional guarantees; and if it also stood for privilege, that was true of constitutional oppositions everywhere, in the seventeenth century.[68] Its consciousness of its *rôle* as mediator, its conception of itself as an Estate of the realm, distinct from that of the nobility, had rather strengthened than otherwise; for the old concept of the mediator had been made fashionable by Althusius under the name of the ephorate, and the old devices of control had become articulate in the new ideal of mixed monarchy.[69] After 1660 the power of the *råd* was sufficiently impressive to make Magalotti sure that Sweden was a pure aristocracy disguised as a monarchy;[70] and in the early 'seventies it seemed to be striving to make good a novel claim to approve or veto royal appointments to the more important offices.[71] The opposition of the Estates, always suspicious of aristocratic influence in the disposal of jobs, had secured the rejection of this pretension; but the old anti-monarchical spirit was sufficiently alive to make credible the story later put about in *Les Anecdotes de Suède* of the existence of a plan to set up an aristocratic republic.[72]

The outbreak of war in 1674 was the turning-point in the fate of the *råd* as it was in that of the former Regents. Wartime administration passed into the hands of the men who surrounded Charles XI in the field, while the *råd* sat in Stockholm despatching dignified trivialities.[73] When the war ended they were politically isolated, discredited by their own internal feuds, distrusted alike by king and Estates. They were not consulted about the peace of 1679, nor about the negotiations with Denmark that followed it, though foreign policy had always been one of their main concerns; they were not consulted about the summoning of the Diet of 1680, though this too had been usual in the past. Indeed, the question was already presenting itself, whether the king was bound to consult them at all? The Land Law, no doubt, bound him to rule with the advice of his council (*med råds råde*); but did it follow that he was bound to seek advice if he felt that he did not need it? And was the *råd* entitled to offer advice unasked? When such questions as these were in the air, it showed a certain lack of realism for members of the *råd* to be talking of the Recess of Kalmar – the most extreme expression of the political pretensions of the mediaeval magnate-class.[74] Already the *råd* had been put in the dock with the Regents, to answer for past mistakes; and they now added a mistake there was no retrieving. They gave Charles unsolicited advice against proceeding with the *reduktion*, and they declined corporate responsibility for past errors on the ground that they were an Estate of the realm, which could not be indicted *en bloc*.[75]

The king saw his chance and took it. He addressed to the *riksdag* an enquiry, in which he asked them whether the Form of Government was binding upon a king of full age; whether the obligation to rule with the advice of his council (*med råds råde*) implied that he could not rule without it; and whether the *råd* was in fact an Estate of the realm. The answers he received were in his favour on every point. The king, they assured him, was bound by the Land Law, and not by the Form of Government, which he was free to alter; consultation with the *råd* was at his own discretion; its claim to be an Estate, as also its pretension to act as an ephorate, was explicitly condemned; and the king was declared responsible only to God.[76] It was a reply which brought to a close three centuries of constitutional controversy; it was the end of *monarchia mixta* in Sweden; it was a bloodless Linköping.[77] In 1682 the official title of the *råd* was changed from *riksråd* (council of state) to *kungligt råd* (king's council), Charles explaining that the older name might suggest some distinction between the service of the king and the service of the state.[78] And though this particular change lasted only as long as the absolutism lasted, the diminution in the power and constitutional authority of the *råd* proved in fact definitive and irreversible. In vain did the constitution-makers of 1719 explain that '*with* the advice of his council' meant 'not *without*, still less *against*':[79] semantics could not put the *råd* back in the position it had occupied in the Age of Greatness. Henceforward the members of the *råd* would be ministers – servants of the king, or of the Estates, as it might happen – but for all their ermined hats and velvet robes, their grave eloquence, composed countenances, and traditional senatorial dignity, they would never be what they had been in the period of Charles XI's minority.[80]

If the utter occlusion of the *råd*, and its meek acceptance of its fate, were sufficiently surprising, what happened to the *riksdag* was scarcely less so. Since 1634 all the signs had seemed to point to a future in which the *riksdag* would gradually take over the function of a constitutional regulator which the *råd* had hitherto discharged.[81] Two long minorities had done much to ripen adolescent parliamentarism to self-conscious maturity: in 1660 the first Estate was claiming for the Diet something like a *pouvoir constituant*.[82] And even in the years since Charles's majority they had shown no lack of enterprise. In 1675 they had taken the initiative in demanding investigation of the Regents' actions; they had claimed the unheard-of right to scrutinize the minutes of the *råd*; they had insisted upon the appropriation of supply.[83] At Halmstad in 1678 they had presented the crown with a comprehensive programme of domestic reforms.[84] Yet now they tumbled over each other to throw away the gains of the last half-century. To loaded questions from the king about the interpretation of the law and the extent of the royal prerogative they sent answers ever more yielding, couched in language ever more servile. By their answer of 1680[85] they in effect declared the king irresponsible before the law. Parliamentary free speech they abandoned without a struggle;[86] the king was suffered to remodel and conflate the resolutions of the several Estates to suit himself;[87] his right to legislate on general matters (and not only on economic affairs, which had always been reserved to him) was half-conceded, and tacitly acquiesced in.[88] When in 1686 Charles promulgated an Ecclesiastical Law without consulting them, they made no objection. With the coming of *indelnings-verket*, as we have seen, their control of troop-raising (and hence of foreign policy) came to an end: no doubt they made the less difficulty about it, because they knew how pacific that foreign policy now was. Only the right to grant or withhold taxes remained, and even that was compromised in 1689.[89] Now it is true that the Estates had scarcely ever taken advantage of their tax-granting power to extort concessions from the monarchy: when they did so in 1675 their purpose was essentially to defend what they conceived to be the crown's interests, by exposing the delinquencies of the former Regents. The king's right to raise money in an emergency had always been tacitly accepted, and the issue implicit in Hampden's case was scarcely even raised. The great social and constitutional crisis of 1650 had demonstrated that the lower Estates, so far from using the crown's necessities to secure parliamentary control of expenditure or policy, were concerned to get a *reduktion* (as the Estates of Brandenburg also were)[90] in order that henceforward the monarch might be enabled to live without parliamentary grants at all: the constitutional opportunity (as it seems to us) was allowed to slip; constitutional progress was secondary to the social struggle.[91] But though the *riksdag* had thus shown no great anxiety to enforce its control of taxation, it had hitherto been vigilant to maintain the position that every new levy of conscripts was a *grant*, and a grant which by this time only the *riksdag* was competent to make. Yet this too they now surrendered.[92] The quarrels between the Nobility and the non-noble Estates put the king in a position where both appealed to him as arbiter. A block of King's Friends terrorized their opponents by delations, threats of royal displeasure, and organized parliamentary uproar.[93] There seemed no limit to the concessions the Estates were prepared to make. They passed an extraordinary act for expunging from their own records (and later extended it to the minutes of the *råd*) every expression which might seem to impugn in the slightest degree the sovereignty of the king: since the dead could not recant, they were to be for ever silenced.[94] And at last, in 1693, they voted a declaration which defined absolutism in the broadest and most uncompromising terms: Charles XI, they resolved, 'is by God, Nature, and the crown's high hereditary right . . . an absolute sovereign king, whose commands are binding upon all, and who is responsible to no one on earth for his actions, but has power and might at his pleasure, as a Christian king, to rule and govern his kingdom'.[95]

The absolutism thus established obviously had features in common with other absolutist *régimes* on the continent. The insistence on Divine Right; the extreme doctrine of *raison d'état*; the interference with municipal, as well as parliamentary liberties; the attempt to impose uniformity upon provincial institutions, in Livonia and in Skåne, and to codify the law; the sinister extension of the Roman law doctrine of *lèse-majesté* so that it became (as Patkul[96] found) a high crime and misdemeanour even to speak against the *reduktion*[97] – all these had parallels elsewhere. But when that turbulent priest Jakob Boëthius denounced it in 1704 as 'a damned French system'[98] he was wide of the mark indeed. For Charles XI's absolutism was throughout permeated by a consistent, if somewhat literal-minded, respect for the law: indeed, it was based upon an *interpretation* of Magnus Eriksson's Land Law, though admittedly an interpretation which was unconventional and probably unhistorical. He did not hesitate to take advantage of legal antiquarianism. He occasionally put pressure on the courts.[99] But on the whole Charles XI was content to take for the state the uttermost farthing that the law allowed, but not one farthing over. His *régime* knew nothing of *évocations*: the common law was good enough for the state's servants, and woe betide the official who tried to strain it in the crown's favour. The civil service was repeatedly reminded that it was their duty to refuse obedience to illegal orders.[100] Charles by no means considered himself, as did his brother of Denmark, absolved from the obligation to conform to the law:

> Although [he wrote] we can in certain cases be said to be above the law, in that we have the power and right to alter, declare or moderate the law when some evident reasonableness or indispensable necessity demands and permits it; yet without such cause, and in the ordinary processes established by us, to make any alteration, or to esteem ourselves so above the law that we should not be willing to permit our subjects to enjoy and use it to their defence and security – that is something quite alien to our kingly office, and incompatible with our subjects' well-being.[101]

Or again, when it was suggested that he confirm a disputed will:

> The crown needs not to confirm the will, if it is in order, for then the law itself confirms it; but if it is not in order, the crown's confirmation cannot make it so.[102]

He would never have decided legal cases according to his own private notions, as Frederick III did; nor conferred an academic degree by prerogative action.[103] He did not claim, as Louis XIV seemed to claim, an ultimate right to his subjects' property.[104] He ruled through the traditional organs of local government: except perhaps in Livonia there was nothing even faintly resembling the *intendants*. His authority did not come to him by violence, nor were his subjects kept in order by a royal army divorced from the feelings of the nation: indeed, no force could have been less suited to support a tyranny than the army which he created, and nothing could be further from the truth than the remark of an English critic that 'He has made Soldiers of one half of his People, to keep t'other half in good Order'.[105] In contrast with many of his European contemporaries, he was not afraid to encourage his peasantry in the frontier provinces to provide themselves with effective arms.[106] Unlike the absolutism of Louis xiv, his authority was based upon, and committed to, the pursuit of peace. Above all, Charles's absolutism was from beginning to end the creation of the *riksdag*. The Danish Estates by one convulsive action put the country into Frederick iii's hands, and thereafter they met no more; the Swedish Estates established absolutism by successive decisions extending over thirteen years. Throughout the period from 1680 to 1693, the collaboration of king and *riksdag* was exceptionally close; and the great columns upon which the *régime* rested – the *reduktion*, the *indelningsverk*, the confiscatory sentences on the Regents and *råd* – were all the Estates' work. It was the old tactic of broadening the basis of responsibility by offloading as much as possible of it upon the *riksdag*: a tactic familiar from many earlier examples.[107] But it was also a line of action which proceeded from a deep-rooted tradition, which held that constitutional changes, if they were to be valid, required the assent of the people. In face of it, the last-ditch aristocratic constitutionalists, the high nobility menaced or rooked by *reduktion*, protested, fell silent, and waited the opportunity of revenge; but the majority of the nation concurred or collaborated in what was done, and an *élite* of fanatical royalists and dynamic civil servants pressed on the work. Swedish absolutism was absolutism by consent of the many, by conviction of the few, and by acquiescence of almost all. As long as Charles xi lived, it was generally popular: Lagerroth went so far as to write that 'His whole government was a realization of his people's innermost wishes'.[108] For they had reached that crux, so familiar in seventeenth-century constitutional history, when men are prepared to forget about liberty for the sake of good government. The political and social crisis, it was recognized, demanded radical remedies.

It was, indeed, the social implications of the crisis which helped to distinguish it from similar transformations elsewhere. The revolution which Charles carried through marked the defeat not only of a political theory but of a social class. The proceedings against the Regents, entailing as they did the downfall of the *råd* also, dealt a shattering blow to the political power and financial resources of almost all of the relatively small number of great families who for decades had provided the political leadership of the nation; and that blow was followed by the long-drawn hammering of the *reduktion*. In Sweden the nobility had never been the natural allies of the monarchy; and in thus basing national solvency upon the financial ruin of some of the richest of them Charles was taking fewer political risks than such a policy would have involved (for example) in France. In 1680 he was the ally, not of the defenders of privilege, but of its assailants; but the very last use he was likely to make of his success was to imitate Louis XIV, and tame the aristocracy by turning it into an ornamental class of court parasites. Impossible to imagine anything less like Versailles than the rude hunting-lodge in the forests at Kungsör, where the king went to ground away from the wits and the diplomats, and where he could shoot bears to his heart's content in the intervals of checking the muster-rolls or testing the saddlery. Nor had he any particular wish that the great magnates should be shut out from major office, once he had stripped them of their ill-gotten gains. For himself he had no strong dislike for the nobility as an order. But the same was not true of most of those that supported him. In Sweden the high nobility attracted to themselves all the odium which in other lands they shared with *gabeleurs*, *traitants*, monopolists and tax-farmers – social pests from whom Swedish society was blessedly free. Royalism in the 'eighties had very strong anti-aristocratic elements: the *reduktion*, after all, marked the conclusion of a 'strife of Estates' which had been raging intermittently for half a century. The Peasantry, as an Estate, had always been strongly royalist, and the coming of absolutism met with no objection from them: 'better one king than many'.[109] Nor did their attitude change when absolutism was later overthrown: in 1720 and 1723 they were staunch for the king's prerogative.[110] But though their support by that time made no difference, that did not mean that the Brahes and the Bondes, the de la Gardies, Horns and Leijonhufvuds, could ever recover the position they had lost. Charles's curbing of the magnate class proved a permanent achievement. His political system might suffer shipwreck, but the shift in the balance of social forces for which he was responsible could not be upset.

The *reduktion* was, no doubt, a measure designed to bring to book landowners who had used the king's necessities to drive a hard bargain with him, and perhaps to cheat him afterwards; and it uncovered and rectified much long-standing abuse and downright swindling. But it was pursued with cruel rigour against innocent heirs, unlucky spouses, and unwitting purchasers, and often the crown's rights meant the subject's wrong. Perhaps it may be not unaptly compared with the hard things that happened to nobles and office-buyers in France, who might on occasion find themselves obliged to repurchase at a higher price, or at least to pay a swingeing contribution. For indeed, alienations in Sweden and sales of offices in France were essentially the same type of finance: in each case the king was in fact raising a loan, the interest being secured either on the revenues of the alienated lands, or on the salary attached to the office; and in each case unspecified benefits, of a social or prestigious kind, sent up the price paid by the buyer. From this point of view the *reduktion* can be seen as a retroactive conversion, or as a partial and selective repudiation, or (in some cases) as a call on shares which had not been fully paid up at the time of issue. It did undoubtedly cause much hardship; but it did not as a rule bring ruin: a timely bankruptcy, a discreet renunciation of an overburdened inheritance, a *separatio bonorum* for one's wife, an agreed composition with the crown, often on the basis of leasing the land which formerly they had owned – saved something for most of the victims.[111] The *reduktion* itself resulted as a rule only in the loss of outlying estates: the ancestral seats were usually preserved.[112] What brought real ruin was not the *reduktion* but the sentences passed upon the Regents and the *råd*, whereby they were obliged to make restitution of enormous sums which (it was alleged)

had been lost to the crown by their negligence or misgovern-
ment. It was the combination of these crushing claims with
the ordinary processes of the *reduktion* which broke the fortunes
of the great magnates, and reduced Magnus de la Gardie,
whose income in 1679 had been equal to one-twentieth of the
revenues of the crown,[113] to living on royal bounty ten years
later – though even so, it was not de la Gardie, but his faithful
archivist, who actually starved to death.[114] Three-quarters of a
century later some of the great families had not yet recovered:
J. G. Oxenstierna, that poetic if spotty youth, was driven to
scrape a living as a clerk to the *riksdag*, and his old aunts
down in Småland were typical specimens of the reduced
gentlewoman.[115]

Nevertheless, the *reduktion* had important effects upon the
general position of the nobility as a landowning class. The
territorial counties and baronies vanished, never to return. No
further manors (*sätesgårdar*), with their special fiscal privileges,
might now be created; and 'noble' land was for ever frozen.
The land-allotment system for the army, and the loss of outlying estates, seriously diminished the available labour force at
the nobility's disposal, and this remained true despite legislation designed to redress the position.[116] Above all, the nobility's
loss of so much of their land went far to deliver the peasantry
from the very real threat of social degradation and political
extinction which had been hanging over it for half a century.
From the king's point of view this was a by-product and a side-
issue, by no means one of the main considerations that had
prompted him to act. But, whether intended or not, it was of
enormous significance. When the *reduktion* was complete,
the number of peasants who were either yeomen farmers or
crown tenants had doubled, while the number of peasants of
the nobility had proportionately declined.[117] Rural society,
which had seemed doomed to sink into the alien serfage of
eastern Europe or the *hoveri* of Denmark, had been violently
wrenched back into traditional Swedish patterns. The freedom
of the peasant would never be threatened again; and in the
century that followed his frugality and thrift would enable him
to add acre to acre, at the expense not only of the nobility but
of the crown.[118]

Meanwhile, the king was once more a great landowner:

better provided, certainly, than at any time since the death of Gustav Adolf. This was in striking contrast with developments in Denmark, where Frederick III's *coup* had been followed by virtual bankruptcy, and by emergency measures which included considerable *alienations* of crown land; so that by the end of the century the share of lands in private hands had risen by nearly 20 per cent.[119] In Copenhagen, absolutism meant financial weakness; in Stockholm, it meant financial strength. By 1697 Charles had reduced the national debt from 44 million *daler s.m.* to 11 million, and had nearly two million put away in the vaults to meet an emergency.[120] He was consequently able not only to free himself from dependence on the foreigner but also to pay his servants: not handsomely, indeed, as he often lamented;[121] but adequately and above all regularly. The famous estimates of 1696 laid down peacetime scales which served Swedish statesmen as the norm for recurrent expenditure until as late as 1809.[122]

As Lagerroth noted,[123] this was the fulfilment of a programme which had originally emanated from the constitutionalists of the *råd*, in protest against the personal and *ad hoc* administrative practices of the earlier Vasas, and it was ironical that it should now be put into effect by the monarch who had struck down that party for ever. From the time of John III the high nobility had demanded the right to serve the state, and therefore demanded also that service be regularly organized and properly paid. In the early seventeenth century they had captured the administration; and this, among other reasons, had prevented the sale of offices by the crown, which would have been intolerable to a class concerned to assert and preserve a monopoly of senior posts.[124] But now that monopoly was for ever ended. The lesser nobility had broken through the barriers, their status was henceforth guaranteed by the Table of Ranks, their wages assured by the solvency of the crown. The professional civil servants, no less than the king, emerged victorious in 1680. And one consequence of the comparative impoverishment of the high nobility was to drive more of them than ever to seek a livelihood in the service of the state.

Thus the absolutism which Charles established was not only a theocratic, but a bureaucratic absolutism. The nomination of Jakob Gyllenborg, a typical bureaucrat, as Marshal of the

Nobility in 1693, was symptomatic of the new age.[125] Hence-forth Sweden was to be essentially a bureaucracy; and perhaps a 'meritocracy' too. The power of making appointments had been wrested from the hands of the magnate-class, and trans-ferred to those of a monarch whom the bureaucrats could trust, because he was in so many respects one of themselves.[126] Office would now be open to all nobles, low or high, and increasingly to all commoners also;[127] it would provide the short cut to enhanced social status, the avenue to ennoblement – which indeed came to be almost automatic upon attainment of a certain grade, and was accorded the more readily because the crown no longer recognized any obligation to provide a peer with an estate capable of supporting his dignity. Office became a sound investment; since with the ending of royal donations (which formerly had served in lieu of pension) office-holders were driven to evolve the *ackord*-system, whereby they were able to sell their offices to their successors.[128] The primitive and highly personal methods of administration of all the monarchs from Gustav Vasa to Charles IX had meant that in Sweden offices were unusually slow to go 'out of court': hence the long persistence of the phenomenon known in Swedish history as 'the rule of secretaries'. But the reign of Charles XI sees the virtual completion of the slow process of evolution which changed the office-holder from a royal instrument into a servant of the state. The king was, no doubt, vividly conscious of the personal relationship between himself as master and his ministers as servants; but he would have been the first to acknowledge that both they and he were the servants of the country: the main difference between them, perhaps, being that he had been appointed to his office by God. Certainly he attended to his duties with the regularity and conscientiousness of the dedicated civil servant. Plodding, accurate, a slave to detail, wedded to routine, too godfearing and too concerned for his subjects' welfare ever to be a tyrant, yet too careful of the state's interests to find magnanimity easy, he had all the gritty qualities of a Joseph II without his intellectual powers or his civilized graces. Unmoved by the hope of glory or the attractions of polite society, ubiquitously vigilant, he struggled ceaselessly against disorder, apathy and corruption. And with success: for the first time (as Emil Hildebrand remarked) the

Swedish subject could be sure that the law would really be enforced.[129] As arch-bureaucrat he looked well after his own: his coadjutors were rewarded with leases of the reduced estates.[130] They were secure against arbitrary dismissal, which would have offended his sense of justice. But he expected from them his own standards of rectitude; and he did not always find them. The very men who had been his chief agents in the establishment of absolutism were themselves later investigated, and stripped of some of their more questionable gains.[131] To the embittered aristocracy, the obvious favour and real power enjoyed by upstarts in office must have looked very like that 'rule of secretaries' against which they had struggled for so long.

But the reality was very different. Charles's financial methods might appear as a relapse into the techniques of a bygone age, but his corps of administrators are the heralds of the Age of Liberty, and indeed of modern times. Monarchy and civil service were fused and blended in intimate collaboration, so that it might at times appear that the country was ruled by a syndicated sovereign; but as long as Charles lived the control of the machine remained firmly in his hands. It was soon to be proved that when such control was wanting the bureaucracy was quite capable of managing the state on its own. For fifteen years Charles XII was to be absent on foreign soil; and in his absence the machine ran as smoothly as ever – provided he let it alone. Towards the close of his life, however, his need for quick results and his contempt for the civil service mind led him to sanction an emergency-administration which challenged and partly superseded the old. Worst of all, Görtz's financial measures, and especially his token-coinage, jeopardized (or seemed to jeopardize) their salaries; and this removed the very basis of their support of the *régime*.[132] At the time of Charles XII's death the bureaucrats were ripe for revolt; and after it they were the main instruments in carrying through the revolution of 1719–20. They killed the absolutism of which they had been both the creators and the creatures.[133] And they survived to dominate the succeeding age, as they had dominated the former.

After 1720 the constitution may appear on paper to be a return to mixed monarchy,[134] with a strictly limited king, a *råd* with once more a share of power, and with the weight of authority transferred to the Estates. But this is an illusion.[135]

By 1720 the men who had been trying to put the constitution back upon the footing of 1634 (or perhaps of 1483) had been decisively defeated. The lower Estates would not suffer a return to the rule of the great families; the notion of an ephorate was emphatically rejected.[136] The monarchy was in fact now so powerless that it could be insulted with impunity and strengthened only by a *coup d'état*; the *råd* soon learned to quail at the prospect of impeachment (*licentiering*); the Estates, whatever their disclaimers, were effectively sovereign, and would presently expressly repudiate responsibility to their constituents. By 1756, in fact, they were in a position not much different from that of Charles XI in 1693, except that they probably bothered less about their responsibility to God; and they could have boasted, with as much propriety as any absolute monarch, *l'état, c'est nous*. King and *riksdag* have changed places: the game goes on as before. And behind and around their authority, as around his, lay the massive, immortal *pondus* of the civil service, which had intervened decisively in 1719 and 1720 to secure victory, not for the *råd*, but for the *riksdag*. And they had taken this line because they did not trust the magnates with control of appointments in 1720 any more than in 1680. Since the monarchy was now out of the question, they wanted that control to lie with the *riksdag*; which meant in fact with themselves.[137] For the bureaucracy by now interpenetrated the three upper Estates, and was dominant in the Nobility and Clergy.[138] In the Age of Liberty the attendance of office-holders at the *riksdag* was so numerous that it sometimes seriously interfered with the ordinary work of justice or administration, and could have disastrous effects on the army in wartime.[139] One sure sign of the relative insignificance of the *råd* was that none of the senior civil servants except the Chancery-President (responsible for foreign policy) might now be a member of that body: a development, incidentally, which had been clearly foreshadowed in the 1680s.[140] And was it not the senior civil service which in 1768 defeated the *råd* by a lightning strike, and so brought the Cap administration to the ground?[141] Of course it was a highly political bureaucracy, as it was bound to be when so many of its members sat in the *riksdag*; and appointments tended to be made on party lines – hence the intolerable expanses of parliamentary time devoted to unedifying and degrading wrangles about vacancies, promotions and 'prejudice'. When one faction was continuously in office for a long period – as the Hats were, from 1739 to 1765 – the civil service eventually became something like the administrative front of the parliamentary party.[142] But even in these circumstances it was strong and independent enough to erect a barrier to the worst excesses of the spoils system: in 1756 the *riksdag* accepted a *Memorandum on the Services* which safeguarded regularity of promotion and gave due weight to the characteristic civil service virtue of longevity.[143] The *riksdag*, for its part – like the monarchy in Charles XI's time – had itself become a part of the bureaucratic apparatus, assuming to itself administrative, investigatory and judicial functions on one slender constitutional pretext after another; and meddling in every department of the central and local government.

Thus the absolutism of Charles XI, by a curious paradox, paved the way for the Age of Liberty, and the bureaucracy provided the bridge between the two. It is clear that as regards the *riksdag* the ground had in many ways been prepared in Charles XI's time, and in part by his actions. No doubt it is true that the meeting of 1693 sees the *riksdag* at its absolute nadir, and that a contemporary might have been forgiven for supposing that it was shortly to die of inanition; but its resurgence in 1713, and its vigour after 1719, were nevertheless due in no small degree to the educative training which Charles himself had provided. He did not follow the example of the absolutist rulers of Germany, and undermine the position of the Estates by persuading them to delegate their powers to a standing committee, though this was a development which had certainly been conceivable in 1634. It was his practice to come to the *riksdag* with a general account of his difficulties rather than with concrete proposals for their acceptance, in the confidence that the problem had been so presented to them that they could hardly fail to suggest the solution he had desired from the beginning. He carried the *reduktion*, for instance, by using the same technique as had enabled Gustav Vasa to confiscate the lands of the church: he simply informed the Estates of the crown's needs, and left it to them (with a little judicious prompting from behind) to provide the remedy. One effect of this way of doing things was that while the royal Proposition became a survey of the state of the nation, the parliamentary initiative passed into the Estates' hands to a greater extent than ever before; and legislation took its rise not so much in the acceptance of the king's proposals as in motions designed to supply his necessities.[144] The harmony between the crown and the *riksdag*, moreover, encouraged royal frankness; and the Estates were kept informed of the details of expenditure with a new particularity: we have here the origins of those 'relations' which in the next century were presented to the Estates, at the beginning of every Diet, by the major offices of government.[145] New responsibilities were placed on the *riksdag*: they were asked, for instance, to formulate economic policy; and though they cannot be said to have discharged the task satisfactorily, it was at least a start.[146] Above all, they were invited by the king to assume inquisitorial and judicial functions which were to develop formidably under his successors. The use of the *riksdag* as a court to judge high offenders had precedents from the sixteenth century, and notably from 1567 and 1600; but what happened in Charles XI's time was of a rather different character. Already in 1675 the Estates had induced the king to permit them to set up a Commission of Enquiry into the conduct of the Regents. In 1680 its place was taken by another – the so-called Great Commission – composed of nine members from each of the four Estates; and to it Charles committed the task not only of investigating, but of passing judgment upon, both Regents and *råd*. It was authorized, moreover, to scrutinize the journals, minutes and records, not only of the *råd* but of the offices of the central government.[147] This amounted in fact to giving royal sanction to something not far removed from the principle of ministerial responsibility to parliament; and Charles himself gave colour to this interpretation when he remarked that if the Regents had kept the *riksdag* properly informed of their proceedings they would have been free of censure.[148] The Great Commission accordingly went systematically through the *råd*-minutes for the years of the Regency, session by session; and any member of that body might find himself called upon to explain or justify an unlucky speech or a heated intervention, made years before in a long-forgotten context. Thus was introduced the particular method of fixing responsibility which was to be characteristic of Swedish parliamentarism throughout the Age of Liberty – the method of examination of written proceedings by a committee of the *riksdag*. At every meeting of the Diet after 1720 the Secret Committee or the Lesser Secret Deputation would comb the journals of the *råd*, while the *Protokollsdeputation*[149] would sift the proceedings of the Colleges, the High Courts, the provincial governors, and at last (after 1760) even of the *Collegium Medicum*.[150] They would extract from them phrases which could be twisted into a deviation from the prevailing constitutional orthodoxy, would judge policies *ex eventu*, would censure or warn the errant speaker or the ill-judging councillor, and in extreme cases of national disaster or political passion would launch at the head of a member of the *råd* an impeachment (*licentiering*)[151] which might result in at least temporary political ruin. The system undoubtedly safeguarded the private citizen against administrative oppressions and delays, and in the end it became a sword of Damocles over the head of every minister; but it was capable of abuse, and it was in fact abused, for party or personal ends – even to the extent of upsetting judgments of the courts. The Swedes of the eighteenth century easily became lachrymose at the mention of 'our Noble Liberty', much as Britons swelled with pride over the Glorious Revolution; but Swedish parliamentarism could at times encroach upon the liberties of the subject with a ferocity which would have staggered Wilkes or Junius. The monstrous proliferation of parliamentary activities, the tyranny of such notorious occasional bodies as the Palmstierna Commission of 1760, stem directly from the action which Charles xi incited the Estates to take against the Regents: it was he who 'nursed the pinion that impelled the steel', never suspecting that seventy-five years later the shaft might glance off the throne itself. As one looks at the *riksdag* in the 1680s, the period of its abasement, one sees everywhere seeds which were to shoot into rank luxuriance in the day of its supremacy. It is now that procedure begins to settle down into the bad habits which make the history of the *riksdag* in the eighteenth century so daunting to the researcher: the ever-mounting flood of paper; the pitiless verbosity, all faithfully reported *verbatim*; the constant transmission of extracts from the minutes of one body for debate in another body; the habit of reading immense documents aloud for hours at a time (one might almost be forgiven for concluding that the invention of printing was still unknown in the Sweden of Linnaeus); the expenditure of parliamentary time in examining the affairs of outside authorities, and in trivialities of a personal nature – all this seems to begin under Charles xi. So do the organization of parliamentary pressure-groups, and the activities of those whom the eighteenth century would call 'operators'; and so too, alas, does the bribery of members of the Diet by foreign powers.[152] These are not legacies for which posterity can feel much gratitude; but they are additional signs that Charles's reign has as much in common with the age of Fersen as with that of Axel Oxenstierna.

It is no easy matter to determine how much of the responsibility for the changes I have been describing is to be assigned to Charles himself. It does not seem that he had any deep insight into the constitutional issues and social problems of his day. His foreign policy has been likened to the instinctive reaction of the hedgehog that rolls itself into a ball as a defence against the outside world; and it is possible to diagnose his domestic policy as arising simply from a relentless determination to clear off the crown's overdraft, and an exaggerated sensitiveness to any threat to his authority. He was ignorant of so much, so little able to deal with complex ideas, so dependent upon advice, that he had necessarily to leave a good deal to ministers better equipped than himself. Dogged and often inflexible as he was, he could be influenced; for he had a streak of real humility which made him respect men who were older and abler than himself: of which the authority of Johan Gyllenstierna, and the prestige of Rutger von Ascheberg, afford the best examples. Yet his violent temper, so easily aroused, as well as his obstinacy and honesty, made him a difficult man to handle: easy to antagonize, impossible to drive. He was quick to resent anything like an affront; and his piety to his father's memory had always to be reckoned with.[153] And though his ideas might be few and elementary, he knew what he believed, and also what he wanted; and on these things he would not compromise. Where the state's interest was concerned, neither family affection, nor old friendship, nor gratitude for past services, availed to move him.[154] In his first instruction to the newly-created Estimates Office (*statskontoret*) he gave an undertaking that he would not in his personal expenditure exceed the budget they laid down; and he kept his promise.[155] As late as 1687 the Exchequer could with impunity venture on sharp criticism of his decisions, for he recognized that they proceeded from zeal for his service;[156] but there was never any question but that he was master. Already in 1677 he was capable of overriding the unanimous objections of his naval experts by insisting on the experiment of wintering the fleet in the Blekinge skerries.[157] If he left the prosecution of the Regents mostly to the Great Commission and its successors,[158] he intervened personally on numerous occasions to steer the course of the *reduktion*. Even on foreign affairs no step could be taken without him, no despatch opened save in his presence.[159] Historians cannot agree upon whether the proceedings at the Diet of 1680 were the result of a deliberate plan for the establishment of absolutism;[160] and they differ upon the extent to which Charles really guided the course of events thereafter. But the guess may be hazarded that the tendency to reduce his share in the revolution has been carried too far. Policy, in the last resort, was his, if only by reason of his choice of ministers and his maintenance of them in office; and upon administration his influence was continuous and astringent. His intelligence may have been of the military variety; but his force of character was a major factor in politics.

To a king such as Gustav III, Charles XI seemed but an ignominious representative of royalty, who soiled his hands in business best left to underlings, and had no notion of spending money on buildings or the arts, as a good king should. This ungentlemanly parsimony was grievous also to his contemporaries,[161] and his shabby clothes, familiar manners, and crude sense of humour repelled the fastidious. Louis XIV dined grandly in public; Charles XI ate one-course meals privately at his mother's house to spare his own pocket.[162] There are moments when, in his paternalistic view of kingship, his wary determination to see for himself, his greed for money – or rather, for the security that money can buy – he recalls the great figure of Gustav Vasa; and certainly his rebukes to the negligent or the peccant at times sound like authentic echoes of the fulminating Vasa style.[163] If Gustav Vasa ran Sweden as though it were his own manor, Charles XI ran it as if it were a quartermaster's stores. But while Gustav Vasa was a man whose very faults and failings were touched with elemental grandeur, there was undeniably something ignoble about Charles: as Anders Schönberg temperately put it, 'It is not easy for posterity to see him in all respects as a great man.'[164] Yet there was something noble about him too: his integrity, his determination to do his best, his strong if narrow piety, his warm devotion to his subjects, his genuine goodness. It was this that moved Geijer to write that 'he was not only the first man in his kingdom, but also the best'.[165] Some of his remarks about his job have a disarming and touching simplicity: 'It is fidelity and righteousness that I have pledged to my subjects, not intelligence or wisdom';[166] or again, 'I do not knowingly do wrong if I can help it'.[167] Not for him the untroubled self-assurance which found the *métier du roi* 'delicious'. But though he shunned embarrassing intercourse with those who were more intelligent, more polished, and more articulate than himself, and though ceremonial dress sat awkwardly upon him except when he was on horseback, he had the Vasas' knack of getting on terms with the common man: as 'King Greycloak' (*Kung Gråkappa*) he is the hero of many a local legend.

I have tried in this lecture to suggest that the reign of Charles XI, so drab in appearance, so difficult of access to the foreigner, was a period when something of real consequence was happening. The Swedish peasant was for ever delivered from the threat of servitude. The bureaucracy moved into the central position in Swedish society. The finances, the administration, the army, the navy, all underwent constructive reform. And Sweden was taught (though the lesson took some time to learn) how to live as a second-rate power. But it was also, of course, a period of destruction, when much that was old and venerable was swept away. The ideals of the *råd*-constitutionalists were blasted. The high aristocracy's grip upon the state was loosened, and they were stripped of the rewards of generations of public service. In 1680 Sweden was still a society in which great peaks of wealth and power towered high above the ordinary man. By 1697 a ruthless process of attrition had ground them down into a smoother and more glaciated landscape. It was the first step towards the egalitarian society of modern Sweden. The men of the Age of Liberty, looking back at Charles XI's years of peace

across the terrible dilapidations for which his son was responsible, could judge him less harshly than their fathers had done,
for they were able to discern, not only the abhorred
'sovereignty', but also the solid achievements which sovereignty
had brought with it. Höpken thought it worth while to compare
Charles xi with Gustav Adolf, not wholly to his disadvantage;[168]
Nils Reuterholm, though an irreconcilable enemy to absolutism,
had no doubt that

he was a great king, who in many respects need not yield pride of
place to Gustav i or ii, and whose like few kingdoms but Sweden
have ever had. Through this sovereign's unwearied, wise and
economical government, Sweden achieved an internal strength and
an external prestige such as she never had before.[169]

But the high nobility, in his own time and long afterwards,
thought otherwise; and they could neither forgive nor forget
what he had done to them. Sooner than they had a right to
hope, their oppressor was struck down: on 5 April 1697 Charles
xi died of cancer of the stomach, aged only forty-one.

While his body lay yet unburied in the old castle of Stockholm, almost all the building, together with much precious
archival material, was destroyed in a fire which contemporaries
obscurely felt to mark the end of an epoch. There is a story[170] – *ben
trovato*, I fear, rather than true – that in the emergency the king's
corpse was hastily transferred to the only portion of the castle
to resist the flames. This was the wing which housed the office
occupied by the officials of the *reduktion*; men said afterwards that no fire could bite on it, for it was drenched with the
tears of the victims. And on the table around which the *reduktion*
had been wont to do its business, they are said to have dumped
the coffin of King Charles xi. To some of his subjects, at least, it
would have seemed an appropriate resting-place.

NOTES

[1] This paper is an expanded version of the Enid Muir Memorial Lecture,
delivered in the University of Newcastle-upon-Tyne on 25 March 1965,
and was published in *History*, 1965.

[2] He wrote, for instance, 'Wrgellan' for Wrangel, 'seiag' for säga, 'hem-
marsien' for 'hemresan': *Karl XI:s bref till Nils Bielke* (Historiska Handlingar,
18, no. 2), Stockholm, 1900, pp. 3, 64, 74.

CHARLES XI

³ Alf Åberg, *Karl XI*, Stockholm, 1958, p. 99.
⁴ See Birgitta Odén, 'Karl x Gustav och det andra danska kriget' *Scandia*, 1961, especially pp. 88–94, 105–7.
⁵ Birger Fahlborg, *Sveriges yttre politik 1660–1664*, Stockholm, 1932, i, 17–18.
⁶ *Ibid.*, pp. 12–13.
⁷ Gustaf Clemensson, *Flottans förläggning till Karlskrona*, Stockholm, 1938, pp. 12, 35, 46.
⁸ Åke Stille, *Studier över Bengt Oxenstiernas politiska system*, Uppsala, 1947, pp. 24, 248; *id.*, 'Några synpunkter på den svenska krigsmaktens historia med särskild hänsyn till sjövapnets roll' (*Skrifter utg. av Sjöhistoriska Samfundet*), Uppsala, 1941, p. 17. In December 1671 the *råd* agreed that it was beyond Sweden's economic capacity to maintain an adequate army on German soil: Birger Fahlborg, 'Sveriges förbund med Frankrike 1672' (*Historisk Tidskrift*, 1935), p. 310.
⁹ Åberg, *Karl XI*, p. 26.
¹⁰ Rudolf Fåhraeus, *Magnus Gabriel de la Gardie*, Uppsala, 1936, p. 128.
¹¹ Georg Wittrock, 'Riksskattmästaren Gustaf Bondes politiska program'. (*Historisk Tidskrift*, 1913), pp. 44–6; Birger Fahlborg, 'Westfaliska folkrättsprinciper och svensk jämviktspolitik' (*Historiska Studier tillägnade Sven Tunberg*) Stockholm, 1942, *passim*. In 1666 de la Gardie said that if Sweden 'wanted not to be in *praedam* for her provinces, she could not at this time disband any troops, or then a mere prince of Lüneburg could make a fool of them. . . . But to keep such troops in being was for Sweden impossible of her own resources, and therefore she must have a powerful alliance which would provide her with money': Frederik Lagerroth, *Frihetstidens författning*, Stockholm, 1915, p. 147.
¹² Georg Landberg, *Den svenska utrikespolitikens historia 1648–1697*, Stockholm, 1952, p. 150.
¹³ All this runs counter to Fahlborg's main contentions: see, e.g., the long argument in 'Sveriges förbund med Frankrike', pp. 321–31 (and contrast *ibid.*, pp. 310 and n. 5, 311–12).
¹⁴ *Ibid.*, p. 311.
¹⁵ Landberg, *op. cit.*, p. 169.
¹⁶ N. Wimarsson, 'Karl Gustaf Wrangel och brytningen med Brandenburg 1674' (*Historisk Tidskrift*, 1920), *passim*; Sven Ulric Palme, 'Sveriges politiska ledning under 1670-talets kris' (*Historisk Tidskrift*, 1937), p. 91; Landberg, *op. cit.*, pp. 175–90, for a clear account of this very complex crisis; Arne Munthe, *Joel Gripenstierna. En storfinansiär från Karl XI:s tid*, Uppsala, 1941, pp. 84–6, 91–2, for French pressure.
¹⁷ Birger Fahlborg, 'Sveriges förbund med Frankrike 1672', p. 373.
¹⁸ O. Varenius, *Räfsten med Karl XI:s förmyndare*, Uppsala, 1910–13, i, 83.
¹⁹ Birger Fahlborg, 'Sverige på fredskongressen i Nijmegen, 1676–78' (*Historisk Tidskrift*, 1944), p. 212.
²⁰ Sir W. Temple, *Works*, Edinburgh, 1754, ii, 7, 12.
²¹ L. André, *Louis XIV et l'Europe*, Paris, 1950, p. 10. On the deterioration of the Swedish army, *cf.* Lorenzo Magalotti, *Sverige under år 1674*, Stockholm, 1912, pp. 16–20; on the general scarcity of money, *ibid.*, pp. 45–6.

[22] S'ils voulaient faire les méchants, on trouverait bien le moyen de faire rentrer dans leurs tanières': André, p. 113; *cf. Recueil des Instructions données aux Ambassadeurs de France: Suède* (1885), i, 41, 44, 132, 137.

[23] André, pp. 133–4; Fahlborg, *HT* 1935, p. 368 n. 3. And *cf.* Colbert de Croissy's view in Sven Grauers, *Bidrag till kännedomen om det karolinska enväldets uppkomst*, Göteborg, 1906, p. 76.

[24] Åke Stille, *Bengt Oxenstiernas politiska system*, p. 136.

[25] On the tactical importance of the special type of sword favoured by Charles xi see Heribert Seitz, 'Den karolinska värjans taktiska betydelse för kavalleriet' *Ny Militär Tidskrift*, 1944, *passim.*

[26] A good biography of him is Alf Åberg, *Rutger von Ascheberg, Fältmarskalk och General-guvernör*, Malmö, 1950.

[27] Göran Rystad, *Johan Gyllenstierna, rådet och kungamakten*, Lund, 1955, pp. 126 ff.

[28] Georg Landberg, *Johan Gyllenstiernas nordiska förbundspolitik*, Uppsala 1931, *passim*; *id.*, 'Nordisk 1600-talspolitik under debatt' (*Historisk Tidskrift* 1939), pp. 328, 339–40; *id.*, *Svenska utrikespolitiska historia, 1648–1697*, for a good survey of the foreign policy of the reign.

[29] Landberg, *Johan Gyllenstiernas nordiska förbundspolitik*, p. 131.

[30] *Karl XI:s bref til Nils Bielke*, p. 48 (16 October 1688). As Dr. John Robinson remarked, 'In Relation to Foreign Affairs, it is apparently the interest of *Sueden* to avoid all offensive War, as being already in the quiet Possession of as many conquer'd Provinces on all sides as it can well defend . . .': [John Robinson] *An Account of Sueden as it was in the Year 1688* (1738), p. 272.

[31] Ingel Wadén, 'Historisk censur under det karolinska enväldet' (*Karolinska Förbundets Årsbok* [*KFÅ*], 1959, p. 65.

[32] This did not prevent Oxenstierna from occasionally evoking such antique bogeys as the danger of a Habsburg tyranny in Germany, or the existence of a sinister international conspiracy fostered by the Jesuits: Åke Stille, 'Bengt Oxenstiernas memorial våren 1690' (*Historiska studier tillägnade Nils Ahnlund*), Stockholm, 1947, p. 208.

[33] See, e.g., *Karl XI:s bref till Nils Bielke*, pp. 77, 84.

[34] F. F. Carlson, *Sveriges historia under konungarne af det pfalziska huset*, Stockholm, 1879, v, 45.

[35] S. E. Åström, *From Stockholm to St. Petersburg*, Helsinki, 1962, p. 47.

[36] Åke Stille, *Bengt Oxenstiernas politiska system*, pp. 29, 44–7, 103–5.

[37] Max Hein, 'Christoph von Brandts relationer om den svenska staten under Karl xi' (*KFÅ*, 1920), p. 60. For the long debate among the nobility as to whether a *reduktion* was preferable to paying taxes, see Sven A. Nilsson, 'Reduktion eller kontribution? Alternativ inom 1600-talets svenska finanspolitik', *Scandia*, 1958, especially pp. 108–14; and R. Swedlund, 'Krister Bonde och reduktionsbeslutet 1655' (*KFÅ*, 1937), pp. 66–9.

[38] For *indelningsverket*, see K. Ågren, *Karl XI:s indelningsverk för armén*, Uppsala, 1922, pp. 1–84: a good English account in Robinson, *An Account of Sueden*, pp. 256–61.

[39] Ågren, pp. 93 ff.

[40] Denmark, with similar financial difficulties, adopted a less radical and

less satisfactory solution. In 1689 Christian V put 7,000 men at the disposal of William III for use in Ireland, on condition they be sent back if Denmark were attacked: Åke Stille, *op. cit.*, p. 93.

[41] See M. Roberts, *Gustavus Adolphus* (1958), ii, 63–79.

[42] Folke Wernstedt, 'Bidrag till kännedomen om den karolinska armens tillkomst' (*KFÅ*, 1954), pp. 60–2; Alf Åberg, 'Rutger von Ascheberg och tillkomsten av den karolinska armen (*KFÅ*, 1951), pp. 190–2.

[43] As the author of *Les Anecdotes de Suède* predicted already in Charles XI's time: *Les Anecdotes de Suède*, The Hague, 1716, p. 164.

[44] Eli Heckscher, *Sveriges ekonomiska historia från Gustav Vasa*, Stockholm, 1936, i, 288 ff. In a later volume Heckscher did however write that 'it can in some ways be said that Charles XI's *reduktion*, with all the consequences it entailed, *presupposed* [my italics] the end of the Age of Greatness': *id.*, *Svenskt arbete och liv*, Stockholm, 1941, p. 161.

[45] *Les Anecdotes de Suède*, p. 162.

[46] Gustav Jonasson, *Karl XII och hans rådgivare*, Uppsala, 1960, pp. 227–8, 262–3. And *cf. Nils Reuterholms journal* (Historiska Handlingar, 36: 2), Stockholm, 1957, p. 66, where he quotes Lillieroot's views, and adds: 'All reasonable and mature men who were not blinded by ambition and their own success were of the same opinion.'

[47] See Alvin Isberg, *Karl XI och den livländska adeln 1684–1695*, Lund, 1953, pp. 14, 74, 86. In Livonia between 45 and 48 per cent. of the total area had been in the hands of the high nobility, besides that held by the lesser nobility: its loss was 'a transference of wealth without parallel before or since': Heckscher, *Sveriges ekonomiska historia från Gustav Vasa*, i, 317.

[48] Ola Lindqvist, *Jakob Gyllenborg och reduktionen*, Lund, 1956, p. 167.

[49] This was not Landberg's opinion: see Georg Landberg, 'Nordisk 1600-talspolitik under debatt' (*Historisk Tidskrift*, 1939), p. 332, where he writes of Swedish policy after 1680 as being only 'superficially' defensive, and considers that the Swedish aristocracy still desired a policy of aggression.

[50] K. Fabricius, *Kongeloven*, Copenhagen, 1920, p. 323.

[51] E. Ingers, *Erik Lindschöld. Biografisk studie*, Lund, 1908, i, 143, 231.

[52] Georg Wittrock, 'Riksskattmästaren Gustaf Bondes politiska program 1661' (*Historisk Tidskrift*, 1913), p. 48.

[53] Göran Rystad, *Johan Gyllenstierna, rådet och kungamakten*, Lund, 1955, pp. 57–8.

[54] *Ibid.*, p. 28.

[55] For these disputes see Severin Bergh, 'Rangstriderna inom adeln under 1600-talet' (*Historisk Tidskrift*, 1896), *passim*; [W. Benson], *A Letter to Sir J— B—, By Birth a S—, . . . Concerning the late Minehead Doctrine* (etc.) (1711). Already in 1674 a shrewd Italian observer saw what might happen: 'it is therefore to be feared that with the help of the new nobility the king of Sweden may succeed in doing what the king of Denmark did with the help of the Burghers, who hated the nobility and therefore served as his instrument to free him from dependence on the Estates, and become absolute. The same can happen in Sweden, where it may easily fall out that the new nobility, which hates the old (from which as a rule members of the *råd* are recruited), will unite with the king (upon whom it mainly depends)

and will destroy and abolish the authority of the *råd* in order to free the king from that yoke': Magalotti, p. 74.

[56] See above, pp. 116–17; and, for *ståndstriden* in general, Birger Lövgren, *Ständstridens uppkomst*, Stockholm, 1915. For the threat to peasant liberty, H. Munktell, 'Till frågan om böndernas ställning vid 1600-talets mitt' (*Historisk Tidskrift*, 1943), *passim*.

[57] The non-noble Estates were embittered by an ordinance issued by the Regents in 1671, which gave the nobility special rights of jurisdiction over their servants. The three lower Estates demanded its withdrawal on the ground that it had not received the assent of the *riksdag*: here, for once, constitutional and class interests coincided. The ordinance was in fact not confirmed, and in 1675 its application was forbidden: Sven Grauers, *Riksdagen under den karolinska tiden*, Stockholm, 1932, pp. 22, 25.

[58] Grauers, p. 69; W. Carlgren, 'Kungamakt, utskott och stånd på 1680- och 90-talens riksdagar' (*Historisk Tidskrift*, 1921), pp. 32–3.

[59] [W. Benson] *A Letter to Sir J— B—*, p. 18.

[60] Nils Runeby, *Monarchia mixta*, Stockholm, 1962, pp. 425–67.

[61] K. Fabricius, *Kongeloven*, pp. 80–5, 314–17.

[62] Magalotti thought that if Charles x had conquered Denmark he would have made himself absolute: Magalotti, pp. 25–6.

[63] S. Bergh, 'Rangstriderna inom adeln', p. 133.

[64] Grauers, p. 17.

[65] Sven Grauers, *Till kännedomen om det karolinska enväldets uppkomst*, Göteborg, 1906, *passim*.

[66] 'The Swedes breed their Clergy at a Place something nearer the Sun than their own Country, call'd Oxford, that is their Seminary; there they suck in all those wholesom Principles, and so 'tis no wonder if we find a Doctrine advanc'd in Sweden at the latter end of our King Charles the Second's Reign, which in his Father's days, and at that time, was so diligently taught in that University': [W. Benson] *A Letter to Sir J— B—*, p. 17; Grauers, *Riksdagen under den karolinska tiden*, p. 52; C. E. Normann, *Prästerskapet och det karolinska enväldet*, Lund, 1948, p. 344 n. 55, is noncommittal, but considers that English *theological* influence was slight.

[67] See above, pp. 21ff.

[68] For a general discussion see Erland Hjärne, *Från Vasatiden till Frihetstiden*, Uppsala, 1929; F. Lagerroth, *Frihetstidens författning*, Stockholm, 1915; and Nils Runeby, *Monarchia mixta*.

[69] Runeby, pp. 18–25: *cf.* the *rôle* of the *parlement* of Paris and the House of Lords: Hjärne, *op. cit.*, p. 222; C. C. Weston, 'The Theory of Mixed Monarchy under Charles i and After' (*EHR*, 1960), p. 420.

[70] Magalotti, p. 2.

[71] Rystad, *Johan Gyllenstierna, rådet och kungamakten*. p. 110; *id.*, 'Med råds råde eller konungens godtycke? Makten över ämbetstillsättningar som politisk stridsfråga under 1600-talet', *Scandia*, 1963, pp. 232–6: *cf.* Ingers, *Erik Lindschöld*, pp. 168, 173.

[72] Jerker Rosén, 'Johan Gyllenstiernas program för 1680 års riksdag', *Scandia*, 1944, pp. 125–31.

[73] Rystad, *Johan Gyllenstierna, rådet och kungamakten*, p. 237.

74 *Ibid.*, p. 292.

75 *Ibid.*, p. 294.

76 Grauers, *Riksdagen under den karolinska tiden*, pp. 78–82; Lagerroth, *Frihetstidens författning*, pp. 223–4.

77 See above, p. 23. Allusions to the blood-bath of Linköping were actually made during the debates of 1680: *Anders Schönbergs historiska bref*, Stockholm, 1850–2, iii, 135.

78 Fåhraeus, *Magnus Gabriel de la Gardie*, pp. 290–1. Charles x had already omitted the prefix *riks-* from the title of the great officers of state; and Frederick iii of Denmark had similarly changed the title of his Council of State to that of Royal Council: Fridericia, *op. cit.*, p. 464.

79 'Konungen eger styra rike sino med och således icke utom, mindre emot, riksens råds råde': Regeringsformen 1719, cl. 13: Emil Hildebrand, *Sveriges regeringsformer 1634–1809*, Stockholm, 1891, p. 67: and see F. Lagerroth, 'Svenska statsrådets ansvarighet i rättshistorisk belysning', *Scandia*, 1934, p. 44.

80 There were plans in 1718–19 for a restoration of the rule of the *råd* (Arvid Horn was said to be thinking in terms of fifteenth-century arrangements); but, significantly, the *riksdag* refused to accept them: Erland Hjärne, *Från Vasatiden till Frihetstiden*, pp. 121, 127.

81 Lagerroth, *Frihetstidens författning*, pp. 166, 176–7, 180–3.

82 *Ibid.*, pp. 176–7, 180–3; Nils Edén, *Den svenska riksdagen under femhundra år*, Stockholm, 1935, p. 107.

83 Grauers, *Riksdagen under den karolinska tiden*, p. 27.

84 *Ibid.*, p. 41.

85 *Supra*, p. 242.

86 Grauers, *Riksdagen under den karolinska tiden*, p. 93.

87 Grauers, pp. 89, 91: perhaps by a straining of the terms of the *riksdagsordning* of 1617, which laid it down that in the event of discrepant resolutions of the Estates the king should select that which seemed best to him.

88 Grauers, p. 94.

89 *Ibid.*, pp. 109–10.

90 F. L. Carsten, *The Origins of Prussia*, Oxford, 1954, p. 166.

91 See above, p. 119.

92 The nobility, indeed, were anxious to maintain the old conscription, which gave them a convenient means of disciplining unruly spirits among their peasants; and in order to avoid the *indelningsverk* they offered to surrender parliamentary sanction altogether – a remarkable instance of the sacrifice of constitutional guarantees for the sake of retaining a class privilege: Ågren, *Karl XI:s indelningsverk*, p. 120.

93 W. Carlgren, 'Kungamakt, utskott och stånd på 1680- och 90-talens riksdagar', p. 43; Lagerroth, *Frihetstidens författning*, pp. 220–5.

94 Among other things deemed objectionable was Axel Oxenstierna's letter to the Estates of December 1632, sending the draft Form of Government: *Anders Schönbergs historiska bref*, iii, 90. Louis xiv had done something like this in regard to the proceedings of the *parlement* of Paris during the Fronde.

ESSAYS IN SWEDISH HISTORY

[95] L. Thanner, 'Suveränitetsförklaring år 1693' (*KFÅ*, 1954), *passim*.

[96] 'That noble foreign Whig', as Benson called him: *A Letter to Sir J—B—*, p. 21.

[97] Isberg, *Karl XI och den livländska adeln*, p. 256.

[98] Thanner, *op. cit.*, p. 20.

[99] Rystad, *Johan Gyllenstierna, rådet och kungamakten*, pp. 238 ff., 246–7.

[100] Lagerroth, 'Det svenska statsrådets ansvarighet i rättshistorisk belysning', p. 57; Folke Wernstedt, 'Bidrag till kännedomen om den karolinska armens tillkomst', p. 59.

[101] *Anders Schönbergs historiska bref*, iii, 122.

[102] *Ibid.*, iii, 125. Even of the Regents Charles said 'that he never intended otherwise than that they should have all the benefit of the laws that other subjects enjoy': Arne Munthe, 'Till förmyndarräfstens historia' (*Historisk Tidskrift*, 1936), p. 237.

[103] J. A. Fridericia, *Danmarks Riges Historie*, iv, 472; Fabricius, *Kongeloven*, p. 347. For Charles XI's participation in the work of the courts, see Robinson, p. 217. Charles XII had fewer hesitations than his father on this point: see Birger Wedberg, *Karl XII på justitietronen*, Stockholm, 1944, *passim*.

[104] Though he came near to it in his contention that municipal revenues were to be considered as revocable loans from the crown: C. F. Corin, *Självstyre och kunglig maktpolitik inom Stockholms stadsförvaltning*, Stockholm, 1958, p. 558.

[105] *A Letter to Sir J— B—*, p. 24.

[106] Carlson, iv, 170.

[107] E.g., 1527, 1567, 1600, 1630.

[108] Lagerroth, *Frihetstidens författning*, p. 230.

[109] They used this argument to urge Charles XII's immediate majority in 1697: Carl-Arvid Hessler, ' "Aristokratfördömandet". En riktning i svensk historieskrivning', *Scandia*, 1943, p. 218.

[110] Erland Hjärne, *Från Vasatiden till frihetstiden*, pp. 105–7.

[111] See Sam Hedar, *Enskilda arkiv under det karolinska enväldet*, Stockholm, 1935, *passim*; Munthe, *Joel Gripenstierna*, pp. 251–5, 263–4, 280; and for examples of leasing lands, Isberg, *Karl XI och den livländska adeln*, p. 52.

[112] Heckscher, i, 353.

[113] *Ibid.*, i, 345. In 1678 de la Gardie had 222 servants on his pay-roll and his estates required the administrative apparatus of a government department: Fåhraeus, *op. cit.*, pp. 252–5.

[114] Hedar, p. 114.

[115] *Dagboks-Anteckningar af Johan Gabriel Oxenstierna*, Uppsala, 1881, pp. 3–4, 32, etc., and (for the aunts), 117.

[116] The *tjänstehjonsstadga* of 1686: for this see Arthur Montgomery, 'Tjänstehjonsstadgan och äldre svensk arbetarpolitik' (*Historisk Tidskrift*, 1933).

[117] Heckscher, i, 355.

[118] For this see E. Ingers, *Bonden i svensk historia*, Stockholm, 1948, ii, 33–5.

[119] J. A. Fridericia, *Danmarks Riges Historie*, iv, 476–82, 492, 631.

[120] Carlson, *op. cit.*, v, 192.

CHARLES XI

¹²¹ *Karl XI:s bref till Nils Bielke*, p. 31.
¹²² Emil Hildebrand, *Svenska statsförfattningens historiska utveckling*, Stockholm, 1896, p. 413.
¹²³ Lagerroth, *Frihetstidens författning*, p. 197.
¹²⁴ Georg Wittrock, 'Riksskattmästaren Gustaf Bondes politiska program 1661' (*Historisk Tidskrift*, 1913), pp. 49–50. And, viewed from the other side, ennoblement through service was soon sufficiently easy to make an alternative route through office-buying unnecessary to those who would otherwise have been interested in it.
¹²⁵ Carlson, v, 239.
¹²⁶ Lennart Thanner, *Revolutionen i Sverige efter Karl XII:s död*, Uppsala, 1953, p. 105.
¹²⁷ On the gradual throwing open of offices to commoners in the eighteenth century, see P. J. Edler, *Om börd och befordran under Frihetstiden*, Stockholm, 1915, and Ingvar Elmroth, *Nyrekryteringen till de högre ämbetena 1720–1809*, Lund, 1962.
¹²⁸ It was characteristic of Charles that he should have disapproved of it when it came to his notice in 1692. It was forbidden in 1723, and several times thereafter, but was too convenient to be suppressed: C. G. Malmström, 'Om ämbetsmännens ställning till riksdagen under Frihetstiden', in *Smärre skrifter rörande sjuttonhundratalets historia*, Stockholm, 1899, pp. 203–7.
¹²⁹ Emil Hildebrand, *op. cit.*, p. 407.
¹³⁰ They also bought a good deal of land which the old aristocracy had been forced to sell in order to meet the crown's claims: Thanner, *Revolutionen i Sverige efter Karl XII:s död*, p. 39.
¹³¹ Carlson, v, 195–9.
¹³² Thanner, pp. 35, 41–5.
¹³³ Thanner, pp. 274–6.
¹³⁴ *Ibid.*, pp. 194, 201: Erland Hjärne, *Från Vasatiden till Frihetstiden*, pp. 155–201.
¹³⁵ Erland Hjärne admitted 'a strong monistic element' in the constitution of 1720.
¹³⁶ Thanner, pp. 186, 233, 255, 263, 273.
¹³⁷ As one of them put it, they wanted 'liberty, but not 24 kings': Thanner, p. 297.
¹³⁸ For some modifications of this view see Sten Carlsson, *Byråkrati och Borgarstånd under Frihetstiden*, Stockholm, 1963, *passim*.
¹³⁹ Malmström, 'Om ämbetsmännens ställning till riksdagen under Frihetstiden', pp. 159–67, 173.
¹⁴⁰ Lagerroth, pp. 211–12.
¹⁴¹ See C. G. Malmström, *Sveriges politiska historia från Karl XII:s död till statshvälfningen 1772*, Stockholm, 1901, vi, 73–8, for this crisis.
¹⁴² Sten Carlsson, *op. cit.*, pp. 81–3.
¹⁴³ For suggestive comments on the implications of the *Memorandum* see Sven Ulric Palme, 'Byråkratien som historiskt problem', *Scandia*, 1948–9, p. 52.
¹⁴⁴ Lagerroth, *Frihetstidens författning*, p. 222.
¹⁴⁵ Carlgren, p. 198; Carlson, iv, 377; v, 240. Charles xi's Testament

envisaged regular reports to the Estates by the Regents for Charles xii: Malmström, 'Om ämbetsmännens ställning . . .,' p. 184.

[146] Sven Grauers, 'Till belysning av det karolinska enväldets näringspolitik' (*KFÅ*, 1960), *passim*.

[147] For the whole question, see Varenius, *op. cit.*, and Rune Blomdahl, *Förmyndarräfstens huvudskede*, Stockholm, 1963.

[148] Lagerroth, 'Det svenska statsrådets ansvarighet . . .', p. 45.

[149] The *Protokollsdeputation* was first constituted in 1734.

[150] Malmström, 'Om ämbetsmännens ställning . . .', pp. 187–96.

[151] An excellent study of *licentiering* is Lennart Linnarsson, *Riksrådens licentiering*, Uppsala, 1943.

[152] See Arne Munthe, *Joel Gripenstierna*, p. 75, for the activities of de Flon.

[153] A good example in Carlson, v, 87.

[154] *Ibid.*, v, 191. The special concessions made to Bengt Oxenstierna (but not to others of the Oxenstierna family) provide one of the few exceptions: *ibid.*, v, 144.

[155] *Ibid.*, iv, 148.

[156] Isberg, *op. cit.*, p. 78.

[157] Clemensson, *Flottans förläggning till Karlskrona*, pp. 85–6.

[158] His participation seems to have been rather greater than used to be thought: see Herman Schück, 'Karl xi och förmyndarräfsten' (*Historisk Tidskrift*, 1964), *passim*.

[159] Åke Stille, *Studier över Bengt Oxenstiernas politiska system*, pp. 49–50.

[160] For typical opposing views see, e.g., Jerker Rosén, 'Johan Gyllenstiernas program för 1680 års riksdag', *Scandia*, 1944, and Sven Grauers, 'Kring förspelet till 1680 års riksdag' (*Historiska studier tillägnade Nils Ahnlund*), Stockholm, 1949.

[161] Robinson, p. 237.

[162] Hein, 'Christoph von Brandts relationer' (*KFÅ*, 1920), p. 56.

[163] See, e.g., the letter in Carlson, iv, 163 n. 2.

[164] *Anders Schönbergs historiska bref*, iii, 103.

[165] Quoted in Carl-Arvid Hessler, ' "Aristokratfördömandet". En riktning i svensk historieskrivning', *Scandia*, 1943, p. 245.

[166] *Anders Schönbergs historiska bref*, ii, 317: perhaps an unconscious echo of Per Brahe's remark on the duty of a member of the *råd*: 'We have sworn, not to be wise, but to be faithful': Varenius, i, 135.

[167] *Karl XI:s bref till Nils Bielke*, p. 78.

[168] *Anders Johan von Höpkens Skrifter*, Stockholm, 1890, i, 248–9.

[169] *Nils Reuterholms journal*, p. 103; and *cf.* his strong approval of the *reduktion*, *ibid.*, p. 35.

[170] *Anders Schönbergs historiska bref*, iii, 252.

9

The Swedish Aristocracy in the
Eighteenth Century[1]

With the death of Charles XII in the trenches before Frederiks-
hald, Sweden entered abruptly upon a new phase in her
history. The Age of Greatness gave place to the Age of Liberty:
'the hand of Sweden's clock' (in the words of the famous
epigram) 'moved from XII to I'. The change was a real revolution; and it was a revolution carried through mainly by the
aristocracy.

The events of 1718–20 represent the culmination of a tradition and the victory of a political principle: the tradition of
aristocratic opposition to the monarchy, the principle of limited
rather than absolute kingship. Since the Middle Ages the
nobility had been the guardians of the nation's liberties. They
had been early converts to the contractualist and monarchomachist theories of the later sixteenth century; and there had
even been occasions when they had evinced some hankerings
after *aurea libertas* on the Polish pattern. Erik Sparre's programme of 1594, the Charter extorted from Gustav Adolf in
1611, the Form of Government of 1634, the *Additament* of 1660,
were all stages in one protracted constitutional debate. In 1680
Charles XI had seized a favourable opportunity to reassert the
rival theory of popular absolutism, and for a generation thereafter constitutionalism had been driven underground. Charles
XI and Charles XII had been 'sovereign', and it was against
'sovereignty' in all its implications that the nobility reacted in

1719 and 1720. The Estates – especially after 1729 – did, no doubt, come to assume to themselves very extensive powers; but even their warmest apologists shrank from terming them 'sovereign': their official designation was simply 'power-owning' (*maktägande*). On paper, indeed, the Constitution of 1720 continued to reserve, in phraseology now somewhat antique, a specific share in the government to king and *råd*; but in fact, as the Age of Liberty settled into its stride, the Estates drew most of the functions of government into the hands of their committees; the king's veto was neutralized by the name-stamp; and the enforcement of ministerial responsibility by the repeated use of something akin to impeachment (*licentiering*) reduced the *råd* at last to a condition of tremulous subjection.

In this growing absolutism the Estate of Nobility had the greatest share. Theoretically, no doubt, each of the four Estates had an equal portion of power: in reality, the weight of the first Estate was for long decisive. The danger of a clash between the Nobility and the lower Estates, which had been serious for some years after 1718, diminished after 1723; and from the late 'thirties to the mid-'sixties the Estate of Burghers, from which the strongest challenge to the Nobility might have been expected, was bound to it by close party ties, since each was usually strongly Hat. The first Estate enjoyed double representation on all those highly developed committees where the real business of the Diet was transacted; its members filled a majority of the more important positions in the king's service; and its Speaker, the Marshal of the Diet, by his position as permanent chairman of the Secret Committee, could do so much to determine the course of parliamentary business that his influence was said to be worth fifty votes. The Nobility even claimed a *votum decisivum*, which would have been tantamount to a veto upon the resolutions of the other Estates; and though it never made this claim good, it could and did block the decisions of the Diet by objecting that they trenched upon its privileges. It is true that the Swedish electoral system was such that as a rule the members of the nobility had little or no influence upon elections for the other Estates: Sweden had no borough patrons. And it is true, too, that the division into Estates precluded the younger son of a nobleman from sitting among the Burghers or Peasants, and that it was extremely rare for the nobility to enter the Church. But even without these aids the Swedish aristocracy was probably in a stronger political position than the English peerage.

The *Riddarhus*, where the Nobility held its debates, was indeed the real centre of Swedish political life. The first Estate, by its size (it was more than three times as big as all the others put together), its political talent, and its constitutional traditions, was the real leader of the nation. The milling crowds of nobles that came up to the Diet (on a critical division the numbers in the *Riddarhus* might exceed a thousand) made party organization a necessity: it was among the nobility that the first party bosses emerged, with their 'operators', their caucus voting and their political clubs. It was in the *Riddarhus* that the notorious corruption of political life was concentrated. It was not that the nobility as a class was less patriotic than the rest of the nation, or more willing to sell itself to a foreign power; the influence of foreign gold upon political behaviour has in any case probably been exaggerated, and it seems likely that many members of the Diet took bribes only for voting according to their own convictions, and chose their paymasters to square with their consciences. But because the Nobility was the most important Estate, it drew to it the greatest share of the foreign ministers' attentions. The election of a Marshal, the securing of suitable benchmen, the gaining of a majority among the noble members of the Secret Committee – these were the great objects for which France and Russia and England spent their money so lavishly. Most of British secret service expenditure in Sweden went upon buying the proxies of peers, or upon paying the travelling expenses and maintenance allowances of impecunious noblemen. Just how poor some of them were, and how cheaply they were prepared to sell their votes upon occasion, may be seen from Sir John Goodricke's estimates for 1765, when no less than two hundred of them were to be paid subsistence allowances at the very modest rate of £3 10s. a month.[2]

The nobility in the eighteenth century was a numerous class: in 1718 it may have numbered some ten thousand members, or something over a thousand families, in a population of one and a half million (or one and three-quarters, if we include Finland). But it was far from being a unified or homogeneous body. It showed marked differences in geographical distribution, paternal origin, material wealth and type of occupation. Geographically, it lay thickest in the Mälar region, in Skåne, and around Jönköping: in Dalarna, and over the whole of Norrland, it was represented only by a handful of resident officials. Between the titled nobility – the counts and barons – and the mass of hungry officers who constituted the majority of the Estate lay a perceptible gulf, and at times a very real antagonism, especially in the period of Arvid Horn's ministry. In 1719 the high aristocracy had tried to entrench their pre-eminence; but the abolition in that year of the division of the nobility into three classes had been the first sign that the 'Riddarhus-democracy' (as it was termed) was resentful of the political pretensions of the magnates; the alteration in 1734 in the method of electing benchmen (whereby procedure by ballot and lot was substituted for open voting) in effect emancipated the lesser nobles from the political influence of the greater; and the fall of Horn in 1738 signified among other things the triumph of 'democracy' over 'aristocracy' within the first Estate. Thereafter the title of count or baron counted for less and less: for the next thirty years it was the lesser nobility that really ruled Sweden.

To some extent the distinction between higher and lower nobility coincided with the distinction (equally important in the politics of the day) between the old landed families and the new nobility of service. Though it is true that there were men of ancient lineage who lived modestly as simple country squires, and though it is no less true that the tradition of state service was deeply implanted in the oldest and wealthiest noble houses, yet on the whole it may be said that the historic families – those Oxenstiernas, Bielkes, Brahes, Posses, Bondes, Sparres, Horns, who in the high summer of Sweden's glory had enjoyed almost a prescriptive right to membership of the Senate – were families whose wealth and consequence came from landed possessions rather than from the emoluments of office. This remained true even after Charles xi's *reduktion* had fallen with capricious severity upon very many of them. But side by side with them there had grown up a new nobility: men who had made a career for themselves in the civil service or the armed forces, and who owed their ennoblement to merits acquired and rank attained in the king's employ. No doubt they very soon became landed proprietors themselves; but in the eyes of the old *råd* families they remained *novi homines*: when Samuel Åkerhielm was made Master of Ceremonies to Frederick I, the appointment provoked a contemptuous snort from Countess Sigrid Bonde.[3] And behind these more eminent *arrivistes* lay troops of nobles in middling or poor circumstances, who 'won their meagre bread' (as they put it) in the service of the crown. For, on the whole, the Swedish aristocracy was a working aristocracy, an aristocracy of bureaucrats, soldiers and sailors; and for many of them their comfort, and even their livelihood, depended upon a good job and fair promotion. Of this bureaucratic aristocracy Charles XI had been the real chief. But Charles XII, in the stress of his closing years, had attempted to override and break through the bureaucratic hierarchy which his father had bequeathed to him; and though he fell before the attempt had made much headway, it gave to the changes of 1718–20 much of their character. The revolution of those years was not only the reaction of a Whiggish aristocracy against absolutism: it was also the reaction of a partly noble bureaucracy against arbitrary interference with the bureaucratic machine.

The number of nobles holding positions in the public service was, both absolutely and relatively, very considerable.[4] In the civil service it varied between about 200 and 300; in the armed forces between about 900 and 1,300. These figures indicate that anything from two-fifths (in 1730) to one-half (in 1720 and again in 1790) of the adult male nobility served the king. In the army, the noble officers accounted for between one-third (in 1719) and almost three-quarters (in 1757) of the whole establishment. In the central offices of government the percentage of nobles was anything from about eighty-five per cent. (in 1720) to about forty-two per cent. (in 1792). In local government they had a monopoly of the office of lord-lieutenant (*landshövding*) and supplied from one-fifth to two-fifths of the sheriffs (*häradshövdingar*); while most of the provincial judges (*lagmän*) were drawn from their ranks. In general, the percentage of nobles tended to fall throughout the period, in all branches; but it did not fall steadily, and even in 1792 the aristocracy was overwhelmingly preponderant in the highest positions. These facts explain the passionate interest, all through the Age of Liberty, in questions concerning appointments and promotions. The great parliamentary crises tended to group themselves round such questions; the inquisitions into the conduct of ministers, undertaken upon an alteration of the party majority in the *riksdag*, paid particular attention to them; and in the years just before 1772 they provided one of the main bones of contention between the Nobility and the lower Estates. But the control of appointments had not only a personal interest for most members of the *Riddarhus*; it had an obvious constitutional aspect too: if the right to appoint were left in the hands of the king, he might gain control of the Diet, since in all Estates, save that of the Peasants, and most especially in the Nobility, a considerable proportion of the members were office-holders. It was a quarrel on just this point that led to the introduction of the name-stamp in 1756. The *Memorandum on the Services* (*Tjänste-betänkande*) of the same year was an attempt to lay down permanent rules for promotion, independently of royal favour, and on a basis of strict seniority. The craving for office among the aristocracy was indeed such that some nobles are said to have sold their land in order to buy an office with the proceeds; many were prepared to accept government posts even though no salary might be attached to them (for the emoluments of an office were often allocated by way of pension to the retiring incumbent); and there grew up in the civil service a trade in offices analogous to the sale of commissions in the army. Moreover, since a state of war brought with it an expansion of the military and naval establishments, and hence brighter prospects of a livelihood for the needier members of the nobility, war (or at least the prospect of war) tended to be popular with such people; and this provides an additional explanation for the bellicosity of the earlier Hats – the party above all of the *Riddarhus*-democracy.

The economic position of many of the nobility thus depended upon salaries and wages: as one of them remarked in 1719, the aristocracy must support itself *'litteris aut armis'*. But the rewards of service were not very brilliant, even when they were punctually paid; and the economic strength of the aristocracy came mainly from other sources, and not least from land. Large-scale agriculture for the market was increasing, especially in Skåne and the Mälar region; but for many nobles the bulk of their income from the land came in rents and labour-services. Noble land was relieved of many burdens, and it could be worked very cheaply, since most of the labour was provided by the obligatory day-work of the tenants on the estate, and noble landlords (especially in the old Danish provinces of the south) had few scruples about making very heavy exactions in this regard; while as to the rest of the labourers, their wages were artificially depressed by legislation (notably in 1723 and 1739) designed to ensure an abundant supply of hands. It was only in the second half of the century that the policy of using mainly wage-labourers began (largely upon noble initiative) to be recognized as an agronomically preferable alternative. But in many parts of Sweden land was valuable not so much for the crops it could produce, or the stock it could support, as for the mineral riches that lay beneath it; and one major source of the wealth of the aristocracy lay in the mining, or the manufacture, of iron. A fair proportion of the leading ironmasters of the eighteenth century were men of noble birth, and perhaps as many had been elevated to the peerage. The ennoblement of great industrialists brought fresh capital into the aristocracy, and enabled it to play a considerable part in financing further industrial enterprises and new mercantile ventures. There were many noble shareholders, for instance, in the Falun copper-mine; the manufactures – at Alingsås, Rörstrand, Vedevåg – upon which the Hats lavished such excessive concessions, had usually plenty of nobles among their directors; and noble iron-masters could find money for investment in new equipment and better processes. Even the East India Company, though established – like most trading ventures – by foreign capital, soon came to be dominated by native directors, many of whom belonged to the aristocracy. The merchant houses of Stockholm were able to raise loans from the industrialists among the nobility, though oftener (as with Grill and C. G. Tessin) it was the merchant who helped the spendthrift noble out of his difficulties. But the free capital of the aristocracy came from the mines and the forges, rather than from agriculture; or it came from marriage into the families of moneyed men (which was of fairly frequent occurrence); or, finally, from the financiers and merchants themselves, who entered the ranks of the peerage, abandoned commerce, and went into iron-manufacturing.

Peerages of this type reflect the fact that the Swedish aristocracy in this century was anything but a closed caste. It was, on the contrary, constantly receiving quite large accessions of fresh blood. The Constitution of 1720 had severely restricted the king's right to create peers; but the limitation was frequently ignored in the course of the next half-century, usually with the connivance of the Estates, or even upon their suggestion. Between 1719 and 1792 some 624 families (or 725 individuals) were ennobled; and though this increase was nearly balanced by the number of peerages that became extinct, it at least assured a perennial rejuvenescence. But it placed an intolerable strain upon the limited seating accommodation of the *Riddarhus*. The nobility steadily resisted all suggestions that they should elect a reasonable number of persons to represent the whole Estate, for they feared electoral corruption of the English type, and gloried in being their own constituents. The consequent crowding of the *Riddarhus* certainly contributed to the tumultuous and unseemly character sometimes assumed by the debates of that assembly. It was partly in order to meet this inconvenience that the Nobility in 1762 took a unanimous resolution not to permit the introduction of any new peers until the membership of the House had fallen to 800. The resolution did not debar new creations: it meant only that for a long time to come no new peers would be able to take their seats. Peer-creating therefore continued; though Gustav III in 1772 promised not to add more than 150 to the existing number.

The new peers were recruited, as to the great majority of them, from reputable sources: it was only rarely that the *Riddarhus* was asked to accept such creations as that of Daniel Schedvin, a simple corporal who was ennobled in 1756 as a reward for betraying Erik Brahe's plot. Much the largest number of peerages went to the army and navy, and to the civil service (as far as possible, in equal proportions): in each of them ennoblement was thought of almost as the necessary consequence of the attainment of a certain grade. But the aristocracy was also supplied from other sources than these. It became usual to ennoble the children of bishops, even in their father's lifetime – a practice which gave some concern to the Estate of Clergy, as compromising their professional solidarity.

It was not uncommon, as we have seen, to ennoble business-men, industrialists and *entrepreneurs*. And there was an admirable readiness to ennoble persons of distinction in the world of learning, science, literature or art: such names as Linnaeus, Olof Dalin, Polhem, Scheele, Lagerbring, Swedenborg, Nordencrantz, Hårleman, are typical of a quite large class. Compared even with the English peerage, the Swedish nobility must seem extraordinarily diverse in origin, various in talent, and in the true sense aristocratic. It was as though Pope and Priestley, James Watt and Gibbon, Adam Smith and Nicholas Hawksmoor had all sat on the same benches with Lord Carrington, Lord Rodney and the first Lord Liverpool.

In Sweden the quality of nobility extended to all the children of a noble, and to all his descendants in the male line. Each noble family sent one representative to the *riksdag* – normally, though not necessarily, its *caput*. Attendance at the *riksdag* was no longer compulsory, and hence it happened that *capita* could entrust their proxies to political allies, or sell them to the highest bidder. Families which had been ennobled, or naturalized, but which had not been introduced into the *Riddarhus*, remained unrepresented there, though in all other respects they shared in the privileges of their order. These privileges were of ancient origin, and were to be considered as the reward for military service rendered in time of war; but that aspect of the question had by this time been almost forgotten. The most important of them was exemption, total or partial, from those basic taxes which formed the ordinary revenues of the crown. The manor (*sätesgård*) inhabited and farmed by its owner was totally exempt: other noble lands paid as a rule at half-rates. On a manor, the tenants rendered to their lord all those dues and services which (if they had been crown-tenants or freeholders) they would have rendered to the crown: on non-manorial lands they rendered half to the landlord and half to the crown. The amount of noble land had been considerably diminished by Charles XI's *reduktion*, and it was now forbidden to increase it; hence, as new families entered the peerage, the competition for noble land, with all the economic advantages it entailed, became keener. The situation was exacerbated by the increasing passage of such land into non-noble hands: an estate might be pawned to a creditor and never redeemed, or an heiress might marry a commoner. From 1719 to 1723 the nobility strove to halt this process by extorting from the monarchy privileges which visited *mésalliance* with severe penalties, and which prohibited the ownership of noble land by commoners. The attempt was a failure. The privileges of 1723 represented a retreat from the extreme claims of 1719: thereafter only peasants were to be debarred from acquiring noble lands; the nobleman's right of pre-emption on any land offered for sale within his family was much curtailed; and the penalties for marriage with a commoner were greatly softened. By collusive actions, special exemptions and simple violation of the law, the transfer of noble land into non-noble hands went briskly on; and though nobles usually managed to prevent commoners from getting hold of manors, there was little to hinder other noble lands from changing hands. And as the aristocracy lost its monopoly of noble land, it found itself more and more forced to buy land which was not noble, since noble land was not to be had. This was particularly true in Skåne and the Mälar provinces, where agriculture for a market encouraged landlords to build up large and unified estates. By 1772 the distinction between noble and non-noble land was already beginning to break down: it has been calculated that whereas in 1718 some 6·7 per cent. of noble land was in the possession of commoners, in 1772 the figure had risen to 16·3 per cent. As to marriage outside the nobility, it seems that at the beginning of the period – thanks mainly to an excess of females which was a consequence of the losses of the nobility in Charles xii's wars – about one-third of all the marriages contracted by the aristocracy was with commoners, while at the end of it the proportion was between two-fifths and one-half.

Other privileges of the nobility included a *forum privilegiatum* for certain offences; the right of presentation to livings in those parishes within which their manors lay; and the monopoly (in certain provinces only) of hunting and fishing on their own lands. As to the last of these, their position was already weakening: attempts to have this privilege entrenched in the new Code of 1734 were defeated; and though hunting rights were not then formally abolished, they remained henceforward upon the uncertain legal basis of ordinance rather than of statute. More important than any of these was the right, firmly established by the privileges of 1723, to a monopoly of the highest appointments in the service of the state. An ordinance of 1714 (suspended in 1766, but renewed in 1774) graded Swedish society into forty classes. In 1723 a line was drawn between the eleventh and twelfth classes, corresponding respectively to the army ranks of colonel and lieutenant-colonel. Henceforward offices in the eleventh class and upwards were to be reserved to the nobility: no one who was not a noble could be appointed, for instance, to the *råd*, nor be made a lord-lieutenant, or an admiral, or a president of one of the Supreme Courts (*hovrätter*). As time went on, however, this limitation was a good deal modified in practice. On the one hand frequent ennoblements opened a way to the highest offices to those not of aristocratic birth; while on the other the bar imposed by the privileges of 1723 was continually weakened by exceptions. By the close of the Age of Liberty the monopoly had become very nearly a dead letter, except as to membership of the *råd*; and even so high an office as that of vice-president of the Supreme Court in Stockholm was from 1758 held by a commoner. These developments explain the violent outburst of indignation on the part of the lower Estates in 1770, when the *råd* excluded a highly qualified commoner from consideration for appointment as vice-president of the Supreme Court at Åbo. It was felt that the aristocracy was trying to revive a privilege already obsolescent; and the controversy about noble privileges became the central point in the bitter internal struggle which in 1772 brought Sweden's constitutional experiment in ruins to the ground.

The constitutional arrangements of 1720 had never been quite as enthusiastically received by the commonalty as by the aristocracy. The Estate of Peasants, shut out (save for a few brief periods of crisis) from the Secret Committee, and made to feel their inferiority, had long been restive. During the rising of the Dalesmen in 1743 there had been evidence of anti-aristocratic feeling, and very clear signs that the lower orders might prefer a popular absolutism on the Danish model to a liberty which advantaged only their betters. In the 'sixties some of these feelings, long suppressed, came to the surface. The great Cap victory of 1765, when the wrongs of a generation were avenged, and the misdeeds of two decades of Hat rule brought to judgment, was essentially the victory of the lower clergy, the smaller towns and the peasants over a nobility and bureaucracy rendered more unpopular than ever by a post-war economic crisis. The Estate of Nobility now found itself, for the first time for forty years, on the defensive. It was increasingly unable to sway the Diet, because it was faced by a solid front of the non-noble Estates. Its resolutions, delayed by the cumbrous procedure which was one effect of its swollen numbers, were now impotent to affect the Diet's decision, since that decision had already been arrived at by the concordant – and speedier – resolutions of the three lower Estates. The days were gone by when the Clergy or Peasants were prepared to alter their resolutions in deference to the appeals or threats or protests of the Nobility. The aristocracy's declining influence now led them to insist, more sharply than for some time past, upon their privileges; and this hardening of their attitude in turn provoked attacks upon them of unprecedented bitterness. Cutting across the party strife of Hats and Caps, there was now emerging a struggle between one Estate and the rest, a struggle of privileged against unprivileged, of 'workers against wasters' (*närande mot tärande*). Popular pamphlets against the nobility appealed to Swedish historical romanticism by idealizing the free yeoman (*odalbonden*) of primitive Scandinavia. The yeoman, it was argued, should have his privileges too; and in 1769–70 there was much discussion of a draft of such privileges, produced by one Kepplerus. The agitation, indeed, showed signs of carrying all before it: in Gustav III's Charter of 1772 the king was forced to promise that all appointments to offices should be made upon merit; and had the Age of Liberty endured much longer, the peasants might well have made good their claim to membership of the Secret Committee, and even of the *råd*. It seemed at least possible, in 1771 and 1772, that Sweden might be on the eve of some such revolution as was to occur in France twenty years later.

From this predicament the aristocracy was saved by Gustav III's *coup d'état*. As long ago as 1742 Olof Dalin, in his so-called epic, *Den svenska friheten* (*Swedish Liberty*), had warned his countrymen that liberty might be lost as well by licence as by servility. The internecine conflicts of the Diet of 1771–2, coming as the climax to so many years' reckless use of power by the Estates, disgusted the nation with parliamentarism, and made men ready for a fresh start. This popular temper, combined with the lively alarms of the aristocracy, gave Gustav the opportunity which his ambition had long been seeking; and the revolution of 1772, thanks to his skill and nerve, was carried through without resistance and without bloodshed. Yet, for all that, it was a revolution weighed down from the start by inherent contradictions. It was at once an action to save Sweden from the fate of Poland, which the king believed to be impending over her; a blow for 'legal despotism' on the model of Mercier de la Rivière; and the rescue of the aristocracy from the dangers which seemed to beset it. The two latter aspects, at least, were fundamentally irreconcilable. Under the influence of their fears, and to preserve their special privileges, the aristocracy in 1772 had renounced their traditional role of champions of constitutionalism. They had turned their backs on two hundred years of history, and aided the monarchy to free itself from the control of the nation. Henceforward the king was to be fettered only by the fragile chains of his own political virtue, and subject only to such restraints as he might think proper to incorporate into his self-drawn constitution. Gustav III might profess to revive kingship in the style of Gustav Adolf; but from the point of view of the nobility it might too easily become a kingship in the style of Charles XI – or even of Charles IX. Once the immediate advantages of alliance with the monarchy had been secured, it was inevitable that the aristocracy should recur to its historic tradition, especially when that tradition, by a discreet eclecticism, could find reinforcement in the writings of French and American political theorists.

Gustav III did not perceive this. All his prejudices predisposed him to favour the aristocracy, and few kings of Sweden have been more sympathetic by temperament to the pretensions of birth. It was his foible to regard himself as the first nobleman in his kingdom, and on more than one occasion he appeared in the *Riddarhus* in the capacity of *caput* of the Vasa family. In 1778 he revived the division of the nobility into three classes, and thus re-established 'aristocracy' within the first Estate. Lesser nobles were not welcomed at court; there was a project to reserve certain regiments exclusively to the higher nobility; and as late as 1785 the king was meditating the elimination of commoners from all commissioned ranks in the army. But this attitude did not extend to the admission even of the highest aristocracy to real political power: the inner ring of the king's advisers, though usually ennobled, were new men, and regarded as upstarts; and Lilliestråle's purification of the local government and the judiciary fell heavily upon noble office-holders. Gustav III, in fact, conceived the aristocracy as Louis XIV had conceived it – as a splendid decoration around the throne. If they were but willing to devote themselves to the mummery of mock orders of chivalry, to immerse themselves in the complexities of court etiquette, and to cultivate an insatiable appetite for amateur theatricals, they had done all that he could require of them.

The Swedish aristocracy soon found this *rôle* unsatisfying. By 1778 the first signs of a revival of constitutional opposition had appeared; by 1786 the first Estate was at loggerheads with the king; by 1788 some of them had pushed contractualist or jusnaturalist theory to its uttermost consequence. The king's breach of his own constitution was answered by the treason of Anjala. The events of 1788–9 in their turn forced Gustav to hasten on the revolution to which he had been tending since 1786. All attempts to conciliate the aristocracy were abandoned, and the Act of Union and Security sealed the alliance of the crown with the lower Estates. In return for new constitutional concessions which made him more nearly absolute, Gustav destroyed the essential privileges of the nobility. Non-manorial lands might henceforth be freely acquired even by peasants; the hunting rights of the aristocracy were extended to all owners of land; and the provision that almost all appointments should be made upon merit alone left little remaining of the noble monopoly of office. Before the end of the reign the *råd* had virtually ceased to exist; and Gustav was considering the replacement of the four Estates by a bicameral legislature on British models.

It was a great social revolution, foreshadowing the end of the old system of politics, and it may well have preserved Sweden from infection by French principles. Yet it probably did no more than give legislative expression to the social situation as it existed. The nobility, who had thus been deprived of their privileged position, had already lost the leadership of which their privileges had been at once the symbol and the reward. The *coup* of 1772 had dammed back the advance of the commons for less than a decade. Soon after 1780 – long before the king was forced into courting them – the non-noble classes were flooding into the services more numerously than ever. By the end of the reign the aristocracy had lost perhaps as much as one-fifth of all the noble land. The political influence of the first Estate was gone, now that the king had tamed the Diet; its social exclusiveness (never as marked as in some other countries) was already breaking down here and there – as, for instance, at the universities, where by the close of the period the nobility were ceasing to keep themselves aloof from other undergraduates and were entering the Nations; and even their cultural leadership was visibly passing into other hands. Thirty or forty years before, the aristocracy had dominated Swedish intellectual life. As a class they were receptive to the great European currents of thought, whether English or (more usually) French, and they developed on their own account an exceptionally advanced body of constitutional theory upon the basis of the Constitution of 1720. They were interested in science and its applications, for many of them had been industrialists or savants themselves. They were liberal patrons of the arts, and their country houses – even though they might be of very modest dimensions – were real centres of culture and enlightenment in the remote backwoods. In C. G. Tessin they produced the Magnus de la Gardie of the age. Tessin, by his intimate ties with Parisian society, did more than any man to implant the passion for all things French – a passion which extended to the adoption of many grotesque Gallicisms into the polite jargon of the day – and for a generation he was the real arbiter of taste. Swedish painting flourished under such patronage; Swedish musical life took shape round the *Riddarhus* concerts; Swedish oratory reached a remarkably high level in the *Riddarhus* debates. And in literature, there was hardly a major author, between 1718 and 1772, who did not bear a noble name. But after 1772 came a gradual change. The influx of learned or ingenious persons – and, not less importantly, of fresh capital – into the peerage declined: in the decade 1781–90 there were only twenty-one new creations, in the last two years of the reign only one. To Tessin's position as arbiter of taste succeeded Tessin's pupil, Gustav III. The rising middle class began to set its stamp upon the arts. A conscious nationalism in culture became apparent, exemplified in Gustav III's dramatic writings, and in his invention of the 'Swedish costume'. The aristocratic predominance in literature came to an end. Creutz and Oxenstierna, no doubt, lived on into the new age, and Oxenstierna is a good example of the king's *penchant* for the old nobility; but the great writers of the Gustavian era were mostly bourgeois: Leopold, Thorild, Kellgren, and above all Bellman, the poet of Stockholm life, who with calculated humour employed the faded aristocratic diction of pastoral poetry to portray the lewd loves of drunken corporals and demireps, and hung a Boucher landscape as background to Hogarthian orgies. When the Swedish Academy was constituted in 1786, six of the Eighteen were commoners – which would have been almost inconceivable a generation earlier. And already, in decorous domestic anonymity, Anna Maria Lenngren – the personification, as a sort of poetic Jane Austen, of the common sense, shrewdness and wit of the upper middle classes – was embarking on those *Attempts at Poetry* which were later to put her in the foremost place among Sweden's women writers.

By 1792, indeed, the role of the Swedish aristocracy was almost played out. Economic power had already been shifting towards the 'Skeppsbro-nobility' of Stockholm, the naturalized merchants of Göteborg, and the non-noble ironmasters. The boom in Sweden's export industries in the 'eighties reinforced this trend. The social and political functions of the aristocracy were passing to those 'persons of standing' (*ståndspersoner*) – the professional men, small gentry, rural industrialists, non-noble civil servants – for whom the old division of society into Estates had been unable to find a place. The nobility still spoke the language of freedom; it still believed itself to be the bearer and custodian of a great historical tradition; it could even profess the fashionable cult of Brutus, and produce a tyrannicide. But its concept of liberty had become narrow and sterile: political liberty for the upper classes, and a Whiggish distrust of the monarchy. Social liberty it strenuously resisted; and equality and fraternity were not among its watchwords. Its obstinate defence of privilege alienated the masses; and its treatment of its tenantry was already attracting the attention of reformers. The heirs of Erik Sparre had gone bankrupt: the future belonged to other men.

NOTES

[1] This essay first appeared in *European Nobility in the Eighteenth Century*, London, A. & C. Black Ltd., 1953.

[2] State Papers, Foreign (Sweden), 95/104, fos. 254–5.

[3] Birger Sallnäs, *Samuel Åkerhielm d.y.*, Lund, 1947, p. 172.

[4] Statistics in this essay are borrowed from Sten Carlsson, *Ståndssamhälle och ståndspersoner, 1700–1865*, Lund, 1949.

10

Great Britain and the Swedish Revolution, 1772–3[1]

On the morning of 19 August 1772 Gustav III seized supreme power in Sweden, overthrew the authority of the Estates, and amid the applause of almost all Swedes outside the circle of professional politicians brought the Age of Liberty to an end. On the morrow of the revolution he explicitly abjured sovereignty for himself; he promised his subjects the constitution of Gustav Adolf; and he did in fact confer on them a liberal and tempered despotism, which may be described as being by Mercier de la Rivière out of *The Patriot King*.[1a] It was a revolution bloodless, popular, and uniquely clement; but it was profoundly disturbing to international relations. Twice in the next nine months it produced crises from which, for a moment, there seemed no issue save a general European war involving all the great powers. It might have been supposed, indeed, that England could stand aside from such a struggle: the country-men of Wilkes and Junius cared little for Swedish liberty, and had but a dim and confused notion of a parliamentary system in some respects more advanced than their own. But by an odd combination of circumstances, the Constitution of 1720 – which Gustav had overthrown on 19 August – had for some years acquired the status of a major British interest; its maintenance had become one of the linchpins of British foreign policy; and its overthrow was a challenge to a whole system of ideas which had prevailed and grown stronger in the years since the Peace of Paris.

In the 1760s and early 1770s, British statesmen were confronted with an international situation which seemed paradoxical, and which was to them quite novel. On the morrow of the most triumphant war this country had ever hitherto waged, they not only found Britain diplomatically isolated – an accidental circumstance which time could perhaps be relied upon to correct; but they found also that the European balance had shifted, and shifted to their disadvantage, in a way which looked like being permanent – and about that it was not in their power to do very much. Victory had given us the empire of the seas; but it had destroyed our ability to control the fate of Europe. By temporarily reducing France to the status of a second-rate power, we had left the Continent to the domination of Russia. Frederick II and Maria Theresa, their resources exhausted by a generation of war, were driven successively to make friends with Catherine, since they dared not do otherwise; and for nearly twenty years she was usually able to play off one against the other. In these circumstances the notion of a Balance of Power ceased to have any meaning. In the mid-1760s perhaps the only statesman in Europe who clearly perceived what had happened was Frederick the Great. Almost everywhere else, the international thinking of the pre-war period persisted in greater or less degree. Men thought of Europe still as broadly divided into two camps: the 'Bourbon Courts' on the one hand, and on the other such a coalition as could be carpentered together to safeguard Europe against the threat of a renewed French domination. The Family Compact had annihilated the Pyrenees. The Habsburgs were now allied with the Bourbons. Nobody in Europe doubted that the struggle of England and France must soon be renewed; nobody doubted – least of all the British ministers – that British policy would be shaped with this prospect in view. It would never have occurred to anybody, in the 1760s, that the old rivalry had become a side issue, and that the political centre of gravity had shifted – at least for the time being – to the East.

For English ministers, therefore, the first concern must be to find a 'System' to set against the 'System' of Choiseul. The obvious alignment, bequeathed by the Diplomatic Revolution and the Seven Years' War, was no longer available to them; for the peace of Bute and Bedford had destroyed the Anglo-Prussian alliance for a generation. Malice, chagrin, and sound political calculation led Frederick not only to reject with contumely every English approach, but also to devote much successful effort to a campaign of vilification directed impartially against all British ministries. His representatives in London – Michell and Maltzan in particular – intrigued with successive opposition factions to provide him with the pabulum of propaganda; and Wilkes and Junius, whether wittingly or not, proved such valuable allies in sinking British prestige, that they may almost be said to have been as important in the history of foreign as of domestic policy.[2] In view of Frederick's attitude, England was eventually forced to look elsewhere than to Prussia for the nucleus around which an anti-Bourbon system could cohere. There were those who hoped still for a restoration of the 'Old System' of King William;[3] but although French policy in Italy and Turkey was displeasing to Vienna, as long as Kaunitz had the ear of his mistress an English alliance was out of the question. There remained, then, only Russia. Russia, closely bound to England by economic ties which the commercial treaties of 1734 and 1766 only made explicit, was widely held to be our 'natural' ally, whose interests were often complementary, rarely antagonistic, to our own. In other circumstances, it might have sufficed simply to maintain the friendly relations which were so obviously to the advantage of either party. But just now, goodwill was not enough: England must have not only Russia's friendship, but Russia's alliance – partly because there was no other alliance open to us; partly because a Russian alliance might provide the basis for a 'Northern System' to balance 'the formidable League of the South'. Choiseul's folly had completed the alienation of Catherine from France; by refusing her the title of 'Imperial Majesty' he sacrificed his country to the genius of the French language.[4] And Catherine not merely disliked, but feared, France: feared French influence in Austria, feared French intrigues in Denmark and Sweden, to say nothing of Poland and the Porte. It became an object of Russian policy, therefore, to construct a system of alliances which should include not only

England and Prussia, but also the Scandinavian kingdoms. Such a league would safeguard Russia from attack by French puppets (as had happened in 1741); it would shut the French out of the Baltic; and it would preserve that 'Tranquillity of the North' which every respectable statesman in that part of Europe alleged it to be his object to maintain.

Nothing could be more welcome to an English secretary of state in search of a policy; and nothing (it might appear) ought to have been easier than to conclude the basic Anglo-Russian alliance upon which the more extended league was to repose. But in fact two obstacles quickly became apparent, and neither pertinacity nor goodwill was ever able to shift them. One lay in the fact that Frederick, after his success in securing Catherine's alliance by the treaty of 1764, was not prepared (if he could help it) to allow any other nation to share that privilege, least of all England; the other was Catherine's determination to use the occasion to extort from England immediate benefits for Russia. The price she demanded varied: now it was British support for her interference in Poland; now it was the payment of subsidies in peacetime to Sweden, or to Denmark; now it was a pledge of aid in case of a Turkish war. For ten years the negotiations for an Anglo-Russian alliance dragged on: hampered by the two months' delay before any query from St Petersburg could get an answer from London; protracted by the marvellous indolence and procrastination of Panin; befuddled by the bumbling garrulity of the well-meaning but credulous Lord Cathcart; and always they stuck fast upon one or other of these difficulties. For no British minister was ever prepared to pay Russia's price. They would not spend the king's money to finance Polish anarchy; and public opinion had by now declared so plainly against subsidies in peacetime that no ministry could risk a treaty which included that obligation.[5] It may be a question whether it was not worth our while to sacrifice our vestigial Levant trade, and accept the Turkish clause, at least till 1769. But the British view was that the alliance without these additions gave an equal advantage to either party; and with every disposition to a closer connection with Russia, ministers were not willing to purchase it by paying what they considered to be blackmail. They may have been mistaken – our representatives in St Petersburg and Stockholm sometimes thought that they were – but it is difficult to find any politician of any party who disagreed with them. If the policy was wrong, Rockinghams and Bedfords, Chathamites, Grenvilles and King's Friends, were all wrong together.

Alliance being unattainable, what remained? Faced with failure in their main objective, ministers very sensibly fell back on the next best thing. Russian and English interests were after all broadly coincident in many fields; and in those fields England proceeded to act as though the alliance had in fact been concluded. Above all, in Scandinavia. Here English and Russian diplomats could work together for common ends, in a common struggle against the friends and agents of France. In Copenhagen the defeat of French influence came soon enough, for Bernstorff's anxiety to arrange the Holstein-Oldenburg exchange overrode all other considerations, and made friendship with Russia the first rule of his policy; and though the blundering ignorance of British diplomacy at first annoyed the Russians, and the rudeness of Saldern and Filosoffof continued to offend Mr Gunning, the French had really no chance, and the Anglo-Russian ascendancy was before long complete.[6] In Stockholm the task was far stiffer. Here England and Russia had a long history of collaboration. For a whole generation they had laboured, at much expense but with small success, to sustain the party of the Caps against the pro-French faction of the Hats. The zeal and indiscretion of Colonel Guydickens had led to his expulsion from Sweden by the Hats in 1748, and for sixteen years thereafter we had been without an accredited representative in Stockholm; but the Caps never wholly lost contact with England, and from 1758 Sir John Goodricke, our minister-designate, had waited impatiently in Copenhagen for the moment when the resumption of diplomatic relations should permit him to proceed to his place of residence. That moment came in 1764; and thenceforward, under Goodricke's able and energetic leadership, the Stockholm legation was perhaps the most active and enterprising of all our foreign missions. Goodricke's relations with Osterman, his Russian colleague, were close and cordial; their collaboration was harmonious even in adversity; and Sweden became the example *par excellence* of the possibilities of joint Anglo-Russian action, the demonstration of an essential community of interests. Here, and perhaps only here, British foreign policy in the 1760s appeared as vigorous and successful.

There was, however, some variation in the attitude of successive Northern Secretaries to Swedish affairs. At first, there is no doubt, the defeat of the Hats was looked upon as a British, no less than a Russian, interest: it was important to ensure that the Swedish navy should not be at France's disposal; the triumph of the Caps, it was hoped, would be followed by a commercial treaty which would do something to redress the very unfavourable balance of trade; and, in the last resort, it was always a British interest to force France to spend more than she could really afford upon the sustentation of her partisans.[7] But on the other hand it was good tactics to profess that our interventions in Sweden had no other motive than to show our goodwill to Russia; for it then became possible to justify our contributing something less than a fair share to the joint expenses of parliamentary corruption.[8] And as time went on, ministers, oblivious of their own earlier arguments, seem to have convinced themselves that this last explanation of their policy was the only true one. At all events, they advanced it so often that they partly defeated their object; for the Russians, far from being grateful for English aid, became resentful of English parsimony. The parsimony, it should be said, was only relative, when compared with the vast sums which Panin placed at Osterman's disposal; and one reason for our comparative meanness was the obvious one, that the Civil List could not conveniently afford more. As George III wrote, with particular reference to the expenditure in Sweden:

as their is no publick mode of obtaining the money that is expended in that corruption it must be taken from my Civil List consequently new Debts incurred and when I apply to Parliament for relieving Me, an odium cast on myself and ministry as if the money had been expended in bribing Parliament.[9]

In 1769 Goodricke paid out no less than £42,000 on secret service;[10] and for the period 1764–71 it seems probable that the Civil List disbursed not far short of £100,000 on Swedish corruption. Figures for 'secret and special service', presented to Parliament in 1770, unfortunately stop at February 1769; but for purposes of comparison it may be noted that the *total* expenditure (domestic as well as foreign) under this head was £43,342 in 1764–5; £54,779 in 1765–6; £38,855 in 1766–7; and £50,806 in 1767–8.[11] It is at least possible that if secret service money could have been provided from some less straitened source, the Russian alliance might have been secured, and the Swedish revolution averted.

As it was, Sir John Goodricke made the best of what he got, and by his skill contributed essentially to the Caps' triumph of 1765, and to their recovery from the electoral disaster of 1769. In these party struggles the Constitution of 1720 was not at first an issue: Hats and Caps – or at any rate their leaders – were by this time prepared to admit that some measure of reform was necessary, if the country were to avoid slipping into a Polish anarchy. France and Russia were both for a time ready to support a moderate reform; though each was suspicious of the good faith of the queen, and neither relished the prospect of a reform carried out under the auspices of the other.[12] In this matter, as in others, British policy conformed to Russian. By 1766, however, the position had changed in two respects. On the one hand, the breach between Osterman and the court had become irreparable: the constitutional amendments which he forced through the Diet in its closing weeks were bitterly disappointing to the queen, and certainly did nothing for the prerogative. On the other hand there came a decisive alteration in the policy of France. Choiseul, upon his return to the conduct of foreign affairs, made a careful review of French exertions in Sweden during the preceding three or four years, and reached the conclusion (which had already been advanced by d'Havrincour as early as 1762) that they had been misdirected. The support of the Hats had been a mistake. For even if France were successful in restoring the Hats to power, it was doubtful whether she would thereby gain an effective or reliable ally: the experience of the Seven Years' War had been disillusioning; and in any case victory in one election might well be followed by defeat in the next. The only sound policy, he decided, was to use French money to support the court; to try to secure such a reform of the constitution as would permit Sweden to emerge from the slough in which she was labouring; and if that attempt failed, to risk everything on a monarchical revolution.[13] This abrupt change in French strategy was soon known to the

British government through the usual interceptions in the Hanoverian post office;[14] and it had obvious consequences for British policy in Sweden. The defence of the Constitution of 1720 (and of most of the amendments which had been tacked on to it since that date) henceforward became a main element in the struggle against French influence; the major danger to be guarded against came to be not so much a victory of the Hats at the polls, but rather a royalist revolt in the capital. Nevertheless, it is clear that for England the constitutional issue was a mere corollary; a consequence of our hostility to France, not a matter interesting in itself. For Russia and for Denmark, on the other hand, the case was very different. For them the preservation of the constitution was felt to be of vital importance. A reform of the constitution which restored real power to the monarchy – especially a reform which gave to the king control of foreign policy and of the armed forces – would make possible a sudden Swedish attack on Norway or Karelia, and offer temptations to a monarch anxious to reinvigorate his people by successful war. Denmark and Russia, in fact, were haunted by the spectre of Charles XII; and if we should be disposed to dismiss these fears as fanciful, the history of the reign of Gustav III serves to demonstrate that they were not without a basis in reality. Hence Bernstorff was glad enough, in his treaties of alliance with Russia, to pledge Denmark to resist any modification of the Constitution of 1720. Hence Catherine's vain attempt to extort a similar undertaking from Frederick in the secret articles of 1769.

But as the 1760s gave way to the 1770s, the difficulty of maintaining Swedish 'liberty', and of resisting the court, visibly increased. The tide of events was plainly working in France's favour. Choiseul's Turkish policy, myopic and cynical as it was, bore fruit in the Russo-Turkish war of 1769; and the consequent drain upon Catherine's military and financial resources must sooner or later limit the effort she could put forth in Sweden. In Denmark, the task that French diplomacy had been unable to compass was effected by the insanity of Christian VII and the tragic infatuation of Caroline Matilda: in September 1770 Bernstorff, the architect of the Holstein exchange, the champion of the Russian system, fell victim to a low intrigue, and was dismissed from his employments; and the dictatorship of Struensee began. Struensee professed a policy of non-intervention in Swedish domestic affairs;[15] and it seemed probable that Osterman and Goodricke would in future no longer be able to count on Denmark's taking her share of the expenses of Swedish corruption. This blow was quickly followed by another: on 12 February 1771 Adolf Frederick of Sweden died unexpectedly from a surfeit of muffins, and Gustav III succeeded him on the throne. The change was in every respect disquieting, for the new king was much abler, more ambitious, and more dangerous than the old. It was known that France had favoured postponing the revolution until his accession. And at the very moment of his father's death, Gustav was in Paris, soliciting supplies, cultivating d'Aiguillon, condescending to Mme du Barry, lobbying the *philosophes*, and inspiring vaguely avuncular emotions in the flaccid bosom of Louis xv.

The change of sovereign in Sweden necessitated a general election; and both parties were caught unprepared. The British Government, however, proved exceptionally generous (at George III's expense), and the returns swept the Caps once more into power. Once in the saddle, however, they showed a disturbing indifference to the counsels and pressures of their old paymasters. The beginnings of a new class struggle were already cutting across the old contest of parties; and the Caps of 1771 stood among other things for the abolition of noble privileges, and for equality of opportunity in the service of the state.[16] Fear of this levelling programme, indignation at the partisan-excesses of the lower Estates – excesses which Osterman, Goodricke and the Cap leaders all vainly tried to restrain – drove many moderate men to look to action by the king as the only hope for Sweden. As ill-luck would have it, Goodricke's chance of controlling his clients was fatally weakened by a sudden access of economy in London, which cut off supplies at the end of 1771.[17] Lord Suffolk, the Northern Secretary – in this as in much else a worthy follower of George Grenville – had come to the conclusion that the king was not getting an adequate return for his expenditure in Sweden. And above all, perhaps, Suffolk was disposed to show his resentment of Russia's attitude in the matter of the negotiations for the alliance. It was felt in England that we had rendered Catherine invaluable services in the Turkish war: by our aid and goodwill her fleet had reached the Mediterranean and won the epoch-making victory of Tchesmé;[18] by the implicit threat of our intervention it had been safeguarded from the very real danger of Spanish or French attack. In every court in Europe we had gone out of our way to be obliging; and on occasion had supplied Russia with secret information of importance. In return, we had seen our proffered mediation in the Turkish war evaded in favour of that of our most notorious ill-wisher, Prussia.[19] For seven years now Goodricke had served Russian interests in Stockholm: our reward had been to be reproached for niggardliness. The alliance negotiations had certainly made no progress; and Lord Suffolk, impatiently cutting through the verbal cotton-wool of Cathcart's despatches, was soon to recall him to England, and send in his place Robert Gunning, a client of his own and no friend to Russia, to administer some salutary cold douches to Panin.[20]

The supplies to Stockholm accordingly came to an end, and with them ended also Goodricke's best chance of saving the Caps from the consequences of their own delirium. Before the Diet ended, Osterman too had exhausted his resources. But there was one contribution that England could still make to the struggle in Sweden: thanks to the Hanover interceptions, Osterman and the Cap leaders were informed in ample time, and in considerable detail, of the king's plans for a *coup d'état*.[21] This, it seemed to Lord Suffolk, should be enough to ensure the failure of the attempt; but after hearing of the preliminary rising in Skåne he so far relented as to send Goodricke permission to draw for £15,000, if that should be necessary to prevent the success of the revolution.[22] To Goodricke's infinite chagrin the permission arrived too late. On the morning of 19 August Goodricke and Osterman confronted the ruin of their policy, and neither the one nor the other had money to bribe with, nor instructions to guide him.[23]

2

The exultation in Paris was great. Mme du Barry shed tears of joy; and the Duc d'Aiguillon preened himself on a success which did something to offset the ignominious desertion of the Polish Confederates.[24] In London, on the other hand, there was

considerable chagrin; and public opinion was generally unfavourable to the revolution. From Horace Walpole and
Princess Amelia, on the one hand, to Burke and the *Annual
Register* on the other (to say nothing of the ripe judgment of the
Prince of Wales), Gustav was condemned as the destroyer of
the liberties of his people.[25] Lord Suffolk was at first of the same
mind. Despite his annoyance at Russian ingratitude, and
despite the moderate tone of his comments to Guines, the
French ambassador,[26] his immediate reaction had been to offer
aid to Catherine II.[27] It was only on 5 September, when Goodricke's despatch of 22 August reached him,[28] with its news of the
king's triumph and the collapse of all resistance, that the full
implications of what had happened began to dawn on him.
Suffolk was a novice in foreign affairs. He had been appointed
to the Northern Secretaryship in June 1771, vainly protesting
his ignorance of French;[29] he was frequently incapacitated by
gout;[30] and he has been unkindly remembered for an unlucky
comment on the partition of Poland which certainly did not
express his real feelings about it; but he was a man of sense
and spirit, with businesslike habits and a high sense of duty,
modestly conscious of inexperience, but determined to learn,
and not at all afraid to trust his judgment.[31] On at least some
of the foreign ministers he made a most favourable impression.[32]
There is certainly nothing in his record in 1772–3 to justify
Temperley's characterization of him as 'the arch-Pecksniff of
diplomacy'.[33] He quickly grasped the probable consequences of
Gustav's *coup*, and realized that they might well prove extremely
grave. The overthrow of Russian influence in Stockholm, the
triumph of France, could hardly be tamely submitted to by
Catherine II.[34] Russia, it seemed certain, would seek to restore
the Constitution of 1720; by diplomatic pressure, or if need be
by force. The Tsarina would demand the assistance which both
Denmark and Prussia were by treaty bound to give; and everything indicated that she would get it. Gustav III on his side
would apply to France for aid; and it was inconceivable that
France should let him down: her recent record in Poland forbade another fiasco of that sort. The Family Compact would be
invoked, and France would be supported by Spain. A French
fleet would appear in the Baltic, a clash with Russia would
follow, and France would call upon her ally Austria – the more

loudly since Prussia's aid to Catherine was likely to take the form of an invasion of Swedish Pomerania, which Austria, by a guarantee of 1757, was bound to protect.[35] The Turkish war might indeed tie the Tsarina's hands for a little; but if the negotiations at Focsany should be successful (as was generally expected) the respite would not be long. A European war, on the largest scale, appeared not merely possible but probable.[36] It was more than ordinarily ironic that on this same 5 September Lord North should have pressed Sandwich to cut the navy vote, on the ground that he stood pledged to economies, and that the peace of Europe seemed secure.[37]

What, then, was to be Britain's attitude to this impending catastrophe? The old policy – support of the Constitution of 1720, solidarity with Russia – led, it seemed, straight to an Anglo-French war, in which England would find herself the ally of Russia, Prussia and Denmark. Had any of these deserved so well of us that we should saddle ourselves with such a burden? Denmark, since the disastrous events of January 1772, was ruled by the persecutors of Caroline Matilda and the executioners of Struensee. Against them we had quite recently been within an ace of sending a naval expedition; and with them no British minister could wish to be upon any other terms than those of the coldest civility.[38] Frederick, our most malignant critic, abhorred as the supposed author of the partition and the corrupter of Catherine, was already alarming the mercantile community with rumours of his designs on Danzig. It was indeed conceivable that the emergency might bring Russia to solicit our alliance on more reasonable terms[39] – Diede von Fürstenstein, the Danish Minister in London, ardently hoped so, and considered that this was Russia's great opportunity[40] – but by this time Suffolk was no longer sure that he wanted it, at least for the present.[41] An unofficial (but inspired) offer of alliance, without either the Turkish clause or subsidies, was at this moment on its way to England; but when Suffolk at last received it (it was lost for two months, and eventually turned up at the Russian legation, wrapped up in a parcel of rhubarb)[42] he dismissed it out of hand, significantly remarking that no British Government would consent to guarantee the integrity of Russia's acquisitions in Poland.[43] And indeed, the question was, whether the alliance on any terms was worth a war with France which neither France nor England desired, and for an issue so remote from our vital concerns as the Constitution of 1720. British foreign policy, it might seem, had come to the end of the road; the logic of the situation demanded that we take fresh bearings. And one way out, perhaps, lay through collaboration with France: with France, whose interest it equally was to avert a European explosion by dowsing the time-fuse in the Baltic.

Lord Suffolk put the thought resolutely behind him. However little he might now be disposed to second Russian ambitions in Sweden, he saw clearly that the traditional hostility to France must force us to intervene, if Louis xv sent a squadron up to Stockholm:[44] we could not suffer the French to dominate the sea from which we drew our naval stores. And, bit by bit, as the autumn of 1772 advanced, Suffolk felt his way towards an alternative policy. On 8 September, in despatches to Goodricke and Gunning, he laid down three principles for their guidance:[45] first, that though we had been ready to collaborate with Russia to *prevent* a revolution in Sweden, it by no means followed that we were ready to assist Catherine to *overthrow* it, now that it had taken place; secondly, that we should 'take no steps nor be involved in any' in support of the Tsarina, until she had offered an alliance on terms acceptable to us (an unlikely contingency); and thirdly, that we should in no circumstances collaborate in any form of common action with France: 'the King' (he told Goodricke) 'will be cautious how he adopts plans of peace that are to arise out of confusion'.[46] At the end of October, alarmed by Panin's explicit statement that Russia intended to feign acquiescence for the moment, but would certainly attack Sweden next spring,[47] he sent urgent instructions to Gunning to find out whether a threat to refuse our aid would deter the Russians from moving; explaining that 'His Majesty, who entertains a different sense of these things from that which has prevailed elsewhere, never did include in his desire to preserve the free constitution of Sweden a wish to diminish its territory and just possessions.'[48] But it was symptomatic of the difficulty and complexity of the situation, that by the same mail Gunning was also enjoined to seek Russia's assistance in putting pressure on Frederick to be reasonable in the affair of the Danzig tolls.[49] It was no doubt true that only

Catherine was in a position to bring Frederick to heel; but to plead and to threaten in the same breath was neither dignified nor wise. Long before these orders could reach St Petersburg, however, Suffolk had gone a step further. In a despatch of 10 November, Gunning was ordered, if necessary, to declare plainly to Panin that if Russia attacked Sweden, England would remain neutral, and would refuse any sort of aid. For Gunning's private ear he added that 'general considerations of policy' might indeed compel us to intervene; but this information he was to keep to himself.[50]

3

The despatch of 10 November coincided with a sudden crisis in Swedish-Danish relations, news of which reached Suffolk from Goodricke on the previous day.[51] For some time there had been reports of military and naval preparations on either side of the Sound; and even if these had been only (as to some extent they were) attributable to the fact that each party was frightened of the other,[52] there was real danger that the guns might go off of themselves. If that happened, the European war was certain: Russia must support Denmark, France must support Sweden. But at the beginning of November it seemed likely enough that the crisis might be precipitated, not by any accident, but by design: Gustav III, it appeared, was determined to eliminate the threat from Denmark before a peace with the Turks should free Russia's hands. His object was the conquest of Norway, whose inhabitants were mistakenly supposed to be so discontented as to be ready to accept Swedish rule.[53] The alarm in Denmark was great; and Count Osten, the Danish foreign minister, bombarded Ralph Woodford with appeals for British diplomatic intervention. By this time Suffolk's attitude both to Denmark and to Sweden had undergone some modification. He had been relieved and somewhat mollified by Osten's categorical assurance that Denmark's line of action would depend on Britain's.[54] And both Suffolk and his co-secretary Rochford were coming round to a more favourable view of the new *régime* in Sweden. They now admitted in private that the abuses of the Age of Liberty had made revolution inevitable;[55] they spoke sympathetically of Sweden's danger; and they went so far (in spite of consistently hostile reports from Goodricke) as to express something like approbation of Gustav's new constitution.[56] For this change of view the patient propaganda and personal popularity of Baron Gustaf von Nolcken, the Swedish Minister in London, seems to have been mainly responsible.[57] And it was von Nolcken who implanted in Suffolk a certain scepticism about the reports of Gustav's aggressive designs upon Denmark – a scepticism which was unhappily not justified by the facts.[58] In the end a European war was avoided in November 1772, not by the anodyne diplomacy of Suffolk, nor by d'Aiguillon's unpromising attempts to reconcile Sweden and Denmark under France's aegis,[59] still less by the comminatory letters of Frederick to his sister and nephew in Stockholm,[60] and least of all by Catherine, whose threats to Sweden arrived only after the crisis had been over for a month,[61] but by the prudence of Osten, who in response to a Swedish declaration of pacific intentions which sounded like an ultimatum (and was meant to be one) gave a reciprocal declaration so explicit that even Gustav could no longer discover a colourable pretext for war.[62]

The Norwegian crisis had revealed very clearly how close was the community of interest of the three European states who, of all the powers, were perhaps the least likely to act in common. Frederick's correspondence with his nephew owed much of its acerbity to his impotent anger at being (as he believed) inevitably dragged into a European struggle which all his efforts since 1763 had been directed to avoid.[63] Yet Anglo-Prussian relations, thanks to the Danzig question, had never been worse; and British ministers quite wrongly suspected Frederick of seeking to provoke an explosion in the North in order that he might have an opportunity of seizing Pomerania.[64] Frederick, on his side, affected to believe that England had incited Russia and Denmark against Sweden.[65] Again, English and French diplomacy in the Scandinavian courts had run on parallel lines since 19 August, and in the Norwegian crisis had been addressed to the same end. But in Stockholm and Copenhagen English and French ministers mined and countermined each other; in St Petersburg Durand's obvious efforts to win Russia's friendship alarmed Robert Gunning; and in London there was nagging anxiety lest France should,

after all, succeed in doing that which England and Russia had
failed to do, and reconcile Baltic rivalries in a general League
of the North.[66] This it was Frederick's interest to prevent, no less
than England's; for he had no intention of allowing other
powers to ally with Russia if he could help it. Yet he hated
England, and he despised France; and he did his best to inflame
their reciprocal animosity. His tactics might well have been
even more successful than they were, had it not been for the
policies of the two men who at this time controlled the tempera-
ture of Anglo-French relations.

4

In June 1771, after an embarrassed interval of some six months,
the Duc d'Aiguillon had succeeded Choiseul in the direction of
French foreign affairs. He had come in as the enemy of Choiseul, and the opponent of Choiseul's 'spirited' policies; and it
was not very surprising that he should soon have decided that
the best hope for a restoration of his country's influence in
Europe lay in a reconciliation with England.[67] D'Aiguillon
accordingly set about making himself agreeable in London: the
long controversy about the Canada Bills was ended by an
acceptable compromise; English alarms about French settle-
ments in Senegal, or about the concentration of troops in
Mauritius, or the employment of the turbulent d'Estaing, were
allayed by swift disclaimers; potentially awkward disputes over
fish-drying in the St Lawrence, or casual clashes in the West
Indies, were resolved upon a footing of goodwill and mutual
forbearance; and France gave no comfort to the revolted
Caribs.[68] D'Aiguillon even indicated a general willingness to
support English policy with regard to Danzig.[69] He had always
claimed credit for contributing to the peaceful solution of the
Falklands crisis; and he now did his best to bring England and
Spain into better relations: indeed, in July 1772, he suggested
to Harcourt the desirability of a triple alliance between them.[70]

The Southern secretary with whom d'Aiguillon had to deal
was the Earl of Rochford. Unlike his colleague Suffolk, Rochford was a career diplomat of considerable experience. He had
been ambassador successively to Madrid and to Paris; and in
Paris, at least, he was well-liked and cordially remembered.[70a]

He seems also to have been trusted and esteemed by the foreign ministers with whom he had to transact business as secretary of state.[71] His policy had hitherto conformed to the general system which England had followed since 1763; but he was perhaps more accessible than some of his colleagues to fresh ideas on foreign affairs: certainly he was inclined to be more civil to the Bourbon courts than Lord Chatham would have approved. His sensible and conciliatory policy was, however, partly offset by a natural vivacity of temper, and above all by a certain proneness to verbal indiscretions.[72] Moreover, any disposition to absorb new ideas on foreign affairs was balanced by an extremely lively sense of the limits which British public opinion imposed upon experiment. He feared the attacks of Shelburne and Chatham;[73] his Falklands settlement (and his defective French) had brought him under the lash of Junius;[74] and he well knew the strength of ignorant prejudice when it is inflamed by ignorant genius. He used his fears and his knowledge as a diplomatic weapon; and was accustomed to protest to Spanish or French ministers (perhaps too often for their patience) that if he fell in with their views, his head would be in danger. It is probably true to say that his policy was affected by the need to avoid risking a bad division in the House of Commons.[75] It is true, too, that he was afraid of war; partly because North wanted economy and Sandwich wanted time for the Navy to recover from the rule of Sir Edward Hawke; but also because some of the ministers, at least, felt their inability to conduct a war effectively – least of all with Chatham hovering above them with unsheathed talons.[76] As to France, Rochford was prepared to believe that d'Aiguillon, for personal and political reasons, had for the moment been forced to renounce the policies of Choiseul. But he did not trust him either as a man or as a minister. He was suspicious of French designs upon India, and infuriated by a tactless suggestion for neutralizing that country in any future war.[77] In March 1772 he had rejected a French proposal to act in common to prevent the partition of Poland; he rejected it again, in October; and in March 1773 was able to dismiss the idea as 'après-diner moutarde'.[78] His early comments to Garnier on the Swedish revolution had a vehemence – not to say a violence – which Suffolk's had avoided; and to an insinuation that England had collaborated secretly with France to bring about the rupture at Focsany he replied in terms which were not merely undiplomatic, but unparliamentary.[79] His brother-secretary Suffolk was inclined to resent what he considered to be Rochford's poaching on his department (though Suffolk's prolonged attacks of gout in the autumn of 1772 must have made this difficult to avoid), and both Suffolk and North are reported to have spoken slightingly of his abilities.[80] Yet he saw very clearly the difficulty of formulating a policy towards Sweden which should be at once practicable, popular and intrinsically sound: if England by menaces deterred France from saving Gustav III, the effect might be to encourage Catherine in aggression; if Catherine were too effectively discouraged, that might 'throw her into the arms of France'.[81] He was irritated by d'Aiguillon's constant attempt to create the impression that England and France were acting in close though unavowed concert. Rochford knew only too well the sort of political capital that the opposition at home would make of such stories. 'It is too romantic,' he wrote to Lord Grantham, 'to suppose we could seriously enter into formal concert with them upon any political transaction whatever.'[82] In March 1772, and again in July, it had been reported that France was fitting out a fleet at Toulon, to operate conjointly with a Spanish squadron in the Mediterranean, presumably against the Russians. On both occasions Rochford warned d'Aiguillon that we could not see him take such a step without ourselves taking counter-measures; and the project (if it ever existed) was thereupon abandoned.[83] In September, there were again reports of a Toulon armament; and again the reaction was swift and trenchant. On 9 October the Cabinet agreed to send word to France that any such measure would be considered a breach of the neutrality which both countries had hitherto observed in the Russo-Turkish conflict, and would, if persisted in, certainly entail action by the British fleet.[84] It was hoped that this warning would restrain d'Aiguillon, as on the earlier occasions, from any provocative heroics.

5

By the end of 1772, then, despite some temperamental difference between the two secretaries, England seemed to have arrived at an agreed and intelligible policy towards the Baltic crisis. Russia was to be restrained (by refusal of aid) from *attacking* Sweden; France was to be deterred (partly by menaces, partly by assurances that England would control Russia) from sending a squadron to *defend* her. Suffolk was to put a damper on Panin; Rochford was to bully d'Aiguillon. But (and this was crucial) the menaces to France were to be kept strictly secret from the Russians; and Panin was to be encouraged to fear that a French fleet might indeed be suffered to appear in the Baltic unchallenged: as Suffolk confessed to Nolcken, 'The preservation of peace for the most part depended on the ability to keep the Russians in ignorance of the English Court's real dispositions.'[85] It was a difficult and risky policy; but it is arguable that it was the best policy available – on the assumption that the old alignments were not to be wholly abandoned. Moreover, it really did seem for a time to meet the case. The Russians were badly shaken by Suffolk's ostentatious coldness; and increasingly they came to fear that the British Navy would let them down.[86] Suffolk was particularly successful in conveying this impression, not only to Mussin-Pushkin, but also to the Danish and Prussian ministers.[87] And though Frederick was rightly sceptical of Maltzan's reports,[88] Panin was obviously troubled:[89] so much so, that in the early months of 1773 he was vainly trying to persuade Prussia to agree to offering England a triple alliance.[90]

Yet it was undeniable that the ministry's policy, even if it were successful, was a mere expedient, devised to meet the peculiar difficulties of the Swedish crisis. It offered no permanent or generally valid solution to the problems which that crisis had so vividly made manifest. It did nothing to restore the European balance, upset in so sinister a fashion by the 'unnatural alliance' of the three eastern monarchies. It offered no real barrier to the possible extension of *le système copartageant*. The challenge provided by the battle of Tchesmé, by the partition of Poland, by the threat to Danzig, by the imminent crisis in Scandinavia, was only evaded: it was not met. Yet there were a few Englishmen who had not merely seen the international situation as it really was, but squarely faced the logical consequences of that confrontation. One of them was the king himself. In a memorandum written in the summer or autumn

of 1772, George III had attempted to put on paper his assessment of the economic and political consequences of the partition
of Poland. The commerce of the Dutch, he argued, would
henceforward be hampered. France's trade to the Levant was
obviously in danger, if Russia should establish a right of access
to the Mediterranean and extort special commercial concessions
from the Turks. Britain would probably be faced with higher
tariff barriers against the export of her textiles to the annexed
provinces. But the day must come, sooner or later, when the
partitioning powers would fall to quarrelling among themselves; and when that moment arrived, the three western powers
must unite to restore the European balance, and to rescue Poland
from tyranny. And the king continued:

This plan may perhaps seem chimerical, but if Britain and France
would with temper examine their respective situations the antient
animosity would appear absurd and that they have by it agrandized
[*sic*] other powers and weakened themselves.[91]

Having reached these conclusions, George III had not hesitated
to act upon them. In July 1772 he had commissioned Lord
Holdernesse to speak on his behalf to the French Ambassador,
the Comte de Guines, and to suggest that Guines obtain
authority from d'Aiguillon to treat directly with him as the
king's representative. The overture, it was emphasized, was
from George III personally. The ultimate objective was an
Anglo-French alliance. And a suitable initial step (Holdernesse
suggested) might be the conclusion of a commercial treaty.[92]
  Guines (who was Choiseul's nephew, and no friend to
d'Aiguillon or his policies) was from the beginning sceptical of
the prospects of success: George III, he warned his government,
did not in this matter speak for Britain.[93] But some of the
English ministers, at all events, were let into the secret, and the
reaction on their side seems to have been not unfavourable.
An Anglo-French merchant in d'Aiguillon's confidence, James
Bourdieu by name, came over in November to begin soundings
on the commercial treaty.[94] Bourdieu had fallen out with the
English East India Company, and no doubt commended himself to d'Aiguillon by his offers to provide financial backing for
a revival of the French company's activities in the east.[95] At
Bourdieu's suggestion, the poet Richard Glover was associated

with him in his mission, partly as an economic expert, partly because he was expected to be *persona grata* to the British Government.[96] D'Aiguillon, no doubt, was interested in the commercial negotiations mainly as preparing the way for a treaty of alliance;[97] but it is clear that the possibility of a commercial treaty, and the terms which France could offer, were seriously considered in Paris. Bourdieu had a cordial, if non-committal, reception from Lord North; and Rochford professed that an agreement of this kind was '*son rêve politique*'.[98] Serious negotiations were delayed, however, by d'Aiguillon's reluctance to take the initiative in formulating proposals for the reduction of duties; and by March 1773 North had to inform Bourdieu that there was no hope of finding parliamentary time for the question in the current session.[99] In the meantime the affair had become entangled in one of those cross-currents so characteristic of French diplomacy of the period. The Comte de Guines, like the Comte de Guerchy before him, was suffering from the attacks of a disappointed and ill-conditioned subordinate, who accused him (among other things) of abusing his position to gamble in British stocks; and d'Aiguillon was pointedly refraining from discountenancing his accuser. It happened also that Guines was heavily in debt to Bourdieu; and it seems clear that one of the rewards for Bourdieu's services as a negotiator was a promise from d'Aiguillon not to intervene to prevent the prosecution of his action at law against the ambassador.[100] It was hardly to be expected, therefore, that Bourdieu should have sought Guines's aid in the conduct of his negotiation, or kept him informed of its progress; and indeed it is far from certain whether Guines was informed of it at all. Nor was it, perhaps, surprising that in February 1773, just at the time when Bourdieu's initial impetus was waning, Guines should himself have produced a rival project, and spontaneously suggested to d'Aiguillon that he be authorized to take soundings for a commercial treaty.[101] But it is significant of d'Aiguillon's real desire to conclude such an agreement, that he approved Guines's initiative, and took some trouble to furnish him with reliable statistics of French trade. As late as mid-April, at a time when the two countries seemed to be on the brink of war, Guines was still giving the idea his serious attention.[102]

We have no knowledge of what, if anything, passed between

Rochford and the king on this subject; but Rochford's un-expectedly warm approval of Bourdieu's mission certainly accords well with the curious ambivalence which characterized his attitude to France in the autumn of 1772. On the one hand he delivered to Garnier[103] emphatic warnings that England would not tolerate a French armament either at Toulon or at Brest – warnings which drew from d'Aiguillon equally emphatic disavowals of any such project;[104] on the other hand he became increasingly confidential with the ministers of the Bourbon courts and their allies. Thus on 12 October the Swedish minister, Nolcken – who was now working in close collaboration with the French embassy – reported Rochford as deeply im-pressed by the French arguments on Sweden.[105] On 23 October Rochford revealed, both to Garnier and to Nolcken, that he had told Mussin-Pushkin (the Russian minister) that if France sent a fleet to the Baltic, Britain would let it go – a declaration which drew a protest from Panin.[106] On the same day he precipitately welcomed a French proposal that England and France should pledge themselves not to give any support to an aggressor in the Baltic (whether the aggressor were Russia or Sweden), remark-ing that he was sure that George III and North would agree to this. He may have been right; but a majority of the Cabinet was of another opinion, and Rochford had next day to eat his words.[107] Nevertheless, on 6 November, in a long and most indiscreet conversation with Nolcken, he spoke of 'the nation's anti-Gallic infatuation'; said that if war came the ministry would be forced to resign, since it was not popular enough to fight it; and agreed wholeheartedly with Nolcken's suggestion that what the situation required was a 'temporary union' of England and France: such a union would make short work of Prussia's pretensions to be a naval power (a bogy with which Nolcken often vainly tried to frighten him), and would probably soon detach Austria from her eastern allies. But at the same time he confessed that such a union was quite impossible, in the existing state of public opinion.[108] Yet a month later he was assuring Guines (who had meanwhile returned to town after an autumn tour which blended sightseeing with espionage) of his earnest desire for a *rapprochement* with France. As Guines wrote:

My lord Rochford m'a dit plusieurs fois dans cet entretien que si l'opposition attaquoit le Gouvernement sur le peu d'influence que

l'Angleterre avoit eue dans tout ce qui venoit de se passer, sa réponse
seroit que le seul remède . . . eût été de se joindre à nous, et qu'il
prendroit cette occasion pour en fair sentir les avantages, et même
la nécessité.[109]

By the end of 1772, then, it seems that side by side with the
official foreign policy there was in existence another, avowable
only intermittently and in confidence; a policy which involved
a revolutionary break with the traditions of the last forty years.
It had been born of the situation produced by the partition of
Poland; it was given fresh impetus by the danger to Sweden.
The ministers who dabbled in it were Hillsborough, Rochford,
Mansfield, and perhaps North: as far as we can see, Suffolk
was not in the innermost circle of confidence. It was a policy
which dared not come into the open, but must work underground. For Rochford, whatever his private opinions, could
never forget the Press and the House of Commons. He took good
care never to put anything of a compromising nature in writing.
No doubt he still had painful memories of the occasion when
there had been a call for papers on the Falkland Islands; nor
could he forget how the final settlement of that affair had been
facilitated by a *verbal* assurance from himself to Masserano
(which he later made no scruple of disavowing)[110] that Spain
could count on an early evacuation of Port Egmont, once it
had been restored to us.[111] Despite his private reservations,
therefore, and despite indiscreet confidences to Guines and
Nolcken, Rochford's despatches for the first few months of 1773
show no deviation from the official anti-French attitude.[112]
The intrigue is known to us almost wholly from French and
Swedish sources. Lord Stormont in Paris never received a
syllable to suggest that Rochford was not thoroughly imbued
with patriotic gallophobia. All forms of international co-
operation with France were ruled inadmissible; French designs
were everywhere to be suspected; French 'insolence' must never
be suffered to escape chastisement. Above all, there must be no
question of a French fleet in the Baltic. And Lord Stormont, or
in his absence Colonel St Paul, did not fail to take his tone
from such instructions. But the Duc d'Aiguillon can scarcely
be blamed for cherishing the hope that, if it came to a
crisis, England might after all be less intractable than her
ambassador.

In this posture affairs remained until the end of March 1773. Ministers became increasingly uneasy with the approach of spring; but they gave little overt sign of any change of attitude. Nolcken certainly found both Suffolk and Rochford sympathetic, and for a moment it seemed at least possible that their sympathy might be translated into action. In January Goodricke, on the basis of conversations with Ulrik and Charles Scheffer, informed his government that a defensive alliance with Sweden might probably now be had for the asking.[113] Rochford, if we may believe the account he gave to Nolcken, urged in Cabinet that the opportunity be seized, and the alliance concluded: already in the preceding November he had hinted that the day might come when a closer connection between the two countries would become possible.[114] But most of his colleagues were not prepared for so bold a step: an alliance with Sweden in 1773 would have been an open provocation of Russia. Suffolk, in particular, was not willing to figure before the public as the friend of France; and his reply to Goodricke was that the time for a Swedish alliance was not yet ripe. But he added that there was no need for Goodricke to inform Osterman that the insinuation had been made.[115] It was certainly not from any lingering regard for Russia that he returned this temporizing answer; for the wish for a Russian alliance had never been fainter. Both Cathcart and Gunning had pointed out that Frederick's annexations of Polish territory had virtually barred Russia's access to north Germany, and had made her in consequence far less desirable as an ally, because far less able to protect Hanover.[116] When in March it seemed that another Russian overture might be impending, Suffolk told Gunning that there could be no alliance unless Catherine renounced all designs upon Sweden, revealed the full extent of her connections with Prussia and Austria, and abandoned any pretensions to a guarantee of the integrity of her newly acquired Polish territories.[117]

Despite the ministry's growing coolness to Catherine, and its growing benevolence to Gustav III, its attitude to France, as expressed in official conversations in Paris or London, continued as intransigent as ever. In December d'Aiguillon had been so hopeful about the prospects that he had recalled Garnier to Paris for verbal instructions. At the beginning of February Garnier had returned, commissioned to prepare the ground for a defensive alliance which was to include both Sweden and Spain.[118] But the official British line was so unyielding that d'Aiguillon was forced to acknowledge to himself that his programme was likely to prove more difficult of attainment than he had at first supposed; and in despatches to Vergennes he accordingly went out of his way to warn the Swedes that they must no longer count on French naval aid.[119] In February 1773 France and Sweden concluded a convention (it had been under discussion since December), whereby Louis xv pledged himself to supply Gustav III with 800,000 *livres* a year for three years from 1 January 1773, on the express condition that the money be used to improve the Swedish army and navy; and further promised that in the event of war France would accelerate her financial aid, and send ten to twelve thousand troops (but not ships) to Sweden's assistance.[120] To the despatch of troops the British Government might well have no great objection: rather the contrary, for it had no wish to see Sweden share the fate of Poland. But it was not apparent how the French units were to be moved from Dunkirk to Göteborg, or how the unarmed transports were to be protected against the Danish and Russian fleets. Guines was disposed to believe that the British Government would not object to a small escort of French warships, provided it received prior notification of the intention to send them, and provided they came straight home after seeing the troops safely landed.[121] D'Aiguillon's solution, repeatedly pressed upon Vergennes, was that the escort should be provided by Sweden, and should meet the transports off the coast of Jutland; and though Ulrik Scheffer continued to point out that if it came to a crisis the Danish navy would never allow Swedish warships to sail from their base at Karlskrona through the Sound, the duke long remained conveniently deaf to this argument.[122]

But it was in St Petersburg, after all, not in Paris or in London, that the fate of Sweden (and perhaps of Europe) would be decided; and as the year drew on neither Suffolk nor d'Aiguillon really knew what Catherine's plans might be. Gustav III and Durand were trying desperately to convince her of Sweden's pacific intentions; Frederick was trying to persuade her that Sweden was so puny that Gustav's intentions did not matter;[123] Suffolk was trying to restrain her by broad hints of desertion if she went to war. Rochford made the interesting suggestion that England and France should jointly offer Catherine their good offices at Bucharest, in return for a Russian pledge not to attack Sweden;[124] though at the same time he was confiding to Nolcken that he hoped the Bucharest negotiations would fail – and was even hinting pretty broadly that he was doing his best to ensure that they should.[125] At various times the idea was mooted of an agreed modification of the new Swedish constitution, to remove those articles which seemed especially dangerous to the Tsarina; but on this Scheffer and d'Aiguillon refused all compromise. Panin, as usual, was profuse of soothing assurances; but there was an uneasy feeling that though he might genuinely desire peace, he was no longer able to restrain Catherine and the Orlovs.[126] Gunning's reports of Russian preparations, it is true, gave no immediate cause for anxiety in London, though there had been a moment in February when he had shown some concern.[127] Vergennes, on the other hand, with his predisposition to see every situation in the darkest colours, predicted a Russian invasion as soon as the ice melted, drew a disheartening picture of the condition of the Swedish armed forces and the misery and discontent of the country, and warned his chief not to expect much in the way of resistance.[128] D'Aiguillon, however, was stubbornly optimistic. In despatch after despatch he asserted that Russia had no aggressive intentions; that Catherine's preparations were merely precautionary; that her difficulties with Turkey forbade any other adventures; and that since Panin had given his word of honour as a gentleman, there was no more to be said.[129] The Comte de Broglie, who provided a running commentary on French foreign policy for the private edification of Louis xv, found d'Aiguillon's credulousness incomprehensible.[130] As late as 21 March d'Aiguillon was confidently asserting to Vergennes that the Russo-Danish and Russo-Prussian treaties 'ne contiennent certainement aucune stipulation qui puisse autoriser toute attaque contre la Suède relativement à la dernière constitution'.[131] It was a bold guess; but (as it happened) a wrong one.

A week later he was rudely awakened. On 28 March Vergennes's despatch of the 9th arrived in Paris. It announced that an invasion of Sweden was now regarded as inevitable in the near future, and reported the embarkation of Russian troops to be imminent.[132] In Stockholm there was extreme alarm. Scheffer wrote urgently to Nolcken to entreat the intervention of England; Gustav III addressed a personal letter to Louis XV, as the patron of the late revolution.[133] The long-expected crisis seemed to have arrived at last. Louis XV, it was reported, felt his honour to be involved,[134] and to save it might even sacrifice the peace; d'Aiguillon's political system – and perhaps his political existence – was now obviously at stake; and at stake too was something more than either: the reputation of France as a great power.[135]

7

The news from Stockholm made it more than ever necessary for d'Aiguillon to make quite sure what England would do, in the event of French intervention in the Baltic. He still hoped for an English alliance,[136] or at the worst for effective English connivance, behind a smoke-screen of gallophobe oratory and truculent diplomatic exchanges. But he had to find out where he stood; and, as it happened, he had already taken steps to do so. Guines was not in his confidence; and perhaps he fancied that Stormont was not in Rochford's. At all events, he had decided to send a secret agent to London to reconnoitre; and on 21 March – one week before the news came from Stockholm – the Chevalier de Martange received instructions for his mission, together with a letter from Mme de Forcalquier to Lord Rochford, which was to serve as the ostensible pretext for his call upon that minister.[137]

Already, however, d'Aiguillon's mind was turning to an alternative line of action. If it became clear that Britain would not tolerate a French fleet in the Baltic, it was still possible to bring pressure to bear on Russia by sending a squadron from Toulon to the Aegean. The Russian fleet in those waters, far from repair facilities or ports of refuge, was highly vulnerable; and it might well be that Spain, who had long ago urged action against it, would be prepared to co-operate now. It is true that

England had thrice warned France of the consequences of arming a squadron at Toulon; but it was reasonable to think that the British public would be less sensitive on this head than in regard to a squadron putting out from Brest. Besides, it was intended to avoid any provocative parade: the armament was to be officially described as a 'flotte d'évolution', destined for one of M. de Boynes's new training-cruises. Such a cruise had actually been carried out, without unpleasant repercussions, in 1772. On 26 March, therefore, the first orders were sent down to Toulon to begin preparations.[138] On the same day Martange arrived in London. It does not seem that the project of a Toulon fleet had been disclosed to him before his departure. And it is eloquent of d'Aiguillon's lack of confidence in Guines that he was not informed of the Toulon armament until 12 April, and that no hint was ever given him that the ostensible purpose of the undertaking was not in fact the real one.[139]

While Martange was making his way across the Channel, events were moving fast in Paris. On 28 March, the day of the arrival of Vergennes's alarming despatch, the king held a council at which d'Aiguillon reported the Swedish request for aid. After stormy debates, it was agreed that aid should be given – mainly, it seems, because d'Aiguillon alleged that England would make no objection – and on the following day he was able to transmit to Vergennes the project of a treaty of alliance, with an important covering despatch.[140] It is obvious that the treaty must have been ready, at least in draft, at the time of the council meeting; but it contained a separate and secret article which cannot have been drawn up much before 26 March. That article, contradicting the general tenor of the treaty, provided that the naval aid which was to be afforded should take the form of action, not in the Baltic, but in the Mediterranean; and the duke's accompanying despatch devoted some space to an elaborate – and specious – attempt to prove that this would really be better for Sweden than a squadron in northern waters.[141]

Two days later (on 31 March) Lord Stormont, who had just returned from leave to find himself unexpectedly in the middle of a major crisis, had a protracted and dramatic interview with d'Aiguillon, of which he transmitted an account to Rochford in an immense and masterly despatch. At this stage Stormont knew nothing of the Toulon squadron, and his arguments were directed to preventing any expedition from Brest. D'Aiguillon did not undeceive him, but offered assurance that a French fleet in the Baltic would do no more than repel attack, and would come straight home after escorting the transports. He was told that this would not be considered satisfactory: Guines's prediction on this point – repeated as late as 9 April[142] – had thus been proved to be mistaken. D'Aiguillon then revived the idea of an Anglo-French pact against any Baltic aggressor: Stormont rejected it out of hand. The duke next asked whether 'Baltic' must be understood to include the North Sea: he was firmly told that it must.[143] It is not surprising that when, on 4 April, Stormont at last learned that the armament had been entirely diverted to Toulon, he should have come to the mistaken conclusion that this change of plan was to be attributed to the vigour of his language four days earlier.[144]

Meanwhile Martange had reached London; had presented himself to Guines as a gentleman travelling for pleasure; and had contrived his first interview with Lord Rochford. Rochford made no bones about declaring 'son entière conviction de la parité d'intérêts qui devoit déterminer l'Angleterre à concerter avec la France dans les circonstances présentes et occasions spéciales, pour empêcher la nouvelle guerre que la Russie se disposoit à porter en Suède'; but he spoke also of 'insurmountable obstacles' in 'the blind antipathy of his impetuous nation': if any administration were to lay before Parliament a treaty of alliance with France, the Commons would 'demand the head of the Chancellor who sealed it, and the minister who had signed it'. Nevertheless, he promised to discuss the situation with the king and his colleagues, and he agreed to meet Martange again. Their interviews were to be kept a close secret. Rochford had seen Martange only after obtaining George III's permission to do so; and the purpose of his mission was to be concealed from everybody else.[145] In fact, however, it proved impossible to conceal it from Lord North;[146] and, as the event was to prove, Rochford by no means kept the king accurately informed of all that passed. To begin with, indeed, he does not seem to have been very forthcoming: at the first two meetings he went no further than to suggest collaboration to detach Austria from Russia, or a 'temperament' of the new Swedish constitution, or the existing English policy of hinting to Catherine that we should not be willing to back her in aggression; and he declared any sort of written engagement, even though it were kept secret, to be 'absolutely impracticable'. But at the close of the second interview, after conceding that France had no notion but to come to Sweden's assistance, he let slip an astonishing remark: 'Je voudrais pour beaucoup que votre escadre passat *et qu'elle battît* la nôtre.'[147] And in the third interview, on 4 April, he came forward with a plan of action which improved on that insinuation. It was his intention, he said, to call a Cabinet for Wednesday, 7 April, in order to discuss Stormont's great despatch of 31 March.[148] That meeting would decide to send him orders which would in fact be England's last word; and at the same time the Lords of the Admiralty would be given preliminary warning to make unostentatious preparations for war. As soon as precise and positive information arrived of French preparations at Brest, ministers would be forced by public opinion to take visible counter-measures. But at the very worst, Rochford calculated, France's preparations would have eight days' start of England's. Martange put his own gloss on this communication: what Rochford meant, he said, was 'Je vais prendre des mesures lentes; prenez-en de promptes; je vous donne les moyens à me gagner de vitesse; concertez-vous avec l'Espagne, et soiez à votre objet, avant que l'on vous oppose de ce côté-cy des obstacles que je ne serois pas le maître de lever, et avec quels au contraire, je paraîtrois concourir.'[149] That this interpretation was correct appeared when they met the next day; for Rochford then promised that he would do his best to delay the orders for arming as long as possible.[150] Of all this it is probable that George III knew nothing; for if he had been informed of it he would not have supposed (as in fact he did) that Martange's report to d'Aiguillon would effectually discourage the duke from pursuing his plans.[151] Rochford's proposal was, to say the least, extraordinary. But it was not quite unprecedented; and to d'Aiguillon it must have seemed the less incredible because in fact something like it had been hinted in the previous December, and reported by d'Aiguillon to Vergennes:

Il paraît [he wrote] par les nouvelles que je viens de recevoir d'Angleterre, que les ministres de cette puissance qui ne veulent pas absolument se brouiller avec nous, sont déterminés dans le cas d'une rupture entre la Russie et la Suède, de mettre tant de lenteurs dans leurs résolutions que nous aurions le temps de passer des troupes à Gothembourg, avant qu'ils puissent s'y opposer, et qu'alors ils entrevoient à exiger de nous de ne point envoyer d'escadre dans la Baltique.[152]

It is clear, from Guines's report to d'Aiguillon, that it had been from Rochford that this suggestion came;[153] and it would therefore seem that his proposal in the following April was no sudden improvisation, but a solution to the political dilemma which had been present in his mind for some time.

There followed two further meetings with Martange, on 6 and 7 April; both of them short. By the time the second of them took place, Rochford had received from Stormont the first intelligence of the transference of the Brest armament to Toulon. The news seems to have made a bad impression on him. He exhorted Martange to urge d'Aiguillon to think twice before committing himself; he impressed upon him the fact that after the cabinet meeting that evening there could be no receding from England's position; that a British fleet at least equal to the French must infallibly sail for the Mediterranean; that the risk of a requisition of aid from Russia, and of an Anglo-French war, was very real. When Martange showed signs of not taking these warnings too seriously, Rochford gave him no encouragement, though he reiterated his promise of collusive delay in the case of an expedition from Brest.[154] Soon afterwards, Martange took an inconspicuous departure – by request: the king was beginning to find his presence too risky.

The distinction which Rochford thus made between a Brest and a Toulon fleet was certainly valid. His immediate object, it seems, was to save Sweden from the fate of Poland. The information at his disposal as to Russian intentions was conflicting; but reports which reached him by way of Paris (not, however, through the embassy) were highly alarming: on 2 April came news that Russian troops had actually embarked for the invasion.[155] In the critical circumstances, therefore, he was prepared to allow Gustav III to be rescued by France, and at the same time to arrange matters so as to avoid an Anglo-French war: he would connive at a swift French expedition to the Baltic, which should do its business and return before England had put the navy on a war footing. But a Toulon fleet was another matter. It would be too late, and too distant, to help Sweden. And Rochford could not forget that we had already committed ourselves to assisting Catherine, if France should attack the Russian fleet in the Aegean.[156]

Nevertheless, he had embarked upon a policy, and he did not abandon it without affording time and opportunity for it to take effect. After the Cabinet of 7 April, he discreetly betook himself into the country for a holiday, with the deprecatory remark to Martange, 'je n'ai que ce temps-là de plaisir':[157] it was an odd moment to choose. He did not return to London for nearly a fortnight. But before he departed, he embodied the decisions of the Cabinet of 7 April in fresh instructions to Stormont. They combined menace with procrastination in nicely judged proportions. No proposal, Stormont was informed, was admissible which tended in any shape to lead us to connive at France's giving naval aid to Sweden(!). A Mediterranean fleet was no less objectionable than a squadron at Brest. If France stirred an oar, we should instantly unbend our sails. Stormont was therefore to ask whether France was arming (a question to which Rochford well knew the answer, but which might at all events waste a little more time); and he was to inform d'Aiguillon that our actions would be governed by his, and that we should hold his silence as justifying any further proceedings.[158] Together with this official letter, Rochford on 8 April sent to Stormont another, marked Most Private. The original appears to have disappeared, but the text has survived in a copy made for the use of Archdeacon Coxe, and now preserved among the Coxe Papers in the British Museum. It ran as follows:

I cannot let the Messenger set off without writing you this confidential Line to tell you that your conduct is thoroughly approved of and that we have all the reason in the world to believe that the French Ministry will be bullied. Stick to your point, and you will gain yourself and us honour – I must trust you a little further and acquaint you that the Duke d'Aiguillon has been using indirect means to tempt us to fall into his views but that he has been told you have the secret of your Court – which you have – and I am persuaded you will make use of the properest method vizt. *fortiter in re* and it does not signify how much *suaviter* you are *in modo.* – Excuse the hurry of this; I will tell you at a proper time the Duke's curious way of negotiating.[159]

The purpose of this letter can hardly be in doubt. Rochford must have realized that it would be difficult, perhaps impossible, to disguise the fact that Martange's visit to London had political implications: as he told Martange on 5 April 'Sur un mot que le Roy m'a dit, je crains qu'on ne vous soupçonne déjà, soit qu'on ne vous aît espionné, soit qu'on aît espionné moy-même.'[160]

And in fact he was right: it was soon known in diplomatic circles that something was afoot in London. Frederick's minister at the Hague, the unpleasant Thulemeier, got hold of the story somehow;[161] Creutz, the Swedish minister in Paris, knew all about it, even to Rochford's proposal to retard English mobilization.[162] There was therefore a good chance that Stormont would hear of it too; and there was certainly much to be said for appearing to take him into Rochford's confidence, rather than allowing him to feel that the real negotiations had been taken out of his hand. But there was another more urgent and more personal reason for writing this letter. Rochford must have been aware that he was taking great risks. If need be, he could have flatly denied the more compromising passages in his conversations with Martange. But unluckily for him there was (as he must have known) one piece of written evidence against him which would certainly have been difficult to shrug off. This was Guines's despatch to d'Aiguillon of 11 December 1772. For by a curious piece of ill-luck, the Secret Office had intercepted, and effectively decyphered, just this particular despatch, and it was highly compromising. It ran as follows, in the decyphered version: Rochford, wrote Guines,

a été jusqu'à me [dire] que quand même nous serions dans le cas de secourir la Suède, son [avis] et [celui] de la plus grande partie du [conseil] seroit de nous laisser le tems d'achever notre besogne, et de reculer la [détermination] à prendre jusqu'au moment où elle ne pour[roit] plus être d'aucune utilité; cette confidence m'a paru forte.[163]

It was not enough, therefore, to safeguard himself by writing despatches in the language of orthodox patriotism; he felt it prudent to provide a second line of defence by taking the same tone in a private and confidential letter which might be supposed to reveal his real thoughts.

While Rochford took his holiday in the country, Suffolk and Stormont, uninformed of the real nature of the activities of the Chevalier de Martange, devoted themselves to saving the peace by frightening France into an abandonment of the Toulon armament. Rochford, we may suppose, was content to leave them to it. If d'Aiguillon did not use the respite that had been contrived for him, it was hardly to be expected that Rochford should take any further risks to help him. In Paris, accordingly, Stormont held a very high and threatening language. It was in vain that d'Aiguillon protested that the Toulon fleet was designed only for a training-cruise similar to that which had taken place without incident in 1772; for he was forced to admit that circumstances might conceivably arise in which it might be ordered to go to Sweden's assistance. Suffolk, at Stormont's suggestion, transmitted a weighty memorial which was intended to alarm Louis xv; Stormont informed d'Aiguillon that England would not, in the existing circumstances, permit France to launch a fleet in *any* sea without taking counter-measures; and the point was rammed home when Stormont assured him that England would not abate her demands, though it should cost a war of thirty years.[164]

Meanwhile, Martange's reports had been reaching Paris: that containing his account of Rochford's proposal probably arrived not later than 8 April. Since England did not announce her mobilization (as we shall see) until 23 April, the French navy was afforded not eight days' start, as Rochford had promised, but fifteen. Yet, as the days slipped by, and the moment drew nearer when the news of England's arming might be expected, there was no sign that the Toulon fleet was coming out. How could it, indeed? It had never been expected to be ready much before the end of May.[165] From the moment when the idea of an expedition from Brest was abandoned, in fact, the concession which Martange had secured in London became of no real significance. Thenceforward the goodwill of Lord Rochford availed France nothing; it was vain for d'Aiguillon to pin his hopes upon him. By the third week of April it came home to the duke that this was so. He began to understand that Stormont's warnings must be taken seriously, and that British policy had returned with a vengeance to familiar channels. He could not now afford to run headlong

319

into a war with England for the sake of making Catherine uncomfortable, and so constraining her to give a tardy redress to the justified complaints of French traders in the Levant.[166] It was not in such a quarrel that Louis xv would feel his honour engaged: Choiseul had been dismissed for less. If the alternatives were a war with England or the acceptance of the English demands, there could be little doubt what the choice must be, however humiliating, and however perilous for Sweden. On 15 April he decided that the Toulon fleet should confine itself to exercises and manœuvres, abstaining not only from an attack on the Russians, but even from the protection of French shipping. On 16 April he ordered the preparations at Toulon to be slowed down.[167] And on 19 April, like the prudent politician that he was, he accepted defeat and informed Guines – in a postscript so elaborately off-hand as to be almost insulting – that the Toulon fleet would not leave port.[168] It remained to devise a graceful retreat, if that were possible, from a false position which (he had some excuse for feeling) was not altogether of his making.

This proved an awkward matter; for though d'Aiguillon informed Stormont on 21 April, 'with an affected casualness', that the training-cruise had been 'suspended', the British Government had on the previous day already decided on partial mobilization. Stormont had for some time been pressing it, as the surest method of preserving the peace, and Suffolk seems to have been of the same opinion.[169] It was not until 20 April, however, that George III's hesitations were resolved by the receipt of a Hanoverian interception of a despatch from Creutz, from which it appeared that d'Aiguillon was determined to avoid war at all costs. The king at once made up his mind. He himself summoned the cabinet; Rochford hurried up to town from St Osyth; and on 21 April orders were sent to the Admiralty to fit out fifteen ships of the line at Spithead, with a 'proportionable number' of frigates, and to commission a further fifteen ships of the line to replace them.[170] On 23 April this resolution was made public, and communicated to all British missions in a circular despatch.[171] Two days later came Stormont's news that the Toulon fleet had been 'suspended'. The king thereupon ordered the secretaries of state to issue a reassuring *communiqué* to the public.[172] But when on 26 April

Guines at last officially communicated to Rochford the substance of d'Aiguillon's orders to him of the 19th, they proved
to be at variance with that minister's language to Stormont; for
the despatch to Guines, as we have seen, said nothing of
'suspension', but announced only that 'l'escadre d'évolution en
armement à Toulon, reste dans ce Port jusqu'à nouvelle
ordre'.[173] The discrepancy was possibly inadvertent; but the
British ministry saw in it a typical example of French duplicity.[174] Orders were at once sent to the *Pomona* frigate to look
into Toulon and ascertain what was really happening there;
and for another week ministers continued in a state of anxiety
and suspense about France's intentions. At last, on 5 May,
Guines notified Rochford officially that the armament had
been 'suspended'; and though Rochford was again thrown into
agitation by another false alarm on 12 May, Stormont was
able to inform him on the 18th that the fleet had been not only
'suspended', but 'countermanded'. With the arrival of this
despatch in London on 21 May the Anglo-French crisis was
over at last, and measures of disarmament could begin.[175] Even
so, Rochford was still wondering at the end of May whether
d'Aiguillon's compliance might not have been designed to lull
him into a false sense of security, while the real blow against
the Russians was preparing in Spain.[176]

Six weeks later, when the last echoes of the crisis had died
away, and Stormont was taking another spell of well-earned
leave, Lord Sandwich provided the appropriate epilogue to
these curious transactions. It took the form of a grand review of
the fleet at Spithead on 22 June. The weather was brilliant;
and the occasion was graced by the presence of the sovereign.[177]
There was a moment, indeed, when Lord Rochford was
expecting, a little nervously, a spectator even more interesting,
and perhaps hardly less interested; for, a week before the event,
one of the British intelligence agents informed him that
d'Aiguillon proposed to embark secretly at Fécamp and witness
the review incognito.[178] This, unfortunately, was too good to be
true; but France did not go unrepresented on the occasion:

The Count de Guines [wrote Rochford to St Paul] partook of the
Fête and had the honour to dine with the King. It would have been
illiberal to have refused him the sight of so brilliant a scene, where

he could not but be pleased, had no opportunity of criticizing, and, without gasconading, could entertain no other ideas than those of admiration.[179]

Suffolk's comment in a private letter to Gunning, if less exuberant, was no less complacent:

A pacific fleet [he wrote] indeed it is, for in my conscience I believe it has preserved the peace of Europe. But how must our Royal Master exult in the proud pre-eminence it gives! How must this display of national strength, these floating bulwarks of his kingdom, strike his maiden view![180]

8

These were heart-warming reflections; but it can hardly be taken for granted that they were justified. The danger which both British and French policy had sought to avert was an interruption of the Tranquillity of the North by a Russian attack on Sweden: France was concerned to protect a political protégé; England was concerned to avoid a European war which from her point of view would have been irrelevant, and in which she would have been an unwilling participant. But no one could feel very confident that that danger had really been eliminated, and not merely deferred; Suffolk himself expected the crisis to recur, once the Turkish war was over.[181] And even though this turned out in fact to be an unduly pessimistic assessment of the situation, it is still quite certain that it was neither the French nor the British armament that saved Sweden. Before ever Anglo-French relations reached a crisis, the danger to Sweden was over. On the very day when Martange arrived in London, Panin's attitude to Sweden began to soften: the cordiality of Catherine's welcome to Frederick von Nolcken,[182] sent by Gustav III to carry the insignia of the Order of the Seraphim to the Grand Duke Paul, was considered to mark the beginnings of a change of policy. This was on 26 March.[183] On 8 April Panin read to Ribbing, the Swedish minister to Russia, the text of a declaration – despatched to Osterman by courier the same day, and presented by him on 24 April – which really ended the Russo-Swedish crisis.[184] Gustav III had in fact relaxed his defensive preparations as early as 3 April, on the news of Nolcken's initial reception.[185] Information of the reversal of Russian policy was contained in Gunning's despatch to Suffolk of 10 April, which enclosed the substance of the declaration which Osterman was to make in Stockholm; and this despatch reached London only on 4 May, when the Anglo-French crisis was effectively over.[186] And though by 10 April Durand's reports from St Petersburg had become more reassuring,[187] d'Aiguillon could not be certain of Sweden's safety until the arrival of Vergennes's despatch of 25 April – and that did not reach Paris till as late as 13 May.[188]

These dates make it clear that the Brest armament, and the French offer of alliance to Sweden (which cannot have been known to the Russian legation in Paris before 29 March) cannot have played any part in producing Panin's change of front. Still less can the Toulon fleet have done so. There is therefore no basis for d'Aiguillon's boast that it was the Toulon fleet that preserved Sweden, or for the attempt by Fraguier and other French historians to represent the outcome as a diplomatic triumph for France.[189] It is true that Gustav III himself said that he owed his deliverance to the Toulon fleet; but this was nothing more than a tactful emollient to salve the feelings of a still indispensable friend.[190] But if France's armaments came too late to affect the issue, this was still truer of England's. By 23 April, when the British mobilization was announced, the risk of war in the Baltic was over. The chance of a clash in the Mediterranean indeed remained; but it is pretty certain that the news of Russia's change of attitude would in any case have led to the countermanding of the preparations in Toulon long before the French fleet could have been ready to put to sea. Suffolk had in fact as little justification for claiming that the British Navy had saved the peace, as d'Aiguillon had for claiming that the Toulon armament had saved Sweden.[191]

Nevertheless, in a broader sense the solution of the crisis could with some reason be credited to British and French *policy*. For there is a good deal to suggest that a main consideration influencing Panin was his belief that the British Navy would leave the Russian galleys to the mercy of the French frigates. No doubt he was also affected by the expectation, and then by the news, of the rupture of the peace negotiations at

323

Bucharest; but that news did not reach St Petersburg until late on 9 April (N.S.), which was the day *after* Panin read his declaration to Ribbing, and in the preceding weeks it seems that Russian official circles had been irrationally optimistic about the outcome of the congress.[192] The notion that England and France were on the brink of an alliance, or perhaps had even secretly concluded one, was very much in the air in the spring of 1773; and in inducing it d'Aiguillon, Rochford and Suffolk had all played a part. Reports of this kind reached Frederick II from London and the Hague.[193] They were freely discussed in the British press.[194] The existence of a triple alliance between England, France and Spain was believed by the Chevalier d'Eon as late as the end of April.[195] An Anglo-French fleet was rumoured to be preparing to go to the aid of Danzig.[196] Mr Birkbeck, a British merchant of Marseilles, was so confident that an Anglo-French commercial treaty was impending, that he applied to be made British consul for Languedoc.[197] And when the order was given for fitting out the Portsmouth squadron, many observers believed that it was destined to act in conjunction with the French, *against* Russia; and indeed Rochford later boasted (apparently truthfully) that he had told Mussin-Pushkin so in plain terms, being afraid that otherwise the news of British mobilization might encourage Catherine in aggression.[198] Nolcken long continued to believe that England, even if unwilling to act in concert with France, might possibly give assistance to Sweden independently.[199] And on 13 May, after all the bitter experience of his interviews with Stormont, d'Aiguillon could still profess to Vergennes a conviction that if he had persisted in the Toulon armament, England would not in fact have molested it.[200]

It may well be true, then, that the salvation of Sweden, and the preservation of the peace, are to be regarded as a demonstration of the validity of the principles of foreign policy which George III had adumbrated in 1772, and which Rochford had secretly attempted to apply; and as the vindication of d'Aiguillon's contention that only an Anglo-French *entente* could set bounds to the system of plunder which the partition of Poland seemed to have inaugurated. But if this was indeed the lesson to be learned from the Swedish crisis, it does not appear that either Englishmen or Frenchmen were willing to learn it. Despite the fact that the suspension of the Toulon armament had preceded by four days the announcement of the British mobilization, public opinion, in France and in Europe, rightly drew the conclusion that d'Aiguillon had climbed down in the face of British menaces. Even Frederick the Great was impressed by this show of vigour.[201] For Frenchmen the sense of national humiliation was keen; and Broglie, Favier and other critics of the minister gave eloquent expression to it.[202] In England there was a corresponding feeling of triumph. As the crisis developed, George III forgot his advocacy of an *entente*, and characteristically insisted on a policy of 'firmness'; while Suffolk seems to have ostentatiously dissociated himself from anything that could be construed as appeasement of France.[203] The Admiralty – even to the 'cream-faced Bradshaw' – was inspirited by the speed and precision of its own preparations; the Portsmouth squadron was manned without a press; Admiral Sir Charles Saunders was spoiling for a fight: as Nolcken remarked, it was a case of *jalousie de métier*.[204] With such feelings on either side of the Channel, what hope was there now for an Anglo-French concert?

Yet the exhilaration in England was itself the revelation of a prevailing *malaise*: the small triumph over France was relished the more, just because it came as a gleam of encouragement after a decade in the doldrums. For in 1773, there can be no doubt, British morale was low, and depression about the country's international position was widespread. The professional diplomats complained that there was now no 'system' in Europe any more; by which they meant, perhaps, that England had none.[205] We stood isolated, without an ally other than Portugal, and almost without a friend; and men found the sensation both unpleasant and inconvenient.[206] The opposition in Parliament railed at the supineness of the ministry; while its friends bewailed its inability to prevent or redress the international iniquities they were forced to witness. Thus that experienced diplomat Sir Joseph Yorke wrote, almost in despair, 'One is tired of being in the right, when one sees wrong prevailing everywhere.'[207] As to remedy, he had none, other than a passive vigilance and the hope of better days: 'What can England do, but keep a good look out and wait for events, for it is not possible for us to join the strongest against the weakest.'[208]

Ministers, on the whole, agreed with him: as Nolcken wrote, their maxim was 'not to meddle with things that don't concern you; keep a sharp eye on your neighbour, and on the economy at home; and for the rest keep the navy in an active and respectable condition'.[209] But it was difficult at times to continue to believe that this was sufficient; and one of the most efficient members of the government, Lord Sandwich, voiced a disquiet which he was not alone in feeling when he wrote:

No man wishes more for the continuance of peace than myself . . . but I dread the consequence of too long an acquiescence in suffering other great powers to take considerable strides without our interfering, as I know that when our proper strength is exerted we are more considerable than any of them, France not excepted.[210]

Suffolk was of the same opinion: as early as 15 September 1772 the Danish minister reported that Suffolk felt that

l'ancien sistème pouvoit convenir à l'Angleterre tant qu'elle étoit déchirée par des Factions, mais maintenant que l'Administration est établie sur un pied stable et solide, elle peut et il lui convient de regarder autour d'Elle; Il n'est pas nécessaire qu'elle se mêle indistinctement de toutes les petites affaires du dehors, mais il est de sa gloire, il peut être nécessaire et utile, qu'Elle se soucie des grandes affaires de l'Europe entière. . . .[211]

And indeed it was high time, for there could be no doubt that European opinion regarded British policy, as it had been manifested since 1763, with contempt. In this matter, Panin, Frederick and Kaunitz were all of one mind. They considered Britain's position to be undermined by the instability of administrations, by the excessive preoccupation of British statesmen with domestic problems, by the ignorant amateurism and indolence of successive secretaries of state, by pennywise and shortsighted views, by the timid and greedy demand of a commercial nation for peace at any price, and lastly by the malign influences of Bedford, Bute and the Princess of Wales – influences which neither the death of two of these nor the political extinction of the third were considered to have diminished. Some, at least, of these criticisms were echoed in the private correspondence of our diplomatists; and towards the end of Cathcart's mission to Russia he sent home (in the guise of an answer to a rash inquiry as to what the Russians thought of us) a tremendous indictment, which provides a convenient compendium of most of them.[212] Even the relatively sympathetic Nolcken in 1773 defined the English system as consisting essentially in timidity varied by spasmodic violence.[213] And at the very moment when ministers were congratulating themselves on the cancellation of the Toulon armament, their former *défaillances* arose to haunt them, and the voice of a victim of their prudence seemed to reproach even their success:

Poor Paoli [wrote Eden] is very low in spirits on this occasion, and could not help saying yesterday, that such a display some years ago would have left him at this moment the head of a free people.[214]

It would be unwise, nevertheless, to attach implicit faith to the sneers of Frederick II, or to accept without question the criticism of opposition factions whose policies when in power had not differed perceptibly from those they were now attacking. The European belief in the feebleness of England was mistaken, then as upon some other occasions, and British ministers found it incomprehensible: they remembered Quiberon and Quebec, and were convinced they could do it again, if need be; they knew that England could afford to fight a war, as no other nation could; and they still believed the Royal Navy to be superior to any rival. If they concentrated their attention on France, that was hardly surprising; nor was it a sign of especial obliquity that they should have seen no threat in the rise of Russia, and even have considered that Russian expansion to the south-east might be attended with benefits to British commerce. For Parliament and the nation the enemy was certainly still France; and there were even those who approved the partition of Poland, as tending to weaken French influence in Europe.[215] Ministers knew well that the country wanted peace and a reduction of taxation; and they knew too that it also expected the French to be kept in order. It was no easy matter to do both; and experience showed that governments which were at variance with public opinion on such issues could not be sure of their majorities. It would have been foolish indeed to go to war over the Canada Bills, or the Manila ransom, or the ditch at Chandernagore, or even the *cunette* at Dunkirk; and if the enemies of England chose to stigmatize a refusal to rush into hostilities on these issues as timidity or decadence, there was no help for it:[216] such things had happened before – in Walpole's time, for instance[217] – and the country had lived it down. Even on Corsica the opinions of experts (both in England and France) about the strategic importance of the island had been sufficiently divided to justify abstention. The Turks Island affair, and the Falklands crisis, and even the divorce of Caroline Matilda, had demonstrated that war would be risked if vital issues were thought to be involved. If England found herself isolated, it was not for want of trying to find an ally; and in so far as ministers were isolationist, it was isolation that made them so, and not the other way round. And lastly, while it may well be true that secretaries such as General Conway or Lord Weymouth were ill-informed and not very competent, it may also be doubted whether a brilliant professional could have done much better in the intractable circumstances of the time.

But though a good deal can thus be said in defence of British foreign policy in the years between 1763 and 1772, it is clear that the first partition of Poland and the Swedish revolution changed the nature of the case, and confronted ministers with a new situation. Choiseul was now politically dead, and his policy seemed to have died with him. Gustav III's *coup d'état* had destroyed the only real common ground between England and Russia. The quest for a Russian alliance had been virtually abandoned, in indignation and chagrin: Catherine's two conversations with Gunning, in the summer of 1773, demonstrated that the negotiation had no prospect of success; Suffolk's final comment on them pronounced its epitaph.[218] And the partition of Poland flung out a challenge to the public law of Europe.[219] Rochford clearly recognized this: he told Garnier in September 1772 that it 'change absolument le sisthème politique de l'Europe', and predicted that one day the partitioning powers might unite against France, as they were now united against Poland.[220] Three months later, Guines reported that

les Ministres Anglais redoutent les suites de la Confédération formidable de ces trois Puissances, ils jugent qu'une Alliance avec la Maison de Bourbon, et des Négotiations qui tendroient à détacher une d'entre elles seroient les seuls moyens d'arrêter le progrès de cette union.[221]

In this situation, those responsible for British foreign policy might seek to keep their courage up by telling each other that the 'unnatural alliance' could not last; but if they were to judge by Austria's attitude to the Swedish crisis, or by Russia's reaction to Frederick's blackmail of Danzig (whose independence Catherine had guaranteed), they could hardly put much faith in their predictions. Never since 1763 had France's influence at Vienna been so low; and never had England's word carried less weight in St Petersburg. To the eastern monarchies England and France were now of importance mainly as makeweights which could tip the uneasy triangular balance between the *pouvoirs copartageants* to one corner or to another. The subsequent course of events was indeed to show that the partitioning system had almost reached its limits; but in 1773 it seemed at least possible that it might be extended, not only to Scandinavia but to Germany.[222] It may be true that Catherine, in particular, was impelled more by her fears than by her ambitions,[223] at least until the Greek Project began to take shape; but this was not a truth that was obvious. In the circumstances, the Swedish crisis of 1772–3 might well have been a turning-point in Anglo-French relations. In the event, it proved nothing of the sort. Ministerial insight was forced to give way to popular prejudice, passion prevailed at the expense of reason, political tradition proved too strong to break. There was only one man in England, wrote Nolcken, who could carry a policy of even temporary and limited concert with France, and that was Chatham; and not Chatham himself could persuade England to a French alliance.[224] But what could be hoped of a statesman who proclaimed himself to be 'quite a Russ', and trusted that 'the Ottoman will pull down the House of Bourbon in his fall'?[225] Rochford's intrigue for an *entente* was submerged in a wave of John Bullish patriotism to which even the king succumbed; and Rochford himself, who had gone to such hazardous lengths to forward it, in the end shrugged his shoulders and drifted with the tide, prepared to be an accessory to the destruction of Sweden, an abettor of Russian aggrandizement, and a combatant in an unwanted war, should d'Aiguillon remain obstinate about the Toulon fleet.[226] Rochford was, no doubt, a political light-weight. He lacked Suffolk's clear, if narrow, understanding; he was much less sure of the principles upon which he acted. His critics (and some of his colleagues) considered him unstable, erratic and indiscreet. Yet it is arguable that, for all his mental confusion, he had a firmer grasp than they of the situation produced by the Swedish revolution. For indeed, France's international position, her interests, her policies, had now much in common with those of Great Britain. No minister of the old *régime* after Choiseul (and perhaps not Choiseul himself) really contemplated the recovery of the losses of 1763 in their full extent:[227] they aspired no higher than to humble British arrogance by achieving a maritime and commercial balance; and Vergennes himself in the hour of triumph was insistent upon the need to preserve England as a great power. The France of Louis xvi desired, as has been well said, 'la cristallisation de l'Europe dans une euphorie générale'.[228] To d'Aiguillon and to Vergennes, as to Suffolk, the *système copartageant* was utterly abhorrent.[229] But for France, as for England, the means to resist it were far from obvious; and both were therefore driven back upon a policy of waiting upon events: 'le rôle passif', wrote d'Aiguillon to Rohan, 'est le seul qui soit assorti aux vœux et aux sentiments du roi.'[230] D'Aiguillon might seem an untrustworthy friend, and his tenure of office (it was not difficult to foresee) might be limited to the lifetime of Louis xv; but for England in 1773 a *rapprochement* with France was not illogical, nor ought it to have been impracticable. Thus Count Bark, the able Swedish minister in Vienna, wrote:

it seems a matter of urgent necessity to provide in good time a counterpoise [to the Partitioning Powers] which might maintain some sort of balance in Europe. This ought not to be difficult of attainment, if only it were possible to suppose that England could overcome her national hatred of France. In a situation of less imminent danger than the present we have seen England and France unite – in the Alliance of Hanover. Might not the partitioning of Poland, and the prospective damage to English trade in the Levant and the Baltic, perhaps avail to produce a closer union of principles between the two powers? Europe might then feel more secure against an aggressiveness which today embarrasses the great powers, and puts the smaller ones in obvious peril.[231]

Gustav iii held very similar views.[232] It is of course true that their opinions were biased by the interests of their own country.

But from a purely British point of view what was the alternative? The alternative, certainly, was now an isolation even more friendless than in the 1760s. Suffolk did not flinch from that prospect: with Sandwich's reorganized navy he was prepared to face France alone, and scramble along in Europe as best he might. He had his way. When the American colonies revolted, George III's appeal to Catherine fell on deaf ears; France dragged Spain into a war of half-hearted revenge; and the Armed Neutrality completed the fiasco of our foreign policy.

Yet the peace of Versailles was not yet signed before Vergennes was trying to secure French and English collaboration in Constantinople in an effort to save the Turks from Russia and Austria.[233] The ending of the colonial struggle brought with it a new situation; and the velleities of George III and Rochford could become the realities of William Pitt. It was Pitt who told Fox (still a typical Chathamite in foreign policy) that the notion of France's being our eternal enemy was 'weak and childish'. It was Pitt who made the commercial treaty which George III had first suggested. It was Pitt who countenanced overt intervention to save Sweden from Catherine's satellite.[234] And it was Pitt, finally, who perceived that the threadbare tenet that Russia was a 'natural' ally was unsupported by the facts; who grasped, by instinct or insight, the possibility that Russian expansion might not be without its inconveniences and dangers; and who vainly tried to brace the country to confront them.

The Spanish minister D'Aranda once remarked that only an absolute monarchy can guide its affairs by pure *raison d'état*; and added that it was one of the essential weaknesses of England that public opinion played so important a part in determining the course of the country's international relations. The crisis of 1773, no less than Ochakov or Jenkins's Ear, provides at least some support for the observation.[235]

NOTES

[1] This essay first appeared in the *Historical Journal*, vii (1), 1964.

[1a] See Gunnar Kjellin, 'Gustav III, den Patriotiske Konungen', in *Gottfrid Carlsson, 18. xii. 1952*, Lund, 1952.

[2] See *Pol[itisches] Corr[espondenz Friedrichs des Grossen]*, xxvii, 193; xxviii,

125, 238, 424, 442; xxix, 31, 281 n. 1; Public Record Office, S.P. 91/88, fos. 123–4: Cathcart to Suffolk, 30 August–10 September 1771. There are signs that Wilkes may have been taking French bribes in 1772: *Correspondance secrète du Comte de Broglie avec Louis XV*, edd. D. Ozanam and M. Antoine, Paris, 1956–61, ii, 356.

[3] E.g. British Museum, Egerton MS. 2701, fo. 308: Sir J. Yorke to Gunning, 14 November 1772; or George III himself: *The Correspondence of George III*, ii, 204. Frederick II suspected Bute of similar views: *Pol. Corr.* xxv, 253 (to Edelsheim, 5 October 1766); and *cf. ibid.*, xxiv, 2.

[4] For Franco-Russian relations, see L. Jacobsohn, *Russland und Frankreich in den ersten Regierungsjahren der Kaiserin Katharina II*, Berlin, 1929).

[5] For the origins of this controversy, see D.B. Horn, 'The Cabinet Controversy on Subsidy Treaties in Time of Peace, 1749—50', *EHR* xlv (1930). Choiseul made an unexpected contribution to this debate when he wrote, in his Memoir to the King, 1765: 'La grande méthode d'Angleterre est la meilleure et la plus sûre, de ne payer que quand on la sert, pour se conserver le crédit prépondérant; de donner avec discernement des présents d'argent dans les occasions aux ministres des Electeurs et Princes de l'Empire. Je crois qu'une somme de cinq mille francs, envoyée par un an dans toutes les cours de l'Empire, les assurera à la France infiniment mieux, si la guerre venait, que le traités de subside les plus onéreux' (*Mémoires de Choiseul*, ed. F. Calmettes, Paris, 1904, p. 244).

[6] For Bernstorff's policy, and the Holstein—Oldenburg exchange, see P. Vedel, *Den aeldre Grev Bernstorffs Ministerium*, Copenhagen, 1882; M. de Bartélémy, *Histoire des relations de la France et du Danemark sous le Ministère du Comte de Bernstorff*, Copenhagen, 1887; Otto von Brandt, *Caspar von Saldern und die nordeuropäische Politik im Zeitalter Katharinas II*, Erlanger–Kiel, 1932.

[7] For these differing views see (e.g.) S.P. 95/104, fo. 135: Sandwich to Goodricke, 6 July 1764; *ibid.*, fos. 165–7: same to same, 3 August 1764; *ibid.*, fos. 356–7: same to same, 18 September 1764: all three views expressed successively by the same minister.

[8] E.g. S.P. 95/106, fos. 84–6: Sandwich to Goodricke, 15 February 1765; or *ibid.*, 110, fos. 211–14: Conway to Goodricke, 19 December 1766.

[9] *Correspondence of George III*, ii, 222. Compare his similar complaint in May 1787 about secret service expenditure in Corsica nearly twenty years before, which had been borne by the Civil List upon a ministerial assurance that the king should be repaid. The repayment was never made, 'which made me consequently appear afterwards in an extravagant light to Parliament' (Alfred Cobban, *Ambassadors and Secret Agents* (1954), p. 134).

[10] SP 95/116, fos. 417 ff.

[11] 32 *Commons Journals*, 555–99.

[12] For the extremely complex history of the attitude of foreign powers and domestic factions to the questions of the Constitution of 1720 see Olof Jägerskiöld, *Hovet och författningsfrågan, 1760–1766*, Stockholm, 1943; Beth Hennings, *Gustaf III som kronprins*, Stockholm, 1953, chapters 13–15; E. Amburger, *Russland and Schweden, 1762–1772*, Berlin, 1934; and the classic work of C. G. Malsmtröm, *Sveriges politiska historia från Konung Karl XII:s död till statshvälfningen, 1772*, Stockholm, 1900–1, vols. v and vi. For Swedish

foreign policy, see Olof Jägerskiöld, *Den svenska utrikespolitikens historia,* *1721–1792,* Stockholm, 1957.

[13] For Choiseul's despatch announcing his change of front see J.B.P.G. Flassan, *Histoire générale et raisonnée de la diplomatie française,* Paris, 1811, vi, 562–70.

[14] S P 95/109, fos. 238–9: Conway to Goodricke, 28 June 1766; and see *Pol. Corr.* xxv, 176 n. 3: Cocceji to Frederick, reporting Goodricke, 18 July 1766.

[15] For Struensee's foreign policy, see E. Holm, 'Styrelsen af Danmark-Norges Udenrigspolitik under Struensee', [Dansk] *Historisk Tidsskrift,* 4R, ii, Bd. (1870–2).

[16] See H. Valentin, 'Det sociala momentet i historieskrivningen om 1772 års statsvälvning', *Scandia,* xiv (1941).

[17] S P 95/119, fos. 142–3: Suffolk to Goodricke, 15 November 1771; *cf. ibid.,* fos. 39–40: Goodricke to Suffolk, 23 July 1771.

[18] See M. S. Anderson, 'Great Britain and the Russian Fleet, 1769–70', *Slavonic and East European Review,* xxxi (1952–3).

[19] M. S. Anderson, 'Great Britain and the Russo-Turkish War of 1768–74', *EHR* lxix (1954), 38–58.

[20] For Suffolk's views on relations with Russia, see S.P. 91/89, fos. 138–9: Suffolk to Cathcart, 7 April 1772; *ibid.,* 90. fos. 5–8: instructions for Gunning, [28] May 1772; *ibid.,* fos. 117, 186–9: Suffolk to Gunning, 4 August, 8 September, 1772; Riksarkivet, Stockholm, [R.A.] Diplomatica, Anglica, Nolcken to Kanslipresidenten, Apostille, 6 September 1771, where he notes that 'the English Court's partiality and inclination towards Russia seems to be notably weakened'. Goodricke denied this in Stockholm, and his language was 'much approved', but Nolcken was correctly informed: S.P. 95/119, fos. 108–9, 116–17: Goodricke to Suffolk, 27 September 1771; Suffolk to Goodricke, 26 October 1771.

[21] For the Hanover intercepts, see Helle Stiegung, *Den engelska under-rättelseverksamheten rörande Sverige under 1700-talet,* Stockholm, 1961, and Bengt Petersson, ' "The Correspondent in Paris" – en engelsk informations-källa under 1700-talet', *Scandia,* xxviii (1961); and S.P. 95/120, fos. 179–84, 190–4: Rochford to Goodricke, 3, 7, 14 July 1772; *ibid.,* 121, fos. 47–9: Suffolk to Goodricke, 4 August 1772; *Corr. of George III,* ii, 363–6.

[22] S.P. 95/121, fos. 122–3: Suffolk to Goodricke, 1 September 1772; *Corr. of George III,* ii, 363–6, 384.

[23] Goodricke had foreseen this possibility nearly a year before: S.P. 95/119, fos. 138–9: Goodricke to Suffolk, 25 October 1771. For his comments to Osterman, see H. Hjärne, 'Sverige inför Europa 1772', in *Ur det för-gångna,* Stockholm, 1912, pp. 159–60. Suffolk's view was that the Caps had brought it on themselves by their inexcusable neglect to act on his warnings: S.P. 95/121, fo. 172: Suffolk to Goodricke, 8 September 1772.

[24] L. Bonneville de Marsangy, *Le Comte de Vergennes. Son Ambassade en Suède,* Paris, 1898, pp. 266–8.

[25] *Letters of Horace Walpole* (ed. Toynbee), viii, 203, 208; *The Annual Register,* 1772, pp. 7, 53–70; Public Record Office, Bliss Transcripts, 31/13/3, fo. 51. The Prince remarked: 'I say . . . his subjects have been in the wrong to permit him' (*Journals of Lady Mary Coke,* Edinburgh, 1896, iv, 109).

[26] Archives du Ministère des Affaires Etrangères, Paris [A.E.], Correspondance Politique [C.P.], Angleterre, 500, fos. 107–8: Guines to d'Aiguillon, no. 96, 4 September 1772.

[27] S.P. 91/90, fos. 168–9: Suffolk to Gunning, 1 September 1772.

[28] S.P. 95/121, fos. 164–5: Goodricke to Suffolk, 22 August 1772.

[29] For the circumstances of his appointment, *Corr. of George III*, ii, 205–7, 251–2. In at least two critical interviews Suffolk was forced to ask his interlocutor to permit him to speak English: Rigsarkivet, Copenhagen [D.R.A.] Dept. f.u.A., England II, Depescher, Diede to Osten, 17, 28 April 1772.

[30] Sir Joseph Yorke wrote: 'Our two Secretaries are of crazy constitutions, the one from his own fault, the other by inheritance. I am very sorry for it because I esteem them both, and they are both attentive and spirited, and want nothing but health to make any figure they please in their departments' (British Museum, Add. MS. 35370, fo. 97: to Lord Hardwicke, 16 February 1773).

[31] See his letters to W. Eden, in Add. MS. 34412, fos. 174, 182, 214; and to Keith, in *Memoirs and Correspondence of Sir Robert Murray Keith* (1849), i, 301.

[32] D.R.A. Dept. f.u.A., England II, Diede to Osten, 3 April 1772: 'Il se fait beaucoup estimer. Il n'aigrira point les choses ... mais je m'attends qu'il me rendra toujours avec franchise et énergie ce qui aura été résolu dans le conseil, ou ce qu'il sera chargé de me dire. Politesse générale, et douceur de caractère, réserve sur les détails, franchise et brièveté dans le propos ministériaux, encore un peu d'embarras, me paroissent être le traits principaux qui le caractérisent. Il conviendra de le ménager.'

[33] H. W. Temperley, *Frederick the Great and Kaiser Joseph* (1915), p. 263. Isabel de Madariaga quotes this judgment, apparently with approval: *Britain, Russia and the Armed Neutrality of 1780* (1962), p. 448; but it is noteworthy that Temperley also considered Suffolk 'a fairly able man ... with a singularly unbiased mind'.

[34] 'Das Ereignis des 19 August 1772', wrote Amburger, 'war überhaupt die schwerste Niederlage, die die Politik Katharinas II bisher erlitten hatte' (Amburger, *op. cit.*, p. 266).

[35] In the event, Kaunitz took care to give no encouragement to the idea that Austria would support her ally on this issue: see AE. CP. Suède, 262, fos. 201, 281, 298: Vergennes to d'Aiguillon, 30 September, 9, 14 November 1773; *ibid.*, fo. 234: copy of Rohan's memorandum of interview with Kaunitz; British Museum, Egerton MS. 2701, fo. 308: Stormont to Gunning, 14 November 1772; R. A. Anglica. Svenska beskickningar till Nolcken. Upplösta chifferbrev (vol. 438): Bark to Nolcken, 6 November 1772.

[36] See especially Add. MS. 35502, fo. 14: Suffolk to Gunning, 30 October 1772; S.P. 91/91, fos. 105–7: same to same, 30 October 1772; Hist. MSS. Comm. *Dartmouth* (1896), iii, 196–7: Suffolk to Dartmouth, 6 September 1772.

[37] *The Private Papers of John, Earl of Sandwich* (Navy Records Soc. 1932), i, 20–3: North to Sandwich, 5 September 1772. Sandwich's pointed reply, alluding to the Swedish revolution, in *ibid.*, 23–4.

[38] S.P. 75/127, fo. 204: Suffolk to Woodford, 8 December 1772; *ibid.*, fos. 231–4: Woodford to Suffolk, 12 December 1772.

³⁹ S.P. 91/91, fos. 13–16: Gunning to Suffolk, 28 August, 4 September 1772.

⁴⁰ D.R.A. Dept. f.u.A., England II, Diede to Osten, 1, 11, 15 September 1772.

⁴¹ S.P. 91/91, fo. 34: Suffolk to Gunning, 2 October 1772.

⁴² For this farcical affair, see S.P. 91/91, fos. 22–3, 25–7, 46–7, etc.

⁴³ S.P. 91/91, fos. 46–7: Suffolk to Gunning, 6 October 1772.

⁴⁴ Compare George III: 'as we are not bound by any treaty of alliance, I cannot see any reason for joining with Russia in a declaration against the changes of the Swedish Constitution; though if Russia is attacked by France, views of general policy [will] not permit our remaining idle spectators' (*Corr. of George III*, ii, 404).

⁴⁵ S.P. 95/131, fos. 169–72; S.P. 91/90, fos. 180–3, 186–9; and see his private letter to Gunning, 8 September, in Egerton MS. 2701, fo. 170.

⁴⁶ S.P. 95/121, fos. 169–70: 8 September 1772.

⁴⁷ S.P. 91/91, fo. 72: Gunning to Suffolk, 14/25 September 1772; *cf.* Add. MS. 35502, fo. 20: same to same, 14 December 1772, for a similar report.

⁴⁸ S.P. 91/91, fos. 105–7: Suffolk to Gunning, 30 October 1772.

⁴⁹ *Ibid.*, fo. 109: Suffolk to Gunning, 30 October 1772, and especially his private letter to Gunning of same date: Egerton MS. 2701, fo. 170.

⁵⁰ S.P. 91/91, fo. 124: Suffolk to Gunning, 10 November 1772; Add. MS. 35502, fo. 16: same to same, 17 November 1772. Gunning seems to have broken it only gradually to Panin: Egerton MS. 2701, fo. 310: Gunning to Goodricke, 7/18 December 1772.

⁵¹ S.P. 95/122, fos. 131–6, 138–40: Goodricke to Suffolk, 27, 30 October 1772; *cf.* Egerton MS. 2701, fo. 235: Goodricke to Gunning, 30 October 1772.

⁵² Sir Joseph Yorke wrote that Sweden and Denmark 'seem like Arlequin and Scapin on the Italian stage, to have big words in their mouths, but at the same time to be horribly afraid of each other': Add. MS. 35370, fo. 70 (to Hardwicke, 17 November 1772).

⁵³ For Gustav's designs on Norway, see *Gustav III:s och Lovisa Ulrikas brevväxling*, Stockholm, 1919, ii, 111; *Konung Gustaf III:s efterlämnade och femtio år efter hans död öppnade papper*, ed. E.G. Geijer, Stockholm, 1843; D.R.A. Ges.-Arkiver, England I, Osten to Diede, 2 November, 28 November (Apostille), 1772; Y. Nielsen, 'Gustav den III:s norske Politik', [Dansk] *Historisk Tidsskrift*, R., 1 Bd. (1877).

⁵⁴ S.P. 75/127, fos. 74–7, 100–9, 113–15: Woodford to Suffolk, 31 October, 3 November 1772; *ibid.*, fos. 98–9: Osten to Woodford, 2 November 1772; *cf.* Egerton MS. 2701, fos. 199–200: Woodford to Gunning, 29 September 1772.

⁵⁵ R.A. Anglica: Nolcken to Kanslipresidenten, 29 September 1772; Hjärne, p. 169 n. 2.

⁵⁶ R.A. Anglica: Nolcken to Kanslipresidenten [K.P.], 29 September, 6 November 1772. Gustav asked d'Aiguillon to use his good offices to have Goodricke recalled (A.E. C.P. Suède 262, fo. 204: Vergennes to d'Aiguillon, 30 September 1772; fo. 233: d'Aiguillon to Vergennes, 20 October 1772);

ESSAYS IN SWEDISH HISTORY

R.A.Kabinettet för utrikes brevväxlingen (Presidentskontoret) Koncept. Ulrik Scheffer to Nolcken, 23 October 1772; to Creutz, 16 October 1772. It was not the first time: see *Corr. of George III*, ii, 249–50. Goodricke believed that a general war could be avoided if Russia attacked Sweden *immediately* (Egerton MS. 2701, fo. 313: Goodricke to Gunning, 1 January 1773).

[57] R.A.Anglica: Nolcken to K.P., 8 December 1772; A.J.Hjelt, *Sveriges ställning till utlandet närmast efter 1772 års statshvälfning*, Helsingfors, 1887, p. 152.

[58] See, for example, S.P. 75/127, fos. 11–12, 125–6: Suffolk to Woodford, 13 October, 17 November 1772; S.P. 91/91, fos. 132–3: Suffolk to Gunning, 17 November 1772; and Nolcken's report of a similar statement by Rochford: R.A.Anglica: Nolcken to K.P., Apostille, 18 December 1772. Scheffer's elaborate pamphlet refuting the allegation of aggressive designs is in R.A.Kabinettet för utrikes brevväxlingen. Cirkulärer 1772.

[59] A.E. C.P. Suède, 262, fos. 57, 200: Vergennes to d'Aiguillon, 21 August, 30 September 1772. D'Aiguillon was as sceptical about Denmark's aggressiveness as Suffolk was about Sweden's: A.E. C.P. Suède, 262, fos. 271, 304–5, 325–6: d'Aiguillon to Vergennes, 5, 15, 26 November 1772.

[60] [L.Manderström], *Brefvexling rörande Sveriges historia under åren 1772–1780*, Stockholm, 1854, pp. 1–2, 8–10, 21–2, 23–4, 42–3, etc.

[61] The delay was due to Panin's indolence: Egerton MS. 2701, fo. 306: Gunning to Goodricke, 16/27 November 1772. Osterman was however threatening Russian intervention as early as 9 November, though without instructions to do so: R.A.Schefferska Samlingen. Skrivelser till Ulrik Scheffer, vol. viii: Falkenberg to Ulrik Scheffer, 9 November 1772. A copy of the declaration Osterman was ordered to make in Stockholm is in Eg. MS. 2701, fo. 237; a copy of the Swedish reply in Add. MS. 35504, fo. 132. The Prussian minister verbally supported the Russian note: Egerton MS. 2701, fo. 282: Goodricke to Gunning, 18 December 1772; D.R.A. Ges.-Arkiver, England I, Osten to Diede, 22 December 1772; H. J. Bull, *Friedrich der Grosse und Schweden in den Jahren 1768–1772*, Rostock, 1933, p. 93.

[62] A.E. C.P. Suède 262, fos. 265–8: Vergennes to d'Aiguillon, 3 November 1772, with copy of Swedish note; *ibid.*, fos. 272–3: Gustav III to Louis xv, 8 November 1772; *ibid.*, fo. 274, the Danish declaration, 9 November 1772; S.P. 75/127, fos. 131–4: Woodford to Suffolk, 10 November 1772. For Danish policy at this period see especially Osten's memorial of 29 August and Schack's observations upon it of 5 September, in 'Aktstykker og Breve til Belysning af Grev Ostens politiske Stilling ... 1772–3', *Danske Magazin*, vR., 4 Bd., Copenhagen, 1900, 194–208.

[63] *Pol. Corr.* xxxiii, 38, 50; Bull, pp. 88–9.

[64] S.P. 91/91, fos. 105–7: Suffolk to Gunning, 30 October 1772; *ibid.*, fos. 213–15: Gunning to Suffolk, 1 December 1772; Egerton MS. 2702, fo. 20: Goodricke to Gunning, 29 January 1773.

[65] *Pol. Corr.* xxxiii, 18, 66. With his usual mendacity Frederick also stated that England and Denmark had offered him an alliance against Sweden (to Prince Henry, 16 October 1772): *Pol. Corr.* xxxii, 570. The story was quite untrue.

336

⁶⁶ *Recueil des Instructions données aux Ambassadeurs . . . de France*, ix, (2): *Russie*, Paris, 1890, p. 286–300; A.E. C.P. Suède 262, fos. 230, 239–42: d'Aiguillon to Vergennes, 20 October 1772; Egerton MS. 2701, fos. 288–9: Woodford to Gunning, 25 December 1772; *ibid.*, fo. 291: Gunning to Murray, 14/25 February 1773; Add. MS. 24158, fo. 197: Rochford to Grantham, 15 December 1772; D.R.A. Ges.-Arkiver, England I, Osten to Diede, 12 September 1772.

⁶⁷ *Cf.* the Abbé Georgel's verdict on d'Aiguillon: 'il avait plus de connoissances [que Choiseul] et autant d'esprit; mais il ne savoit pas comme lui être tranchant et braver les obstacles. De petites ruses, de petits moyens, le talent des petites intrigues, voilà ce qui le caractérisoit. Il prenait l'opiniâtreté pour l'énergie, et il a montré qu'il étoit peu propre à manier le timon des affaires dans un grand état': *Mémoires de l'Abbé Georgel*, Paris, i, 1820, i, 150.

⁶⁸ See, for example, S.P. 78/283, fos. 66, 139, 148, 150, 263; S.P. 78/284, fos. 35, 331–2; S.P. 78/285, fos. 320–2; S.P. 78/286, fos. 150–3; S.P. 78/287, fos. 119–20; B. de Fraguier, 'Le Duc d'Aiguillon et l'Angleterre', *Revue de l'Histoire diplomatique*, xxvi (1912), 609–27. Mercy commented: 'je le soupçonne d'idées chimériques sur son prétendu crédit en Angleterre' (*Correspondance secrète du Comte de Mercy-Argenteau avec l'Empéreur Joseph II et le prince de Kaunitz*, Paris, 1891, ii, 412: Mercy to Kaunitz, 16 October 1772); *cf.* S.P. 91/90, fo. 133: Cathcart to Gunning, 6/17 July 1772, where Cathcart reports French approaches to him. But French espionage with a view to the invasion of England continued in 1771 (G. Lacour-Gayet, *La marine militaire de la France sous le régne de Louis XV*, Paris, 1910, p. 456).

⁶⁹ A.E. C.P. Angleterre, 500, fo. 299: d'Aiguillon to Guines, no. 55, 6, December 1772.

⁷⁰ S.P. 78/285 fo. 295: Harcourt to Rochford, 16 July 1772.

⁷⁰ᵃ Though he seems to have been on bad terms with Choiseul: R.A. Anglica, Nolcken to K.P., 23 October 1768.

⁷¹ E.g. Tchernichev: F. de Martens, *Recueil des Traités . . . conclus par la Russie*, St Petersburg, 1892, ix (x), 280; and Favier wrote 'My lord Rochefort est homme de plaisir, mais encore plus homme d'honneur': E. Boutaric, *Correspondance secrète inédite de Louis XV*, Paris, 1866, ii, 186 n. 1; *cf.* Add. MS. 35370, fo. 16.

⁷² J. Goebel, *The Struggle for the Falkland Islands*, New Haven, 1927, p. 356, n. 78. George III wrote to Suffolk of 'your Brother Secretary who, though possessed of many amiable qualities, is not very prudent' (*Corr. of George III*, ii, 370). And Garnier wrote: 'Milord Rochford est sujet en affaires ou plutôt en discours à de petites vivacités qui ne signifient rien' (A.E. C.P. Angleterre, 500, fo. 221: Garnier to d'Aiguillon, no. 106, 30 October 1772). For a less favourable estimate see the reports of Haneken and Diede: D.R.A. Dept. f.u.A. England II, 3 April, 17 April 1772, where he is accused of using his influence on foreign policy to assist his stock-exchange manœuvres.

⁷³ *Cf.* his anxiety about d'Aiguillon's talks with Shelburne when Shelburne was in Paris (S.P. 78/283, fo. 313).

⁷⁴ *The Letters of Junius* (ed. C.W.Everett) (1927), p. 190, n. 1.

337

[75] Suffolk found it necessary to deny this to Nolcken (Bliss transcripts 31/13/3, fos. 14–16).

[76] R.A. Anglica, Nolcken to K.P., 6 November 1772.

[77] S.P. 78/284, fos. 282–4; 286, fos. 67–71; d'Aiguillon had compared British and French behaviour in India, and suggested that sooner or later the British were bound to be evicted by the outraged Indians. Rochford called this 'as extraordinary a performance as ever issued from the pen of the most insolent French Minister that ever existed'.

[78] S.P. 78/286, fos. 95–6; 287, fos. 102–4; Fraguier, pp. 610–12.

[79] *Pol. Corr.* xxxii, 611, Jeanneret to Frederick, 16 October 1772, where he reports Rochford as saying, 'C'est donc un mensonge affreux et une impertinence indigne de la France de débiter une pareille nouvelle, et, par conséquent, même de nous prêter des sentiments que nous n'avons point.'

[80] D.R.A. Dept f.u.A., England II, Diede to Osten, 27 November 1772, 19 February 1773; *cf.* the remarks of Mussin-Pushkin (the Russian Minister to Great Britain), *ibid.*, 13 April 1773.

[81] *Sandwich Papers*, i, 30–3.

[82] Add. MS. 24158, fo. 197: Rochford to Grantham, 15 December 1772.

[83] S.P. 78/284, fos. 161–2; 285, fos. 263–4, 271–2.

[84] S.P. 78/286, fos. 24–5: Blaquière to Rochford, 9 September 1772; fos. 80–2: Rochford to St Paul, 9 October 1772 (*cf.* a previous instruction to Blaquière of 11 September: 286, fos. 18–19); Add. MS. 24158, fos. 144, 182: Rochford to Grantham, 11 September, 13 November 1772; R.A. Anglica: Nolcken to K.P., Apostille, 30 June 1772.

[85] R.A. Anglica: Nolcken to Gustav III, 22 January 1773.

[86] Add. MS. 35502, fos. 18–19: Gunning to Suffolk, 1 December 1772.

[87] *Pol. Corr.* xxxiii, 325: Maltzan to Frederick, 16 February 1773, where he reports Suffolk as saying: 'que la France étoit déterminée qu'en cas que la Russie attaquât la Suède d'envoyer une escadre dans la Baltique; qu'eux ne l'empêcheraient pas, dût-elle y faire passer toute sa marine'; D.R.A. Dept. f.u.A., England II; Diede to Osten, 18 December 1772: 'C'est de la Russie qu'on se méfie plus que de la France, et c'est elle qu'on blâme ... et si elle [*sc.* a Russian attack on Sweden] arrive, on laissera faire la Cour de France': *cf.* Osterman's comments to Goodricke, S.P. 95/113, fos. 24–5; and Sir J. Yorke's to Gunning, 15 March 1773: Egerton MS. 2702, fo. 16. There seems no doubt that Panin believed that these were Suffolk's views; though the trend of Diede's later despatches was to the effect that it was Rochford rather than Suffolk that held such language; and in mid-April (when it was too late to matter) Mussin-Pushkin told Diede that hitherto he had treated such remarks as of no importance: see D.R.A. Dept. f.u.A., England II; Diede to Osten 12 and 19 February, 13 April 1773.

[88] *Pol. Corr.* xxxiii, 308; *cf. ibid.*, xxxii, 568.

[89] S.P. 91/92, fo. 149: Gunning to Suffolk, 12/23 March 1773.

[90] *Pol. Corr.* xxxiii, 238, 239, 246; *cf. ibid.*, 338, 347, 393.

[91] *Corr. of George III*, ii, 428–9.

[92] Fraguier, p. 615.

[93] *Ibid.*, p. 619.

[94] A.E. C.P. Angleterre 500, fos. 249–51: Bourdieu to d'Aiguillon, 20 November 1772.

[95] *Ibid.*, 500, fos. 258–61: Bourdieu to d'Aiguillon, 24 November 1772.

[96] A.E. C.P. Angleterre 500/249–51, 501, fos. 5–6: Bourdieu to d'Aiguillon, 20 November 1772, 5 January 1773.

[97] *Ibid.*, 500, fo. 276: d'Aiguillon to the Abbé de Terray, 30 November 1772.

[98] Fraguier, pp. 616, 619–20.

[99] A.E. C.P. Angleterre 501, fo. 121: Bourdieu to d'Aiguillon, 2 March 1773.

[100] *Ibid.*, 501, fos. 18–19, 21–3, 87–92, etc., for this affair: Bourdieu was also a creditor of the French Government for goods and services in the Windward Islands (*ibid.*, 501, fo. 374).

[101] A.E. C.P. Angleterre 501, fos. 112–14: Guines to d'Aiguillon, no. 120, 26 February 1773.

[102] *Ibid.*, 501, fos. 133–4: d'Aiguillon to Guines, no. 63, 7 March 1773; *ibid.*, fo. 132: d'Aiguillon to de Terray, 6 March 1773; fos. 238–40: d'Aiguillon to Guines, 29 March 1773; fos. 328–36: Guines to d'Aiguillon, no. 125, 16 April 1773.

[103] Principal Secretary to the French Embassy, *chargé d'affaires* during Guines's absence on holiday.

[104] A.E. C.P. Angleterre, 500, fos. 167–70: Garnier to d'Aiguillon, 9 October 1772; fo. 194: d'Aiguillon to Garnier, 18 October 1772.

[105] R.A. Anglica: Nolcken to K.P., 12 October 1772.

[106] R.A. Anglica: Nolcken to Gustav III, 23 October 1772; Hjelt, p. 63. He told Mussin-Pushkin that 'sa Cour ferait très-bien de ne pas penser à former aucune tentative contre la Suède, parcequ'elle trouveroit sûrement la France sur son chemin et que l'Angleterre ne s'en mêleroit pas attendu qu'elle ne vouloit point entrer en guerre': *cf.* A.E. C.P. Suède 262, fos. 272, 276; Add. MS. 35502, fos. 18–19; Add. MS. 24158, fg. 182.

[107] A.E. C.P. Angleterre, 500, fos. 199–203, 208–11, 214–20: Garnier to d'Aiguillon, 23 and 30 October 1772. The idea of a non-aggression pact was Garnier's own, approved by d'Aiguillon: *ibid.*, 500, fos. 150–1, 177: *cf.* R.A. Anglica: Nolcken to K.P., 23 October 1772, and d'Aiguillon's account to Creutz: E. Tegnér, *Bidrag till kännedomen om Sveriges yttre politik närmast efter statshvälfningen 1772* (*Valda skrifter*, v), Stockholm, 1906, p. 119 n. 1.

[108] R.A. Anglica: Nolcken to Gustav III, 6 November 1772.

[109] A.E. C.P. Angleterre, 500, fos. 208–11; Garnier to d'Aiguillon, 23 October 1772.

[110] For his denials, see e.g. S.P. 78/283, fos. 269, 301, 312.

[111] For the 'promise' see Goebel, *op. cit.*, pp. 360–3; but see too the judicious discussion in M.H. Nieto, *La Cuestion de las Malvinas*, Madrid, 1947, pp. 227–30, 264, 269; Nieto doubts whether anything Rochford said could be considered binding.

[112] See, e.g., S.P. 78/287, fos. 46–48: Rochford to St Paul, 12 February 1773.

[113] S.P. 95/123, fos. 33–4: Goodricke to Suffolk, 29 January 1773.

[114] R.A. Anglica: Nolcken to Gustav III, 16 March 1773, 6 November 1772.

[115] S.P. 95/123, fos. 39–41: Suffolk to Goodricke, 26 February 1773.

[116] S.P. 91/90, fos. 145–6: Cathcart to Suffolk, 12/23 January 1772; 91/92, fo. 71: Gunning to Suffolk, 16 January 1773.

[117] S.P. 91/92, fos. 119–21: Suffolk to Gunning, 26 March 1773.

[118] *Correspondance secrète de Broglie avec Louis XV*, ii, 396 n. 2. For d'Aiguillon's optimism about England, see A.E. C.P. Suède, 262, fos. 147, 153, 229, 362. D'Aiguillon told Creutz (the Swedish ambassador in Paris) about his offers to England: Hjelt, pp. 154–5.

[119] A.E. C.P. Suède, 263, fos. 113–14, 202: d'Aiguillon to Vergennes, 18 February, 21 March 1773. When Bougainville, deprived for the moment of royal support for another voyage of exploration, and finding himself unemployed, suggested to de Boynes (the Minister of Marine) that he might be temporarily commissioned to a frigate and sent on a cruise to the Baltic so that French officers could be trained in the navigation of those waters, d'Aiguillon replied that at present it was 'nullement convenable' to send *any* French warship to the Baltic (A.E. C.P. Suède, 263, fos. 155–6: d'Aiguillon to de Boynes, 7 March 1773).

[120] A.E. C.P. Suède, 262, fos. 344–9: Creutz to Gustav III (copy), 13 December 1772; 263, fos. 170 ff.: Vergennes to d'Aiguillon, 15 March 1773. In return for French subsidies, Sweden engaged to have an army of 47,000 men, and 21 ships of war, in readiness by 1 January 1776.

[121] A.E. C.P. Angleterre 501, fo. 219: Guines to d'Aiguillon, 23 March 1773.

[122] A.E. C.P. Suède, 263, fos. 35–41, 103, 179–80: Vergennes to d'Aiguillon, 16 January, 15 February, 15 March 1773; *ibid.*, 263, fos. 113–14, 202: d'Aiguillon to Vergennes, 18 February, 21 March 1773; P. Véou, 'Un chapitre inédit des Mémoires de Barthélémy: La Révolution suèdoise de 1772', *Revue des Etudes Historiques*, civ (1937).

[123] He also tried to deter the British Government from sending a fleet to the Baltic by spreading rumours of concentrations of troops on the Hanover border: *Pol. Corr.* xxxiii, 313 (to Prince Henry, 23 February 1773); *cf.* Add. MS. 35505, fo. 136: Harris to Keith, 6 April 1773. The rumours caused Suffolk some concern: A.E. C.P. Angleterre, 501, fo. 276: Guines to d'Aiguillon, no. 123, 2 April 1773. Suffolk, like Frederick, realized that Sweden's weakness would for some time to come make her innocuous as an enemy and a liability as an ally: D.R.A. Dept. f.u.A. England II: Diede to Schack-Rathlou, 26 March 1773. Osterman seems in the end to have realized it too (Bull, *op. cit.*, p. 99).

[124] A.E. C.P. 501, fo. 227: Guines to d'Aiguillon, no. 122, 23 March 1773.

[125] R.A. Anglica: Nolcken to Gustav III, 16 March 1773: 'dess [*sc.* the British government's] bearbetande därwid wore nu mera af hel annan beskaffenhet än tillförene.'

[126] A.E. C.P. Suède, 263, fos. 31, 230–2, 238–40: Vergennes to d'Aiguillon, 16 January, 29 March, 5 April 1773; Add. MS. 35370, fo. 112: Sir J.Yorke to Hardwicke, 6 April 1773.

[127] Egerton MS. 2702, fo. 30: Gunning to Goodricke, 25 January/5 February 1773.

[128] See, e.g. A.E. C.P. Suède, 263, fos. 9, 35–41, 122, 176.

[129] A.E. C.P. Suède 263, fos. 3–4, 16–17, 49, 61–2, 158–60: d'Aiguillon to Vergennes, 3, 14, 20, 24 January, 18 February, 7 March, 21 March 1773.

[130] *Correspondance secrète de Broglie avec Louis XV*, ii, 387. For Broglie's very pertinent criticisms of d'Aiguillon's policy in the northern crisis, see H. Stiegung, *Louis XV:s hemliga diplomati och Sverige*, pp. 281–8; and Bengt Petersson, 'Louis xv:s hemliga diplomati – några reflexioner', *Scandia*, xxviii (1962), 407–12.

[131] A.E. C.P. Suède, 263, fo. 198: d'Aiguillon to Vergennes, 21 March 1773.

[132] A.E. C.P. Suède, 263, fos. 161–6: Vergennes to d'Aiguillon, 9 March 1773; *cf.* Barthélémy's account in Véou, *op. cit.*, p. 423; Hjelt, p. 176. Already in February Gustav had told Goodricke that 'the Ballance of Europe was in the hands of the King of Great Britain': S.P. 95/123, fos. 49–50: Goodricke to Suffolk, 19 February 1773.

[133] R.A. Kabinettet för utrikes brevväxlingen: U. Scheffer to Nolcken, 26 March 1773; A.E. C.P. Suède, 263, fo. 185: Gustav III to Louis xv, 17 March 1773: printed but misdated in L. Manderström, *op. cit.*, p. 63.

[134] S.P. 78/287, fo. 56: St Paul to Rochford, 17 February 1773.

[135] Compare Mercy's comment (to Maria Theresa, 17 February 1773): 'La France, . . . par des désordres aussi inouïs qu'inexcusables, s'est réduite pour le moment dans l'estat d'anéantissement où elle se trouve, n'ayant ni la volonté ni le pouvoir d'offrir à son allié des secours, des moyens pour barrer les vues ambitieuses des deux puissances formidables' (A. d'Arneth and A. Geffroy, *Marie Antoinette. Correspondance secrète entre Marie-Thérèse et le Cte de Mercy-Argenteau*, Paris, 1875, i, 420–1).

[136] The marginal minute on Martange's report of 29 March reads: 'conversation avec M^d Rochford relativem^t au projet d'Alliance avec l'Ang^trre (A.E. C.P. Angleterre, 501, fo. 241: Martange to d'Aiguillon, 29 March 1773).

[137] *Correspondance secrète du Comte de Broglie avec Louis XV*, edd. D. Ozanam and M. Antoine, Paris, 1956–61, ii, 386 n. 3; *Correspondance inédite du Général-Major de Martange*, Paris, 1898, pp. 508 ff.

[138] *Correspondance . . . de Broglie avec Louis XV*, ii, 384–5 n. 2.

[139] A.E. C.P. Angleterre, 501, fos. 320–1: d'Aiguillon to Guines, no. 66, 12 April 1773; *ibid.*, fos. 338–9: same to same, no. 67, 19 April 1773.

[140] S.P. 78/287, fos. 166–7: Stormont to Rochford, 4 April 1773; A.E. C.P. Suède 263, fos. 216–27; Hjelt, pp. 184–90.

[141] When de Broglie protested that a Toulon fleet would be useless to Sweden, Louis xv noted at the foot of his letter: 'Dans la Baltique, si nous y paroissions, l'Angleterre y paraîtroit aussytost. Dans la Méditerranée, cela n'est pas si sûr mais pouroit être. Dans quelques jours nous en serons éclaircis' (*Corr. de Broglie avec Louis XV*, ii, 386). *Cf.* the comment of Bonneville de Marsangy: 'Une démonstration maritime, en faveur de la Suède, ayant pour théâtre la Méditerranée, devait paraître à tous . . . une conception aussi platonique qu'illusoire' (L. Bonneville de Marsangy, *Le Comte de Vergennes. Son ambassade en Suède*, Paris, 1898, p. 377).

[142] A.E. C.P. Angleterre, 501, fo. 309: Guines to d'Aiguillon, no. 124, 9 April 1773.

¹⁴³ S.P. 78/287, fos. 140–61: Stormont to Rochford, 31 March 1773.

¹⁴⁴ S.P. 78/287, fos. 166–9: Stormont to Rochford, 4 April 1773.

¹⁴⁵ *Correspondance . . . de Martange*, 508–16; *Corr. of George III*, ii, 467–8.

¹⁴⁶ As appears from *ibid.*, ii, 476.

¹⁴⁷ *Corr. de Martange*, p. 525: italics mine.

¹⁴⁸ *Ibid.*, 525–7. Rochford gave Martange a version of Stormont's despatch of 31 March heavily coloured to demonstrate that Stormont, like himself, was the friend of France. He told him, for example, that Stormont had argued strongly that it was unjust and unwise of England to prevent France from sending aid to Sweden; and added, 'Imaginez-vous . . . qu'il a été jusqu'à mettre dans sa dépêche que la Grande Bretagne alloit se rendre la fable de l'Europe en armant en faveur de la Russie.' This was quite untrue. All that Stormont had said was that if we were going to be driven to fight on the same side as Russia, we had better make sure of an alliance on decent terms beforehand.

¹⁴⁹ *Corr. de Martange*, pp. 526–7.

¹⁵⁰ *Ibid.*, 527–8.

¹⁵¹ *Corr. of George III*, ii, 476: King to North, 25 April 1773.

¹⁵² A.E. C.P. Suède 262, fo. 362 for d'Aiguillon's despatch; A.E. C.P. Angleterre, 500, fo. 305: Guines to d'Aiguillon, 11 December 1772.

¹⁵³ Though Guines believed himself to have received a hint nearly to the same effect from Mansfield: A.E. C.P. Angleterre, 500, fo. 339: Guines to d'Aiguillon, no. 114 (*bis*), 27 December 1772.

¹⁵⁴ *Corr. de Martange*, pp. 530–4. Dumouriez in his *Mémoires* has a story to the effect that since the device of delaying British mobilization was found on examination to be impracticable, Rochford and Martange agreed that French troops in French transports should be convoyed by a British naval escort, and Martange was to report this verbally in Paris. D'Aiguillon is said to have hesitated; meanwhile the plan leaked out and came to Dumouriez's knowledge; and Dumouriez, who had a grudge against d'Aiguillon, revealed it to Monteynard, who was properly indignant: the scheme thereupon dropped: *Mémoires du Général Dumouriez*, Paris, 1848, i, 154–5. The story was accepted by de Broglie, though he admitted there was no documentary evidence for it other than Dumouriez, and though he himself remarked that Dumouriez 'ne paraît avoir eu ni une mémoire fidèle ni un vif scrupule de la vérité': de Broglie, *Le Secret du Roi*, Paris, 1878, ii, 417 ff. and 422 n. 1. It cannot, however, be true; for it would have required the consent of the whole cabinet, and would have disastrously compromised the ministry in the eyes of the public. But it may well be that d'Aiguillon played with the notion on his own account: in his interview with Stormont on 31 March he threw out the suggestion, as if in jest, but dropped it at once when it met with no response: S.P. 78/287, fo. 155: Stormont to Rochford, 31 March 1773.

¹⁵⁵ S.P. 78/287, fo. 137: Rochford to Stormont, 2 April 1773. It is true that both Rochford and the king professed themselves sceptical of this, but on Rochford at least the story seems to have made some impression (*ibid., loc. cit.*); *Corr. de Martange*, p. 521.

[156] S.P. 91/86, fo. 44: Cathcart to Rochford, 19 October 1770: *cf. ibid.*, 85, fos. 59–72: Rochford to Cathcart, 25 August 1770.

[157] *Corr. de Martange*, p. 527.

[158] S.P. 78/287, fos. 170–6: Rochford to Stormont, 7 April 1773.

[159] Add. MS. 9242, fo. 154.

[160] *Corr. de Martange*, p. 528.

[161] *Pol. Corr.* xxxiii, 434: it is possible, however, that the reference to 'un homme de confiance du duc d'Aiguillon' applied not to Martange, but to Garnier or Bourdieu: the letter is dated 30 March, which would imply very prompt intelligence if Martange was intended.

[162] Tegnér, v, 175, 176 n. 1.

[163] Add. MS. 32258 fo. 433: lacunae supplied from A.E. C.P. Angleterre, 500, fos. 305 ff.: Guines to d'Aiguillon, 11 December 1772.

[164] S.P. 78/287, fos. 200, 191–2: Stormont to Rochford, 7 April 1773; *ibid.*, fos. 220–6: Suffolk to Stormont, 14 April 1773; *ibid.*, 288, fos. 11–20, 21–5: Stormont to Rochford, 14 April 1773.

[165] S.P. 78/287, fo. 189: Stormont to Rochford, 7 April 1773.

[166] S.P. 78/287, fos. 203–15: Stormont to Rochford, 10 April 1773.

[167] *Correspondance de Broglie avec Louis XV*, ii, 384–5 n. 2.

[168] A.E. C.P. Angleterre, 501, fo. 338: d'Aiguillon to Guines, no. 67, 19 April 1773; S.P. 78/288, fos. 59–60: Guines to Rochford, 26 April 1773; *Correspondance de Broglie avec Louis XV*, ii, 396 n. 3; Fraguier, p. 622. As early as 11 April, Stormont received the impression that d'Aiguillon was 'looking for a proper way of getting off': S.P. 78/287, fos. 216–19: Stormont to Rochford, 11 April 1773.

[169] S.P. 78/287, fos. 201, 216–19; 288, fos. 21–5: Stormont to Rochford, 7, 11, 14 April; 287, fos. 228–30: Suffolk to Stormont, 16 April 1773; *Corr. of George III*, ii, 472–3; Suffolk to King, 14 April 1773.

[170] *Corr. of George III*, ii, 474; S.P. 78/288, fos. 26–7: the Toulon fleet was of twelve ships of the line and six frigates.

[171] S.P. 91/92, fo. 156: Suffolk to Gunning, Circular, 23 April 1773. Guines thought the delay of two days in the announcement indicated that the British Government was deliberately dragging its feet (A.E. C.P. Angleterre, 501, fos. 362–4: Guines to d'Aiguillion, no. 128, 23 April 1773).

[172] *Corr. of George III*, ii, 476.

[173] S.P. 78/288, fos. 59–60: Guines to Rochford, 26 April 1773.

[174] S.P. 78/288, fo. 65: Rochford to Stormont, 27 April 1773; *Corr. of George III*, ii, 478–9.

[175] Add. MS. 36800, fo. 3: Rochford to Cooke, 27 April 1773; S.P. 78/288, fos. 104–5: Guines to Rochford, 5 May 1773; *ibid.*, fos. 139–43: Rochford to Stormont, 12 May 1773; *ibid.*, fos. 165–8: Stormont to Rochford, 18 May 1773; *ibid.*, fos. 169–70: Rochford to Stormont, 21 May 1773; *Corr. of George III*, ii, 488.

[176] Guines himself had wondered too: A.E. C.P. Angleterre, 501, fo. 340: Guines to d'Aiguillon, no. 126, 19 April 1773. For the alarm about Spain see Add. MS. 24159, fo. 39: Suffolk to Grantham, 12 April 1773; S.P. 78/288, fos. 129–35: Stormont to Rochford, 5 May 1773, enclosing copy of Grantham to Stormont, 27 April; Add. MS. 9242, fo. 196: Rochford to

Grantham, 28 May 1773; S.P. 78/288, fos. 206–9: Stormont to Rochford, 2 June 1773.

¹⁷⁷ 'Well imagined and fortunately executed', was Conway's verdict: Add. MS. 35505, fo. 336.

¹⁷⁸ *Corr. of George III*, ii, 494, 508–9; S.P. 78/289, fo. 20: Rochford to Stormont, 18 June 1773. Stormont's sceptical reply, 23 June, *ibid.*, fo. 38.

¹⁷⁹ S.P. 78/289, fo. 45: Rochford to Grantham and St Paul, 26 July 1773.

¹⁸⁰ Egerton MS. 2702, fo. 48: Suffolk to Gunning, 11 June 1773 (referring to an earlier visit which the two secretaries had made to the fleet before its disarmament).

¹⁸¹ *Cf.* Favier's view, in his *Conjectures raisonées*: Boutaric, i, 481; ii, 23, 32.

¹⁸² He was the brother of the Gustaf Adam von Nolcken who was minister in London.

¹⁸³ R.A. Muscovitica. Baron F. von Nolckens Depescher. Nolcken to K.P. 15/26 March 1773.

¹⁸⁴ R.A. Muscovitica, Ribbing to K.P., 28 March/8 April 1773.

¹⁸⁵ Gustav must have interpreted Nolcken's despatches a good deal more optimistically than a dispassionate reading of them would seem to warrant: R.A. Muscovitica, Nolcken to K.P., 8/19, 15/26, 19/30 March 1773. The initial step towards a *détente* probably came from Vergennes, who on 18 March pressed Scheffer to give a formal *démenti* to rumours that France was urging Sweden to attack: R.A. Schefferska Samlingen. Skrivelser till Ulrik Scheffer: Vergennes to Scheffer, 18 March 1773.

¹⁸⁶ S.P. 91/93, fos. 10–12: Gunning to Suffolk, 10 April 1773; *cf.* S.P. 95/123, fos. 111–13: Goodricke to Suffolk, 27 April 1773.

¹⁸⁷ S.P. 78/287, fos. 203–15: Stormont to Rochford, 10 April 1773.

¹⁸⁸ A.E. C.P. Suède, 262, fos. 283–5.

¹⁸⁹ Add. MS. 35505, fo. 303: Suffolk to Keith, 11 June 1773: 'The Court of France continues perfectly quiet, and is satisfied with the Russian declaration; on which the French Minister plumes himself highly; having, in defiance of stubborn facts and inconsistent dates, placed it to the account of the Toulon preparations': Fraguier, p. 626; Bonneville de Marsangy, *Le Comte de Vergennes*, p. 381; E. Bourgeois, *Manuel historique de politique étrangère*, Paris, 1928, i, 443; G. Zeller, *Histoire des Relations internationales*, iii. *Les temps modernes*, ii, 303.

¹⁹⁰ A.E. C.P. Suède, 263, fo. 299: Gustav III to Creutz (copy), 14 May 1773. The Danish ministers, with equal tact, attributed the preservation of the peace to the British armament (Egerton MS. 2702, fo. 118: Woodford to Gunning, 9 May 1773). They may even have believed it, for A.P. Bernstorff conveyed congratulations in cypher, as well as *en clair* (D.R.A. Ges.-Arkiver, England I: Bernstoff to Diede, 8 May 1773).

¹⁹¹ Wolfgang Michael was too charitable when he wrote 'In London hatte dieses Mal die Entscheidung über Krieg und Frieden Europas gelegen, durch die fest Haltung des britischen Kabinetts war der Friede erhalten worden' (W. Michael, *Englands Stellung zur ersten Teilung Polens*, Hamburg, 1890, p. 77).

¹⁹² S.P. 91/93, fos. 7–12: Gunning to Suffolk, 10 April 1773; R.A. Muscovitica, Ribbing to K.P., 8/19 March, 13/24 March 1773.

[193] *Pol. Corr.* xxxiii, 161, 461, 500; *cf.* Egerton MS. 2702, fo. 62: Sir J. York to Gunning, 15 March 1773; S.P. 78/286, fo. 152: St Paul to Rochford, 4 November 1772.

[194] See the account in D.B.Horn, *British Public Opinion and the First Partition of Poland*, Edinburgh, 1945, pp. 20–3, 47–64; and *cf. The Letters of Horace Walpole*, viii, 258 (to W.Mason, 27 March 1773).

[195] *Correspondance secrète de Broglie avec Louis XV*, ii, 396; and *cf.* Favier's remarks in Boutaric, ii, 177 and n. 3.

[196] Egerton MS. 2702, fo. 54: Suffolk to Gunning, Private, 9 March 1773.

[197] S.P. 78/288, fo. 159: Birkbeck to Rochford, 3 May 1773.

[198] R.A.Anglica: Nolcken to Gustav III, 16, 23, 27 April 1773. Suffolk, too, took care to instruct Gunning to profess ignorance of the orders given to the fleet, and of its destination: S.P. 91/92, fos. 158–9: Suffolk to Gunning, Confidential, 23 April 1773. Guines (C.P. Angleterre, 501, fo. 385, 29 April 1773) confirms Rochford's story. But Rochford also successfully persuaded Diede (after the crisis was over) that the rumours to this effect had never had any foundation: D.R.A. Dept. f.u.A. England II: Diede to Schack-Rathlou, 7 May 1773.

[199] R.A. Anglica: Nolcken to K.P., 5 and 9 March 1773; A.E. C.P. Suède, 263, fos. 279–82: Vergennes to d'Aiguillon. Draft. Private, 24 April 1773.

[200] A.E. C.P. Suède, 263, fo. 296: d'Aiguillon to Vergennes, 13 May 1773.

[201] *Pol. Corr.* xxxiii, 551: to Goltz, 24 May 1773: '. . . je ne vous dissimulerai point que j'ai tout lieu d'être surpris de la fermeté du Lord Stormont. . . . Je le connais de longue main, et jamais je lui en aurais supposé une aussi forte dose pour parler avec autant de hauteur et, en même temps, de dignité à un ministère étranger.'

[202] *Correspondance secrète de Broglie avec Louis XV*, ii, 395, 404; Boutaric, i, 448; ii, 177: Broglie, *Le Secret du Roi*, ii, 438: Guibert to Dumouriez, [May] 1773: 'J'ai vu maintenant les trois grandes puissances qui balancent les destinées de l'Europe. Nous, nous sommes morts. Mande-moi si le nom français est une parure là où tu es; je n'ai pas encore trouvé à m'en vanter depuis que je voyage.' *Cf. Mercy–Kaunitz Corr.* ii, 419, and Comte de Saint-Priest, *Mémoires*, Paris, 1929, i, 144–5.

[203] *Corr. of George III*, ii, 470; R.A. Anglica: Nolcken to K.P., 4 May 1773.

[204] S.P. 78/288, fos. 121–2; *Sandwich Papers*, i, 35; Add. MS. 35505, fo. 187: R.Bradshaw to Keith, 23 April 1773; *ibid.*, fo. 239: W.Eden to Keith, 7 May 1773; *Correspondence of William Pitt, Earl of Chatham* (1839), iv, 261, n. 1: Mrs Alexander Hood to Lady Chatham, 25 April: 'Upon its being said, that our equipment would be only a fleet of observation, Sir Charles said, "If I sail, it will be a war," '

[205] Add MS. 35505, fos. 205–6: Stormont to Keith, 24 April 1773; Add. MS. 35370, fos. 46–7: Sir J.Yorke to Hardwicke, 28 August 1772.

[206] Thus de Visme wrote to Gunning, 5 January 1772: 'I cannot but consider it as a great misfortune for a publick minister, that we have no particular connection or alliance with any one Power in Europe except Russia, so that we cannot concert measures with any other minister, and compare intelligence, and discuss the news and business of the day so as to

receive mutual helps and lights from each other' (Egerton MS. 2701, fo. 7).

[207] Add. MS. 35370, fo. 86: to Hardwicke, 12 January 1773.

[208] *Ibid.*, fo. 105: to Hardwicke, 9 March 1773.

[209] R.A. Anglica, Nolcken to K.P. Apostille, 19 June 1772.

[210] *Sandwich Papers*, i, 29: Sandwich to Rochford, 15 November 1772; *cf.* a similar sentiment in *The Annual Register*, 1772, p. 3.

[211] D.R.A. Dept. f.u.A., England II: Diede to Osten, 15 September 1772; *cf.* same to same, 19 January 1773.

[212] S.P. 91/88, fo. 109: Cathcart to Suffolk. Most Secret. 20/31 August 1771. Among other home truths, he wrote '. . . that the fearing a War with France prevented her [England] holding at Paris a language which, without a War would have prevented the loss of Corsica; – and that the same policy, and a desire of having friends everywhere, and enemies nowhere, occasioned England to hold a middle conduct, in many other instances, expensive and disadvantageous for herself, ineffective for her friends and the common cause, and highly convenient for her enemies'. And *The Annual Register* for 1771 admitted (p. 12) that 'Our unhappy intestine divisions, which had gradually spread into almost every part of the British Empire, had so filled the hands, and engaged the thoughts of government, that little attention either had, or could for some time past have been given to our foreign interests.'

[213] R.A. Anglica: Nolcken to K.P., 5 March 1773. This long despatch contains an exceptionally shrewd analysis of British policy.

[214] Add. MS. 35505, fo. 239: W. Eden to Keith, 7 May 1773.

[215] *Annual Register*, 1771, p. 6.

[216] Compare George III's comment on Dunkirk: 'You may think me pro-lix, but it is from not desiring that the heat of a Boy may throw me so much off my guard as to draw this country into another addition of 50 millions to the National Debt; we must get the Colonies into order before we engage with our Neighbours': *Corr. of George III*, ii, 372: to North, 1 August 1772. And perhaps there was something to be said for the view of Sabathier de Cabres, who considered that 'Le plus grand bien en Politique, c'est d'être crus moins que nous sommes; de faire couver pour ainsi dire sous la cendre un pouvoir réel qui ne sort que pour s'affermir et qui étonne en enlevant subitement par son éclat et par ses actes les moyens de lui mettre un frein' (Sabathier de Cabres, *Cathérine II, sa Cour et la Russie*, Berlin, 1862, p. 99).

[217] On 30 July 1733, Horatio Walpole had written to Baron Gedda: 'Si nous marquons du déplaisir de voir l'Europe en danger d'une guerre générale, à l'occasion d'une dispute qui intéresse si peu l'équilibre de cette partie du monde, et de l'empressement à maintenir la paix et à prévenir une rupture, il [Chavigny] va aussitôt représenter à ceux qui le veulent bien écouter les bonnes intentions du Roy et de ses ministres comme l'effet de leur faiblesse et de leur timidité, se trouvant dans l'incapacité de remplir leurs engagemens; d'où il infère qu'il n'y a rien à craindre de l'Angleterre ni de la Hollande dans l'abaissement où elles sont présentement' (quoted in J. H. Plumb, *Sir Robert Walpole*, ii, 286–7).

[218] S.P. 91/93, fos. 102–6, 191: Gunning to Suffolk, 4 June–3 August 1773, for Gunning's remarkable conversations with Catherine. Suffolk

replied: 'I will frankly own to you, that I feel so much indignation at the style the Court of Petersburg has behaved in, towards this country, that I am exceedingly less concerned for the Impediments that obstruct the Alliance, than I once thought I should ever have been. . . . A subsidy to Denmark can never make the foundation of a treaty with Russia. A guaranty of the usurpations in Poland can never compose a part of it. Nor will His Majesty, contrary to established usage, admit the Turkish clause' (*ibid.*, fo. 195: Suffolk to Gunning, 27 August 1773).

[219] The partition, wrote *The Annual Register* for 1772 (p. 2), 'is to be considered as the first very great breach in the modern political system of Europe'.

[220] A.E. C.P. Angleterre, 500, fo. 141: Garnier to d'Aiguillon, no. 100, 25 September 1772.

[221] *Ibid.*, fo. 340: Guines to d'Aiguillon, no. 114 (*bis*), 27 December 1772.

[222] Prince Henry, for instance, 'saw the confusion in Europe as a chance for Prussia to profit – perhaps even to divide up the Germanies between Austria and Prussia' (Herbert H. Kaplan, *The First Partition of Poland*, New York, 1962, p. 131).

[223] As Ribbing, for instance, repeatedly advised his government: see, for example, his remarkably forceful statement in R.A. Muscovitica: Ribbing to K.P., 21 December/1 January 1772/3, Apostille.

[224] R.A. Anglica: Nolcken to K.P., 4 May 1773. Compare Burke's view: *The Correspondence of Edmund Burke*, Cambridge, 1960, ii, 429.

[225] *Chatham Papers*, iv, 298–9: Chatham to Shelburne, 20 October 1773.

[226] See in particular his private letter to Stormont of 12 May 1773: Add. MS. 9242, fo. 174.

[227] Pierre Rain, *La diplomatie française d'Henri IV à Vergennes* (1945), pp. 252–3.

[228] *Ibid.*, p. 323.

[229] See Vergennes's memoir of 8 December 1774, quoted in R. Salomon, *La Politique Orientale de Vergennes* (1935), pp. 30–1.

[230] Rain, p. 286.

[231] R.A. Anglica. Svenska beskickningar till Nolcken. Upplösta chifferbrev (vol. 438): Bark to Nolcken, 6 November 1772.

[232] R.A. Kabinettet för utrikes brevväxlingen. Gustav III to Nolcken, autog. draft, 14 May 1773.

[233] M.S. Anderson, 'The Great Powers and the Russian Annexation of the Crimea, 1783–4', *The Slavonic and East European Review*, xxxvii (1958–9); Salomon, pp. 255 ff.

[234] On this episode see, most recently, Signe Carlsson, *Sverige och Storbritannien, 1787–90*, Lund, 1944.

[235] R. Konetzke, *Die Politik des Grafen Aranda*, Berlin, 1929, p. 39.

Index

349

Germany, *see also* the various German states
strategy of Gustav Adolf in, 203
political objectives of Gustav Adolf in, 82–102
Gersdorff, Joachim, 157
Giavarina, Venetian envoy, 174
Gilds, Swedish, 3
Glover, Richard, poet, 306
Goodricke, Sir John, English diplomat, 298, 299
collaboration with Russia, 290
bribes Swedish Diet, 271, 291–2
deprived of funds, 294–5
on possible alliance with Sweden, 309
Görtz, Baron Georg Heinrich von, 252
Government, Form of, *see* Form of Government
Great Britain, *see also* Cromwell, Oliver; Baltic
diplomatic isolation after Seven Years' War, 287
interest in maintaining Swedish constitution, 286
and Russia, 288–90
co-operation with Russia in Sweden, 291–5
European attitude to British foreign policy, 326–7
Great Commission
investigates Regents and *råd*, 255, 258
Greatness, Age of, *see* Age of Greatness
Grotius, Hugo, 112, 216–17
influence on Gustav Adolf, 95—6
on alliances, n. 107
code for conduct of war, 216–17
Grubbe, Lars, 89, 120
Guines, Comte de, French Ambassador, 305 ff., 312, 318, 321, 328
suggests commercial treaty with Britain, 306
Gunning, Robert, British diplomat, 290, 299, 300, 309, 311, 328

sent to Russia, 295
Gustav I Vasa, King of Sweden, 3, 4, 5, 8, 13, 16, 19, 20, 34, 46, 119
comparison with Charles XII, 258
Testament of, 20
Gustav II Adolf, King of Sweden, 3, 5, 11, 12, 13, 23, 24–5, 35, 41, 149, 150, 202, 204, 212, 234, 235, 260
tactics and strategy, 64–75, 203, 215
in Germany, 72–4, 82–102
policy, 87–92, 94–7
influence of Grotius, 95
Gustav III, King of Sweden, 5, 6, 11, 13, 37, 258, 276, 283, 294, 296, 310, 331
seizes power, 280–1, 286
and Nobility, 281–2
threatens Denmark, 299–300
British support, 309
and France, 316–17
Gustav IV, King of Sweden, 10
Gustavus Adolphus, *see* Gustav II Adolf
Gyllenborg, Jakob, 250–1
Gyllenstierna, Johan, 23, 238, 257
foreign policy of, 231
Gyllenheim, Karl Karlsson, 26, 120

Hague Concerts, 171, 229
Hanover, 309
Hanseatic merchants, 2
Hats, the (political party), 10, 13, 254, 270, 274; *see also* Caps
concessions to industrialists, 275, 279–80
British interest in defeat of, 291
France withdraws support, 292
Heckscher, Eli, historian, 1, 3, 235
Hesse-Cassel, 88
Hildebrand, Emil, historian, 252
Hoghusen, Johan, 38
Holland
Cromwell's attitude to, 139–40
attempts to improve Anglo-French relations, 147

Manorial system, 17, 37, 277, 282
  extended under Christina, 115–16
  checked under Charles XI, 249
Maria Theresa, Empress of Austria, 287
Marine Treaty, Nieupoort's, 155, 158
Martange, Chevalier de, 312 ff.
Maurice of Orange, 12, 196, 211, 212
  contribution to military tactics, 60–2
  new drill system introduced by, 197
  development of standing army, 201
Mazarin, Cardinal, 146, 157, 158, 161, 230
Meadowe, Philip, Cromwell's envoy to Denmark, 164, 165, 167, 170
Mecklenburg, 84, 95
Memorandum on the Services, 254, 274
Messenius, Arnold, 121, 131–2, 134–5
Messenius, Arnold Johan, 112, 121, 131–2
Michael, Wolfgang, historian, 139, 140
Milton, John, 145
Monarchy, Swedish
  elective, 15, 32
  hereditary, 18, 19
  mixed, 26
  popular character, 37, 119
  freed from oligarchical control, 130
  limited, 269
Monro, Robert, soldier, 63, 200, 212
Mun, Thomas, 213
Muscovy Company, 151

Napier, John, mathematician, 211
Narva, Battle of, 235
Navigation, first Act of, 147
Navy
  English, reliance on Baltic area, 148

French, prevented from operating in Baltic, 313–14, 321
  Swedish, 12
  factors leading to permanent, 202
Nieupoort, Dutch diplomat, 141, 142, 143, 145, 147, 149, 156
Nilsson, Nils, 128, 131, 132
Nobility, the 5, 7: *see also* Estates
  aristocratic constitutionalism, 14–44
  patents of, 24
  restriction of office to, 30, 279
  failure in opposing monarchy, 32–3, 43
  privileges, 37–9, 41, 277, 278–9
  patriotism, 43, 125
  respect for law, 44
  opposition from the other estates, 113, 121, 127–8
  acquisition of crown land, 114–15
  power, 117, 125–6, 270
  new creations, 123–4
    by Christina, 128
    in eighteenth century, 276
  minor
    grievances of, 237
    transfer of power to, 126
    and high, compared, 272–3
    urge *reduktion*, 238
  high
    defeated by crown, 240
    ruined by Charles XI, 247
    characteristics in eighteenth century, 271–2
    participation in industry and trade, 275
    loss of privileges, 282
Noble land
  tax position, 277
  sales to commoners, 278, 282
Nolcken, Baron Gustaf Adof von, 300, 304, 307, 308, 309, 311, 325, 326, 327, 329
Nolcken, Frederick von, 322
Norma futararum actionum, 91, 98
North, Lord, 297, 302, 303, 306
Norway, 293, 299, 300
Nystad, Peace of, 235